Naugatuck, Connecticut

Congregational Church Records

1781–1901

Helen S. Ullmann

HERITAGE BOOKS
2012

HERITAGE BOOKS
AN IMPRINT OF HERITAGE BOOKS, INC.

Books, CDs, and more—Worldwide

For our listing of thousands of titles see our website
at
www.HeritageBooks.com

Published 2012 by
HERITAGE BOOKS, INC.
Publishing Division
100 Railroad Ave. #104
Westminster, Maryland 21157

Copyright © 1987 Helen S. Ullmann

All rights reserved. No part of this book may be reproduced or transmitted in any form or by any means, electronic or mechanical, including photocopying, recording or by any information storage and retrieval system without written permission from the author, except for the inclusion of brief quotations in a review.

International Standard Book Numbers
Paperbound: 978-1-55613-045-8
Clothbound: 978-0-7884-9429-1

INTRODUCTION

The following abstract of the records of "The Church of Christ in Salem" in Waterbury, Connecticut, now known as "The Congregational Church of Naugatuck," was taken from a microfilm copy of the original. The microfilm is available at the Connecticut State Library in Hartford and through branch libraries of the Genealogical Department of The Church of Jesus Christ of Latter-day Saints in Salt Lake City. Although established as the Salem Society in 1773, the church was not organized until 22 Feb 1781 (*The Town and City of Waterbury, Conn.* Joseph Anderson, D.D., ed., [New Haven, 1896], v. 1, p. 642-3). Naugatuck was a part of the town of Waterbury until May 1844.

Every single name in volumes I and II was abstracted with the exception of the frequent appearance of the name of the current Moderator (minister) or Clerk. In some cases church business regarding an individual continues for several pages but is only referenced on the first page of the discussion. The "Church Proceedings" in volume III were not abstracted although they have been referred to in a few cases.

A resume of the contents of the three volumes appears below. In many cases it would be helpful to refer to this list if an entry appears ambiguous. For example, a typical entry for a woman might read "Hotchkiss, Temperance, 1817, adm ch, wife of Zina Andrus: dis 1835 to Prospect, 3:18." It is not apparent from this entry whether Temperance and Zina married before or after 1817 except for the fact that it does appear under Temperance's maiden name. Such entries should be interpreted carefully with regard to other entries for the same person and by noting whether the page reference refers to a compiled list of members or to the original entry in a church business meeting. However, admissions and dismissions do not always appear in the records of meetings. In Temperance's case her admission appears only on lists. There seem to have been a number of admissions during the early 1800's which do not appear in the records.

It is important to realize that the several compiled membership lists contain annotations after the original entry. Deaths, dismissals, husbands, excommunications were all added information and are extremely valuable for determining, for example, whether a death date refers to one Sally Smith or another.

There are a few entries on p. 1:13 dated 1813 with the comment that they may actually have occurred in 1820. Later study has shown that 1820 is almost certainly the correct date. The confusion is caused by the fact that there are two different hands on the page with the lower handwriting evidently continuing from a previous page.

Cross referencing has been done only when alternate spellings of the same surname are not adjacent to each other in these abstracts.

The deaths in Volume III have been annotated at some later date with reference to headstones in Hillside Cemetery.

At times the records, particularly around pages 1:52-60 and in the 1890's have been very difficult to read. In this case it has been very helpful to use the "Find" commands in Appleworks to seek out all those with similar given names and several puzzles have been solved in that way. Hopefully errors have been minimized but there are surely a few.

In the records Columbia parish was in the town of Prospect, Gunntown was a section of Naugatuck, and Humphreyville was an old name for Seymour. East Plains and Mt. Carmel were the two religious societies in Hamden.

The cover drawing by Sally Gardner, art student at Brigham Young University, is taken from an 1870 photo on file at the Howard Whittemore Library in Naugatuck. The Salem Society almost immediately erected a building in 1782. It remained for 49 years and then was moved in 1831 to land given by Daniel Beecher. In 1853, then 71 years old, the old meeting house was again moved to give place to the building depicted here (*Ibid.*, p. 644-45; also, Constance McL. Green, *History of Naugatuck. Connecticut*, [New Haven, 1948], p. 113).

                                                    Helen S. Ullmann
                                                    713 Main St.
                                                    Acton, MA 01720

ERRATA

1.   Porter, "Asa" bp 27 Aug 1815 should probably be "Asa Henry" and "Henry" deleted as a separate entry. The original reads "Aug 27th [1815] Baptized the children of widow Sarah Porter: Names Harriet, Asa [space] Henry, Harrietta & Sarah." The probate of Asa Porter, Waterbury, 1816, #6571, divided his real property between the widow and four children, none of whom are named.

2.   Pardee, "Asa" should be "Ada" bp 20 Oct 1791.

3.   Hoadley, "Asa" should be "Ada" bp 9 Aug 1788.

CONTENTS OF THE
NAUGATUCK CONGREGATIONAL CHURCH RECORDS

1:1-6	Constitution of the Church in 1781, and Covenant.
1:5	Names of original members, 22 Feb 1781.
1:6-51	Business of the church, 1781-1810, includes admissions, baptisms, discipline, decisions, dismissions, etc.
1:53-59c	List of members made in 1811, with later additions through 1830. Numbering on pages 51-59 on top differs from that on the bottom. The top numbers were used for these pages.
1:60-61	Baptisms 1817-1818. Very difficult to read.
1:62-63	Church business 1811-1813.
1:63	Baptisms 1813 [or possibly 1820 (see 1:84)] through 1821. The handwriting on this page makes it look like a continuation from page 61 with the business on 62-63 in very different handwriting.
1:64-67	A special paper on the case of Irijah Terril, 1812.
1:67-80	Church business continues, 1813-1822. At the bottom of p. 80 it says "see 96."
1:81-83	Members of the Church, Aug. 1822, with annotations, continues to 1829, then cont. on p. 94. Very difficult handwriting.
1:84-89	Baptisms 1819, 1822-31.
1:87	A few deaths 1820-22.
1:94	Members of the church (in 1822) continued from p. 83.
1:96-120	Business 1822-32.
1:143	A few dismissions.
1:144-46	Deaths continued from page 163, 1826-1832.
1:151-154	Marriages 1800-1803, 1810, 1823-30.
1:155	Deaths, 1801-1813, 1817, 1822-1828. At end says "see page 144.
1:164-176	Baptisms 1785-1817.
2:4	Historical notes and Index.
2:5	Articles of Faith.
2:9-72	"Votes of the Church" 1832-1850. Includes some baptisms, admissions, dismissals, discipline, committees, etc.
2:79	List of officers, 1781-1834.
2:81-100	List of members 1781-1834, 1834-37, 1837-43, 1843-49. Made in several stages in different handwriting, probably started in 1834.
2:104-108	Baptisms 1832-49.
2:114-115	Deaths, 1832-1838.
3:1	Pastors & Deacons 1849-1899.
3:2-59	Church Members, 1781-1901. This section was compiled approximately alphabetically.
3:60-72	Additions by Profession 1850-1901.
3:90-99	Additions by Letter, 1850-1901.
3:120-129	Dismissions, 1850-1899.
3:150-165	Baptisms, 1850-1901.
3:200-228	Marriages, 1850-1900.
3:250-261	Deaths, 1850-1901.
3:320-335	Religious Charities. Basically organizations and amounts of money. Not abstracted.
3:340-436	Church Proceedings, 1850-1900. Does not contain any information about admissions or dismissions except in cases of church discipline and two occasions, in 1885 and 1900, when a number of members were considered erased. Not abstracted, but was sometimes referred to for clarification.

ABBREVIATIONS

adm	admitted
bp	baptized
cand	candidate
certif	"certified" to another church
ch	church, or child or children
comm	committee
d	died, or days
dau	daughter
dea	deacon
dec	deceased
dism	dismissed
exc	excommunicated
Irr	irregularly dismissed, usually when it is to the Episcopals
m	months
marr	married
memb	member, membership
poss	possibly
prob	probably
rec	recommended to another church
rem	removed to another place
S.S.	Sabbath School
wid	widow
wks	weeks
y	years

RECORDS OF THE CONGREGATIONAL CHURCH, NAUGATUCK, CONNECTICUT

1781-1901

Surname	Given Name	Date		Event	Page
-	-	-	1785	paragraph of ch business, illegible on microfilm	1:10
--	Barbara	28 May	1865	d, 72	3:255
unknown	-	20 Jan	1807	d "an infant of a stranger unnown"	1:158
unknown	-	Dec	1824	man fr Plymout, fell under wheel of loaded cart...liquor...22	1:162
--adley	Jonathan N.	3 Oct	1828	of Middlebury, marr Phebe Lewis of Waterbury	1:153
Abel	Warren D.	-	1899	adm ch from Cambridge Ms; also wife	3:2
Abel	Warren D.	3 Sep	1899	adm ch	3:72
Abel	Warren D.	5 Nov	1899	Mrs., adm fr 1st Pres, Cambridge NY	3:98
Adams	Amanda	19 Jun	1823	marr Major Terril "Waty" [she of Wat(erbur)y?]	1:152
Adams	Andrew	12 Sep	1830	d, 52, belonged to Gunntown	1:146
Adams	Betsey	12 May	1851	marr Willard Hopkins, both of Naug	3:200
Adams	Eli	29 Jul	1830	d, 74, belonged to Gunntown	1:146
Adams	Hannah	-	1787	wife of Abm, adm ch; dec 181-	3:2
Adams	Hannah	27 May	1787	wife of Abraham, adm ch; died 21 Feb 1817	2:83
Adams	Hannah	27 May	1787	wife of Abram adm ch	1:11
Adams	Hannah	27 May	1787	Ab, adm ch, d 21 Feb 1817 ["Abraham" added]	1:54
Adams	Nancy	-	-	adm ch; dec 18--; Wolcottville; [inserted later]	3:2
Ainsworth	Mary E.	-	1885	adm ch	3:2
Ainsworth	Mary E.	5 Jul	1885	adm ch	3:67
Albro	Oliver	26 Feb	1829	marr Amanda Hoyt of Salem	1:153
Allan	Cora M.	24 Aug	1898	21 marr Wm F. Frinn 21	3:226
Allen	Betsy	17 Mar	1811	d, 24	1:160
Allen	Frederick A.	22 Oct	1860	of Hamden marr Ann Lewis of Derby	3:204
Allen	Lyman	28 Feb	1866	d, 59, intemperance, Hillside	3:255
Allen	Margaret	1 Jan	1861	of Naug marr J. Camp of Bristol	3:204
Allen	Nathalie Ruth	11 Jun	1899	inf bp; John E. & Elnora Bowers	3:164
Allen	Wid	26 May	1827	grandchild d, 5 weeks	1:144
Allerton	G.M.	-	-	husband of Alida Leggett	3:26
Allerton	George M.	24 Jan	1877	marr Mary Alida Leggett of Naug	3:211
Alling	Abraham	2 Dec	1800	Revd Elder attending Consociation at Salem, from East Plains	1:19
Alling	Abraham	29 Sep	1801	Rev. Elder attending consociation in Salem, from East Plains	1:25
Alling	Hannah O.	10 Dec	1826	of Salem, marr George Palmer of New Haven	1:153
Alling	Liman	5 Jun	1801	son of Lemuel, d, 14y 3m 28d	1:155
Alvord	Geo B.	18 Sep	1895	24 marr Winnifred L. Warner 25	3:223
Anderson	-	Mar	1812	wife of --, d	1:160
Anderson	Anna	-	1896	Mrs., adm ch	3:2
Anderson	Anna	6 Sep	1896	Mrs., adm fr M.E., Portland Ct	3:98
Anderson	Carl P.	-	1896	adm ch	3:2

NAUGATUCK, CONNECTICUT, CONGREGATIONAL CHURCH RECORDS

Anderson	Carl P.	6 Sep	1896	adm fr M.E. Portland Ct	3:98
Anderson	Chas Oscar	24 Jul	1888	an inf, bp	3:159
Anderson	Gustave E.	24 Apr	1886	28 marr Matilda Olson 28, both of Naug	3:217
Anderson	Lillian Sultiff	21 Sep	1898	Mrs, 24 marr Lewis Hokenson 25	3:226
Anderson	Martin	24 Jul	1888	an inf, bp	3:159
Andras	Reuben Gilbert	Nov	1831	bp, ch of Mis Nony [prob Nancy; see Androus]	1:89
Andress	Tempa	4 Mar	1825	wife of Zina, adm ch from Columbia [see Andrews, Andrus]	1:101
Andrew	Amelia T.	-	1866	wife of S.N., adm ch; dec 1885	3:2
Andrew	Amelia T.	2 Sep	1866	adm ch	3:63
Andrew	Amelia T.	22 May	1885	Mrs, d, dyspepsia	3:259
Andrew	Ella	-	-	see Smith, Brainard Andrew	-
Andrew	Ella A.	-	1869	adm ch	3:2
Andrew	Ella A.	2 May	1869	adm ch	3:64
Andrew	Esther Louisa	2 Sep	1866	ch bp; Saml. N. & Amelia T.	3:154
Andrew	Ettie	-	1876	adm ch; dis 1892	3:2
Andrew	Ettie	7 May	1876	adm ch	3:65
Andrew	Ettie L.	14 Dec	1881	marr Warren L. Hall, both of Naug	3:213
Andrew	F.S.	-	-	husband of Julia Cutler	3:8
Andrew	Frank S.	-	1858	adm ch; dis 1869	3:2
Andrew	Frank S.	5 Sep	1858	adm ch	3:62
Andrew	Frank S.	17 May	1866	marr Julia Cutler, both of Naug	3:207
Andrew	Frank S.	18 Apr	1869	dism to West Cong, New Haven	3:124
Andrew	Fred S.	21 May	1885	24 of Naug marr Ida M. Hine 21	3:216
Andrew	Frederick Stephen	2 Sep	1866	ch bp; Saml N. & Amelia T.	3:154
Andrew	Jennie	21 Jul	1858	ch bp; Wm W. & --	3:152
Andrew	Julia	18 Apr	1869	[wife of] Frank S. dism to West Cong, New Haven	3:124
Andrew	N.T.	-	-	husband of Jane E. Lewis	3:26
Andrew	Noyes T.	11 Nov	1875	marr Jennie E. Lewis, both of Naug	3:211
Andrew	Saml N.	-	1866	adm ch; dec 1895	3:2
Andrew	Saml N.	2 Sep	1866	adm ch	3:63
Andrew	Samuel	14 Jan	1875	d, 74, kidney disease, Hillside	3:256
Andrew	Samuel	19 Jul	1884	Mrs, d [note says "cannot identify, March 1908"]	3:259
Andrew	Samuel N.	9 Jul	1895	d, 70	3:260
Andrew	W.W.	-	1885	erased	3:409
Andrews	Anna	-	1802	wife of Simeon, adm ch; dec 184-	3:2
Andrews	Anna	-	1822	wife of Simeon, on list of members	1:82
Andrews	Anne	17 Oct	1802	wife of Simeon adm ch	1:34
Andrews	Anne	27 Feb	1803	bp, ch of Simeon	1:171
Andrews	Charles H.	28 Dec	1876	marr Lillie A. Stevens, both of Naug	3:211
Andrews	Cndwin[sic]	17 Dec	1899	23 marr Charles Kling 21	3:228
Andrews	Frank Smith	3 Nov	1843	bp, ch of Samuel	2:107
Andrews	Hiram A.	20 Feb	1898	20 marr Lucy E. Hubbell 20	3:226
Andrews	Isaac	27 Feb	1803	bp, ch of Simeon	1:171
Andrews	Jenny	31 Jul	1858	d, inf of W.W., 10 wks	3:252
Andrews	Lucretia	27 Feb	1803	bp, ch of Simeon	1:171
Andrews	Mary	4 Dec	1806	d, 91y	1:158
Andrews	Milo	2 May	1801	ch of Simeon, d, 1y 10m 14d	1:155
Andrews	Mrs.	11 Jul	1841	adm ch from Woodbridge	2:37
Andrews	Nancy A.	Sep	1831	w of Reuben T. adm ch; rem 24 Dec 1836 to New Hartford N.	2:93
Andrews	Nancy A.	24 Dec	1836	w of Reuben T., dism to Cong, North New Hartford	2:20
Andrews	Plyne	27 Feb	1803	bp, ch of Simeon	1:171
Andrews	Ruth	27 Feb	1803	bp, ch of Simeon	1:171
Andrews	Ruth	-	1822	female, on list of members	1:82
Andrews	Selina	-	1841	adm ch; dec 188-	3:2

NAUGATUCK, CONNECTICUT, CONGREGATIONAL CHURCH RECORDS

Surname	Given	Date	Notes	Ref
Andrews	Selina	11 Jul 1841	adm ch from Woodbridge	2:97
Andrews	Temperance	14 Jun 1835	Mrs, letter to ch in Watertown, Conn.	2:19
Andrews	Wm W.	5 Sep 1858	adm fr Meth Ch, Naug	3:91
Andrews	Zina	27 Feb 1803	bp, ch of Simeon	1:171
Andrews	Zina	Oct 1825	male, on list of members; adm Oct 1825	1:81
Andrews	Zina	9 Sep 1825	adm ch from Columbia	1:101
Androus	Milow	27 Apr 1806	bp, son of Simeon, bp in the right of his wife	1:173
Androus	Nancy	Sep 1831	approved as cand for memb	1:114
Androus	Zina	3 Sep 1819	adm ch	1:59
Andrus	-	30 May 1827	d, from Meriden, fever, 20	1:144
Andrus	Anna	17 Oct 1802	wife of Simeon, adm ch; died Nov 1849	2:86
Andrus	Anna	17 Oct 1802	Sim., adm ch	1:56
Andrus	Darwin C.	26 Dec 1853	of Norfolk marr Jane E. Cook of Winsted	3:201
Andrus	Milo	15 Jun 1829	d, consumption, lingered for 4 y, confined to house and bed, 23	1:145
Andrus	Nancy A.	- 1831	wife of R.T., adm ch; dis 183-	3:2
Andrus	Ruth	- 1818	wife of E. Woodruff, adm ch; dis 184-	3:2
Andrus	Ruth	15 Mar 1818	wife of Woodruff, adm ch; rem 3 May 1840 to Episcopalians	2:89
Andrus	Ruth	15 Mar 1818	adm ch	1:59
Andrus	Temperance	- 1825	wife of Zina, adm ch; dis 183-	3:2
Andrus	Temperance	4 Mar 1825	wife of Zina, adm ch from Prospect; rem 14 Jun 1835 to Watertown	2:94
Andrus	Wm W.	- 1858	adm ch; care withdrawn 1885	3:2
Andrus	Zina	- -	husband of Temperance Hotchkiss	3:18
Andrus	Zina	- 1816	adm ch; Dis	3:2
Andrus	Zina	5 Jul 1816	cand for memb	1:73
Andrus	Zina	25 Aug 1816	adm ch; rem to Prospect	2:87
Andrus	Zina	25 Aug 1816	adm ch, dism Jun 1821	1:57
Andrus	Zina	25 Aug 1816	adm ch	1:73
Andrus	Zina	- 1819	adm ch; dec 183-	3:2
Andrus	Zina	3 Sep 1819	adm ch; rem	2:91
Andrus	Zina	9 Sep 1825	adm ch from Prospect; died 10 Sep 1833	2:94
Andrus	Zina	Aug 1833	died, 44	2:114
Andruss	Tempa	- 1822	female, member adm after 1822	1:83
Arandhaltz	Lydia	26 Dec 1885	24 marr John Hermanson 28, both of Naug	3:217
Arandholtz	Maria	14 Oct 1886	Mrs, 49 marr Theodore S. Erwin 55, both of Naug	3:217
Armstrong	Julia	- -	see Douglas, Raymond	-
Arnold	Cornelia J.	26 Apr 1863	(Beardsley) dism to Cong, Birmingham	3:122
Arnold	Gideon	- -	husband of Cornelia J. Beardsley	3:5
Arnst	Fraderic Dehemon	16 Sep 1804	[sic] bp, ch of John	1:172
Arnst	John	3 Jan 1808	ch bp	1:174
Arnst	Margaret	24 Aug 1800	wife of John, adm ch; ex May 1834	2:85
Arnst	Margaret	24 Aug 1800	Jo, adm ch	1:56
Arnst	Margaret	4 Jan 1818	adm ch	1:58
Arnst	Marget	4 Apr 1834	Mrs., her case discussed, she moved to NY, excomm.	2:15
Arnst	Polly	12 Jun 1803	bp, dau of John	1:171
Arnt	Daniel	Sep 1800	bp, ch of John	1:169
Arnt	Harshal	Sep 1800	bp, ch of John	1:169
Arnt	John	24 Aug 1800	wife bp & adm ch	1:15
Arnt	John H.	Sep 1800	bp, ch of John	1:169
Arnt	Margaretta	Sep 1800	bp, ch of John	1:169
Arnt	Marshal	Sep 1800	bp, ch of John	1:169
Arnt	Ruth	29 Nov 1810	of Salem, marr Cabeb [sic] Grannis of Cheshire	1:151
Arnt	Ruthe	Sep 1800	bp, ch of John	1:169
Arnt	Shelden	Sep 1800	bp, ch of John	1:169
Arnts	Barsillai	- 1848	adm ch; dis 183-	3:2

NAUGATUCK, CONNECTICUT, CONGREGATIONAL CHURCH RECORDS

Surname	Given	Date	Event	Ref
Arnts	Barzilla	1 Mar 1801	bp, ch of John	1:169
Arnts	Barzillai	16 Apr 1848	adm ch from Litchfield	2:100
Arnts	Barzillai	1 Jun 1851	dism to Cong, Litchfield	3:120
Arnts	Garry	17 Nov 1826	marr Catharine J. Phelps of Salem	1:153
Arnts	John	15 Jan 1829	his wife complained against for intoxication and countenancing adultery	1:107f
Arnts	Margaret	- 1800	wife of John, adm ch; Exc 1834	3:2
Arnts	Margaret	- 1818	adm ch; dis 183-	3:2
Arnts	Margaret	4 Jan 1818	adm ch ["Arnst" crossed out]	2:89
Arnts	Margaretta	- 1822	wife of John, on list of members	1:82
Arnts	Margaretta Jr	- 1822	female, on list of members	1:82
Arnts	Mary H.	- 1848	adm ch; dis 183-	3:2
Arnts	Mary H.	16 Apr 1848	adm ch from Litchfield	2:100
Arnts	Susan	- 1848	adm ch; dis 183-	3:2
Arnts	Susan	16 Apr 1848	wife of Barzillai, adm ch from Litchfield	2:100
Arnts	Susan	1 Jun 1851	w. of B[arzillai] dism to Cong, Litchfield	3:120
Arthur	Nettie	- 1881	adm ch; dis 188-	3:2
Arthur	Nettie	2 Dec 1881	adm fr M.E. Church, Birmingham Ct	3:94
Arthur	Nettie	9 Oct 1885	dism to 2nd Cong, Waterbury	3:126
Atkins	Josiah	3 Jun 1792	bp, ch of Mrs. Culver	1:166
Atkins	Sally	3 Jun 1792	bp, ch of Mrs. Culver	1:166
Atwater	Beele	Apr 1833	on committee for SS	2:9
Atwater	Bela	- 1818	adm ch; withdrawn 184-	3:2
Atwater	Bela	4 Sep 1818	infant ch bp	1:61
Atwater	Bela	- 1822	male, on list of members	1:81
Atwater	Bela	20 Dec 1842	to be visited and laboured with	2:42
Atwater	Bela	10 Aug 1845	excomm, having joined Episcopal Ch in this place	2:51
Atwater	Bela	7 May 1859	d, 72, Hillside	3:252
Atwater	Bele	15 Mar 1818	adm ch; withdrawn to Episcopal	2:89
Atwater	Bele	15 Mar 1818	adm ch	1:58
Atwater	Br	6 Nov 1829	voted to attend future conf	1:109
Atwater	Jane	- 1822	wid, on list of members	1:82
Atwater	Lucinda	28 Apr 1828	of Salem, marr Emery Mason	1:153
Atwater	Moses	6 May 1827	d, long helpless in consequence of epilepsy, 75	1:144
Atwater	Nancy Miriam	31 Aug 1832	bp, ch of Bele, b 24 Dec 1831	2:104
Atwater	Naomi	- 1818	wife of Bela, adm ch; withdrawn 184-	3:2
Atwater	Naomi	15 Mar 1818	wife of Bele, adm ch; withdrawn to Episcopal	2:89
Atwater	Naomi	- 1822	wife of Bela, on list of members	1:82
Atwater	Naomi	10 Aug 1845	Mrs., excomm, having joined Episcopal Ch in this place	2:51
Atwater	Neomia	15 Mar 1818	wife of Bele, adm ch	1:58
Atwater	William	1 Jan 1809	infant ch d, 3d	1:159
Atwood	Mary L.	3 Apr 1828	of Watertown, marr Henry Sandland of Birmingham, Eng.	1:153
Averill	Eliphalet	- 1856	adm ch; dis 1858	3:2
Averill	Eliphalet	2 Nov 1856	adm ch	3:61
Averill	Eliphalet	21 Mar 1858	dism to Chapel St Ch, N. Haven	3:121
Averill	Lucy E.	- 1885	adm ch from Branford Ct; dis 1891	3:2
Averill	Lucy E.	3 May 1885	Mrs., adm fr 1st Cong, Branford Ct	3:95
Averill	Lucy E.	6 Sep 1891	dism to Cong, Branford Ct	3:127
Ayers	Alvin D.	19 Sep 1877	of Syracuse NY marr M. Lizzie E.[crossed out] Patterson of Naug	3:211
Ayres	Priscilla	5 Feb 1855	of Poughkeepsie NY marr Cornelius H. Porter of Naug	3:202
Babcock	Ivan Edwin	- 1890	adm ch; dis 1891 to Cincinnatus	3:7
Babcock	Ivan Edwin	9 Mar 1890	bp, adult, immersed in Bapt Ch Waterbury	3:159
Babcock	Ivan Edwin	9 Mar 1890	adm ch	3:70
Babcock	Ivin	6 Nov 1891	dism to Baptist, Cincinnatus NY	3:127

NAUGATUCK, CONNECTICUT, CONGREGATIONAL CHURCH RECORDS

Back	Geo D.	-	-	2nd husband of Emily J. Smith	3:44
Bailey	Cora E.	1 May	1880	marr Wm L. Pond, both of Naug	3:216
Bailey	Emma L.	4 Mar	1877	adm ch	3:65
Bailey	Emma L.	17 May	1895	Miss, dism to 2nd Cong, Waterbury	3:128
Baily	Emma L.	-	1877	adm ch; dis 1895 to 2nd ch, Waterbury	3:6
Baker	J.J.	2 May	1886	adm ch; dis 1895 to Newark NJ [day was copied wrong]	3:7
Baker	J.J.	7 Nov	1886	adm ch	3:69
Baker	John J.	16 Aug	1895	dism to 1st Cong, Newark NJ	3:128
Baldwin	-	-	-	see Balwin	-
Baldwin	Abigail	-	1794	adm ch, wife of Matthew; dec 1812	3:4
Baldwin	Abigail	14 Oct	1794	wife of Matthew, adm ch; died 11 Jul 1812	2:84
Baldwin	Abigail	94 Oct	1794	adm ch, d 11 Jul 1812 [day written "94 Oct"]	1:55
Baldwin	Abigail	11 Jul	1812	d, widow of Mathew	1:160
Baldwin	Abigal	19 Oct	1794	adm ch	1:13
Baldwin	Amy	-	1845	adm ch from Waterbury; dec 1854	3:5
Baldwin	Amy	31 Oct	1845	adm ch from Waterbury	2:100
Baldwin	Amy	13 Feb	1854	d, 77, Burned [?]	3:250
Baldwin	Ana	30 Sep	1787	adm ch	1:11
Baldwin	Anna	-	1787	adm ch, wife of A. Mills; dis to Canton	3:4
Baldwin	Anna	30 Sep	1787	wife of Amasa Mills, adm ch; rem to Canton	2:83
Baldwin	Anna	30 Sep	1787	adm ch, dism [to "Canton" added]	1:54
Baldwin	Augusta L.	-	1867	adm ch; care withdrawn 1885	3:6
Baldwin	Augusta L.	6 Jan	1867	adm ch	3:64
Baldwin	Elizebeth S.	3 Jul	1825	d, Hydrocephalus, 5	1:162
Baldwin	Ellen	19 May	1861	of Naug marr Alfred E. Fuller of New Milford	3:205
Baldwin	Elvira	27 Sep	1863	(Hotchkiss) dism to Cong, Prospect	3:122
Baldwin	Jerusha M.	2 Jan	1853	of Naug marr Thos K. Small of Truro, Mass	3:201
Baldwin	Joseph	30 Aug	1863	his inf d, 1	3:254
Baldwin	L.	-	-	husband of Elvira Hotchkiss	3:18
Baldwin	L.	-	-	husband of Susan M. Hoadley ["L" written over "A."]	3:18
Baldwin	Leonard	-	-	husband of Susan M. Hoadley	2:92
Baldwin	Leonard	19 Oct	1829	of Torrington, marr Susan M. Hoadley of Salem Bridge	1:153
Baldwin	Lucian	17 Jun	1826	wife d, swelling in throat, 20	1:163
Baldwin	Lucius	-	-	husband of Elvira Hotchkiss	2:95
Baldwin	Matthew	4 Jul	1817	d, 50	1:161
Baldwin	Miles	23 Sep	1810	d, ch of Matthew, 2y	1:160
Baldwin	Nancy	3 Feb	1850	wife of Wm, dism to Cong, Cheshire	3:120
Baldwin	Susan	-	1830	dism to Winchester	1:143
Baldwin	Susan	5 Sep	1830	rec to ch in Wincester	1:111
Baldwin	Susie	7 Jun	1876	["Carrie" crossed out] marr Robert M. Smith of Naug	3:211
Baldwin	Theo.	-	-	husband of Millissent Pardee	2:91
Baldwin	W.J.	-	-	husband of Nancy Stone	3:43
Baldwin	W.J.	-	1845	adm ch from Cheshire; dis 1850 to Cheshire	3:5
Baldwin	William	3 Feb	1850	dism to Cong, Cheshire	3:120
Baldwin	William J.	21 Dec	1845	adm ch from Cheshire; dism 3 Feb 1850	2:100
Ball	Austin C.	-	1898	adm ch from Cornwall, wife also adm	3:7
Ball	Austin C.	6 Nov	1898	Mr., adm fr Cong, Cornwall Ct; wife also	3:98
Balwin	Anna	28 May	1823	of Woodbridge, marr Earl Sperry	1:152
Barlow	Gertrude R.	25 Aug	1887	21 marr Willis R.R. Smith 23, both of Watertown	3:218
Barlow	Mary	13 Mar	1878	marr Lester E. Terrell, both of Naug	3:212
Barnam	-	-	-	see Barnum	-
Barnam	E.C.	-	-	husband of Eliza Jane Ward	3:54
Barnam	Eli C.	29 Dec	1868	marr Elisa J. Ward of Naug	3:208
Barnes	Harrietta	-	1869	adm ch; dis 1886 to Cong ch, Wallingford	3:6

NAUGATUCK, CONNECTICUT, CONGREGATIONAL CHURCH RECORDS

Barnes	Harrietta [sic]	2 May 1869	adm ch	3:64
Barnes	Philo P.	9 Aug 1870	d, 28, typhoid	3:256
Barnum	-	-	see Barnam	-
Barnum	Alice Eliza	7 Jan 1855	bp, 4 yrs; Edwd & Hannah	3:151
Barnum	Hannah F.	- 1854	adm ch fr North Cornwall; w of Edwd; dis 1859 to Mt Vernon NY	3:5
Barnum	Hannah F.	3 Sep 1854	adm from North Cornwall	3:90
Barnum	Hannah F.	3 Jul 1859	dism to Ref Prot Dutch Ch, Mt. Vernon NY	3:121
Barnum	Henry C.	- 1896	adm ch from Southport; dis 1896 to Beacon Falls	3:7
Barnum	Henry C.	1 Mar 1896	adm fr Cong, Southport, Ct	3:98
Barnum	Henry C.	4 Dec 1896	dism to M.E. Ch, Beacon Falls, Ct	3:128
Barnum	Henry C.	28 Aug 1896	dism to Cong, Bethany Ct [crossed out] "letter not used"	3:128
Barnum	Mary Ella	16 Jul 1854	d, dau of Edwd & Hannah, 19 mos, whooping cough	3:251
Barret	Mary	11 Mar 1881	dism to 1st Cong, Waterbury	3:125
Barrett	Mary	- 1878	adm ch from 1st Cong, Waterbury; dis 1881 to 1st Cong Waterbury	3:6
Barrett	Mary	3 Mar 1878	adm fr Waterbury 1st Cong	3:94
Bartlemas	Rose	10 Jan 1893	23 marr William Saunders 23	3:222
Bartlemas	Rose M.	- 1891	adm ch, wife of Wm Saunders	3:7
Bartlemas	Rose M.	1 Mar 1891	Miss, adm ch	3:70
Bartlett	Stephen C.	22 Sep 1869	marr Julia B. Pickett, both of Naug	3:208
Basham	Hattie A.	18 Aug 1891	marr Edford C. Seeley	3:221
Bassett	Delia L.	- 1877	adm ch; care withdrawn 1885	3:6
Bassett	Delia L.	4 Mar 1877	adm ch	3:66
Bassett	Theophilus	29 Sep 1801	Delegate to consociation in Salem, from East Plains	1:25
Bateman	Esther	30 Oct 1829	ch of Stephen, bp	1:88
Bateman	Frances Eleanor	16 Mar 1834	bp, ch of Wiliam [surname looks like "Betom-"]	2:15
Bateman	Haritt	5 Oct 1828	ch of Stephen, bp	1:88
Bateman	Maria	- 1828	adm ch, wife of Stephen; dis 1838 to Blackwoodtown NJ	3:4
Bateman	Maria	4 Jul 1828	St., adm ch	1:59b
Bateman	Maria	6 Jul 1828	wife of Stephen, adm ch; rem 9 Jun 1838 to Blackwoodtown NJ	2:93
Bateman	Maria	6 Jul 1828	member	1:94
Bateman	Maria	6 Jul 1828	wife of Stephen, adm ch	1:106
Bateman	Mr.	13 Mar 1838	on comm	2:31
Bateman	St	6 Nov 1829	voted to attend future conf	1:109
Bateman	Stephen	20 Sep 1826	marr Maria Benham of Salem	1:152
Bateman	Stephen	- 1828	adm ch; dism 1838 to Blackwoodtown NJ	3:4
Bateman	Stephen	4 Jul 1828	adm ch	1:59b
Bateman	Stephen	6 Jul 1828	adm ch; rem 9 Jun 1838 to Blackwoodtown NJ	2:93
Bateman	Stephen	6 Jul 1828	member	1:94
Bateman	Stephen	6 Jul 1828	adm ch	1:106
Bateman	Steven	30 Dec 1832	on comm	1:119
Bateman	Wiliam	30 Dec 1833	on comm	2:14
Bateman	William	Apr 1833	Librarian for SS	2:9
Bateman	Wm	- -	husband of Fanny Stevens	2:93
Bateman	Wm	- 1828	adm ch; dis 1838 to Blackwoodtown NJ	3:4
Bateman	Wm	6 Jul 1828	adm ch; rem 14 Sep 1838 to Blackwoodtown, NJ	2:92
Bateman	Wm	6 Jul 1828	adm ch	1:59a
Bateman	Wm	6 Jul 1828	member	1:94
Bateman	Wm	6 Jul 1828	adm ch	1:107
Bateman	Wm	6 Nov 1829	voted to attend future conf	1:109
Bateman	Wm	26 Aug 1832	Librarian for SS	2:11
Bates	Edward Henry	11 Jun 1899	inf bp; Edwd C. & Laura B., Millville Chapel	3:164
Batterman	-	- -	husband of Paulina Beecher	2:91
Batterman	Paulina	15 Dec 1844	dism to Presbyterian Ch in Guilderland NY	2:50
Baumer	Cassie	10 Nov 1897	21 marr Peter J. Quinn 24	3:225

NAUGATUCK, CONNECTICUT, CONGREGATIONAL CHURCH RECORDS

Surname	Given	Date	Event	Ref
Bavier	Chas H.	5 Sep 1888	22 marr Susie J. Hawley 16	3:219
Beach	Fannie	26 Apr 1877	of Naug marr Joseph Divine	3:211
Beach	George W.	4 Oct 1855	of Naug marr Sarah Upson of Seymour	3:202
Beach	Mary E.	10 Feb 1872	of Naug marr Evan Lewis of Waterbury	3:209
Beach	Theodore B.	9 Oct 1879	marr Libbie O. Lockwood, both of Seymour	3:212
Beach	Wesley Henry	- 1900	adm ch; dec 1901	3:7
Beach	Wesley Henry	1 Jul 1900	adm ch	3:72
Beach	Wesley Henry	13 Jan 1901	d, 21, spinal meningitis	3:261
Beacher	-	-	see Beecher	-
Beacher	Abiah	26 Jun 1803	bp, ch of Daniel	1:171
Beacher	Anna	26 Jun 1803	bp, ch of Daniel	1:171
Beacher	Argus	26 Jun 1803	bp, ch of Daniel	1:171
Beacher	Baldwin	26 Jun 1803	bp, ch of Daniel	1:171
Beacher	Baldwin	4 Jan 1818	adm ch	1:58
Beacher	Calvin	19 Apr 1807	bp, son of Daniel & Clarissia	1:173
Beacher	Clarissa	16 Sep 1804	bp, ch of Daniel	1:172
Beacher	Clarissa	15 Mar 1818	adm ch, dism 1829	1:58
Beacher	Daniel	3 Jul 1818	on committee to est. Sabbath School	1:76
Beacher	Daniel	4 Jan 1818	adm ch	1:58
Beacher	Elizia Hooker	4 May 1817	ch of Baldwin, bp	1:60
Beacher	Fanny	26 Jun 1803	bp, ch of Daniel	1:171
Beacher	Julia Ann	6 Sep 1818	dau Daniel, bp	1:61
Beacher	Julias	29 Sep 1803	d, son of Daniel, "ten years" [sic]	1:156
Beacher	Julius	26 Jun 1803	bp, ch of Daniel	1:171
Beacher	Luke	19 Mar 1799	bp, ch of Daniel	1:169
Beacher	Maria	15 May 1808	bp, dau of Daniel & Clarissia	1:174
Beacher	Parsons	26 Jun 1803	bp, ch of Daniel	1:171
Beacher	Susan	26 Jun 1803	bp, ch of Daniel	1:171
Beale	Cora Mabel	5 Jul 1885	inf bp; J.E. & Hattie	3:157
Beale	Florence Phoebe	5 Jul 1885	inf bp; J.E. & Hattie	3:157
Beale	J.E.	31 Dec 1886	Mrs., dism to Cong, Wallingford	3:126
Beardley	Wm D.	12 Mar 1823	infant ch d, 5d	1:161
Beardslee	James H.	5 Jul 1839	adm ch from Syracuse NY	2:97
Beardsley	-	-	see Bersley	-
Beardsley	--nius Lyon	21 Oct 1827	ch of Wm D., bp [name could be "Penius" or "Genius"]	1:87
Beardsley	Alvira	- 1822	wife of Wm D, on list of members	1:82
Beardsley	Ann M.	6 Nov 1853	dism to 2d Cong, Bridgeport	3:120
Beardsley	Ann Maria	- 1844	adm ch from Plymouth; dis 1853	3:5
Beardsley	Ann Maria	1 Mar 1844	wife of Samuel, adm ch from Plymouth	2:99
Beardsley	Br	6 Nov 1829	voted to attend future conf	1:109
Beardsley	Chs L.	19 Jul 1868	d, 26, asthma, Hillside	3:256
Beardsley	Cornelia J.	- 1854	adm ch; wife of Gideon Arnold; dis 1863 to Birmingham	3:5
Beardsley	Cornelia J.	5 Mar 1854	adm ch	3:61
Beardsley	Cornelia Jane	31 Aug 1832	bp, ch of Wm D., b 3 Jan 1832	2:104
Beardsley	Elvira	- 1819	adm ch, wife of Wm D.; dec 1854	3:4
Beardsley	Elvira	3 Jan 1819	wife of Wm D., adm ch	2:91
Beardsley	Elvira	25 Mar 1854	d, wife of Wm D., 56, Hillside	3:250
Beardsley	Emma C.	- 1876	adm ch; dis 1890 to Goshen Ct	3:6
Beardsley	Emma C.	7 May 1876	adm ch	3:65
Beardsley	Emma C.	24 Jan 1890	Miss, dism to Cong, Goshen Ct	3:127
Beardsley	Esther	- 1841	adm ch; dis 1862 to Deep River [see Southworth]	3:5
Beardsley	Esther	11 Jul 1841	adm ch	2:98
Beardsley	Esther Stevens	15 Jun 1823	ch of Wm, bp	1:85
Beardsley	James	6 Feb 1841	on comm	2:36

NAUGATUCK, CONNECTICUT, CONGREGATIONAL CHURCH RECORDS

Surname	Given	Date	Event	Ref
Beardsley	James	29 Mar 1850	and wife, requested to make their own statements before the Ch	2:63
Beardsley	James H.	- 1839	adm ch from Syracuse NY; exc 1851	3:5
Beardsley	Maria	1 Mar 1844	adm from Cong Ch Plymouth Hollow	2:49
Beardsley	Nancy	- 1841	adm ch; wife of Danl Pratt; dis 1849 to Southington	3:5
Beardsley	Nancy	11 Jul 1841	adm ch; [m] Mr. Pratt; dism 1 Jan 1849 to Southington	2:98
Beardsley	Nancy Devom [sic]	9 Sep 1825	ch of Wm, bp	1:86
Beardsley	W.D.	4 Oct 1863	watch & fellowship withdrawn	3:122
Beardsley	William Junius	29 Jun 1838	bp, ch of Wm D.	2:105
Beardsley	Wm D	3 Jan 1819	adm ch	2:91
Beardsley	Wm D.	- 1819	adm ch; withdrawn 1863	3:4
Beardsley	Wm D.	- 1822	male, on list of members	1:81
Beardsley	Wm D.	10 Apr 1825	on committee	1:101
Beardsley	Wm D.	20 Dec 1842	to visit and labour with Brother Selden Woodruff	2:42
Beardsley	Wm D.	9 Sep 1868	d, 77, apoplexy, Hillside	3:256
Beardsley	Wm J.	- 1857	adm ch; dis 1866 to Sandusky, Ohio	3:5
Beardsley	Wm J.	5 Jul 1857	adm ch	3:61
Beardsley	Wm J.	28 Oct 1866	dism to Cong, Sandusky, Ohio	3:123
Beardsley	Wm Kirk	30 Apr 1830	ch of Wm, bp	1:88
Beardsly	Wm	7 Oct 1827	on committee	1:103
Beatty	Augusta	27 Nov 1890	marr Frank Foster	3:221
Bebee	-	-	see Beebe	-
Bebee	Amzi	28 Mar 1802	of Salem, marr Jerusha Summers of Milford	1:151
Bebee	Caroline	4 Sep 1814	bp, ch of Jerusha wife of Amzi	1:176
Bebee	Chester	15 Mar 1818	adm ch; rem to Ridgeville O.	2:89
Bebee	Desire	3 Dec 1786	wife of Zera, adm ch; rem 20 Oct 1805 to Prospect	2:83
Bebee	Desire	3 Dec 1786	Zera, adm ch, dism 20 Oct 1805	1:54
Bebee	Elias Brister	23 Jun 1811	bp, ch of Jerusha, wife of Amzi	1:175
Bebee	Esther	18 Sep 1791	wife of Joseph, adm ch; rem 6 Sep 1806 to Colebrook	2:84
Bebee	Esther	18 Sep 1791	Jo[seph], adm ch, dism 6 Sep 1806	1:55
Bebee	Hannah	22 Feb 1801	wife of Reuben, adm ch; died 25 Feb 1807	2:86
Bebee	Hannah	22 Feb 1801	Ru, adm ch, d 25 Feb 1807	1:56
Bebee	Hannah	22 Feb 1801	wife of Reuben adm ch	1:21
Bebee	Jemima	23 Apr 1786	wife of Ira, adm ch; withdrawn to Baptist	2:83
Bebee	Jemima	23 Apr 1786	Ira. adm ch, ["Ira - Baptist" added] certificated	1:54
Bebee	Jerusha	18 Sep 1808	Amz, adm ch [year omitted in record]	1:56
Bebee	Jerusha	18 Sep 1808	wife of Amzi, adm ch; rem 3 May 1839, joined the Baptists	2:86
Bebee	Joseph	18 Sep 1791	adm ch; rem 6 Sep 1806 to Colebrook	2:84
Bebee	Joseph	18 Sep 1791	adm ch, dism	1:55
Bebee	Joseph Jr.	- -	husband of Rhoda Todd	2:83
Bebee	Joseph Jr.	3 Jun 1787	adm ch; rem 6 Sep 1806 to Prospect	2:83
Bebee	Joseph Junr	3 Jun 1787	adm ch, dism 6 Sep 1806	1:54
Bebee	Maria	15 Mar 1818	wife of Chester, adm ch; rem to Ridgeville O.	2:89
Bebee	Reuben	22 Feb 1801	adm ch; died 20 Jul 1812	2:86
Bebee	Reuben	22 Feb 1801	adm ch, d 20 Jul 1812	1:56
Bebee	Reuben	22 Feb 1801	adm ch	1:21
Bebee	Reuben	20 Jul 1812	d	1:160
Bebee	Reuben Chittenden	4 Jul 1813	bp, ch of Jerusha wife of Amzi	1:176
Bebee	Sally	18 Sep 1808	Is., adm ch, dism [year omitted in record]	1:56
Bebee	Sally	18 Sep 1808	wife of Isaac, adm ch; rem to Torrington	2:86
Bebee	Zera	30 Sep 1787	adm ch; rem 20 Oct 1805 to Prospect	2:83
Bebee	Zera	30 Sep 1787	adm ch, dism	1:54
Becker	Jacob	21 Feb 1882	marr Catharine Bohem [sic], both of Naug	3:214
Becker	Margarette	6 Apr 1889	marr Daniel Larsch	3:220
Beckwith	E.G.	22 Feb 1881	at centennial exercises	3:300

NAUGATUCK, CONNECTICUT, CONGREGATIONAL CHURCH RECORDS

Beebe	-	-	-	see Bebee	-
Beebe	Abram Warner	5 Apr	1787	bp, ch of Zera [definitely says "April"]	1:164
Beebe	Abram Warner	5 Aug	1787	bp ["Agust"][entry crossed out]	1:11
Beebe	Amzi	15 Dec	1828	d, in consequence of intemperance, 53	1:145
Beebe	Ansel	5 Apr	1801	bp, ch of Reuben	1:170
Beebe	Augustus	24 Nov	1859	d, 74, burned in a fit of intoxication, Hillside [or 25 Nov]	3:252
Beebe	Benjamin	5 Apr	1787	bp, ch of Zera [definitely says "April"]	1:164
Beebe	Benjamin	5 Aug	1787	bp [Agust"][entry crossed out]	1:11
Beebe	Chester	-	1818	adm ch; dis to Ridgeville O.	3:4
Beebe	Chester	15 Mar	1818	adm ch, dism 26 Aug 18--	1:58
Beebe	Chester	15 Mar	1818	bp	1:60
Beebe	Clarissa	Oct	1818	ch of Amzi, bp	1:61
Beebe	David Jr	4 Mar	1808	infant ch d	1:158
Beebe	Desire	-	1786	wife of Zera, adm ch; dis 1805 to Prospect	3:4
Beebe	Desire	20 Oct	1805	relict of Zere, given certificate	1:39
Beebe	Ephraim	5 Apr	1801	bp, ch of Reuben	1:170
Beebe	Esther	-	1791	adm ch, wife of Joseph; dis 1806 to Colebrook	3:4
Beebe	Esther	18 Sep	1791	wife of Joseph, adm ch	1:12
Beebe	Esther	6 Sep	1806	wife of Joseph, rec to ch at Colebrook	1:45
Beebe	Eunice	5 Apr	1801	bp, ch of Reuben	1:170
Beebe	Ezra	18 Oct	1791	bp, ch of Joseph	1:166
Beebe	Hannah	-	1801	adm ch, wife of Reuben; dec 1807	3:4
Beebe	Hannah	25 Feb	1807	d, wife of Reuben, 57y	1:158
Beebe	J. Jr.	-	-	husband of Rhoda Todd	3:48
Beebe	Jane S.	1 Mar	1829	of Salem, marr Burr Benham	1:153
Beebe	Jemima	-	1786	wife of Ira, adm ch; Irr. to Baptist	3:4
Beebe	Jemima	23 Apr	1786	wife of Ira adm ch	1:10
Beebe	Jerusha	-	1808	adm ch, wife of Amsi; Irr. 1839 to Baptist	3:4
Beebe	Jerusha	18 Sep	1808	bp, wife of Amzi	1:174
Beebe	Jerusha	18 Sep	1808	wife of Amei [sic], adm ch	1:48
Beebe	Jerusha	-	1822	wife of Amzi, on list of members	1:82
Beebe	Joseph	-	1791	adm ch; dis 1806 to Colebrook	3:4
Beebe	Joseph	18 Oct	1791	bp, ch of Joseph	1:166
Beebe	Joseph	18 Sep	1791	adm ch	1:12
Beebe	Joseph	6 Sep	1806	rec to ch at Colebrook	1:45
Beebe	Joseph Jr.	-	1787	adm ch; dis 1806 to Prospect	3:4
Beebe	Joseph Junr	3 Jun	1787	adm ch	1:11
Beebe	Laurel Calkins	28 Jun	1818	ch of Chester, bp	1:61
Beebe	Leve	5 Apr	1801	bp, ch of Reuben	1:170
Beebe	Levi	6 Apr	1788	bp, ch of Zera	1:165
Beebe	Levisa	4 Jan	1830	of Salem, marr Sylvester Clark of Watertown	1:154
Beebe	Lockey	1 Jan	1825	of Waterbury, marr Charles A. Russel	1:152
Beebe	Lovwel Newel	28 Jun	1818	ch of Chester, bp	1:61
Beebe	Maria	-	1818	adm ch, wife of Chester; dis to Ridgeville O.	3:4
Beebe	Maria R.	15 Mar	1818	wife of Chester adm ch, dism 26 Aug 18--	1:58
Beebe	Moses Cook	30 Nov	1794	bp, ch of Joseph	1:167
Beebe	Reuben	-	1801	adm ch; dec 1812	3:4
Beebe	Reuben	5 Apr	1801	bp, ch of Reuben	1:170
Beebe	Salla [sic]	18 Oct	1791	bp, ch of Joseph	1:166
Beebe	Sally	-	1808	adm ch, wife of Isaac; dis to Torrington	3:4
Beebe	Sally	18 Sep	1808	wife of Isaac adm ch	1:48
Beebe	Sally	-	1822	wife of Isaac, on list of members; dism	1:82
Beebe	Selden	5 Apr	1801	bp, ch of Reuben	1:170
Beebe	Thankful	5 Apr	1801	bp, ch of Reuben	1:170

NAUGATUCK, CONNECTICUT, CONGREGATIONAL CHURCH RECORDS

Beebe	William W.	14 Jan 1806	d, son of David Jr, 2y	1:157
Beebe	Zera	3 Dec 1786	wife adm ch	1:10
Beebe	Zera	1787	adm ch; dis 1805 to Prospect	3:4
Beebe	Zera	30 Sep 1787	adm ch	1:11
Beebe	Zere	20 Oct 1805	relict Desire given certificate	1:39
Beecher	-	-	see Beacher	-
Beecher	A.	-	husband of Mary A. Lewis	3:25
Beecher	A.	-	husband of Sarah Scott	3:42
Beecher	Abigail	18 Jan 1856	of Prospect marr Luther Gaylord of Naug	3:203
Beecher	Abraham	-	husband of Mary A. Lewis	2:93
Beecher	Argus	21 Jul 1829	ch d, dysentery, 3	1:145
Beecher	Argus	1879	widow died, see Sarah Scott	3:258
Beecher	Baldwin	1818	adm ch; dis 1843 to Broad Alban	3:4
Beecher	Baldwin	4 Jan 1818	adm ch; rem 1843 Brod Albin "21 - 1843" [see Hannah & Eliza H.]	2:88
Beecher	Baldwin	1822	male, on list of members	1:81
Beecher	Baldwin	9 Dec 1827	to attend conf at Darien	1:105
Beecher	Baldwin	6 Nov 1829	voted to attend future conf	1:109
Beecher	Bennet	18 Aug 1816	bp, ch of Hannah wife of Baldwin	1:176
Beecher	C., Mrs.	5 May 1837	on comm "to attend to cases of unchristian walk...among	2:25
-	-	-	female members"	-
Beecher	Clara	1854	adm ch fr Edinburgh Center NY; w of Ira; dis 1860 to	3:5
-	-	-	1st ch Waterbury	-
Beecher	Clara	5 Nov 1854	w of I, adm fr Edingburgh [sic] Center NY (Cong)	3:90
Beecher	Clara	29 Apr? 1860	dism to 1st Cong, Waterbury	3:121
Beecher	Clara	4 Mar 1877	Mrs, adm fr Waterbury Ct 1st Cong	3:94
Beecher	Clara	1878	widow, adm ch from 1st Cong, Waterbury; dec 1887	3:6
Beecher	Clara	19 Jan 1887	Mrs, d, 84, pneumonia	3:259
Beecher	Clarissa	20 Jan 1811	her ch bp, wife of Daniel	1:175
Beecher	Clarissa	1818	adm ch, wife of C. Goodyear; dis 1829 to Philadelphia	3:4
Beecher	Clarissa	15 Mar 1818	wife of Charles Goodyear, adm ch; rem to Philadelphia	2:91
Beecher	Clarissa	1822	wife of Daniel, on list of members	1:82
Beecher	Clarissa	25 Aug 1824	of Salem, marr Charles Goodyear	1:152
Beecher	Clarissa	6 Nov 1829	on comm	1:109
Beecher	Clarissa Jr.	1822	female, on list of members, "C. Goodyear" [prob. husband]	1:82
Beecher	D.	-	husband of Clarissa Porter	3:35
Beecher	D.	-	husband of Sena Hoadley	3:18
Beecher	D.[?]	-	husb of Asinetty ["Sena" crossed out] her 1st husb Hiel Hoadley	2:89
Beecher	Daniel	-	husband of Clarissa Porter	2:85
Beecher	Daniel	-	husband of Clarissa Porter	1:55
Beecher	Daniel	1818	adm ch; dec 1848	3:4
Beecher	Daniel	4 Jan 1818	adm ch; died 10 Mar 1848	2:88
Beecher	Daniel	1822	male, on list of members	1:81
Beecher	Daniel	4 May 1828	Mrs, on comm	1:106
Beecher	Daniel	30 Dec 1832	meeting at his house	1:119
Beecher	David	23 Jun 1855	d, 77, diabetis, Hillside	3:251
Beecher	Eleanor	1861	adm ch from Derby; wife of Saml; dis 1866 to 1st ch Milford	3:6
Beecher	Eleanor	3 Nov 1861	adm fr 1st Ch, Derby	3:91
Beecher	Eleanor	28 Oct 1866	dism to 1st Ch, Milford	3:123
Beecher	Elect	14 May 1802	wife of Daniel, d, 28y 11m 4d, Hillside	1:155
Beecher	Elisa Z. [sic]	1836	adm ch; wife of H.W. Spencer; dism 1843 to Broad Alban	3:5
Beecher	Elisabeth	1832	adm ch from Prospect; dis 1864	3:4
Beecher	Elisth	25 Mar 1864	voted dism, eligible for letter if asked for [see 3:367]	3:122
Beecher	Eliza H. [sic]	3 Jan 1836	adm ch; [m] H.W. Spencer; dism 9 Apr 1843 to Brod Albin	2:96
Beecher	Elizabeth	9 Sep 1832	adm ch from Prospect	2:93

NAUGATUCK, CONNECTICUT, CONGREGATIONAL CHURCH RECORDS

Beecher	Elizabeth H.	25 Mar 1868	d, (Mrs. Guy), 43, cancer, Hillside	3:256
Beecher	Emily	- 1833	adm ch; wife of M. Upson; dism 1837	3:5
Beecher	Emily	5 May 1833	wife of Martin Upson, adm ch; rem to Waterbury 18 Jun 1837	2:93
Beecher	Franklin	- -	husband of Mary Jane Milson	3:29
Beecher	Franklin K.	- 1856	adm ch; dec 1864	3:5
Beecher	Franklin K.	2 Nov 1856	adm ch	3:61
Beecher	Franklin K.	6 Oct 1864	d, 32, yellow fever, Hillside, d in Newb... N.C.	3:255
Beecher	George Bennet	4 Apr 1813	bp, ch of Clarissa wife of Daniel	1:176
Beecher	Guy	17 Mar 1858	marr Elisabeth Scott, both of Naug	3:203
Beecher	Guy	15 Oct 1861	d, 40, typhoid, Hillside	3:253
Beecher	Hannah	- 1816	adm ch, wife of Baldwin; dis 1843 to Broad Alban	3:4
Beecher	Hannah	3 May 1816	wife of Baldwin, cand for memb	1:72
Beecher	Hannah	6 May 1816	adm ch	1:72
Beecher	Hannah	26 May 1816	wife of Baldwin, adm ch; rem [9?] Apr 1843 to Brod Albin NY	2:87
Beecher	Hannah	26 May 1816	adm ch	1:57
Beecher	Hannah	- 1822	wife of Baldwin, on list of members	1:82
Beecher	Helen Maria	- 1849	bp, ch of John	2:108
Beecher	Herbert	5 Sep 1861	d, ch of Frank & Mary, 2 y, dysentery, Hillside	3:253
Beecher	Ira	- 1854	adm ch from Edinburgh Center NY; dec 1864	3:5
Beecher	Ira	5 Nov 1854	adm fr Edingburgh Center NY (Cong.)	3:90
Beecher	John J.	7 May 1854	dism to Cong, Woodbridge	3:120
Beecher	Julia Ann	- 1833	adm ch; wife of G. Spencer; dec 1843	3:5
Beecher	Julia Ann	5 May 1833	wife of Gustavus Spencer, adm ch; died 28 Jan 1843	2:93
Beecher	L.N.	22 Feb 1881	at centennial exercises, and Mrs.	3:300
Beecher	Laura F.	- 1857	adm ch; dis 1858 to Clinton Ave. Cong, Brooklyn NY	3:5
Beecher	Laura F.	1 Mar 1857	adm ch	3:61
Beecher	Laura F.	4 Jul 1858	dism to Clinton Ave Cong, Brooklyn NY	3:121
Beecher	Laura Francelia	1 Mar 1857	bp, adult	3:151
Beecher	Maria	11 Apr 1827	of Salem, marr Laurence S. Spencer	1:153
Beecher	Maria	- 1850	adm ch; wife of John; dis 1854 to Woodbridge	3:5
Beecher	Maria	6 Jan 1850	wife of John, adm ch	3:60
Beecher	Maria	7 May 1854	wife of John J. dism to Cong, Woodbridge	3:120
Beecher	Martha M.	- 1856	adm ch	3:5
Beecher	Martha Melissa	4 May 1856	bp, adult	3:151
Beecher	Martha Melissa	4 May 1856	adm ch	3:61
Beecher	Mary A.	24 Mar 1837	Mrs., certificate to Episcopal ch	2:24
Beecher	Mary J.	11 May 1889	d, "diebatis" [see Milson]	3:259
Beecher	P.	13 Mar 1838	Miss, on comm	2:31
Beecher	Paulina	- 1826	adm ch; dis 1844 to Guilderland	3:4
Beecher	Paulina	Apr 1826	adm ch	1:59a
Beecher	Paulina	5 Feb 1826	propounded for membership	1:101
Beecher	Paulina	23 Apr 1826	adm ch, w of -- Batterman; rem 15 Dec 1844 to Guilderlund, NY	2:91
Beecher	Paulina	23 Apr 1826	female, member	1:83
Beecher	Paulina	23 Apr 1826	adm ch	1:101
Beecher	Polina	29 Jan 1826	examined for membership	1:101
Beecher	Polly	23 Aug 1827	of Salem, marr Alonzo Neal of Southington	1:153
Beecher	Saml N.	28 Oct 1866	dism to 1st Ch, Milford	3:123
Beecher	Samuel N.	- 1861	adm ch from Derby; dis 1866 to 1st ch Milford	3:6
Beecher	Samuel N.	3 Nov 1861	adm fr 1st ch, Derby	3:91
Beecher	Sena	2 Nov 1851	dism to 1st Cong, Waterbury	3:120
Beecher	Susan	21 Apr 1836	died, 42	2:115
Beeley	Evaline Ruth	7 Nov 1900	inf bp; Chas Wm & Augusta	3:165
Beers	Edward	1 Mar 1844	bp, ch of Smith	2:107
Beers	Edwin	30 Jul 1864	d, 29, suicide	3:254

NAUGATUCK, CONNECTICUT, CONGREGATIONAL CHURCH RECORDS

Beers	Henrietta	-	1869	adm ch; wife of Hubert; dis 1885 to Cong ch, Cheshire	3:6
Beers	Henrietta	2 May	1869	bp, adult	3:154
Beers	Henrietta	2 May	1869	adm ch	3:64
Beers	Henrietta	20 Mar	1885	now Mrs. Hanaford Smith, dism to Cong, Cheshire	3:126
Beers	Hubert	1 Mar	1844	bp, ch of Smith	2:107
Beers	Hubert	-	1859	adm ch; dec 1864	3:5
Beers	Hubert	2 Jan	1859	adm ch	3:62
Beers	Hubert	1 Jun	1864	d, 27, shot in battle in Va.	3:254
Beers	Nancy	-	1836	adm ch; wife of Smith; dism 1870 to New Haven 1st	3:5
Beers	Nancy	3 Jan	1836	wife of Smith, adm ch	2:95
Beers	Nancy Warner	21 Aug	1870	dism to 1st Cong, New Haven	3:124
Beers	Smith	12 Sep	1841	bp, adult	2:106
Beers	Smith	-	1842	adm ch; dec 1860	3:5
Beers	Smith	10 May	1842	adm ch	2:98
Beers	Smith	3 Oct	1860	d, fever, Hillside	3:253
Belden	Laura E.	28 Apr	1844	dism to ch in Bridgeport	2:49
Belden	Laura Evelina	-	1843	adm ch; dis 1844	3:5
Belden	Laura Eveline	14 May	1842	bp, adult	2:106
Belden	Laura Eveline	14 May	1843	adm ch; dism 6 May [sic] 1844	2:99
Benham	Burr	1 Mar	1829	marr Jane S. Beebe of Salem	1:153
Benham	Burr	19 Nov	1862	d, 57, Found dead in chair	3:254
Benham	Charles	-	1841	adm ch; dec 1888	3:5
Benham	Charles	11 Jul	1841	adm ch	2:97
Benham	Charles	11 Jul	1841	bp, adult	2:106
Benham	Chas	15 Apr	1884	Mrs, d, apoplexy	3:259
Benham	Chas	8 Dec	1888	d, 75, lung fever	3:259
Benham	Desire	12 Aug	1798	bp, ch of Elihu	1:168
Benham	Desire	21 Sep	1803	d, dau of Elihu, 5y	1:156
Benham	Edwin	-	1876	adm ch; dec 1892	3:6
Benham	Edwin	7 May	1876	and wife adm ch	3:65
Benham	Edwin	8 Sep	1892	d (in Waterbury) 71	3:260
Benham	Edwin	22 Aug	1897	Mrs, d in Waterbury, 72	3:261
Benham	Elihu	-	1790	adm ch; dec 1836	3:4
Benham	Elihu	21 Mar	1790	adm ch; died 28 Feb 1836	2:93
Benham	Elihu	21 Mar	1790	adm ch	1:12
Benham	Elihu	-	1822	male, on list of members	1:81
Benham	Elihu	29 Sep	1827	appointed to attend consocial at West Haven	1:103
Benham	Elihu	Sep	1831	on Visiting Committee	1:115
Benham	Elihu	28 Feb	1836	died, 88	2:115
Benham	Elihu	20 Dec	1842	to be visited and laboured with	2:42
Benham	Elihu	11 Jan	1843	difficulties with, statement by Milo Lewis	2:43f
Benham	Elihu	26 Feb	1843	protest against him voted withdrawn	2:46
Benham	Elihu	10 Apr	1846	consideration of his allegations	2:54
Benham	Elihu	29 Mar	1846	says "the chh. was corrupt" and wished to speak	2:53
Benham	Elihu	18 Oct	1848	advised by Consociation to think no more of his case	2:59
Benham	Elihu Jr	Sep	1813	ch d	1:160
Benham	Elihu Jr	19 Mar	1828	ch d, influenza, 8 months	1:144
Benham	Elihu Jr	19 Feb	1862	d, 85, casualty, Hillside	3:253
Benham	Elihu Jr.	-	1828	adm ch; dec 1862	3:4
Benham	Elihu Jr.	-	1828	male, on list of members, adm 1828	1:81
Benham	Elihu Jr.	4 May	1828	adm ch	1:59a
Benham	Elihu Jr.	4 May	1828	adm ch	1:106
Benham	Elihu Jr.	4 May	1828	adm ch	2:92
Benham	Elihu Jr.	20 Mar	1828	propounded for adm	1:106

NAUGATUCK, CONNECTICUT, CONGREGATIONAL CHURCH RECORDS

Benham	Elisa A.	-	1841	adm ch; dis 1845 to New Haven	3:5
Benham	Eliza A.	11 Jul	1841	adm ch; dism 21 Sep 1845 to N. Haven	2:97
Benham	Eliza Ann	11 Jul	1841	bp, adult	2:106
Benham	Eliza Ann	21 Sep	1845	Miss, dism to 3d Cong Ch in New Haven	2:52
Benham	Esther	-	1833	adm ch, wife of Elihu; dec 1841	3:4
Benham	Esther	6 Jan	1833	wife of Elihu Jr, adm ch; died Jul 1841	2:93
Benham	Eva	-	1866	adm ch; dis 1876 to 1st Presb, Jamesburg NY	3:6
Benham	Eva	2 Sep	1866	bp, adult	3:153
Benham	Eva	2 Sep	1866	adm ch	3:63
Benham	Eva	20 Aug	1876	dism to 1st Presb, Jamesburg NJ	3:124
Benham	Harriet L.	-	1876	Mrs. adm ch from Middlebury; dis 1892 to 2nd Cong, Waterbury	3:6
Benham	Harriet L.	7 May	1876	Mrs., adm fr Cong, Middlebury	3:93
Benham	Harriet L.	8 Apr	1892	Mrs., dism to 2nd Cong, Waterbury	3:127
Benham	Joseph	2 Dec	1800	Delegate at Consociation at Salem, from East Plains	1:19
Benham	Leveret	30 May	1826	wife d, delirium, 47	1:163
Benham	Lewis	1 May	1796	bp, ch of Elihu	1:167
Benham	Lewis	26 Sep	1850	inf dau d, 16 [15?] mos, dysentery	3:250
Benham	Lois H.	-	1840	adm ch; wife of Chas.; dec 1884	3:5
Benham	Lois H.	12 Jul	1840	wife of ClS [sic], adm ch	2:97
Benham	Lois H.	12 Jul	1840	bp	2:106
Benham	Louisa M.	-	1858	adm ch; erased 27 Apr 1900	3:5
Benham	Louisa Maria	4 Jul	1858	bp, adult	3:152
Benham	Louisa Maria	4 July	1858	adm ch	3:62
Benham	Maria	20 Sep	1826	of Salem, marr Stephen Bateman	1:152
Benham	Maria	6 Jul	1828	adult, bp	1:87
Benham	Mehetable	-	1790	adm ch, wife of Elihu; dec 1834	3:4
Benham	Mehetable	21 Mar	1790	wife of Elihu, adm ch; died 28 Oct 1834	2:94
Benham	Mehitable	21 Mar	1790	wife of Elihu adm ch	1:12
Benham	Mehitable	-	1822	wife of Elihu, on list of members	1:82
Benham	Mehitable	28 Oct	1834	died, 79	2:114
Benham	Mrs.	-	1876	adm ch [wife of Edwin]; dec 1897	3:6
Benham	Philina	10 Jul	1791	bp, ch of Elihu	1:166
Benham	Ransom	16 May	1790	bp, ch of Elihu	1:165
Benham	Rsuke[?]	16 May	1790	bp, ch of Elihu [Rhusa? (Je)rusha?]	1:165
Benham	Sarah	-	1784	wife of D. Webb, adm ch; dec 1834	3:4
Benham	Sarah	?	1784	adm ch	1:7
Benham	Sarah	Sep	1784	wife of Daniel Webb, adm ch; died 19 Jul 1834	2:82
Benham	Sarah	Sep	1784	adm ch, ["d 19 Jul 1834 Daniel Webb" added]	1:53
Benham	Selina	-	1838	adm ch; wife of Jay; dec 1879	3:5
Benham	Selina	2 Sep	1838	bp, adult	2:105
Benham	Selina	21 Sep	1838	wife of Jay, adm ch	2:97
Benham	Selina	16 Jan	1879	d, widow of Jay, 70, apoplexy	3:258
Benham	Sena	24 Nov	1793	bp, ch of Elihu	1:166
Benham	Walter L.	5 Jun	1885	23 of Naug marr Mary S. Wilcox	3:216
Benley	Elvira	3 Jan	1819	wife of William, adm ch	1:59
Benley	William D.	3 Jan	1819	adm ch, [see Penley]	1:59
Benley	William D.	27 Apr	1834	Asst. Super. in SS	2:16
Bennet	Harry Hotchkiss	19 Mar	1899	inf bp; Harry Ashley & Cora	3:164
Bennett	Cora Hotchkiss	16 Jun	1893	dism to Bethany Presb, NY City	3:128
Bennett	Harry A.	5 Sep	1889	22 marr Cora J. Hotchkiss 20	3:220
Bennett	Ira P.	8 Sep	1880	marr Eliza M. Tolles, both of Naug	3:213
Bennett	Lucius Hotchkiss	5 Jul	1891	an inf, bp; Harry A. & Cora J.	3:160
Benson	Ernest William	2 Sep	1888	an inf, bp	3:159
Benson	Nellie Esther	4 May	1900	22 marr Adelbert S. Clark 36	3:228

NAUGATUCK, CONNECTICUT, CONGREGATIONAL CHURCH RECORDS

Berger	Charles Louis	9 Mar 1890	bp, adult	3:159
Berger	Charles Louis	9 Mar 1890	adm ch	3:70
Berger	Chas Louis	- 1890	adm ch	3:7
Berger	Sherwood Isbell	9 Jun 1901	ch bp; Charles E. & Maud (Isbell)	3:165
Bersley	Wm D	Apr 1833	Assistant Super. for Sabbath School [see Beardsley]	2:9
Bidwell	Frederick	4 Jan 1852	adm ch	3:60
Bidwell	Frederick	1857	adm ch; dis 1861 to Litchfield	3:5
Bidwell	Frederick	3 May 1857	adm fr 1st Ch Litchfield	3:91
Bidwell	FredK	1852	adm ch; dis 1852 to Litchfield	3:5
Bidwell	FredK	13 Jun 1852	dism to Cong, Litchfield	3:120
Bidwell	FredK	1 Sep 1861	dism to Cong, Litchfield	3:121
Bidwell	Mary H.	13 Jun 1852	[wife of] FredK, dism to Cong, Litchfield	3:120
Bidwell	Mary H.	1857	adm ch; wife of FredK; dis 1861 to Litchfield	3:5
Bidwell	Mary H.	3 May 1857	w of F., adm fr 1st Ch Litchfield	3:91
Bidwell	Mary H.	1 Sep 1861	[wife of] FredK dism to Cong, Litchfield	3:121
Biengton	Jared	3 Aug 1803	ch of Jared, d, abt 2 y [see Byington]	1:156
Bigalow	John W.	31 Jan 1825	marr Electa Judd of Salem	1:152
Bigalow	Polly	16 Aug 1824	d at Plymouth, fever, 23	1:162
Bigelow	Caroline A.	1852	adm ch	3:5
Bigelow	Caroline A.	7 Mar 1852	adm ch	3:60
Biggin	Fred W.	29 Sep 1890	marr Lillian A. Gyde	3:221
Biggins	James Frederick	10 Jun 1900	inf bp; Fred W. & Lillian (Gyde)	3:165
Biggins	Lillian (Gyde)	1899	Mrs., adm ch	3:7
Biggins	Lillian (Gyde)	5 Mar 1899	bp, adult	3:164
Biggins	Lillian Gyde	5 Mar 1899	Mrs., adm ch	3:72
Biland	Carrie	14 Jun 1894	26 marr Jacob Mersey 33	3:223
Bilham	Fanny	21 Apr 1868	d, 34, consumption	3:256
Billam	Fanny	1868	adm ch from B. Presbn, Bridgewater PA; dec 1868	3:6
Billam	Fanny	22 Mar 1868	adm fr Presb, Bridgewater Pa.	3:92
Bilson	Eva Jane	3 May 1885	inf bp; John & Louisa	3:157
Bilson	John	1873	adm ch fr 2nd Cong, Rockville Ct; dis 1877 2nd Cong, Rockville	3:6
Bilson	John	12 Apr 1878	dism to Rockville Ct 2nd Cong	3:125
Bilson	John	1 Jul 1881	adm fr 2nd Cong, Rockville Ct	3:94
Bilson	John	1 Jul 1881	adm ch from 2nd Cong, Rockville; care withdrawn 1891	3:7
Bilson	John	21 Aug 1890	Mrs, d, at hospital in New Haven	3:260
Bilson	John	1 Mar 1891	"conduct...beyond reach of any influence"	3:416
Bilson	John H.	2 Nov 1873	adm fr 2nd Cong, Rockville Ct	3:93
Bilson	John H.	1 Mar 1891	watch and care withdrawn	3:127
Bilson	Louisa	12 Apr 1878	wife of John dism to Rockville Ct, 2nd Cong	3:125
Bilson	Louisa	1 Jul 1881	Mrs, adm fr 2nd Cong, Rockville Ct	3:94
Bilson	Louisa	1 Jul 1881	adm ch; wife of John; dec 1890	3:7
Bilson	Louisa N.	1873	adm ch, w of John; dism 1877 [sic] to 2nd Cong, Rockville Ct	3:6
Bilson	Louisa N.	2 Nov 1873	w of John H., adm fr 2nd Cong, Rockville Ct	3:93
Bilson	Maud Louisa	3 May 1885	inf bp; John & Louisa	3:157
Bingham	Ada Francis	12 Oct 1892	23 marr Harry Arthur Soper 26	3:222
Birch	Ida I.	27 Sep 1887	18 marr Chas A. Robinson 25	3:218
Bird	Henry	- -	husband of Daisy Widge	3:55
Bird	Henry P.	22 Nov 1888	28 marr Daisey A. Widge 22	3:219
Birdsall	B. Morris	1899	adm ch from Gill, Mass.	3:7
Birdsall	B. Morris	2 Jul 1899	adm fr Cong, Gill Mass	3:98
Birdsall	Ella	1876	adm ch, wife of -- Curry; dec 1894	3:6
Birdsall	Ella	7 May 1876	adm ch	3:65
Birdsall	Frederic Fremont	9 Jun 1901	ch bp; Warren A. & Elizabeth (Meyers)	3:165
Birdsall	Geo G.	5 Jul 1885	adm ch	3:7

NAUGATUCK, CONNECTICUT, CONGREGATIONAL CHURCH RECORDS

Birdsall	George G.	5 Jul 1885	bp, adult	3:158
Birdsall	George G.	5 Jul 1885	adm ch	3:68
Birdsall	Ida F.	Sep 1882	adm ch from M.E. ch, Orange NJ; dis 1884	3:7
Birdsall	Ida F.	1 Sep 1882	Miss, adm fr 1st M.E. Ch, Orange NJ	3:95
Birdsall	Ida F.	2 May 1884	dism to M.E., Naugatuck	3:126
Birdsall	Lydia B.	14 Apr 1881	marr Henry J. Hart, both of Naug	3:213
Birdsall	Lydia Bannister	- 1880	adm ch; wife of J.R. Saunders	3:6
Birdsall	Lydia Bannister	4 Jul 1880	bp, adult	3:156
Birdsall	Lydia Bannister	4 Jul 1880	adm ch	3:67
Birdsall	W.J.	7 May 1883	Mrs, d, cancer on liver	3:258
Birdsall	Warren William	9 Jun 1901	ch bp; Warren A. & Elizabeth (Meyers)	3:165
Birdsall	Wm J.	- 1876	Mrs., adm ch from Baptist, Newark NJ.; dec 1883	3:6
Birdsall	Wm J.	7 May 1876	Mrs., adm fr 1st Baptist, Newark NJ	3:93
Birdsall	Wm J.	2 Jul 1877	d, 46, Malignant Erysipela	3:258
Birge	Edwin	- -	husband of Myretta Porter	3:35
Birge	Edwin	- -	husband of Myretta Porter	2:92
Bishop	--	- -	husband of Betsey Hotchkiss	3:18
Bishop	Betsey	7 Jun 1835	Mrs., letter of dism to ch in Woodbridge	2:19
Bishop	Lois A.	29 Dec 1861	dism to Cong, Litchfield	3:122
Bishop	Lois Ann	- 1860	adm ch; dis 1861 to Litchfield	3:5
Bishop	Lois Ann	1 Jan 1860	bp, adult	3:152
Bishop	Lois Ann	1 Jan 1860	adm ch	3:62
Bishop	Polly M.	8 Dec 1852	of Woodbury marr Aaron Osborn of Naug	3:201
Bissell	Lilly A.	- 1876	adm ch from Prospect, wife of Geo D.	3:6
Bissell	Lilly A.	2 Jan 1876	w of Geo D.B., adm fr Cong, Prospect	3:93
Blackman	Berkley	2 May 1886	inf bp; Rev. W.F. & Lucy	3:158
Blackman	Enos B.	10 Jun 1868	of Middlebury marr Sarah E. Kervan of Williamsburg NY in Middlebury	3:208
Blackman	Marjorie	9 Mar 1890	an inf, bp	3:159
Blackman	W.F.	- 1885	Rev, adm ch from Steubenville O.; dis 1891 to Ithaca NY	3:7
Blackman	W.F.	- 1885	Mrs., adm ch [see him for adm & dis]	3:7
Blackman	W.F.	1 Jan 1885	settled as Pastor; dism 13 Sep 1891	3:1
Blackman	W.F.	3 May 1885	Rev and wife adm fr 1st Cong, Steubenville Ohio	3:95
Blackman	W.F.	25 Sep 1891	Rev and Mrs. dism to Cong, Ithaca NY	3:127
Blackman	Worthington	6 Nov 1887	an inf, bp	3:158
Blake	Lillie J.	7 Jun 1890	25 marr Geo M. Rice 32	3:221
Blake	Mary A.	17 Jun 1883	marr Rufus E. Munger, both of Naug	3:215
Blansfield	Augusta V.	29 Jun 1893	20 marr Frank M. Mudge 23	3:223
Blansfield	Gussie	5 Jul 1885	adm ch	3:67
Blansfield	Gussie	5 Jul 1885	adm ch	3:7
Blansfield	Lillian May	- 1896	adm ch	3:7
Blansfield	Lillian May	3 May 1896	bp, adult	3:162
Blansfield	Lillian May	3 May 1896	adm ch	3:71
Blish	Hiram H.	4 Dec 1858	d, 41, consumption, Hillside	3:252
Blish	Mary Ann	- 1857	adm ch; dis 1862	3:5
Blish	Mary Ann	5 Jul 1857	adm ch	3:61
Blish	Mary Ann	18 Apr 1862	(Cowles) dism to Cong, Union Village	3:122
Bodfish	C.J.	25 Sep 1891	dism to Presb, Camden NJ	3:127
Bodfish	Clarence J.	- 1890	adm ch; dis 1891 to 1st Pres, Camden NJ	3:7
Bodfish	Clarence J.	9 Mar 1890	adm ch	3:69
Bodfish	Hattie Griggs	9 Mar 1890	an inf, bp	3:159
Bodfish	Minnie S.	- 1890	adm ch; wife of C.J.; dis 1891 to 1st Pres, Camden NJ	3:7
Bodfish	Minnie S.	9 Mar 1890	adm fr Union Cong, Rockville Ct	3:96
Bodfish	Minnie S.	25 Sep 1891	dism to Presb, Camden NJ	3:127

NAUGATUCK, CONNECTICUT, CONGREGATIONAL CHURCH RECORDS

Bodin	Venda C.	14 Jan 1896	17 marr Benj Johnson 26	3:224
Boehm	Derwood H.	17 Jun 1888	an inf, bp	3:158
Boehm	Helen L.	- 1887	adm ch fr New Britain, w of J. Henry; dis 1893 to Howard Av,	3:7
-	-	- -	New Haven	-
Boehm	Helen L.	3 Jul 1887	adm fr So. Cong, New Britain Ct	3:96
Boehm	J. Henry	- 1887	adm ch from New Britain; dis 1893 to Howard Av, New Haven	3:7
Boehm	J. Henry	14 Apr 1893	and wife dism to Howard Ave, New Haven	3:128
Boehm	J. Henry Jr.	3 Jul 1887	adm fr So. Cong, New Britain Ct	3:96
Bohem [sic]	Catharine	21 Feb 1882	marr Jacob Becker, both of Naug	3:214
Booth	Albert Winnifred	26 Jan 1898	inf bp; Albert & Margaret (Wallace)	3:163
Booth	Canfield	- -	husband of Catharine E. Roberts	3:39
Booth	Chas C.	4 Mar 1896	26 marr Mary Stillson 28	3:224
Booth	Clifford H.	2 May 1886	adm fr College St., Cong, New Haven Ct.	3:95
Booth	Clifford H.	2 May 1886	adm ch from College St., New Haven; dis 1891 to New Haven	3:7
Booth	Clifford H.	11 Dec 1891	dism to College St, New Haven	3:127
Boughton	-	- -	see Bouten, Bouton	-
Boughton	Adelia	6 Jul 1828	wife of Wm Smith, adm ch; withdrawn 5 Jan 1838 to Episcopalians	2:92
Boughton	Hannah	17 May 1801	bp, ch of John	1:170
Boughton	James	17 May 1801	bp, ch of John	1:170
Boughton	Lausa [sic]	17 May 1801	bp, ch of John	1:170
Boughton	Lowman	17 May 1801	bp, ch of John	1:170
Boughton	Olive	- 1800	adm ch, wife of John; dec 1806	3:4
Boughton	Olive	14 Dec 1800	wife of John, adm ch; died 6 Dec 1806	2:85
Boughton	Olive	14 Dec 1800	Jo., adm ch, d 6 Dec 1806	1:56
Boughton	Olive	14 Dec 1800	wife of John adm ch	1:20
Boughton	Olive	17 May 1801	bp, ch of John	1:170
Boughton	Polly	17 May 1801	bp, ch of John	1:170
Boughton	Sally	17 May 1801	bp, ch of John	1:170
Boughton	Thalia J.	10 Mar 1850	marr Wm C. Scott, both of Naug	3:200
Bourne	Benjn T.	- 1860	adm ch fr West 23 St Presb; dis 1865 Central Cong, Lawrence MA	3:6
Bourne	Benjn T.	1 Jan 1860	adm fr West 23 Str Presb, N. York	3:91
Bourne	Benjn T.	5 Mar 1865	dism to Central Cong, Lawrence Ms, joined Eliot Cong.	3:122
Bourne	Hannah E.	- 1862	adm ch from Providence RI; dis 1865 to Cen. Cong Lawrence [MA]	3:6
Bourne	Hannah E.	2 Mar 1862	adm fr Central Cong, Providence RI	3:91
Bourne	Hannah E.	5 Mar 1865	dism to Central Cong, Lawrence Ms	3:122
Bourne	Harriet A.	- 1860	adm ch; w of Benj T. [see him for adm & dis]	3:6
Bourne	Harriet A.	1 Jan 1860	adm fr West 23 Str Presb, N. York	3:91
Bourne	Harriet A.	5 Mar 1865	dism to Central Cong, Lawrence Ms	3:122
Bourne	Helen Sherburne	20 Nov 1864	inf bp; B.T. & H.A.	3:153
Bourne	Henrietta Wardwell	20 Nov 1864	inf bp; B.T. & H.A.	3:153
Bourne	Robert Wardwell	4 May 1862	inf bp; B.T. & H.A.	3:152
Bouten	-	- -	see Boughton	-
Bouten	Olive	6 Dec 1806	d, wife of John, 33y	1:158
Bouten	Sally	3 May 1818	adm ch; excomm. 10 Jan 1830	1:59
Bouten	Sally	10 Jan 1830	fornication, "long course of unbecoming conduct", exc	1:110
Bouton	Adelia	- 1828	adm ch, wife of Wm Smith; Irr. 1838, Episcopal	3:4
Bouton	Adelia	4 Jul 1828	adm ch	1:59b
Bouton	Adelia	6 Jul 1828	adult, bp	1:87
Bouton	Adelia	6 Jul 1828	member	1:94
Bouton	Adelia	6 Jul 1828	adm ch	1:107
Bouton	Asa Smith	12 Jun 1803	bp, son of John	1:171
Bouton	John	3 Dec 1806	infant ch d, 3 week	1:157
Bouton	Sally	- 1818	adm ch; exc 1830	3:4
Bouton	Sally	3 May 1818	adm ch; excomm 10 Jan 1830	2:89

NAUGATUCK, CONNECTICUT, CONGREGATIONAL CHURCH RECORDS

Surname	Given	Date	Notes	Ref
Bouton	Sally	- 1822	female, on list of members; excluded	1:82
Bouton	Silas	12 Oct 1823	marr Julia A. Hotchkis of Salem	1:152
Bower	Charles H.	16 Jan 1868	of Greenfield, Mass marr Martha Career of Naug	3:208
Bracket	Lydia	5 Oct 1825	of Waterbury, marr Smith Miller of Annsvill, Oneida Co, NY	1:152
Bradbury	Frank Lucas	- 1889	adm ch	3:7
Bradbury	Frank Lucas	7 Jul 1889	bp, adult	3:159
Bradbury	Frank Lucus	7 Jul 1889	adm ch	3:69
Bradley	Anna E.	- 1878	adm ch fr Park St. Cong, Bridgeport, w of John; dis 1888 Seymour	3:6
Bradley	Anna E.	2 Mar 1888	Mrs. J.S., dism to Cong, Seymour Ct	3:127
Bradley	Anna E.W.	3 Mar 1878	adm fr Park St Cong, Bridgeport	3:94
Bradley	Carrie L.	30 Oct 1899	29 marr Isaac V. Jones 29	3:227
Bradley	Deborah	- 1789	adm ch; dis to Middlebury	3:4
Bradley	Deborah	19 Sep 1789	Wd, adm ch; rem to Middlebury	2:84
Bradley	Deborah	29 Sep 1789	Wid. adm ch, dism [see Bra(dley), date should be 19 Sep]	1:55
Bradley	E.	- -	husband of Lydia C. Lewis	3:25
Bradley	Eldad	- -	husband of Lydia C. Lewis	2:91
Bradley	Enos	- -	husband of Sarah Ells	3:11
Bradley	Enos	- -	husband of Sarah Ells	2:83
Bradley	Fred K.	27 Dec 1894	23 marr Agnes Thompson 21	3:223
Bradley	Jennet	Sep 1825	of Southbury, marr Robert Goodyear of Waterbury	1:152
Bradley	Lydia C.	4 May 1845	dism to Methedist Ch in Bridgeport	2:50
Bradley	Maud Van Ness	5 Jul 1885	an inf, bp	3:157
Bradley	Mrs.	26 May 1830	d, childbed fever, 21	1:146
Bradley	Nelson	- -	husband of Phebe Lewis	2:92
Bradley	Phebe	- 1866	adm ch from Middlebury; dec 1872	3:6
Bradley	Phebe	1 Jul 1866	adm fr Cong, Middlebury	3:92
Bradley	R.G.	17 Dec 1877	d, 32, consumption	3:258
Bradley	Sally	- 1866	adm ch from Middlebury; dec 1890	3:6
Bradley	Sally	1 Jul 1866	adm fr Cong, Middlebury	3:92
Bradley	Sally	16 Aug? 1890	Miss, d [date taken fr previous entry]	3:260
Bradley	Sarah	19 Jun 1856	d, 92, dysentery	3:251
Bradley	Stella Elizabeth	5 Jul 1885	Mrs., adm fr Cong, Roxbury Conn	3:95
Bradley	Stella Elizabeth	5 Jul 1885	Mrs., adm ch from Roxbury	3:7
Bray	George Richard	6 Sep 1888	an inf, bp	3:159
Bray	Gideon F.	29 Aug 1883	marr Minnie Smith	3:215
Bray	Gideon F.	5 Jul 1885	and wife adm ch	3:68
Bray	Gideon F.	5 Jul 1885	adm ch; wife also adm same day	3:7
Bray	Howard Benjamin	2 May 1886	inf bp; Gideon F. & Mrs.	3:158
Bray	Morris P.	3 Oct 1865	of Funkville, Pa marr Isabella Fenn of Ansonia	3:207
Bra[dley]	Deborah,	19 Sep 1790	widow, adm ch, [with Abraham & Ruth Lewis]	1:12
Bridges	Almira Adeline	26 Aug 1857	bp, adult; at Beacon Falls in sickness	3:151
Briggs	Chas	20 Apr 1876	of Waterbury marr Alice Ward of Naug	3:211
Bristol	A.	31 May 1853	d, 14, Bilious Cholic	3:250
Bristol	B.H.	2 Feb 1897	Mrs, d	3:261
Bristol	Benjamin H.	5 Jul 1885	Mrs, adm fr 1st Cong, Waterbury	3:95
Bristol	Benjamin H.	5 Jul 1885	Mrs., adm ch from Waterbury; dec 1897	3:7
Bristol	Benjamin Hiel	20 Nov 1897	inf bp; Edgar H. & May (Rexford)	3:163
Bristol	Bennett B.	5 Jul 1885	bp, adult	3:157
Bristol	Bennett B.	5 Jul 1885	adm ch	3:7
Bristol	Bennett B.	5 Jul 1885	adm ch	3:67
Bristol	Bertha Pauline	- 1890	adm ch	3:7
Bristol	Bertha Pauline	9 Mar 1890	bp, adult	3:159
Bristol	Bertha Pauline	9 Mar 1890	adm ch	3:70
Bristol	Carleton Wm	12 Jun 1892	an inf, bp	3:160

NAUGATUCK, CONNECTICUT, CONGREGATIONAL CHURCH RECORDS

Surname	Given Name	Date		Notes	Ref
Bristol	Charles E.	30 Dec	1877	ch bp; John	3:155
Bristol	Cora F.	6 Jul	1890	adm fr 2nd ch, Waterbury Ct	3:96
Bristol	Cora F.	6 Jul	1890	adm ch from Waterbury 2nd, wife of Frank	3:7
Bristol	Edgar Hial	-	1890	adm ch	3:7
Bristol	Edgar Hial	9 Mar	1890	bp, adult	3:159
Bristol	Edgar Hial	9 Mar	1890	adm ch	3:70
Bristol	Eleanor	9 Jun	1901	ch bp; Edgar H. & May (Rexford)	3:165
Bristol	Frank B.	6 Oct	1882	dism to 2nd Cong, Waterbury	3:125
Bristol	Frank B.	6 Jul	1890	adm fr 2nd ch, Waterbury	3:96
Bristol	Frank B.	6 Jul	1890	adm ch from Waterbury 2nd	3:7
Bristol	Franklin B.	-	1877	adm ch; dis 1882 to 2nd Cong, Waterbury	3:6
Bristol	Franklin B.	4 Mar	1877	adm ch	3:66
Bristol	Franklin Benjamin	9 Jun	1901	ch bp; Franklin B. & Cora (Russell)	3:165
Bristol	Fredk C.	5 Sep	1859	d, 2y 8m, cholera infantum	3:252
Bristol	Gertrude	20 Nov	1897	inf bp; Edgar H. & May (Rexford)	3:163
Bristol	Gertrude Rexford	-	1899	adm ch from Winsted, wife of "BBB"	3:7
Bristol	Gertrude Rexford	2 Jul	1899	adm fr 1st Cong, Winsted Ct	3:98
Bristol	Helen	9 Jun	1901	ch bp; Bennett B. & Gertrude (Rexford)	3:165
Bristol	John	7 Jul	1873	bur, 1 yr 16 d, Hillside, died 6 Jul	3:257
Bristol	John	4 Mar	1877	Mrs, adm fr S.Britain Ct, Cong	3:94
Bristol	John	5 Feb	1883	Mrs, d, inflammation Bowels	3:258
Bristol	Laura May	30 Dec	1877	ch bp; John	3:155
Bristol	Marion	11 Jun	1899	inf bp; Edgar H. & May Rexford	3:164
Bristol	Mary Louise	11 Jun	1899	inf bp; Bennett B. & Gertrude Rexford	3:164
Bristol	May Rexford	-	1895	adm ch	3:7
Bristol	May Rexford	3 Nov	1895	adm fr --	3:97
Bristol	Mrs.	-	1878	adm ch from So. Britain, Conn; wife of John; dec 1883	3:6
Bristol	Paulina S.	-	1864	adm ch; wife of Benj; dec 1877	3:6
Bristol	Paulina S.	1 May	1864	bp, adult	3:153
Bristol	Paulina S.	1 May	1864	adm ch	3:63
Bristol	Pauline S.	21 Mar	1877	d "1840 Dec 5 1877 Mar 22" pneumonia, Hillside	3:257
Bristol	Sadie A.	25 May	1887	22 marr Frederick A. Phelps 22	3:218
Bristol	Samuel Russell	-	1901	adm ch	3:11
Bristol	Samuel Russell	6 Jan	1901	adm ch	3:72
Bristol	Sarah A.A.	Nov	1881	adm ch	3:7
Bristol	Sarah Anna Abigal	6 Nov	1881	adm ch	3:67
Bristol	Wm H.	8 Sep	1885	25 marr J. Louise Wright 21, both of Naug	3:217
Bristor	Esther	-	1794	adm ch; dis to Milford	3:4
Bristor	Esther	14 Oct	1794	adm ch; rem to Milford	2:84
Bristor	Esther	19 Oct	1794	adm ch	1:13
Bristor	Esther	94 Oct	1794	[date sic] adm ch, dism	1:55
Brixy	William	6 May	1880	marr Francis DeWolf, both of Seymour	3:212
Broadbent	Myrtle Elizabeth	9 Aug	1897	inf bp; Bernice & Jennie	3:163
Brockway	Justine Morgan	21 Sep	1892	25 marr Harris Whittemore 27	3:222
Bronson	-	-	-	see Brownson	-
Bronson	John	20 Jul	1834	ch died, 1y 2m	2:114
Bronson	Seth	29 Apr	1817	Deacon, from Middlebury, at Council re Rev. Dodd's removal	1:74
Bronson	Seth, Dn	29 Sep	1801	Delegate to consociation in Salem, from Middlebury	1:25
Bronson	Stephen, Dn	29 Sep	1801	Delegate to consociation in Salem, from Waterbury	1:25
Brooks	Charity	4 Feb	1873	bur, 93	3:257
Brooks	Chas M.	24 Oct	1894	27 marr Annie M. Gibbud 21	3:223
Brooks	George	24 Dec	1864	marr Margaret Stacey, both of Naug	3:206
Brooks	Walter	21 Aug	1889	43 marr Mrs. Lizzie Lewis 40	3:220
Brothers	A.H.	-	1878	adm ch; erased 27 Apr 1900	3:6

NAUGATUCK, CONNECTICUT, CONGREGATIONAL CHURCH RECORDS

Surname	Given	Date	Notes	Ref
Brothers	A.H.	3 Mar 1878	bp, adult; also wife	3:156
Brothers	A.H.	3 Mar 1878	and wife adm ch	3:66
Brothers	Mrs.	- 1878	adm ch, wife of A.H.; erased 27 Apr 1900	3:6
Brown	E.	10 Mar 1854	d, inf dau Mr Brown (English) 2 years, fit	3:250
Brown	Eliza I.	5 May 1861	dism to South Cong, Bridgeport	3:121
Brown	George	- 1877	adm ch; care withdrawn 1885	3:6
Brown	George	4 Nov 1877	adm ch	3:66
Brown	John Henry	2 Dec 1877	of Waterbury marr Henrietta Dorsey of Naug	3:212
Brown	William E.	- 1858	appt'd Deacon; removed 1861 Dec	3:1
Brown	Wm	1 Sep 1882	Mrs, dism to Park St Ch, Bridgeport	3:125
Brown	Wm E.	- -	husband of Eliza Jane Hotchkiss	3:19
Brown	Wm E.	- 1852	adm ch; dis 1861 to Bridgeport	3:5
Brown	Wm E.	2 May 1852	adm ch	3:60
Brown	Wm E.	17 Oct 1854	marr Eliza Jane Hotchkiss, both of Naug	3:202
Brown	Wm E.	5 May 1861	dism to South Cong, Bridgeport	3:121
Brown	Wm E.	- 1876	widow, adm ch fr 2nd Cong, Bridgeport; dis 1882 Park St. Bpt	3:6
Brown	Wm E.	2 Jan 1876	Mrs., adm fr 2nd Cong, Bridgeport, Ct	3:93
Brownlow	Annie Elizabeth	31 May 1900	inf bp; Thomas & Annie (Platt)	3:165
Brownlow	James Alfred	5 Aug 1897	inf bp; Thomas & Annie	3:163
Brownson	-	- -	see Bronson	-
Brownson	David	2 Dec 1800	Revd Elder attending Consociation at Salem, from Oxford	1:19
Brownson	Seth, Dn.	2 Dec 1800	Delegate at Consociation at Salem, from Middlebury	1:19
Bruce	Mary Katherine	30 Nov 1899	inf bp; Michael J. & Emma Steiber	3:164
Bruce	Michael J.	15 Nov 1898	23 marr Emma Steiber 23	3:226
Brundage	J.D.	- 1874	Dr, adm ch from Goshen; dis 1882 General Letter	3:6
Brundage	J.D.	6 Sep 1874	Dr, adm fr 2nd Cong, Goshen Ct; also wife	3:93
Brundage	J.D.	20 Oct 1882	Dr, dism by General Letter; also wife	3:126
Brundage	Minnie	- 1876	Miss, adm ch; dis 1882 to Northfield Min.	3:6
Brundage	Minnie	2 Jul 1876	adm ch	3:65
Brundage	Minnie	20 Oct 1882	dism to Northfield Cong, Minn	3:126
Brundage	Mrs.	- 1874	adm ch from Goshen; dis 1882 General Letter	3:6
Brush	Charles Edgar	- 1897	adm ch	3:7
Brush	Charles Edgar	2 May 1897	adm ch	3:71
Brush	Gabriella	22 Nov 1887	21 marr George Wheeler 22	3:218
Brush	Mary J.	- 1890	Mrs, adm ch	3:7
Brush	Mary J.	5 Jan 1890	Mrs., adm ch	3:69
Buckingham	Ellen	15 Oct 1855	d (Hoadley) in N. Milford, 27, Typhoid fever, Hillside	3:251
Buckingham	George	18 Oct 1830	d, "1 - 8 months"	1:146
Buckingham	Mary E.	19 Apr 1862	d, 8 y, diphtheria, Hillside	3:253
Buckingham	Mary Ellen	2 Nov 1856	ch bp; Selden & Lucretia Hoadley, guardians	3:151
Buckingham	Nathan	29 Sep 1801	Delegate to consociation in Salem, from Oxford	1:25
Buckley	-	- -	see Bukley, Bulkley	-
Buckley	Gordon Lewis	7 Dec 1788	bp, son of Doct Daniel	1:165
Buckley	Levi	17 May 1795	bp, ch of Doct	1:167
Budrow	Carrie	3 Nov 1864	marr Merrett C. Saunders, both of Naug	3:206
Budrow	Carrie L.	- 1863	adm ch; wife of M.C. Saunders; dis 1881 to Ansonia	3:6
Budrow	Carrie L.	1 Nov 1863	bp, adult	3:153
Budrow	Carrie Lucretia	1 Nov 1863	adm ch	3:63
Budrow	Olive E.	- 1863	adm ch from Bridgeport Ct; dis 1870 to Olivet Mission	3:6
Budrow	Olive E.	1 Nov 1863	bp, adult	3:153
Budrow	Olive Ellen	1 Nov 1863	adm ch	3:63
Bukley	-	- -	see Buckley, Bulkley	-
Bukley	Daniel	9 Dec 1787	adm ch; rem 30 Mar 1817 to Green, YN [sic]	2:84
Bukley	Daniel	9 Dec 1787	adm ch, dism 29[?] Mar 1817[?] [written over]	1:55

NAUGATUCK, CONNECTICUT, CONGREGATIONAL CHURCH RECORDS

Surname	Given	Date	Notes	Ref
Bukley	Daniel	9 Dec 1787	Doct, adm ch	1:11
Bukley	Daniel	30 Mar 1817	Doct, letter of rec voted	1:73
Bukley	Flora	18 Jul 1791	bp, ch of Do- Daniel	1:166
Bulkley[sic]	Daniel	- 1787	adm ch; dis 1817	3:4
Bull	Benedict	2 Dec 1800	Delegate at Consociation at Salem, from 2nd Milford	1:19
Bull	Benedict	29 Sep 1801	Dn, Delegate to consociation in Salem, from 2nd Milford	1:25
Bull	Benjamin	29 Sep 1801	Dn, Delegate to consociation in Salem, from 1st Milford [sic]	1:25
Bull	Clara Chapman	- 1891	adm ch; wife of Dr. T.M.	3:7
Bull	Clara Chapman	6 Sep 1891	adm fr 1st Baptist, Pittsfield Mass	3:97
Bull	T.M.	2 Nov 1890	Dr., adm ch from New York	3:7
Bull	Thos. M	2 Nov 1890	Dr, adm fr Pres Ch, University Place NY	3:96
Bunce	Louis E.	- 1854	adm ch; dis 1864 to Manchester	3:5
Bunce	Louis E.	5 Mar 1854	adm ch	3:61
Bunce	Louis E.	21 Feb 1864	dism to Cong, Manchester	3:122
Bunnel	Clarissa	- 1828	adm ch, wife of Wm; dec 1835	3:4
Bunnel	Clarissa	4 Jul 1828	Wm, adm ch	1:59b
Bunnel	Clarissa	6 Jul 1828	wife of Wm, adm ch; died 2 Nov 1835	2:93
Bunnel	Clarissa	6 Jul 1828	adm ch	1:107
Bunnel	Clarissa	2 Nov 1835	died, 43	2:115
Bunnel	Clasissa [sic]	6 Jul 1828	member	1:94
Bunnel	Elizebeth	19 Jul 1829	ch of Wm, bp	1:88
Bunnel	Frideric William	19 Jul 1829	ch of Wm, bp	1:88
Bunnel	Harriot	19 Jul 1829	ch of Wm, bp	1:88
Bunnel	Minerva S.	- 1854	adm ch; dec 1880	3:5
Bunnel	Minerva S.	5 Mar 1854	adm ch	3:61
Bunnel	Mr.	20 Oct 1826	his ch d, canker, 3	1:144
Bunnell	Elizabeth	22 Mar 1875	bur, 57, Hillside	3:257
Bunnell	Jennie A.	10 Jun 1894	bp; Roland & Nellie A.	3:161
Bunnell	Mary	22 Sep 1861	(Woodruff) dism to Cong, Terryville	3:122
Bunnell	Minerva	30 Mar 1880	d, 49, consumption	3:258
Bunnell	Minerva Stevens	2 May 1833	bp, ch of Wm, b 11 Dec 1830	2:104
Bunnell	Mr.	24 Sep 1825	ch d, dysentery, 6m[?]	1:163
Burbank	James H.	2 Nov 1882	marr Ida F. Norton, both of Naug	3:214
Burleigh	Emily A.	5 Mar 1854	adm ch	3:60
Burleigh	Emily Ann	5 Mar 1854	bp, profession	3:150
Burleigh	Emily E.	- 1854	adm ch; Erased 1866	3:5
Burleigh	Emily E.	30 Mar 1866	voted dismissed, eligible for letter if asked [see 3:369]	3:123
Burnham	Egbert R.	4 Aug 1850	of Naug marr Polly L. Sanford of Oxford	3:200
Burrett	-	-	husband of Adeline Hotchkiss	3:20
Burwell	Catharine C.	- 1857	adm ch from Seymour Ct; dis 1866 to Seymour	3:5
Burwell	Catharine C.	5 Jul 1857	adm fr Cong, Seymour Ct	3:91
Burwell	Catharine C.	28 Oct 1866	dism to Cong, Seymour	3:123
Burwell	Nathan	- 1836	adm ch from So. Britain; dism [prob.] 1838 to Middlebury	3:5
Burwell	Nathan	3 Jul 1836	adm from ch in South Britain	2:20
Burwell	Nathaniel	1 Apr 1838	dism to ch in Middlebury	2:32
Burwill	Nathan	3 Jul 1836	adm ch from S. Britain; dism 1 Nov 1838 to Middlebury	2:96
Bush	Ernest Mennis	25 Feb 1894	bp, 1 yr; Geo & Alice	3:161
Bush	Wm Wallace	25 Feb 1894	bp, 4 yrs; Geo & Alice	3:161
Butts	Frances	3 Jan 1850	d, 19, Consumption	3:250
Butts	James A.	11 Aug 1861	d, brot from New York, 20, consumption	3:253
Byington	-	-	see Biengton	-
Byington	Anna	8 Apr 1792	bp, ch of Jared	1:166
Byington	Asahel	2 Dec 1787	bp, ch of Jared	1:164
Byington	Clarissa	18 May 1788	bp, dau of Jared	1:165

NAUGATUCK, CONNECTICUT, CONGREGATIONAL CHURCH RECORDS

Byington	Esther	13 Jun	1806	wife of Isaac, testified against Thomas Porter	1:40f
Byington	Isaac	2 Dec	1787	bp, ch of Jared	1:164
Byington	Isaac	13 Jun	1806	testified against Thomas Porter	1:40f
Byington	Jared	-	1787	adm ch; exc 1802	3:4
Byington	Jared	18 Nov	1787	adm ch; excomm 12 Nov 1802	2:84
Byington	Jared	18 Nov	1787	adm ch	1:11
Byington	Jared	18 Nov	1787	adm ch, excomm 12 Nov 1802	1:54
Byington	Jared	4 Apr	1799	chosen Clerk	1:14
Byington	Jared	4 Sep	1801	brought complaint against John Lewis	1:24
Byington	Jared	12 Feb	1801	brought complaint against Samuel Scott for slander	1:21f
Byington	Jared	15 Oct	1801	on committee	1:32
Byington	Jared	22 Feb	1801	bp, ch of Jared	1:169
Byington	Jared	29 Sep	1801	consociation held regarding his difficulties with the ch	1:25f
Byington	Jared	16 Apr	1802	re confession; excommunicated	1:34f
Byington	Jesse	2 Dec	1787	bp, ch of Jared	1:165
Byington	Mehittabel	13 Nov	1796	bp, ch of Jared	1:168
Byington	Orin	2 Dec	1787	bp, ch of Jared	1:164
Byington	Rebeckah	4 Apr	1790	bp, ch of Jared	1:165
Byington	Salley	23 Sep	1798	bp, ch of Jared	1:168
Byington	Stephen	9 Nov	1794	bp, ch of Jared	1:167
Byington	Submit C.	-	1802	adm ch, wife of L. Townsend; dis to Middlebury	3:4
Byington	Submit C.	17 Oct	1802	wife of Larman Townsend, adm ch; rem to Middlebury	2:86
Byington	Submit C.	17 Oct	1802	adm ch	1:56
Byington	Submit Clarissa	17 Oct	1802	bp & adm ch	1:34
Cable	Erwin W.	25 Dec	1899	22 marr Libbie Peck 23	3:228
Cable	Julia M.	8 Mar	1892	19 marr Alfred Judson Nichols 29	3:221
Calking	Cloe	2 Oct	1796	bp, ch of Roswel	1:168
Calkings	Eunice	-	1787	adm ch, wife of Roswell; dis	3:8
Calkings	Eunice	30 Sep	1787	wife of Rosswell, adm ch; rem	2:83
Calkings	Marcia	1 May	1791	bp, ch of Roswel	1:166
Calkings	Rosswell	30 Sep	1787	adm ch; excomm	2:83
Calkings	Roswell	-	1787	adm ch; exc	3:8
Calkins	Amira [sic]	14 Oct	1787	bp, ch of Roswell [see Caulkins]	1:164
Calkins	Eunice	30 Sep	1787	wife of Roswell adm ch	1:11
Calkins	Eunice	30 Sep	1787	R., adm ch, Dism [to "Ohio" added]	1:54
Calkins	Julia	27 Jul	1794	bp, ch of Roswell	1:167
Calkins	Lovewell	14 Oct	1787	bp, ch of Roswell	1:164
Calkins	Lucy	17 May	1789	bp, ch of Roswell	1:165
Calkins	Rossil	30 Sep	1787	adm ch, excommunicated	1:54
Calkins	Roswell	30 Sep	1787	adm ch	1:11
Camp	George	1 Apr	1858	of New Milford marr Mary Jane Johnson of Middlebury, both colored	3:203
Camp	J.	1 Jan	1861	of Bristol marr Margaret Allen of Naug	3:204
Camp	Salome	15 Oct	1862	d, Middlebury, 61	3:253
Campbell	Robert	3 Jan	1900	45 marr Mrs Elizabeth A. Teator 50	3:228
Cande	-	28 Feb	1826	d, consumption, 20	1:163
Candee	-	-	-	see Condee	-
Candee	-	-	-	husband of Sarah Ellen Potter	3:36
Candee	-	-	-	husband of Lucy A. Roberts	3:39
Candee	B.	-	-	husband of Lois Judd	3:22
Candee	Bird	-	-	husband of Lois Judd	2:89
Candee	Lois	-	1856	adm ch from Episcopal Naug, w. of B.; dec	3:8
Candee	Lois	6 Jan	1856	Mrs, adm from Episcopal, Naug	3:90
Candee	Lucy A.	24 Sep	1873	d, typhoid, Hillside	3:256

NAUGATUCK, CONNECTICUT, CONGREGATIONAL CHURCH RECORDS

Surname	Given	Date	Event	Ref
Candy	Lois	— 1822	wife of B. Candy, on list of members	1:82
Candy	Mrs.	12 Jan 1824	d, wife of --, jaundice, 47	1:161
Candy	Verus	16 Feb 1825	ch d, 5m	1:162
Candy	Wid	28 Jun 1824	d, 82	1:161
Canfield	Mary A.	— 1847	adm ch fr Meriden, w of Jared; dis 1866 to Center, Meriden	3:8
Canfield	Mary A.	5 Sep 1847	wife of Jared, adm ch from Meriden	2:100
Canfield	Mary J.	28 Oct 1866	dism to Center Ch, Meriden	3:123
Career	Martha	16 Jan 1868	of Naug marr Charles H. Bower of Greenfield, Mass	3:208
Carey	—	— —	see Cary	—
Carey	James	7 May 1891	marr Mary Wistim [sic]	3:221
Cariall[?]	Mary Mix	15 Mar 1818	infant ch of Nathaniel, bp [see Caroll, Carrol, etc.]	1:60
Carn	Susan	11 Dec 1882	marr Samuel Gibson, both of Naug	3:214
Caroll	Nathan	17 Dec 1830	on comm	1:112
Caroll	Nathanel	Sep 1831	on Visiting Committee	1:115
Carr	Agnes	25 Jun 1859	of Waterbury marr Manwaring Green of Woodridge in Woodbridge	3:204
Carrington	E.H.	— 1877	Mrs., adm ch	3:8
Carrington	E.H.	4 Mar 1877	Mrs., adm ch "Re-affirmation of Faith"	3:66
Carrol	—	— —	see Cariall, Caroll	—
Carrol	Br	6 Nov 1829	voted to attend future conf	1:109
Carrol	Br.	6 Nov 1829	on comm	1:109
Carrol	Br. & Sister	9 Nov 1838	act of excommunication 9 Nov 1837 reconsidered, upheld	2:32
Carrol	Lucy	— 1812	adm ch from W. Hartford, wife of Nathl; Irr 1837 Episcopal	3:8
Carrol	Lucy	3 May 1812	w of Nathaniel, adm ch fr West Hartford; withdrawn, see p 2:33	2:87
Carrol	Lucy	3 May 1812	adm ch	1:57
Carrol	Lucy	3 May 1812	adm ch	1:62
Carrol	Lucy	15 Apr 1812	wife of Nathaniel, cand for memb, from ch in West Hartford	1:62
Carrol	Mr.	14 Oct 1837	and wife, comm to draft allegations against them, he excomm	2:28f
Carrol	N.	19 Aug 1832	appointed delegate to ordination at Orange	1:120
Carrol	Nathaniel	3 May 1812	adm ch fr West Hartford; withdrawn, see p 2:33 [also Br & Sis]	2:87
Carrol	Nathaniel	3 May 1812	adm ch	1:57
Carrol	Nathaniel	3 May 1812	adm ch	1:62
Carrol	Nathaniel	15 Apr 1812	cand for memb, from ch in West Hartford	1:62
Carrol	Nathl	— 1812	adm ch from W. Hartford; Irr. 1837 to Episcopal	3:8
Carrol	Samuel Valentine	23 Jun 1811	bp, ch of Nathaniel & Lucy	1:175
Carrol	Wm Henry	22 Oct 1815	bp, ch of Nathaniel & Lucy	1:176
Carroll	Lucy	— 1822	wife of Nathl, member	1:82
Carroll	Mr.	4 May 1828	on comm	1:106
Carroll	N.	12 Mar 1828	on comm	1:106
Carroll	N.	7 Oct 1833	his case considered	2:14f
Carroll	Nahanel	Apr 1833	on committee for SS	2:9
Carroll	Nathaniel	30 Apr 1830	on Sabb School board, Superintendent	1:111
Carter	Addie M.	16 Jan 1896	19 marr Chas H. Smf [sic] 25 [see Sumpf, Zumpf]	3:224
Carter	Isabell T.	1 Oct 1854	marr Chs H. Porter, both of Naug	3:202
Carter	Solon F.	24 Nov 1858	of Boston marr Augusta C. Gaylord of Naug	3:204
Cary	—	— —	see Carey	—
Cary	Edwin T.	— 1900	adm ch; dec 1901	3:9
Cary	Edwin T.	6 May 1900	bp, adult	3:165
Cary	Edwin T.	6 May 1900	adm ch	3:72
Cary	Edwin T.	18 Apr 1901	d, 22, apendicitis	3:261
Casey	Maggie	14 May 1891	marr Chas T. Squire	3:221
Casey	Mary	— 1876	adm ch; dis 1879 to Wallingford	3:8
Casey	Mary	7 May 1876	adm ch	3:65
Casey	Mary	23 Dec 1879	dism to Cong, Wallingford	3:125
Casier	Mathias, Rev.	7 Jun 1804	requested to return and labour 1 yr, 28 Jun apptd Moderator	1:38

NAUGATUCK, CONNECTICUT, CONGREGATIONAL CHURCH RECORDS

Castle	Jehiel	20 Jan	1802	marr Mary Johnson, both of Woodbridge	1:151
Castle	Seth	28 Dec	1800	marr Olive Stephens, both of this place	1:151
Caulkins	Amica	27 Mar	1803	marr David Lewis, both of this place [see Calkins]	1:151
Cerrick	Heinrich S.	18 Oct	1877	d, 2 mon, Chol Inf [surname also written Katick]	3:258
Chadwick	Holland Weeks	19 May	1802	"my son" [Rev. Jabez'] bp by Mr. Weeks	2:2
Chadwick	Jabez	3 Dec	1800	Pastor, dism Mar 1803 [see also 2:2]	2:79
Chadwick	Jabez	6 Oct	1800	voted to return and take charge of church	1:17
Chadwick	Jabez	17 Mar	1803	presented petition to be dismissed	1:36
Chadwick	Jabez, Jr.	2 Dec	1800	settled; dismissed March 1803	1:13
Chadwick	Jane	28 Apr	1855	d, dau of Robert, 2 1/2, croup	3:251
Chadwick	Mr.	2 Dec	1800	approved and ordination appointed for 3 Dec	1:194
Chadwick	Sarah	-	1803	adm ch, wife of Jabez; dis 1803 to Lee, Mass.	3:8
Chadwick	Sarah	27 Feb	1803	wife of Jabez, adm ch; rem 8 Apr 1803 to Lee, Mass.	2:86
Chadwick	Sarah	27 Feb	1803	adm ch, dism 8 Apr 1803	1:56
Chadwick	Sarah	27 Feb	1803	wife of Jabez adm ch	1:36
Chamberlain	Asa Lewis	20 Sep	1899	28 marr Mary Edith Webster 23	3:227
Chamberlain	Frank E.	21 Jul	1880	marr Hannah D. Watkins, both of Seymour	3:212
Chamberlain	Hubert	24 May	1871	marr Estella Wilmot, both of Naug	3:209
Chamberlain	Lilian Jane	15 Mar	1893	20 marr Louis Howard Wilmot 23	3:222
Chapman	Annie Sarah	-	1897	adm ch	3:9
Chapman	Annie Sarah	2 May	1897	Mrs., adm ch	3:71
Chapman	Barton James	24 Feb	1898	21 marr Hattie M. Farrell 21	3:226
Chapman	Bertha	7 Apr	1897	21 marr Wm E. Hoadley 25	3:225
Charlesworth	Florence	2 Nov	1898	21 marr Arthur Holmes 22	3:226
Chase	Frances E.	-	1860	adm ch fr Presb NJ, w of Saml N.; dis 1862 Blackwoodtown NJ	3:8
Chase	Frances E.	4 Nov	1860	w of Saml N, adm fr Presb Blackwoodtown NJ	3:91
Chase	Frances E.	21 Dec	1862	[wife of] Saml N. dism to Presb, Blackwoodtown NJ	3:122
Chase	Martha	10 Sep	1897	21 marr Howard N. Howland 22	3:225
Chase	Saml N.	-	1857	adm ch; dis 1862 to Blackwoodtown NJ	3:8
Chase	Saml N.	5 Jul	1857	adm ch	3:61
Chase	Saml N.	21 Dec	1862	dism to Presb, Blackwoodtown NJ	3:122
Chase	Saml Noyes	5 Jul	1857	bp, adult	3:151
Chatfield	Eshir [sic]	5 Sep	1805	d, ch of Josiah, abt 1y	1:157
Chatfield	Esther	12 Aug	1804	bp, ch of Josiah	1:172
Chatfield	Josiah	-	-	husband of Olive Tuttle	3:48
Chatfield	Josiah	-	-	husband of Olive Tuttle	2:86
Chatfield	Lydia	-	1787	adm ch, wife of Saml; dec	3:8
Chatfield	Lydia	18 Nov	1787	wife of Samuel, adm ch; died	2:84
Chatfield	Lydia	18 Nov	1787	wife of Samll adm ch	1:11
Chatfield	Lydia	18 Nov	1787	adm ch, Sam, dead	1:54
Chatfield	Lyman	1 Dec	1805	bp, son of Josiah	1:173
Chatfield	Olive	4 May	1806	letter of rec to ch at Windom, Greens Co., NY	1:40
Chatfield	Polly Ann	24 Nov	1857	of Waterbury marr Thos French Jr of Naug	3:203
Chatfield	Saml	-	1787	adm ch; dec	3:8
Chatfield	Samll	18 Nov	1787	adm ch	1:11
Chatfield	Samuel	18 Nov	1787	adm ch; died	2:84
Chatfield	Samuel	18 Nov	1787	adm ch, dead	1:54
Chidacy	Heriet	17 May	1826	of East Haven, marr Abijah H. Rogers of Branford	1:152
Chittenden	Ophelia	19 Mar	1861	of Waterbury marr John T. Moulthrop of Bridgeport	3:205
Chittendon	Ann	30 Sep	1824	of Columbia, marr David M. Platt	1:152
Chittendon	Ann	30 Sep	1824	"& David M. Platt" [this is among deaths, smudged over]	1:162
Church	Agnes	-	-	see Higgins	-
Church	Clarrissa S.	29 May	1897	35 marr Adna D. Warner 37	3:225
Church	Homer	2 May	1886	adm ch	3:69

NAUGATUCK, CONNECTICUT, CONGREGATIONAL CHURCH RECORDS

Surname	Given	Date	Event	Ref
Church	Homer	2 May 1886	adm ch	3:9
Church	Homer R.	26 Sep 1888	25 marr Clarissa S. Lewis 26	3:219
Churchill	Frank Burton	3 Sep 1852	inf bp; Saml M. & Hester E.	3:150
Churchill	Hester E.	- 1852	adm ch fr Woodbury, w of Saml; dis 1855 1st Pres, Dunleith Ill.	3:8
Churchill	Hester E.	21 Mar 1852	wife of Saml M, adm ch from North Cong, Woodbury	3:90
Churchill	Hester E.	17 Jun 1855	wife of S[aml] M. dism to 1st Presb, Dunleith Ill	3:121
Churchill	John	- 1867	adm ch from New Hartford; dis 1877 to 2nd Cong Winsted	3:8
Churchill	John	3 Mar 1867	adm fr New Hartford	3:92
Churchill	John	11 Feb 1877	dism to 2d Cong, W. Winsted Ct.	3:125
Churchill	Lucy R.	- 1867	adm ch from New Hartford, w of John; Irr 1872 Episcopal	3:8
Churchill	Lucy R.	3 Mar 1867	adm fr New Hartford	3:92
Churchill	Saml M.	- 1852	adm ch; dis 1855 to 1st Presb ch in Dunleith Ill.	3:8
Churchill	Saml M.	7 Mar 1852	bp, profession	3:150
Churchill	Saml M.	7 Mar 1852	adm ch	3:60
Churchill	Saml M.	17 Jun 1855	dism to 1st Presb, Dunleith Ill.	3:121
Ciderholm	Yugue	20 Nov 1896	25 marr Lima Milberg 20 [Nulberg?]	3:225
Clark	-	10 Feb 1829	ch d, [crossed out]	1:145
Clark	Adelbert S.	4 May 1900	36 marr Nellie Esther Benson 22	3:228
Clark	Adulla	3 Mar 1878	bp, adult; wife of Miles S.	3:156
Clark	Chas R.	3 May 1885	30, of Waterbury marr Hattie E. Smith 25	3:216
Clark	Ellen K.	- 1898	adm ch from Ovid NY	3:9
Clark	Ellen K.	6 Nov 1898	Miss, adm fr Pres, Ovid NY	3:98
Clark	Isabella	- 1893	adm ch; dis 1894 to New Milford, Ct	3:9
Clark	Isabella	5 Nov 1893	Miss, adm ch	3:71
Clark	Isabella	28 Dec 1894	dism to Cong, New Milford	3:128
Clark	Maria P.	21 Apr 1851	Mrs, marr Israel Upson, both of Waterbury	3:200
Clark	Martha J.	22 Jun 1859	marr David W. Curtiss of Huntington Ct	3:204
Clark	Miles S.	29 Sep 1872	marr Adeline E. Platt, both of Waterbury	3:209
Clark	Miles S.	- 1878	adm ch, and wife	3:8
Clark	Miles S.	3 Mar 1878	bp, adult [but crossed out]	3:156
Clark	Miles S.	3 Mar 1878	and wife adm ch	3:66
Clark	Mr.	22 Apr 1818	of Oxford proposed to be engaged by church	1:76
Clark	Nelson D.	19 Jan 1887	marr Katie F. Steele	3:218
Clark	Sally	11 Apr 1827	of Waterbury, marr Bezaleel Scott	1:153
Clark	Sarah	- 1845	adm ch from Waterbury; dec 1848	3:8
Clark	Sarah	31 Oct 1845	adm ch from Waterbury; died 1848	2:99
Clark	Sylvester	4 Jan 1830	of Watertown, marr Levisa Beebe of Salem	1:154
Clark	Thomas	2 Dec 1800	Delegate at Consociation at Salem, from Oxford	1:19
Clark	Timothy	2 Dec 1800	Delegate at Consociation at Salem, from Waterbury	1:19
Clegg	Wm	- 1891	adm ch from Schaghticoke NY	3:9
Clegg	Wm	1 Nov 1891	adm fr 1st Presby, Schatagcoke NY	3:97
Clemens	Huldah M.	8 Feb 1866	d, 67, lung fever	3:255
Clifford	-	-	husband of Jane G. Russel	3:39
Cline	Hattie Katharine	28 Feb 1894	an inf, bp	3:161
Cline	Roy Henry	7 Nov 1895	inf bp; Henry & Helen Aderson	3:161
Cobleigh	Elizabeth Cone	- 1901	adm ch from Norwich Ct	3:9
Cobleigh	Elizabeth Cone	6 Jan 1901	adm fr 2nd ch, Norwich Ct	3:99
Cobleigh	Irving V.	- 1901	adm ch from Pleasantville NY	3:9
Cobleigh	Irving V.	6 Jan 1901	adm fr 1st Ch, Pleasantville NY	3:99
Coe	Andrew	6 Jul 1858	d, son of Robt & Emily J, 11, drowned	3:252
Coe	Augusta	1 Dec 1844	wife of Isaac, dism to Methedist Ch in Waterbury	2:50
Coe	Emily J.	29 Jun 1862	[wife of] Robert dism to Cong, Ansonia	3:122
Coe	Isaac	- -	husband of Augusta Hoadley	2:95
Coe	R.	- -	husband of Emily J. Horton	3:19

NAUGATUCK, CONNECTICUT, CONGREGATIONAL CHURCH RECORDS

Coe	Robert	-	-	husband of Emily J. Horton	2:97
Coe	Robert	-	1851	adm ch from Meth Naug; dis 1862 to Ansonia	3:8
Coe	Robert	9 Mar	1851	adm ch from Methodist Episcopal, Naug.	3:90
Coe	Robert	29 Jun	1862	dism to Cong, Ansonia	3:122
Cole	Mary A.	4 Jul	1875	marr Wm J. White, both of Naug	3:211
Coleman	Harriet A.	2 May	1886	bp, adult, "Mrs."	3:158
Coleman	Harriet A.	2 May	1886	Mrs., adm ch	3:69
Coleman	Harriet A.	2 May	1886	adm ch, wife of J.S.	3:9
Collins	Ann	27 May	1860	marr George Sanford, both of Naug	3:204
Collins	Mary	-	1866	adm ch from Meth Naug, wife of --; dec 1871	3:8
Collins	Mary	6 May	1866	Mrs, adm fr Methodist, Naug	3:92
Collins	William	12 May	1868	d, 56, lung fever, Hillside	3:256
Condee	-	21 Mar	1828	ch d, 0 [see Candee]	1:144
Condee	Bird	15 Mar	1818	wife Lois adm ch	1:59
Condee	Lois	19 Dec	1834	wife of Bird, dism to Episcopal Ch	2:18
Condict	F.H.	24 Nov	1899	and wife dism to Center Moriclus LI NY	3:129
Condict	Fletcher H.	-	1894	adm ch; dis 1899 to Centre Moriclus NY	3:9
Condict	Jennie H.	-	1894	Mrs., adm ch; dis 1899 to Centre Moriclus NY	3:9
Condit	Fletcher H.	1 Jul	1894	adm ch	3:71
Condit	Jennie H.	1 Jul	1894	Mrs., adm ch	3:71
Conklin	Fanny	3 Nov	1878	w of J.P., adm fr Anagansett Presb	3:94
Conklin	James P.	3 Nov	1878	adm ch	3:67
Conkling	Bessie	14 Feb	1899	19 marr Wm Dunham Martin 23	3:227
Conkling	Della	1 Dec	1897	28 marr Geo E. Fairchild 22	3:225
Conkling	Della J.	-	1885	adm ch	3:9
Conkling	Della J.	5 Jul	1885	bp, adult	3:158
Conkling	Della J.	5 Jul	1885	adm ch	3:68
Conkling	Fanny	-	1878	adm ch, wife of James P., from Anaganset Pres Ch.	3:8
Conkling	James P.	-	1878	adm ch	3:8
Conkling	Phoebe E.	-	1885	adm ch	3:9
Conkling	Phoebe E.	5 Jul	1885	bp, adult	3:158
Conkling	Phoebe E.	5 Jul	1885	adm ch	3:68
Cook	-	-	-	husband of Maria Payne	3:36
Cook	J.	4 Apr	1834	Mr, involved in case of Mrs. Marget Arnst	2:15
Cook	Jane E.	26 Dec	1853	of Winsted marr Darwin C. Andrus of Norfolk	3:201
Cook	Julius B.	2 Mar	1851	of Cheshire marr Polly C. Hopkins of Naug	3:200
Cook	William R.	5 Oct	1870	of Wallingford marr Maria Payne of Naug	3:209
Cooke	Gertrude E.	-	1897	adm ch from New Haven	3:9
Cooke	Gertrude E.	7 Nov	1897	adm fr College St, New Haven	3:98
Cooke	Harry Ludlow	-	1897	adm ch from New Haven	3:9
Cooke	Harry Ludlow	7 Nov	1897	adm fr College St, New Haven	3:98
Cooper	Frederick W.	6 Oct	1886	31 of Waterbury marr Ida J. Waite 26 of Naug	3:217
Corker	George	15 Oct	1877	marr Mattie Kerston, both of Southington	3:212
Cosier	Olive	13 Feb	1855	of Woodbury marr Alson Wooster of Naug	3:202
Couch	Elethea B.	13 Oct	1857	of Redding Ct marr Samuel L. Thompson of New Milford	3:203
Cowets[sic]	James	18 Jul	1810	wife d, 51y	1:160
Cowles	Maryann	-	-	see Blish	-
Cowles[?]	Carrie	27 Aug	1897	(Marsland) dism to 2nd Cong, Waterbury	3:129
Cowley	Sally N.	25 Jan	1861	d, 60, cancer	3:253
Cox	Arthur N.	3 Dec	1874	of Boston marr Alice J. Gaylord of Naug	3:210
Craft	Edward	29 Apr	1817	Deacon, from Derby, at Council re Rev. Dodd's removal	1:74
Crampton	Chas Schenck	9 Jun	1895	inf bp; Harry I. & Mary F.	3:161
Crampton	Ellen M.	-	1885	adm ch, wife of W.H.	3:9
Crampton	Ellen M.	5 Jul	1885	bp, adult	3:158

Crampton	Ellen M.	5 Jul	1885	adm ch	3:68
Crampton	Esther	13 Sep	1896	inf bp; W.D.	3:162
Crampton	Mary Francis	-	1888	adm ch from Williamsport Pa, wife of Harry	3:9
Crampton	Mary Francis	24 Aug	1888	adm fr 3d Presb, Williamsport Pa	3:96
Crampton	Susie Pierce	-	1887	adm ch from Pittsfield Mass., wife of Geo C.	3:9
Crampton	Susie Pierce	1 May	1887	Mrs., adm fr 1st Baptist, Pittsfield Mass	3:95
Crampton	Wm D.	-	1889	adm ch from Southington, and wife adm	3:9
Crampton	Wm D.	5 May	1889	adm fr Cong, Southington; also wife	3:96
Crampton	Wm Dewitt	13 Sep	1891	an inf, bp	3:160
Crampton	Wm H.	-	1885	adm ch; dec 1896	3:9
Crampton	Wm H.	5 Jul	1885	bp, adult	3:158
Crampton	Wm H.	5 Jul	1885	adm ch	3:68
Crampton	Wm H.	3 Apr	1896	d, Brights disease	3:261
Crane	Harvey	25 Nov	1851	of Bethlehem Ct marr Cornelia Sperry of Waterbury	3:201
Cray	Emily	-	1874	adm ch fr Baptist, Tiverton, Eng; w of James; dism [see James]	3:8
Cray	Emily	4 Jan	1874	adm fr Baptist Ch, Tiverton, England	3:93
Cray	Emily	18 Mar	1877	dism to 1st Freewill Baptist, Olneyville, Providence RI	3:125
Cray	James	-	1875	adm ch fr [see Emily]; dis 1877 Baptist, Orneyville, Prov., RI	3:8
Cray	James	3 Jan	1875	adm fr Baptist Ch, Tiverton, Eng.	3:93
Cray	James	18 Mar	1877	dism to 1st Freewill Baptist, Olneyville, Providence RI	3:125
Crich	Dorothy	11 Jun	1899	inf bp; John A. & Elizabeth Newton	3:164
Crich	John A.	-	1888	adm ch from Waterbury	3:9
Crich	John A.	4 Nov	1888	adm fr 2nd Cong, Waterbury Ct	3:96
Crich	John A.	3 Jul	1894	marr Elizabeth Newton	3:223
Cross	George	-	1836	adm ch; dis 1839 to Bridgeport	3:8
Cross	George	3 Jan	1836	adm ch; dism 2 Mar 1839 to Bridgeport	2:95
Cross	Nancy L.	-	1836	adm ch; dec 1838	3:8
Cross	Nancy L.	3 Jan	1836	wife of George, adm ch; died 1838	2:95
Cross	Nancy L.	3 Jan	1836	bp, adult	2:105
Crouch	Mr.	8 Aug	1824	dau d, consumption, 12	1:162
Culver	Amos	-	1787	adm ch; dec 1830	3:8
Culver	Amos	30 Sep	1787	adm ch; died 30 Jun 1830	2:83
Culver	Amos	30 Sep	1787	adm ch	1:11
Culver	Amos	30 Sep	1787	adm ch, d 30 Jun 1830	1:54
Culver	Amos	14 Sep	1801	on committee	1:24
Culver	Amos	-	1822	male, on list of members	1:81
Culver	Amos	30 Jun	1830	d, 82	1:146
Culver	Aner	-	1800	adm ch, wife of Stephen; dec 1844	3:8
Culver	Aner	14 Dec	1800	wife of Stephen, adm ch; died 3 Feb 1844	2:85
Culver	Anner	14 Dec	1800	St., adm ch	1:56
Culver	Anner	14 Dec	1800	wife of Stephen adm ch	1:20
Culver	Brother	19 Jun	1841	comm to visit him re "ardent spirits"	2:37
Culver	Clarissa	3 Jun	1792	bp, dau of Mrs Amos Culver	1:166
Culver	Clarissa	17 May	1808	d, 16y	1:159
Culver	Curtis	1 Mar	1801	bp, ch of Stephen	1:169
Culver	Eliza	-	1822	wife of Ransom, on list of members	1:82
Culver	Elizabeth	8 Oct	1843	wife of Ransom, requested letter to Episcopal Ch	2:48
Culver	Elizabeth, Mrs.	1 Mar	1844	excomm, having joined Episcopal Ch	2:49n
Culver	Hannah	-	1822	wife of Stephen, on list of members	1:82
Culver	Hannah Weeks	19 May	1805	bp, dau of Steven, bp in right of wife	1:172
Culver	J.	3 Feb	1842	case suspended	2:40f
Culver	Jonah	1 Oct	1826	appointed as delegate to consociation at Milford	1:102
Culver	Jonah	31 Oct	1827	appointed to conference at New Canaan	1:104
Culver	Josiah	12 May	1799	bp, son of Amos	1:169

NAUGATUCK, CONNECTICUT, CONGREGATIONAL CHURCH RECORDS

Culver	Josiah	-	1818	adm ch; exc 1842	3:8
Culver	Josiah	15 Mar	1818	adm ch; excomm 21 Jul 1842	2:89
Culver	Josiah	15 Mar	1818	adm ch	1:58
Culver	Josiah	-	1822	male, on list of members	1:81
Culver	Josiah	13 Aug	1827	appointed messenger to conference at Southbury	1:103
Culver	Josiah	2 Sep	1832	appt'd delegate to consociation in Oxford	2:12
Culver	Josiah	5 May	1837	SS Comm	2:25
Culver	Josiah	5 Feb	1843	case continued	2:45
Culver	Marshal	5 Jun	1785	bp, ch of Amos	1:164
Culver	Martin	3 Jan	1802	bp, ch of Stephen	1:170
Culver	Martin	5 Jun	1804	d, son of Steven, 2y	1:157
Culver	Mary	22 Oct	1815	bp, adopted ch of Anner	1:176
Culver	Mary L.	-	-	see Hubbell, Mary L.	-
Culver	Mershal[sic]	5 Jun	1785	bp	1:9
Culver	Mr.	30 Dec	1841	discussion of case against his trafficking in ardent spirits	2:39
Culver	Mrs.	3 Jun	1792	children bp, surname Atkins	1:166
Culver	R.	22 Mar	1833	Appt'd Asst. librarian for SS	2:13
Culver	Ransom	-	-	husband of Elisabeth Hull	3:18
Culver	Ransom	-	-	husband of Elizabeth Hull	2:88
Culver	Ransom	15 Jan	1797	bp, ch of Amos	1:168
Culver	Ransom	-	1818	adm ch; Irr. 1844 Episcopal	3:8
Culver	Ransom	15 Mar	1818	adm ch; withdrawn to Episcopay [sic]	2:89
Culver	Ransom	15 Mar	1818	adm ch	1:58
Culver	Ransom	-	1822	male, on list of members	1:81
Culver	Ransom	7 Oct	1827	appointed to attend conference at Newton	1:103
Culver	Ransom	17 Dec	1830	on comm	1:112
Culver	Ransom	30 Apr	1830	Mrs., on Sabb School board	1:111
Culver	Ransom	Sep	1831	on Visiting Committee	1:115
Culver	Ransom	30 Dec	1832	on comm	1:119
Culver	Ransom	30 Dec	1833	on comm	2:14
Culver	Ransom	20 Dec	1842	to visit and labour with Brother Elihu Benham	2:42
Culver	Ransom	8 Oct	1843	requested letter of dism to Episcopal Ch	2:48
Culver	Ransom	11 Jan	1843	visited Mrs. Fowler with Milo Lewis	2:44
Culver	Ransom	1 Mar	1844	excomm, having joined Episcopal Ch	2:49n
Culver	Ransome	24 Feb	1843	on comm	2:46
Culver	Sarah	-	1785	adm ch, wife of Amos; dec 1789	3:8
Culver	Sarah	17 Feb	1785	["Amos" added] d 24 Nov 1789	1:53
Culver	Sarah	20 Feb	1785	wife of Amos C., adm ch; died 24 Nov 1789	2:82
Culver	Sarah	20 Feb	1785	wife of Amos adm ch	1:9
Culver	Sarah	-	1792	adm ch, wife of Amos; dec 1845	3:8
Culver	Sarah	19 Feb	1792	2nd wife of Amos, adm ch; died 1 May 1845	2:84
Culver	Sarah	19 Feb	1792	wife of Amos adm ch	1:12
Culver	Sarah	19 Feb	1792	A[mos], adm ch	1:55
Culver	Sarah	-	1822	wife of Amos, on list of members	1:82
Culver	Stephen	-	1818	adm ch, dec 1849	3:8
Culver	Stephen	4 Jan	1818	adm ch	2:88
Culver	Stephen	4 Jan	1818	adm ch	1:58
Culver	Stephen	-	1822	male, on list of members	1:81
Culver	Stephen Hopkins	17 Mar	1811	bp, ch of Stephen, on account of his wife	1:175
Culver	Susanna	27 Jul	1794	bp, ch of Amos	1:167
Currie	John M.	7 May	1897	24 marr Ruby Estelle Wilmot 26, both of Waterbury	3:225
Curry	Ella Birdsall	18 Jul	1894	Mrs, d, 35, heart failure	3:260
Curry	Ellis C.	-	1895	adm ch	3:9
Curry	Ellis C.	Sep	1895	bp, adult, immersed in Bapt Ch, Waterbury	3:161

27

NAUGATUCK, CONNECTICUT, CONGREGATIONAL CHURCH RECORDS

Surname	Given	Date	Event	Ref
Curry	Ellis C.	1 Sep 1895	adm ch	3:71
Curry	Ellis C.	28 Nov 1900	22 marr Adaline E. Reffelt [sic] 20 at Beacon Falls	3:228
Curtis	Caroline Irene	2 Nov 1866	ch bp; Ames R. & Ellen H.	3:154
Curtis	Charles Henry	31 Aug 1860	ch bp; Ames R. & Ellen H.	3:152
Curtis	Cyrus Osborn	27 May 1869	ch bp; Ames R. & Ellen H.	3:155
Curtis	Eliza Henrietta	1 Jan 1860	bp, adult	3:152
Curtis	Eliza Henrietta	1 Jan 1860	adm ch	3:62
Curtis	Ellen [sic] H.	- 1860	adm ch, wife of Ames R.	3:8
Curtis	Emily Barber	30 Aug 1861	inf bp; Ellen H.	3:152
Curtis	Emma	2 May 1886	adm ch, wife of Samuel	3:9
Curtis	Freddie	7 Sep 1862	d, 5, diphtheria, Hillside	3:253
Curtis	George	7 May 1876	Mrs, adm ch	3:65
Curtis	Harriet	- 1876	adm ch, wife of George	3:8
Curtis	Harriet M.	8 Mar 1865	of Middlebury marr Charles T. Yale of Cornwall at Middlebury	3:206
Curtis	Hattie	25 Apr 1863	d, inf Ames & Ellen, 4 mos, diphtheria, Hillside	3:254
Curtis	Julia Lucina	31 Aug 1860	ch bp; Ames R. & Ellen H.	3:152
Curtis	Lillie Evangeline	3 Aug 1887	an inf, bp	3:158
Curtis	Louis Lambert	- 1890	adm ch	3:9
Curtis	Louis Lambert	9 Mar 1890	bp, adult	3:159
Curtis	Louis Lambert	9 Mar 1890	adm ch	3:70
Curtis	Mary E.	3 Mar 1856	of Middlebury marr Joseph Woodbridge of Stonington in Middlebury	3:203
Curtis	Miriam Atwater	12 Jun 1898	inf bp; Louis L. & Mabel Curtis	3:163
Curtis	Samuel	2 May 1886	adm ch	3:9
Curtis	William	16 Sep 1798	bp, ch of Clarissa	1:168
Curtiss	Ames R.	26 Nov 1872	bur, 49, Hillside	3:257
Curtiss	C.B.	Apr 1894	Mrs, d	3:260
Curtiss	Caroline B.	- 1885	adm ch from San Bernardino Cal, wife of -- Jennings	3:9
Curtiss	Caroline B.	3 May 1985	adm fr 1st Bap, San Bernardino Cal	3:95
Curtiss	Carrie B.	1 Apr 1886	21 marr Ralph R. Jennings 25, both of Naug	3:217
Curtiss	David W.	22 Jun 1859	of Huntington Ct marr Martha J. Clark of Waterbury	3:204
Curtiss	Emma	2 May 1886	wife of Samuel, adm ch	3:69
Curtiss	Emma J.	12 Apr 1865	marr Martin Reed, both of Newtown	3:206
Curtiss	Fred	2 Jun 1899	18 marr Sarah Kirk 21	3:227
Curtiss	S.B.	- 1885	adm ch; dec 1895	3:9
Curtiss	S.B.	- 1885	Mrs., adm ch; erased 27 Apr 1900	3:9
Curtiss	S.B.	13 Sep 1885	and wife adm ch	3:69
Curtiss	Samuel	2 May 1886	adm ch	3:69
Cushman	Ella	26 Nov 1873	marr Chas Daniels, both of Naug	3:210
Cutler	Julia	- 1865	adm ch, wife of F.S. Andrew; dis 1869 to New Haven	3:8
Cutler	Julia	7 May 1865	bp, adult	3:153
Cutler	Julia	7 May 1865	adm ch	3:63
Cutler	Julia	17 May 1866	marr Frank S. Andrew, both of Naug	3:207
Cutler	Mary J.	11 Jun 1868	marr Dwight W. Lewis, both of Naug	3:208
Cwick	Lucius	14 Mar 1864	marr Delia Russel, both of Naug [see Zwick]	3:205
Cwick	Phillip	14 Jun 1870	marr Elizabeth Kutze, both of Naug	3:209

NAUGATUCK, CONNECTICUT, CONGREGATIONAL CHURCH RECORDS

Dalby	Harry A.	-	1887	adm ch from Steubenville O.; dis 1890 to So Norwalk	3:10
Dalby	Harry A.	4 Sep	1887	adm fr Cong, Steubenville O.	3:96
Dalby	Harry A.	8 Sep	1889	22 marr Etta A. Terrill 19	3:220
Dalby	Harry A.	26 Sep	1890	dism to Cong, So Norwalk, Ct; also wife (Etta Terrell)	3:127
Dalby	Harry Andrew	1 Jul	1888	adult, bp; ["previously baptized in infancy" crossed out]	3:159
Daniels	Chas	26 Nov	1873	marr Ella Cushman, both of Naug	3:210
David	Adolph N.	23 Apr	1898	37 marr Gussie Linz 24	3:226
Davis	Emma (Noble)	Feb	1893	Mrs, d, consumption	3:260
Davis	Etta Rose	22 Nov	1877	ch bp; Nelson H. & Mary E.	3:155
Davis	Isabella Lizzie	1 Aug	1897	a ch, bp; chapel at Millville	3:162
Davis	Minnie Sophia	1 Aug	1897	a ch, bp; chapel at Millville	3:162
Davis	Sophia	-	1855	adm ch from Milford; wife of Truman; dis 1873 to Milford	3:10
Davis	Sophia	4 Nov	1855	w of Truman, adm fr 2d Cong Milford	3:90
Davis	Walter Barrett	22 Nov	1877	bp, Nelson H. & Mary E.	3:155
Day	Alida	1 Nov	1896	Miss, adm ch	3:71
Day	S. Alida	-	1896	Miss, adm ch	3:10
Day	S. Alida	1 Nov	1896	bp, adult	3:162
Dayton	Martha	28 Dec	1864	d, 84, lung fever	3:255
Deabler	Jacob	23 Sep	1858	of Bethany marr Josephine Zels of Naug	3:203
Dean	Sally	-	1818	adm ch; dis 1825 to New Haven	3:10
Dean	Sally	6 Sep	1818	adm ch; rem 10 Apr 1825 to New Haven 1st Ch	2:91
Dean	Sally	6 Sep	1818	adm ch, dism	1:59
Dean	Sally	-	1822	Wid, on list of members; dism	1:82
Dean	Sara	10 Apr	1825	Wid, rec to 1st ch in New Haven	1:101
Decker	Theodore	27 Mar	1869	of Watertown marr Margaret J. Sloan of Bethany	3:208
Delavan	Mary Ann	28 May	1850	d, wife of J. Smith Delavan, 22 Consumption	3:250
Demeer[sic]	John	20 Mar	1882	marr Henrietta Doisey [Dorsey?], both of Naug	3:214
Demo[sic]	Essie May	21 Jan	1894	inf bp; Wm & Annie	3:161
Dencer[?]	Villa Adeline	1 Oct	1883	marr Francis Lathrop Hosmer [Honner?], both of Naug	3:215
Dennen	Fred	5 Apr	1884	marr Lilly McCrumb[?], both of Naug	3:216
Dennin	Caroline S.	15 Dec	1885	49 marr Samuel F. Dennin 50, both of Naug	3:217
Dennin	Samuel F.	15 Dec	1885	50 marr Caroline S. Dennin 49, both of Naug	3:217
Denniston	H.G.	5 Nov	1893	and wife adm ch	3:71
Dethlefsen	Chas Reuckert	20 Mar	1887	an inf, bp	3:158
Dethlefson	Henry W.	31 Dec	1885	28 marr Lizzie Schatzman 19, both of Naug	3:217
Dettuel	Louis	21 Sep	1981	marr Barbara Scusceur, both of Naug	3:216
Deutsch	Hattie	-	1891	Mrs., adm ch from Brookville, Kan	3:10
Deutsch	Hattie	4 Jan	1891	Mrs., adm fr Cong, Brookville Kan	3:97
DeVoir	A.H.	-	1887	Mrs., adm ch from Steubenville O.	3:10
DeVoir	A.H.	4 Sep	1887	Mrs., adm ch fr Cong, Steubenville O	3:96
Dewalt	Willie Albert	15 Aug	1869	ch bp, Mr. & Mrs. Dewalt (German)	3:155
DeWolf	Francis	6 May	1880	marr William Brixy, both of Seymour	3:212
Dews	Jane A.	-	1885	adm ch from Middlebury; dis 1899 Oakville Ct	3:10
Dews	Jane A.	3 May	1885	Mrs., adm fr Cong, Middlebury Ct	3:95
Dews	Jane A.	23 Jun	1899	dism to Union Ch, Oakville Ct	3:129
Dibble	Clara Ella	12 Jun	1898	inf bp; Robert W. & Ida Fenn	3:163
Dibble	Robert W.	1 Jan	1882	marr Ida B. Fenn, both of Naug	3:213
Dibble	Robt W.	27 Apr	1898	42 marr Anna E. Terrill 38	3:226
Dibble	Ruth Westcott	17 Jun	1888	an inf, bp	3:158
Dibble	Stanley Emmett	12 Jun	1898	inf bp; Robert W. & Ida Fenn	3:163
Dicamon[sic]	Benonia	16 Apr	1807	infant ch d, 2 wks	1:158
Distler	Emma	12 Nov	1899	20 marr John C. Valentine 29	3:227
Divine	Joseph	26 Apr	1877	marr Fannie Beach of Naug	3:211
Dodd	Phebe	-	1811	adm ch from Bloomfield NJ, wife of Stephen; dec 1815	3:10

NAUGATUCK, CONNECTICUT, CONGREGATIONAL CHURCH RECORDS

Dodd	Phebe	5 Jul	1811	wife of Rev. Stephen, cand for memb, from Bloomfield, NJ	1:62
Dodd	Phebe	13 Oct	1811	wife of Stephen, adm ch from Bloomfield NJ; died 27 Feb 1815	2:87
Dodd	Phebe	13 Oct	1811	adm ch, d 27 Feb 1815	1:57
Dodd	Phebe	13 Oct	1811	adm ch	1:62
Dodd	Stephen	2 Oct	1810	Rev, chosen Moderator; installation as pastor discussed	1:51
Dodd	Stephen	5 Aug	1810	Rev., voted to return to settle here	1:50
Dodd	Stephen	-	1811	Rev., ordained; dism 1817	2:2
Dodd	Stephen	-	1811	Pastor, dism 29 Apr 1817	2:79
Dodd	Stephen	-	1811	Rev, settled; dismissed April 1817	1:13
Dodd	Stephen	8 Apr	1817	Rev., requested a council to consider his resignation	1:74
Dodd	Stephen	29 Apr	1817	Rev., Ministerial connection dissolved	1:75
Dohering	Mrs.	25 Nov	1874	bur, 37	3:257
Doisey [sic]	Henrietta	20 Mar	1882	[Dorsey?] marr John Demeer[sic], both of Naug	3:214
Donkersley	Elsie May	12 Jun	1892	an inf, bp	3:160
Donkersley	Howard Herbert	26 Jul	1897	twin bp; Herbert H. & Ida G.	3:162
Donkersley	Maud Alice	26 Jun	1897	twin bp; Herbert H. & Ida G.	3:162
Donnan[?]	Walter W.	12 Oct	1880	[Dorman?] marr Martha A. Osborn, both of Seymour	3:213
Doolittle	-	-	-	husband of Laura Horton	3:19
Doolittle	-	-	-	husband of Laura Horton	2:97
Doolittle	Abigail	16 Mar	1826	of Cheshire, marr Joseph H. Payne of Waterbury	1:152
Doolittle	Jeanette A.	12 Jun	1899	24 marr Wm H. Watson 26 at New Haven	3:227
Dorsey	Henrietta	2 Dec	1877	of Naug marr John Henry Brown of Waterbury [see Doisey]	3:212
Dougal	Jane A.	15 Jun	1854	of Naug marr Edward Jewett of Newburyport Mass	3:201
Dougall	Emerett	8 Mar	1862	marr Merritt Wheeler, both of Naugatuck	3:205
Douglass	David K.	27 Jun	1853	of Naug marr Nancy M. Newcomb of Plymouth	3:201
Douglass	Julia Elizabeth	-	1900	Mrs., adm ch	3:10
Douglass	Julia Elizabeth	4 Mar	1900	adm ch	3:72
Douglass	Maria A.	10 Oct	1853	of Naug marr Wheaton S. Plumb of Wallingford	3:201
Douglass	Raymond	9 Jun	1901	ch bp; Elisha A. & Julia (Armstrong)	3:165
Dover	Clara	16 Nov	1875	marr Fremont W. Tolles, both of Naug	3:211
Downes	Mary A.	-	1877	adm ch; dec 1889, reported dead in Wolcott	3:10
Downes	Mary A.	22 Aug	1889	reported died in Wolcott	3:261
Downes	Nellie Charlotte	25 Dec	1898	inf bp; Fred F. & Nellie	3:163
Downes	Robert Walter	10 Jun	1894	bp; Fred F. & Nellie A.	3:161
Downs	James	12 Aug	1818	[Name is blank but was his wife] adm ch fr Milford,	2:91
-	-	-	-	rem to Southington	-
Downs	James	13 Aug	1818	his wife adm ch	1:59
Downs	James D.	-	1818	wife adm ch from Milford; dis to Southington	3:10
Downs	Mary A.	4 Mar	1877	adm ch	3:66
Draper	Elizabeth	5 Jul	1865	marr William Oxby, both of Naug	3:206
Dugg	Raymond Curtis	20 Nov	1898	an inf, bp	3:159
Dumiston	H.G.	-	1893	Maj & Mrs. adm ch	3:10
Dunder[?]	Anne	16 Aug	1882	marr Peter Settler, both of Naug	3:214
Dyson	Clara E.	-	1885	adm ch	3:10
Dyson	Clara E.	5 Jul	1885	adm ch	3:68
Dyson	Florence	-	1885	adm ch	3:10
Dyson	Florence	5 Jul	1885	adm ch	3:68
Dyson	Florence	7 Jun	1893	26 marr Herbert V. Gooding 26	3:223
Eames	Mr.	13 Jan	1842	on comm, Rev.	2:40
Eastman	Peter	29 Sep	1801	Capt, Delegate to consociation in Salem, from N. Haven	1:25
Easton	D.A.	-	1876	Rev., adm ch fr 2nd Danbury; dis 1879 to 2nd ch in Portland Me	3:11
Easton	D.A.	2 Jul	1876	Rev., adm fr 2nd Cong, Danbury Ct	3:93
Easton	D.A.	5 Mar	1876	settled as Pastor; dism 31 Jan 1879	3:1
Easton	D.A.	22 Dec	1878	Rev, dism to 2nd Cong, Portland Me [crossed out]	3:125

NAUGATUCK, CONNECTICUT, CONGREGATIONAL CHURCH RECORDS

Surname	Given	Date	Notes	Ref
Easton	D.A.	23 Jan 1879	Rev, dism to 2nd Portland Maine	3:125
Eaton	Alice	20 Aug 1861	d, inf of Mr & Mrs of St Louis, 6 ms, Hillside	3:253
Eaton	Delia B. [sic]	7 Sep 1890	Mrs., adm fr Cong, Watertown Ct	3:96
Eaton	Delia E.	- 1890	Mrs., adm ch from Watertown; dis 1895 to New Haven	3:11
Eaton	Delia E.	21 Jun 1895	dism to United Cong, New Haven	3:128
Eckart	Richard Wm	17 May 1891	an inf, bp	3:160
Eckert	-	4 Sep 1891	an inf, bp	3:160
Edmonds	Lucinda	- 1854	adm ch from Southbury; dis 1855 to 2d ch Waterbury	3:11
Edmonds	Lucinda	19 Mar 1854	adm from Cong, Southbury	3:90
Edmonds	Lucinda	12 Aug 1855	dism to 2d Cong, Waterbury	3:121
Edwards	Mr.	29 Sep 1801	referred to in Saml Scott's confession	1:30
Edwards	Philip	1 Aug 1897	ch bp; Benjamin D.; chapel at Millville	3:162
Eells	-	- -	see Ells	-
Eells	Daniel	24 Jul 1785	bp, ch of Leut	1:164
Eells	Daniel	24 Jul 1785	bp [entry crossed out]	1:10
Eells	Mary	17 Jul 1785	wife of Leut, adm ch	1:9
Eels	Sarah	30 Sep 1787	adm ch	1:11
Eggert	Lena	25 Nov 1896	Mrs. 41 marr Winand Rasquin 35	3:225
Eggleston	Emma L.	21 Dec 1882	marr Chas W. Hoadley, both of Naug	3:215
Ellis	-	- -	husband of Emily N. Hoadley	3:20
Ellis	-	3 Aug 1887	an inf, bp	3:158
Ellis	Emily N.	- 1886	adm ch from Middlebury	3:11
Ellis	Emily N.	3 Jan 1886	Mrs, adm fr Cong, Middlebury Ct	3:95
Ellis	Eugene Hoadley	7 Mar 1886	an inf, bp	3:158
Ellis	Hattie	3 Oct 1897	ch bp in Parish House at opening exercises of Sunday School	3:163
Ellis	Walter	5 Nov 1897	24 marr Lottie Saylor 23	3:225
Ells	-	- -	see Eels	-
Ells	Diana	14 Dec 1800	adm ch; rem 5 [sic] Jul 1811 to Middlebury	2:85
Ells	Diana	14 Dec 1800	adm ch, dism 6 Jul 1811	1:56
Ells	Diana	14 Dec 1800	adm ch	1:20
Ells	Diana	5 Jul 1811	rec & certif	1:51
Ells	Dinah [sic]	- 1800	adm ch; dis 1811 to Middlebury	3:11
Ells	Julia	4 Jan 1801	bp, ch of Diana	1:169
Ells	Mary	- 1785	adm ch, wife of Leut; dis 1815	3:11
Ells	Mary	17 Jul 1785	wife of Leut, adm ch; rem Jun 1815	2:82
Ells	Mary	17 Jul 1785	Leut, adm ch [d "1815" crossed out] dism Jun 1815	1:54
Ells	Mary	Jun 1815	certif, moving out of state	1:69
Ells	Sarah	- 1787	adm ch, wife of Enos Bradley; dis to Middlebury	3:11
Ells	Sarah	30 Sep 1787	wife of Enos Bradley, adm ch; rem to Middlebury	2:83
Ells	Sarah	30 Sep 1787	adm ch, dism	1:54
Ely	Calvin	19 Sep 1868	d, 81	3:256
Englehardt	Louise	- 1899	Miss, adm ch	3:11
Englehardt	Louise	5 Nov 1899	Miss, adm ch	3:72
Ericson	Augusta Elizabeth	12 Nov 1898	inf bp; Edward & Emma Staub	3:163
Ericson	Raymond Edward	24 Aug 1897	inf bp; Edwd & Emma	3:163
Erwin	Theodore S.	14 Oct 1886	55 marr Mrs. Maria Arandholtz 49, both of Naug	3:217
Erwin	W.S.	22 Feb 1881	at centennial exercises	3:300
Fairchild	Elizabeth Hard	10 Jun 1900	inf bp; Geo E. & Della (Conkling)	3:165
Fairchild	Geo E.	1 Dec 1897	22 marr Della Conkling 28	3:225
Fairchild	Jennie E.	- -	see Hopkins	-
Fairchild	Willis Conkling	10 Jun 1900	inf bp; Geo E. & Della (Conkling)	3:165
Fanning	Col.	29 Apr 1837	ch died, 3	2:115
Fanning	Sarah	12 Mar 1837	died, 29	2:115
Fanning	Sarah R.	- 1835	adm ch; dec 1837	3:13

NAUGATUCK, CONNECTICUT, CONGREGATIONAL CHURCH RECORDS

Surname	Given	Date	Event	Ref
Fanning	Sarah R.	20 Dec 1835	adm ch; died 12 Mar 1837	2:95
Farrell	Hattie M.	24 Feb 1898	21 marr Barton James Chapman 21	3:226
Fenn	Ella D.	29 Jun 1884	marr Hobart M. Hill, both of Naug	3:216
Fenn	Ida B.	1 Jan 1882	marr Robert W. Dibble, both of Naug	3:213
Fenn	Isabella	3 Oct 1865	of Ansonia marr Morris P. Bray of Funkville, Pa	3:207
Fenton	-	-	see Talmage	-
Fenton	Elizabeth	- 1885	Mrs., adm ch, wife of Jas	3:13
Fenton	Elizabeth	3 May 1885	Mrs, adm ch	3:67
Fish	Alice B.	- 1900	adm ch	3:13
Fish	Alice B.	7 Jan 1900	adm ch	3:72
Fisk	Mrs.	10 May 1875	bur, 24	3:257
Fitts	Florence Emma	- 1897	adm ch	3:13
Fitts	Florence Emma	2 May 1897	bp, adult	3:162
Fitts	Frederick A.	20 Jun 1892	36 marr Harriet L. Pease 27	3:222
Fitz	E.	- 1894	Mrs., adm ch from Lebanon NH	3:13
Fitz	E.	7 Jan 1894	Mrs, adm fr Baptist, Lebanon NH	3:97
Fitz	Florence Emma	2 May 1897	adm ch	3:71
Fitz	Jennie E.	- 1894	adm ch	3:13
Fitz	Jennie E.	7 Jan 1894	adm ch	3:71
Fitzgerald	Edward Senior	30 Dec 1877	bp	3:155
Fitzgerald	Mary Ann	30 Dec 1877	a ch, bp	3:155
Fitzgerald	Sarah Senior	30 Dec 1877	a ch, bp	3:155
Flinn	Angeline	- 1854	adm ch; dis 1864	3:13
Flinn	Angeline	5 Mar 1854	bp, profession	3:150
Flinn	Angeline	5 Mar 1854	adm ch	3:60
Flinn	Angeline	25 Mar 1864	voted dism, eligible for letter if asked for [see 3:367]	3:122
Flint	-	-	husband of Harriette Hopkins	3:20
Flint	Wm H.	9 Jun 1886	marr Hattie L. Hopkins, both of Naug	3:217
Flor	Annie	28 Oct 1879	marr August Shultz, both of Beacon Falls	3:212
Ford	Capt [sic]	20 Feb 1809	infant d, 4m	1:159
Ford	Delia J.	14 Apr 1865	marr Isaac S. Sanford, both of Waterbury	3:206
Ford	Elias	Sep 1813	infant d	1:160
Ford	James	19 May 1864	of New Haven marr Zelia S. Rowley of Naug	3:205
Ford	John	2 Feb 1876	of New York, marr Emma J. Gould of Naug	3:211
Ford	Rebecca	- 1878	adm ch; care withdrawn 1885	3:13
Ford	Rebecca	3 Mar 1878	adm ch	3:66
Forgul	Francis	28 Feb 1825	d, debility, interesting comments in original, e.g.	1:162
-	-	-	"infidel," 58	-
Forrest	Bellmont	19 Apr 1869	of Waterbury marr Nettie H. Lewis of Naug	3:208
Foster	Edith	- 1887	adm ch	3:13
Foster	Edith	3 Jul 1887	adm ch	3:69
Foster	Frank	27 Nov 1890	marr Augusta Beatty	3:221
Foster	Irene C.	- 1900	adm ch	3:13
Foster	Irene C.	6 May 1900	adm ch	3:72
Foster	Jane Charlotte	- 1878	adm ch, wife of Wm S.	3:13
Foster	Jane Charlotte	5 May 1878	wife of William S., adm ch	3:67
Foster	Mary A.	- 1887	adm ch; dis 1894 to Broad Brook, Ct	3:13
Foster	Mary A.	3 Jul 1887	adm ch	3:69
Foster	Mary A.	14 Sep 1893	24 marr Chas N. Wood 25	3:223
Foster	Mary A. (Wood)	28 Dec 1894	dism to Cong, Ch, Broad Brook Ct	3:128
Foster	William S.	5 May 1878	adm ch	3:67
Foster	Wm S.	- 1878	adm ch; dec 1888	3:13
Foster	Wm S.	16 Jun 1888	d, chronic diarrhoea	3:259
Fowler	Abraham	- 1785	Rev, ordained; dism 1799	2:2

NAUGATUCK, CONNECTICUT, CONGREGATIONAL CHURCH RECORDS

Fowler	Abraham		Jan	1785	Pastor, dismissed Mar 1799	2:79
Fowler	Abraham Cap	19 Jun	1785	bp, "my own son"	1:164
Fowler	Abraham, Rev		Jan	1785	was settled; dismissed March 1799	1:13
Fowler	Abraham, Rev	18 Jul	1802	his wife given certificate as member	1:34
Fowler	Abram	5 Sep	1794	Moderator	1:12
Fowler	Arabella	-	1898	Mrs., adm ch from So Amenia NY	3:13
Fowler	Arabella	4 Sep	1898	Mrs, adm fr Pres, South Amenia NY	3:98
Fowler	Benjamin	9 Mar	1878	marr Mrs. Urania B. Norton, both of Naug	3:212
Fowler	Fanney	-	1822	wife of Abra, on list of members	1:82
Fowler	Fanny	-	1817	adm ch, wife of Abm; dec 1861	3:13
Fowler	Fanny	16 Nov	1817	wife of Abraham C., adm ch	2:88
Fowler	Fanny	16 Nov	1817	adm ch	1:57
Fowler	Fanny	20 Dec	1842	Mrs, to be visited and laboured with	2:42
Fowler	Fanny P.	27 Feb	1861	d, 72, apoplexy, Hillside	3:253
Fowler	Fanny Prudencia	15 Mar	1818	ch of Abraham C., bp [could be 2 children]	1:60
Fowler	Henry Porter	15 Mar	1818	ch of Abraham C., bp [could be 2 children]	1:60
Fowler	Julia Anne	15 Mar	1818	ch of Abraham C., bp [could be 2 children]	1:60
Fowler	Marion	-	1901	adm ch from Norwich Ct.	3:13
Fowler	Marion	6 Jan	1901	adm fr 2nd ch, Norwich Ct	3:99
Fowler	Mary	-	1787	adm ch; dis 1802	3:13
Fowler	Mary	18 Nov	1787	adm ch; rem 18 Jul 1802	2:84
Fowler	Mary	18 Nov	1787	adm ch	1:11
Fowler	Mary	18 Nov	1787	adm ch ["Rev Abraham" added] dis 18 Jul 1802	1:54
Fowler	Mrs.	11 Jan	1843	visited by Milo Lewis and Ransom Culver	2:44
Fowler	Rebecca	-	1797	adm ch, wife of Rev. Abm; dis 1802 to Ridgefield	3:13
Fowler	Rebecca	14 May	1797	wife of Rev. Abraham, adm ch; rem 18 Jul 1802 to Ridgefield	2:85
Fowler	Rebecca	14 May	1797	[Rev.], adm ch, dism 18 Jul 1802	1:55
Fowler	Rebeckah	14 May	1797	wife of Abram adm ch	1:13
Fowler	Sarah	18 Sep	1785	wife of Abraham, adm ch; died 26 Jan 1795	2:82
Fowler	Sarah	18 Sep	1785	adm ch	1:10
Fowler	Sarah	18 Sep	1785	adm ch, d 6 Jan 1795	1:54
Fowler	Sarah Rebeckah	15 Mar	1818	ch of Abraham C., bp [could be 2 children]	1:60
Fowler	Stern Humphrey	15 Mar	1818	ch of Abraham C., bp [could be 2 children]	1:60
Fox	Lucy A.	4 Jan	1860	marr John G. Patterson, both of Naug	3:204
Fox	Nancy	-	1857	adm ch, wife of O. Hitchcock; care withdrawn 1885	3:13
Fox	Nancy	5 Jul	1857	bp, adult	3:151
Fox	Nancy	5 Jul	1857	adm ch	3:61
Fox	Nancy	4 Jan	1860	marr Oliver Hitchcock, both of Naug	3:204
Freeman	Arthur	1 Oct	1885	22 marr Ida McKinney 21, both of Naug	3:217
Freeman	Charles	18 Feb	1858	of Bridgeport marr Mary Ann Weston of Naug, both colored	3:203
Freeman	Hanford D.	26 Oct	1882	marr Cathrine Wylie, both of Naug	3:214
Freeman	James	-	1843	adm ch; dec 1863	3:13
Freeman	James	4 May	1849	residence and condition to be ascertained	2:59
Freeman	Mary	-	1877	adm ch from Pres Ch Astoria NY, wife of Wm Jr	3:13
Freeman	Mary F.	4 Mar	1877	Mrs., adm fr Astoria NY Pres	3:94
Freeman	Watson Wylie	Sep	1885	bp	3:158
Freman	James	2 Jul	1843	adm ch	2:99
Freman	James	2 Jul	1843	bp, adult	2:107
French	David	29 Sep	1801	Dn, Delegate to consociation in Salem, from 2nd Woodbridge	1:25
French	Gertrude	23 May	1883	marr Franklin J. Gunn, both of Naug	3:215
French	Kate Jenner	11 Jun	1899	inf bp; Geo N. & Alice Jenner	3:164
French	Thos Jr.	24 Nov	1857	of Naug marr Polly Ann Chatfield of Waterbury	3:203
Frey	Joseph	14 Dec	1876	inf bp; Godfred Frye	3:155
Frey	Mary Ann	22 Jan	1879	inf bp; H.G.	3:156

NAUGATUCK, CONNECTICUT, CONGREGATIONAL CHURCH RECORDS

Surname	Given	Date	Event	Ref
Frey	Olti [sic]	14 Dec 1876	inf bp; Godfred Frye	3:155
Frick	Agnes	6 Jul 1890	an inf, bp	3:159
Frick	Anna S.	9 Jun 1893	dism to Swedish Ch, Naug	3:128
Frick	Annie S.	- 1885	Mrs., adm ch, wife of Joseph; dis 1893 to Sweedish Ch	3:13
Frick	Annie S.	5 Jul 1885	Mrs, adm ch	3:68
Frick	Joseph	- 1886	adm ch; dis 1893 to Sweedish Ch	3:13
Frick	Joseph	7 Mar 1886	adm ch	3:69
Frick	Joseph	9 Jun 1893	dism to Swedish Ch, Naug	3:128
Frinn	Wm F.	24 Aug 1898	21 marr Cora M. Allan 21	3:226
Frisbe	-	Sep 1813	ch d	1:160
Frisbe	Jonah	22 Mar 1789	adm ch	1:12
Frisbe	Jonah	22 Mar 1789	adm ch, dism 27 Jan 1805	1:55
Frisbe	Thirza	21 Mar 1790	bp, ch of Jonah	1:165
Frisbee	Alpha	10 May 1795	bp, ch of Jonah	1:167
Frisbee	Trena	18 Sep 1791	bp, ch of Jonah	1:166
Frisbie	-	-	husband of Annie L. Wertz	3:56
Frisbie	Ama	27 Jan 1805	wife of Jonah, of Deary, Shenango Co., NY, letter of rec	1:38
Frisbie	James	20 Sep 1808	d, 37	1:159
Frisbie	Jonah	-	husband of Amy Smith	3:41
Frisbie	Jonah	-	husband of Amy Smith	2:83
Frisbie	Jonah	- 1789	adm ch; dis 1805 to Gorman NY	3:13
Frisbie	Jonah	22 Mar 1789	adm ch; rem 27 Jan 1805 to Gorman NY	2:84
Frisbie	Jonah	27 Jan 1805	of Deary, Shenango Co, NY, letter of rec	1:38
Frisbie	Sally	3 May 1804	d, dau of James, 2y	1:157
Frost	Anna C.	- 1894	adm ch	3:13
Frost	Anna C.	6 May 1894	Mrs., adm ch	3:71
Frost	Mertie	6 Aug 1873	bur, 17 mos, Hillside	3:257
Frye	-	-	see Frey	-
Fullar	David	2 Dec 1800	Revd Elder attending Consociation at Salem, from 2nd Milford	1:19
Fullar	David	29 Sep 1801	Rev. Elder attending consociation in Salem, from 2nd Milford	1:25
Fuller	Alfred E.	19 May 1861	of New Milford marr Ellen Baldwin of Naug	3:205
Fuller	Calvin E. [sic]	3 Mar 1878	adm ch	3:66
Fuller	Calvin R.	- 1878	adm ch	3:13
Fuller	Catharine M.	- 1872	adm ch, wife of Calvin R.	3:13
Fuller	Catharine M.	3 Nov 1872	Mrs., adm ch	3:64
Fuller	Catharine M.	3 Nov 1872	bp, adult	3:155
Fuller	Frankie	13 Mar 1877	d, 3 y, cerebro-spinal menengitis, Hillside	3:257
Fyfe	Thos Harper	25 May 1892	26 marr Helen Harriet Henderson 29	3:222
Garnsey	Irenia	16 Nov 1817	adm ch	1:57
Garnzy	-	-	see also Gearnsey, Girnsy, Gurnsey	-
Garnzy	Irena	- 1817	adm ch; dec 1834	3:15
Garnzy	Saml	- 1801	adm ch; lrr 1820 Baptist	3:15
Garnzy	Samuel	22 Feb 1801	adm ch; withdrawn Jul 1820 to Baptist	2:86
Garnzy	Samuel	22 Feb 1801	adm ch, d Jul 1820, certificated	1:56
Garnzy	Samuel	22 Feb 1801	adm ch	1:21
Garrison	Louise	-	wife of Tracy W. North	3:31
Gay	Addie	23 Feb 1889	31 marr A.A. Painter 19	3:220
Gaylord	Abbe	- 1869	adm ch, wife of Luther G.; "this name not entered elsewhere"	3:15
Gaylord	Abbe	2 May 1869	adm ch	3:64
Gaylord	Agnes A.	25 Jan 1857	d, 4 y, scarlet fever	3:251
Gaylord	Alice J.	3 Dec 1874	of Naug marr Arthur N. Cox of Boston	3:210
Gaylord	Augusta C.	24 Nov 1858	of Naug marr Solon F. Carter of Boston	3:204
Gaylord	Luther	18 Jan 1856	of Naug marr Abigail Beecher of Prospect	3:203
Gearnsey	Irena	- 1822	female, on list of members	1:82

NAUGATUCK, CONNECTICUT, CONGREGATIONAL CHURCH RECORDS

Geisler	-	-	-	see Schwitz	-
Geisler	Henry John	5 Jul	1891	an inf, bp	3:160
Genish[?]	W.E.	-	1893	Dr., adm ch [Gerrish?]	3:15
Genish[?]	W.E.	3 Sep	1893	Dr., adm ch [Gerrish?]	3:71
Germer	Herman G.	-	1886	adm ch; dis 1896 to Chicago Ill	3:15
Germer	Herman G.	7 Nov	1886	bp, adult	3:158
Germer	Herman G.	17 Apr	1896	dism to Lake View Cong, Chicago Ill	3:128
Germer	Hermann G.	7 Nov	1886	adm ch	3:69
Gherst	Ida L.	-	1880	adm ch from Rockville Ct	3:15
Gherst	Ida L.	5 Mar	1880	Miss, adm fr 2nd Cong, Rockville Ct	3:94
Gibbard	-	-	-	see Gibbud	-
Gibbard	Clarissa	-	1818	adm ch, wife of Merritt; lrr 1825 Baptist	3:15
Gibbard	Clarissa	4 Jan	1818	wife of Merit, adm ch; withdrawn 16 Feb 1825 to Baptist	2:89
Gibbard	Clarissa	4 Jan	1818	adm ch	1:58
Gibbard	Clarissa	-	1822	wife of Merit, on list of members; dism	1:82
Gibbard	Esther	-	1818	adm ch, wife of Lyman; dis 1833 Hamden	3:15
Gibbard	Esther	3 May	1818	wife of Lyman, adm ch; rem Aug 1833 to Hamden E.P.	2:89
Gibbard	Esther	3 May	1818	adm ch	1:59
Gibbard	Esther	-	1822	wife of Lyman, on list of members	1:82
Gibbard	Friend Smith	30 Jun?	1826	wife of Lyman, bp [prob means a ch of the wife of Lyman, bp]	1:86
Gibbard	Luther	11 Dec	1857	d, 32, congestion of the lungs	3:252
Gibbard	Rejoice	-	1817	adm ch; dec 1843	3:15
Gibbard	Rejoice	16 Nov	1817	adm ch	1:57
Gibbard	Rejoice	16 Nov	1817	adm ch; died Mar 1843	2:87
Gibbard	Rejoice	-	1822	wife of Tim, on list of members	1:82
Gibbard	William Carloss	7 Sep	1823	ch of Lyman & Esther, bp	1:85
Gibbud	-	-	-	see Gibbard	-
Gibbud	Alsop	4 Sep	1818	ch of Lyman, bp	1:61
Gibbud	Annie C.	-	1885	adm ch	3:15
Gibbud	Annie C.	5 Jul	1885	bp, adult	3:157
Gibbud	Annie C.	5 Jul	1885	adm ch	3:68
Gibbud	Annie M.	24 Oct	1894	21 marr Chas M. Brooks 27	3:223
Gibbud	Brockel[?]	4 Sep	1818	ch of Lyman, bp	1:61
Gibbud	Carrie Jane	27 May	1869	ch bp, (adop); Israel & Mary A.	3:155
Gibbud	Charles	18 Oct	1834	died, 3y	2:114
Gibbud	Clarissa	16 Feb	1825	wife of Merit, requested letter to Baptist ch	1:100
Gibbud	Edson	26 Jun	1860	d, 18 m, dropsy, Hillside	3:252
Gibbud	Harris	4 Sep	1818	ch of Lyman, bp	1:61
Gibbud	Harry	12 Oct	1862	d, 7, diphtheria	3:253
Gibbud	Henry Morril	15 Mar	1818	ch of M-- [could be Morril], bp	1:60
Gibbud	Luther	13 Sep	1825	ch d, fits, 1y 3m[?]	1:163
Gibbud	Luther	8 Sep	1826	d, fever, 41	1:163
Gibbud	Lyman	4 Sep	1818	ch of Lyman, bp	1:61
Gibbud	Lyman	12 Aug	1820	ch died, aged 1 y	1:87
Gibbud	Mary A.	-	1861	adm ch, wife of Israel T. ["Luther" crossed out]	3:15
Gibbud	Mary A.	6 Jan	1861	bp, adult	3:152
Gibbud	Mary A.	6 Jan	1861	adm ch	3:62
Gibbud	Mary Clara	15 Mar	1818	ch of M--, bp	1:60
Gibbud	Mason	4 Sep	1818	ch of Lyman, bp	1:61
Gibbud	Merit	15 Feb	1829	wife d, deranged for several years, 33	1:145
Gibbud	Obedience	4 Sep	1818	ch of Lyman, bp	1:61
Gibbud	Pauline	-	-	see Richards	-
Gibbud	Susan	4 Sep	1818	ch of Lyman, bp	1:61
Gibbud	Timothy	4 Sep	1818	ch of Lyman, bp	1:61

NAUGATUCK, CONNECTICUT, CONGREGATIONAL CHURCH RECORDS

Gibbud	Timothy	26 Nov 1825	d, Capt., fever, 64	1:163
Gibson	Samuel	11 Dec 1882	marr Susan Carn, both of Naug	3:214
Gidley	Mary	- 1870	adm ch; dis 1875 M.E. Verbank NY	3:15
Gidley	Mary	May 1870	bp, adult	3:155
Gidley	Mary	7 Mar 1870	adm ch	3:64
Gidley	Mary A.	24 Jan 1875	dism to M.E. Ch, Verbank NY	3:124
Gilbert	Jane	12 Nov 1857	marr Erwin Peck, both of Naug	3:203
Gillet	Miseander	22 Feb 1781	supervised organization of ch	1:6
Gillet	Miseander	22 Feb 1781	one of the ministers constituting the church, from Wolcott	2:79
Gillette	Grace Camp	- 1897	Mrs., adm ch from New Britain; dis 1899 to New London	3:15
Gillette	Grace Camp	3 Jan 1897	w of J.P., adm fr South Cong, New Britain Ct	3:98
Gillette	Grace Camp	19 May 1899	dism to 3d Cong, New London	3:129
Gillette	Joseph P.	- 1890	adm ch; dis 1899 to New London Ct	3:15
Gillette	Joseph P.	9 Mar 1890	bp, adult	3:159
Gillette	Joseph P.	9 Mar 1890	adm ch	3:70
Gillette	Joseph P.	19 May 1899	dism to 3d Cong, New London	3:129
Gilmore	Caroline	7 Oct 1862	Mrs, d, 39, consumption, Hillside	3:253
Gilpin	Wm	2 Jul? 1877	d, 35, consumption [no day, taken from entry above]	3:258
Girnsy	Samuel	20 Jun 1820	died, aged 82 [see also Garnzy, Garnsy, Gearnsey]	1:87
Glilly	Elisa	26 Jun 1813	dau of Silas, bp [see Grilley] [perhaps 1820]	1:63
Goddard	Jennie	- 1876	adm ch; dis 1878 to So. Hadley Falls, Mass	3:15
Goddard	Jennie	7 May 1876	adm ch	3:65
Goddard	Jennie	8 Dec 1878	dism to So Hadley Falls Cong	3:125
Godfrey	W.H.K.	- 1882	adm ch from 2d Waterbury; dis 1891 3d ch Torrington	3:15
Godfrey	W.H.K.	27 Jan 1882	adm fr 2nd Cong, Waterbury	3:94
Godfrey	W.H.K.	24 Apr 1891	dism to 3d Cong, Torrington Ct	3:127
Golding	Charles	14 Oct 1856	d, 10 ms, complica. diseases, Hillside	3:251
Golding	George Kossuth	1 Mar 1857	ch bp; Wm F. & Martha A.	3:151
Golding	Martha A.	1 Mar 1857	adm ch [see Goulding]	3:61
Golding	Martha Ann	1 Mar 1857	bp, adult	3:151
Golding	William James	1 Mar 1857	ch bp; Wm F. & Martha A.	3:151
Goodell	Helen M.	- 1866	adm ch; care withdrawn 1885 [3:409 says "Goodale"]	3:15
Goodell	Helen Matilda	2 Sep 1866	bp, adult	3:153
Goodell	Helen Matilda	2 Sep 1866	adm ch	3:63
Goodhue	Rev. Mr.	24 May 1834	voted to be invited to settle here	2:16
Gooding	Herbert V.	7 Jun 1893	26 marr Florence Dyson 26	3:223
Gooding	Lilian Ethel	19 Jun 1898	inf bp; Herbert V. & Florence Dyer	3:163
Goodrich	Annie Alberta	3 Mar 1897	inf bp; Chas [sic, error? next entry is also Chas] & Annie	3:162
Goodrich	Geo W.	- -	husband of Anna L.C. Miller	3:29
Goodrich	Geo W.	2 May 1896	28 marr Annie L.C. Miller 19	3:224
Goodrich	Lillian Pauline	21 Jun 1900	inf bp; Geo W. & Annie (Miller)	3:165
Goodspeed	Clara B.	11 Oct 1888	18 marr Geo A. Stevens 21	3:219
Goodyear	Amasa Munson	22 May 1814	bp, ch of Cynthia wife of Amasa	1:176
Goodyear	C.	- -	husband of Clarissa Beecher	3:4
Goodyear	C.	- 1822	husband of Clarissa Beecher Jr.	1:82
Goodyear	Carrie L.	- 1876	adm ch from Chicago, wife of Edwd B.	3:15
Goodyear	Charles	- -	husband of Clarissa Beecher	2:91
Goodyear	Charles	- 1822	adm ch; dis 1829 to Philadelphia	3:15
Goodyear	Charles	- 1822	male, on list of members, adm since 1822	1:81
Goodyear	Charles	Sep 1822	adm ch; rem to Philadelphia	2:91
Goodyear	Charles	Sep 1822	adm ch, dism 1829	1:59
Goodyear	Charles	Sep 1822	adm ch	1:96
Goodyear	Charles	25 Aug 1824	marr Clarissa Beecher of Salem	1:152
Goodyear	Charles	23 Sep 1827	appointed to attend conference at Derby	1:103

NAUGATUCK, CONNECTICUT, CONGREGATIONAL CHURCH RECORDS

Goodyear	Clarissa	17 Jan	1858	ch bp; George & Cynthia	3:151
Goodyear	Cynthia	-	1813	adm ch from New Haven, wife of Amasa; dis 1838 to New Haven	3:15
Goodyear	Cynthia	16 May	1813	wife of Amasa, adm ch from New Haven; rem Oct 1816 to New Haven	2:87
Goodyear	Cynthia	16 May	1813	adm ch, dism Oct 1816	1:57
Goodyear	Cynthia	16 May	1813	wife of Amasa, adm ch	1:67
Goodyear	Cynthia	30 Apr	1813	wife of Amasa, cand for memb	1:67
Goodyear	Cynthia	-	1822	wife of Amasa, on list of members	1:82
Goodyear	Cynthia	7 Jul	1822	wife of Amasa, adm ch; rem 22 Jul 1838 to Mass.	2:91
Goodyear	Cynthia	7 Jul	1822	adm ch	1:59
Goodyear	Cynthia	24 Mar	1828	ch of Charles, bp	1:87
Goodyear	E.B.	9 Mar	1879	Mrs., adm fr 1st Pres, Chicago Ill	3:94
Goodyear	Ellen Maria	18 Sep	1825	ch of Charles, bp	1:86
Goodyear	Hannah	21 Dec	1862	(Tuttle) dism to 3d Cong, New Haven	3:122
Goodyear	Hariet	-	1822	female, on list of members	1:82
Goodyear	Hariet	7 Jul	1822	adm ch	1:59
Goodyear	Harriet	18 Jul	1813	bp, ch of Cynthia wife of Amasa G.	1:176
Goodyear	Harriet	-	1822	adm ch; dis 1834 to Episcopal	3:15
Goodyear	Harriet	7 Jul	1822	adm ch; rem to Episcopalian	2:91
Goodyear	Henry	-	1828	adm ch; exc 1837	3:15
Goodyear	Henry	6 Jul	1828	adm ch; excomm 3 Feb 1837	2:92
Goodyear	Henry	6 Jul	1828	adm ch	1:59a
Goodyear	Henry	6 Jul	1828	member	1:94
Goodyear	Henry	6 Jul	1828	adm ch	1:107
Goodyear	Henry	3 Feb	1837	disregards covenants, cut off	2:21
Goodyear	Henry	5 Feb	1837	sentence of excommunication publicly read	2:24
Goodyear	Henry Bateman	18 Jul	1813	bp, ch of Cynthia wife of Amasa G.	1:176
Goodyear	Maria	7 Jun	1827	of New Haven, marr Stephen Hotchkiss	1:153
Goodyear	Nelson	18 Jul	1813	bp, ch of Cynthia wife of Amasa G.	1:176
Goodyear	Robert	Sep	1825	of Waterbury, marr Jennet Bradley of Southbury	1:152
Goodyear	Robert	27 Oct	1836	ch died, 10 days	2:115
Goodyear	Stephen	2 Dec	1800	Delegate at Consociation at Salem, from 1st Hamden	1:19
Goodyear	Stephen, Dn	29 Sep	1801	Delegate to consociation in Salem, from Hamden	1:25
Gordecke	Herminim	10 Oct	1886	an inf, bp	3:158
Gorham	Mahitabal	20 May	1838	adm ch from Bridgewater; died 13 Dec 1843	2:97
Gorham	Mahitable	-	1838	adm ch from Bridgewater; dec 1843	3:15
Gorton	Carrie	-	1893	Mrs., adm ch from Bridgeport	3:15
Gorton	Carrie	5 Nov	1893	Mrs., adm fr No Main St M.E., Bridgeport	3:97
Gorton	H.H.	-	1893	Dr., adm ch from Bridgeport	3:15
Gorton	H.H.	5 Nov	1893	Dr, adm fr No Main St. M.E., Bridgeport	3:97
Gould	Emma J.	2 Feb	1876	of Naug marr John Ford of New York	3:211
Goulding	Martha A.	-	1857	adm ch, wife of Wm F.; dis 1861 to So Groton Mass	3:15
Goulding	Martha A.	28 Jul	1861	dism to Cong, So. Groton, Mass. [see Golding]	3:121
Govan	Kate G.	28 Aug	1897	inf bp; Wm G. & Clara K.	3:163
Graf	Magdalena	10 Oct	1886	an inf, bp	3:158
Graf	Willhelmina	12 Sep	1888	an inf, bp	3:159
Granes	Ruth	4 Apr	1834	dau of Mrs. Marget Arnst [named in disciplinary case, see	2:15
-	-	-	-	Grannis]	-
Grannis	-	-	-	see Granes	-
Grannis	Cabeb [sic]	29 Nov	1810	of Cheshire, marr Ruth Arnt of Salem	1:151
Grannis	Caleb	5 Mar	1826	d, 35	1:163
Granniss	Stella D.	16 Oct	1867	marr Isaac S. Hine, both of Waterbury	3:207
Grant	Arthur M.	12 Apr	1866	of Plymouth marr Caroline A. Wright of Derby	3:207
Green	Manwaring	25 Jun	1859	of Woodbridge marr Agnes Carr of Waterbury in Woodbridge	3:204
Greider	Christina	24 Aug	1869	d, 3ms, whooping cough	3:256

Grenman	Bridget	4 Jun 1871	of Waterbury marr William Kennedy of New York	3:209
Grieder	Annie	6 Dec 1867	a ch, bp	3:154
Grieder	Christiana	8 Apr 1866	d, 9, convulsions [see Greider]	3:255
Grieder	Christina	1 Aug 1869	ch bp; Mr. & Mrs. Grieder (German)	3:155
Grieder	Emma	2 Jul 1888	19 marr Max Schubert 23	3:219
Grieder	Henry	6 Dec 1867	a ch, bp	3:154
Grieder	John	6 Dec 1867	a ch, bp	3:154
Grilley	-	-	see Glilly	-
Grilley	Frederic	16 Oct 1826	ch of Silas, d, canker, 1	1:144
Grilley	Silas	19 Mar 1823	infant ch d, fever, 30[d]	1:161
Grilley	Silas Mortimer	4 Jun 1826	ch of Silas, bp	1:86
Grilley	Triphina	- 1818	adm ch, wife of Silas; dis 1834 Episcopal	3:15
Grilley	Tryphena	- 1822	wife of Silas, member	1:82
Grilly	Charles Thomas	24 Jun 1821	ch of Silas, bp	1:63
Grilly	Triphena	3 May 1818	wife of Silas, adm ch; rem 7 Mar 1834 to Episcopalian	2:89
Grilly	Tryphina	3 May 1818	adm ch	1:59
Grinnels	Benjamin	24 Nov 1825	of Litchfield, marr Harriet Johnson of Middlebury	1:152
Griswold	Carrie	30 Jan 1883	marr Geo W. Mason, both of Naug	3:215
Griswold	Clarence Raymond	18 May 1901	ch bp; James S. & Lottie (Handle)	3:165
Griswold	James Henry	26 Nov 1899	inf bp; James L. & Lottie (Handle)	3:164
Grudzus	Mary	- 1887	adm ch	3:15
Grudzus	Mary	3 Jul 1887	adm ch	3:69
Gunn	Anna Judd	16 Aug 1890	Mrs. Frank, d, 32	3:260
Gunn	Arthur Edward	17 Jul 1862	ch bp; Silas & Maria	3:153
Gunn	Cilas 2d [sic]	Apr 1833	on committee for SS	2:9
Gunn	Esther Sophia	1 Nov 1835	bp, ch of Silas Jr., b 30 Jun 1835	2:105
Gunn	Fannie E.	16 Mar 1872	marr Russell J. Sanders, both of Naug	3:209
Gunn	Flora Philinda	11 Oct 1829	ch of Silas, bp	1:88
Gunn	Frank	- -	husband of Anna Judd	3:22
Gunn	Frank B.	- 1897	adm ch from New Haven, wife also	3:15
Gunn	Frank B.	2 May 1897	and wife adm fr 2nd Cong, New Haven	3:98
Gunn	Franklin J.	23 May 1883	marr Gertrude French, both of Naug	3:215
Gunn	Franklin L.	20 Oct 1886	28 marr Anna M. Judd 28, both of Naug	3:217
Gunn	George	3 May 1865	d West Haven, 22	3:255
Gunn	Hariet Luezach[?]	31 Aug 1828	ch of Silas, bp	1:88
Gunn	Harriet Louisa	5 Jun 1854	marr Ezra Osborn, both of Naug	3:201
Gunn	Henrietta	27 Nov 1868	of Naug marr Robert C. Kelly of Meriden	3:208
Gunn	Louisa	- 1842	adm ch, wife of Ezra Osborn; dis 1866 Sugar Grove, Iowa	3:15
Gunn	Louisa	13 Nov 1842	adm ch	2:98
Gunn	Luserne	13 Jul 1851	ch bp, Silas Jr. & Theodosia	3:150
Gunn	Luther Enoch	17 Jul 1862	ch bp; Silas & Maria	3:153
Gunn	Maria	16 Jul 1862	d, w of Silas, 53, paralysis, Gunntown	3:253
Gunn	Mary M.	- 1854	adm ch; dec 1865	3:15
Gunn	Mary M.	5 Mar 1854	adm ch	3:61
Gunn	Mary M.	16 Sep 1865	d, 28, Gunntown	3:255
Gunn	Mary Melissa	7 Mar 1839	bp, ch of Silas Jr.	2:105
Gunn	Silas	26 Nov 1826	marr Theodotia Johnson of Salem	1:153
Gunn	Silas	6 Jul 1828	adm ch	1:59a
Gunn	Silas	Sep 1831	on Visiting Committee	1:115
Gunn	Silas	30 Apr 1847	penitent	2:56
Gunn	Silas	4 May 1849	to be visited	2:59
Gunn	Silas Jr	20 Mar 1828	propounded for adm	1:106
Gunn	Silas Jr.	- 1828	adm ch; dec 1866	3:15
Gunn	Silas Jr.	6 Jul 1828	member	1:94

NAUGATUCK, CONNECTICUT, CONGREGATIONAL CHURCH RECORDS

Surname	Given Name	Date	Event	Ref
Gunn	Silas Jr.	6 Jul 1828	adm ch	1:107
Gunn	Silas Jr.	6 Jul 1828	adm ch	2:92
Gunn	Silas Jr.	5 May 1837	SS Ass. Lib.	2:25
Gunn	Silas Jr.	20 Feb 1838	confessed violating pledge of temperance Society	2:31
Gunn	Silas Jr.	14 Sep 1866	d (West Haven) 61, cholera morbus, bur Gunntown	3:255
Gunn	Silas Wilson	14 Sep 1834	bp, ch of Silas, b 12 Oct 1834	2:104
Gunn	Theodocia	1 Mar 1835	wife of Silas, adm ch; died 5 Aug or Sep 1841	2:95
Gunn	Theodoria [sic]	- 1835	adm ch, wife of Silas Jr.; dec 1841	3:15
Gunn	Thompson	13 Jul 1851	ch bp, Silas Jr & Theodosia	3:150
Gunn	Wm Andrew	13 Jul 1851	ch bp, Silas Jr & Theodosia	3:150
Gurnsey	Irena	16 Nov 1817	adm ch; died 1834 [see also Garnzy, etc.]	2:88
Gyde	Annie E.	4 Jun 1890	19 marr Fairwell Schofield 24	3:221
Gyde	Emma	- 1887	adm ch, wife of James	3:15
Gyde	Emma	3 Jul 1887	Mrs., adm fr 1st Ch of Christ, East Haven Ct	3:96
Gyde	Leroy James	11 Jun 1893	an inf, bp; Mr. & Mrs. James	3:160
Gyde	Lillian A.	29 Sep 1890	marr Fred W. Biggin	3:221
Hagadas	John	16 Mar 1899	inf bp; John & Lizzie	3:164
Haigh	Jane E.	20 May 1855	of Naug marr Elihu H. Norton of Litchfield	3:202
Haight	Ethel Frances	19 Jun 1898	inf bp; Charles & Dora Riggs	3:163
Hakenson	Louis	27 Jun 1889	marr Carrie Neilson	3:220
Hakes	D.C.	16 Nov 1884	dism to Presby, Cohoes NY	3:126
Hakes	Dewitt C.	- 1881	adm ch from Pitcher NY; dis 1884 to Presby Cohoes NY	3:21
Hakes	Dewitt C.	23 Sep 1881	adm fr Union Cong, Pitcher NY	3:94
Hakes	Dewitt C.	- 1891	adm ch; dis 1898 ["So. Terry Miss" added]	3:21
Hakes	Dewitt C.	4 Jan 1891	adm fr Cong, Pitcher NY	3:97
Hakes	Dewitt C.	6 Mar 1898	dism to M.E. Ch, South Terry Miss	3:129
Halbert	Jameson L.	- 1889	adm ch from Canastota NY; dis 1890 to Canistota NY	3:21
Halbert	Jameson L.	6 Jan 1889	adm fr Pres, Canaslota[sic] NY	3:96
Halbert	Jamison L.	13 Jun 1890	dism to Presby, Canastota NY	3:127
Halbert	Lester T.	- 1887	adm ch from Pitcher NY; dec 1895	3:21
Halbert	Lester T.	1 May 1887	adm fr Cong, Pitcher NY	3:96
Halbert	Lester T.	Oct 1895	d, in Canistota NY, 28, consumption	3:260
Hall	Anna Abell	- 1900	Mrs, adm ch, wife of Edwd C.	3:23
Hall	Anna Abell	7 Jan 1900	Mrs, adm fr 1st Cong, Lebanon Ct	3:98
Hall	B.C.	- -	husband of Adelaide Smith	3:44
Hall	B.C.	22 Aug 1899	Mrs, d, 56, paralysis	3:261
Hall	Billeous C.	2 Apr 1862	marr Addie E. Smith, both of Naug	3:205
Hall	Billious C.	- 1864	adm ch from Wallingford	3:20
Hall	Billious C.	3 Jul 1864	adm fr 1st Cong, Wallingford	3:92
Hall	Clarence Dwight	27 May 1869	ch bp; B.C. & Adelaide Hall	3:154
Hall	Clarence L.	12 Oct 1863	d, 4, dyphtheria, Hillside	3:254
Hall	Curtis	10 Jun 1877	Mrs, dism to Plymouth Ch, Milford	3:125
Hall	Edward C.	- 1893	adm ch	3:21
Hall	Edward C.	2 Jul 1893	adm ch	3:70
Hall	Edward Clinton	31 Aug 1884	ch bp; B.C. & Addie	3:157
Hall	Esther	29 Jan 1858	d, 27, consumption, Hillside	3:252
Hall	Francis	27 Jun 1867	d, 40, Hillside	3:255
Hall	Francis L.	8 Mar 1867	marr Augusta A. Stevens, both of Naug	3:207
Hall	Grace	25 Apr 1861	d, w of Billious C., 26, Hillside	3:253
Hall	Hermione	- 1894	adm ch from Baltimore	3:21
Hall	Hermione	2 Sep 1894	adm fr Presb, Baltimore Md	3:97
Hall	Lamonte Andrew	5 Jul 1885	inf bp; Warren & Etta	3:157
Hall	Louis H.	- 1893	adm ch	3:21
Hall	Louis H.	2 Jul 1893	adm ch	3:70

NAUGATUCK, CONNECTICUT, CONGREGATIONAL CHURCH RECORDS

Surname	Given	Date	Day	Year	Notes	Ref
Hall	Louis Harrison	31 Aug		1884	ch bp; B.C. & Addie	3:157
Hall	Martha	-		1869	adm ch, wife of Curtis; dis 1877 to Plymouth Ch, Milford Ct	3:20
Hall	Martha	2 May		1869	adm ch [but crossed out]	3:64
Hall	Martha	4 Jul		1869	adm ch	3:64
Hall	Rufus	-		-	husband of Emily A. Smith	3:44
Hall	Rufus W.	18 Oct		1869	of Bridgeport marr Emily A. Smith of Naugatuck	3:208
Hall	Susan	6 Jul		1851	of Waterbury marr Nathanl Merrell of Naug	3:200
Hall	Warren L.	14 Dec		1881	marr Ettie L. Andrew, both of Naug	3:213
Hall	Warren L.	-		1886	adm ch from 2nd Waterbury; dis 1892 to 2nd Waterbury	3:21
Hall	Warren L.	2 May		1886	adm fr 2nd Waterbury	3:95
Hall	Warren L.	5 Feb		1892	and wife dism to 2nd Cong, Waterbury	3:127
Hallock	Emma M.	20 Aug		1887	Mrs, 34 marr Luther E. Hart 42	3:218
Ham	Conrad Seymour	9 Jun		1895	inf bp; Geo C. & Grace Seymour	3:161
Ham	Geo	-		-	husband of Grace Seymour	3:45
Ham	George C.	9 Jun		1892	25 marr Grace Seymour 27	3:222
Hamilton	Edna Josephina	4 Sep		1898	Miss, adm ch	3:72
Hamilton	Edna Josephine	-		1898	adm ch	3:23
Hamilton	Grace	-		1898	adm ch	3:23
Hamilton	Grace	4 Sep		1898	adm fr Goodwill M.E., Oceania NJ	3:98
Hamilton	Isabelle	15 Aug		1897	inf bp; Henry W. & Julia T.	3:163
Hamilton	Julia A.	-		1898	Mrs., adm ch	3:23
Hamilton	Julia A.	4 Sep		1898	Mrs., adm ch	3:72
Hammil	W.	-		-	husband of Dorcas T. Sanford	3:42
Hammill	Wm	8 Jul		1828	of Little Fall, NY, marr Dorcus Thomas Sanford of Salem	1:153
Hancock	Archibald V.	-		1901	adm ch	3:23
Hancock	Archibald V.	5 May		1901	adm ch	3:72
Hancock	Fred	2 May		1897	Mrs., adm ch	3:71
Hancock	Frederick W.	-		1897	adm ch; also wife	3:23
Hancock	Frederick W.	4 Jul		1897	adm ch	3:72
Handle	Lottie	-		-	see Griswold	-
Hannahe	Walter L.	29 Nov		1881	marr Mary E. Tyler, both of Naug	3:213
Hannon	Margaret	-		1854	adm ch; dis 1861 to New Preston	3:19
Hannon	Margaret	5 Mar		1854	bp, profession	3:150
Hannon	Margaret	5 Mar		1854	adm ch	3:60
Hannon	Margaret	1 Sep		1861	dism to New Preston	3:121
Hard	Eudora E.	-		1885	adm ch, wife of Wm G.	3:21
Hard	Eudora E.	5 Jul		1885	adm ch	3:68
Hard	Frank Nelson	5 Jul		1885	inf bp; Wm G. & Eudora E.	3:157
Hard	Irma Eudora	5 Jul		1891	an inf, bp	3:160
Hard	Mildred Holt	11 Jun		1899	inf bp; Wm G. & Eudora Holt	3:164
Hard	Myron	-		1886	wife adm ch	3:21
Hard	Myron	2 May		1886	Mrs, adm ch	3:69
Hard	Wm G.	-		1885	adm ch	3:21
Hard	Wm G.	5 Jul		1885	bp, adult	3:157
Hard	Wm G.	5 Jul		1885	adm ch	3:68
Harkins	Marguerite Copelan	9 Jun		1901	ch bp; Thomas B. & Margaret	3:165
Harkins	Thomas B.	-		1901	adm ch	3:23
Harkins	Thomas B.	5 May		1901	adm ch	3:72
Harrington	Arabella Clarissa	9 Mar		1890	Mrs., adm ch	3:70
Harrington	Arabelle Clarrissa	9 Mar		1890	bp, adult	3:159
Harrington	Asa E.	-		1890	adm ch	3:21
Harrington	Asa Edgerly	9 Mar		1890	bp, adult	3:159
Harrington	Asa Edgerly	9 Mar		1890	adm ch	3:69
Harrington	Barbara	2 Sep		1864	d, 62, dropsy	3:254

Harrington	Isabelle C.	-	1890	adm ch, wife of A.E.	3:21
Harris	Adaline Amelia	12 Jul	1840	bp, ch of John	2:106
Harris	Amos Pettingill	30 Jul	1837	bp, ch of John W.	2:105
Harris	Charles Richardson	5 Jan	1824	ch of John, bp	1:85
Harris	David Stevens	30 Oct	1825	ch of John, bp	1:86
Harris	Frances Harriot	12 Jul	1829	ch of John, bp	1:88
Harris	Hariet	-	1822	wife of John, member	1:82
Harris	Hariet	Feb	1844	Mrs., dism to Church St Ch, New Haven	2:48
Harris	Henry Elisha	16 Jul	1843	bp, ch of John	2:107
Harris	J.W.	-	-	husband of Harriet Stevens	3:42
Harris	John	-	-	husband of Harriet Stevens	2:89
Harris	John	Apr	1826	ch d, sudden	1:163
Harris	John	2 Nov	1827	ch bp [or could be John himself bp]	1:87
Harris	John Stevens	21 Sep	1834	bp, ch of John, b 6 Mar 1834	2:104
Harris	John W.	Sep	1831	ch d, ocationed by a Teakettle of hot water turned onto it.	1:146
Harris	John W.	5 Oct	1832	ch died, 2 mo.	2:114
Harris	Mary	Feb	1844	dism to Church St Ch, New Haven	2:48
Harris	Mary E.	-	1836	adm ch; dis 1844 to New Haven	3:18
Harris	Mary Esther	12 May	1822	ch of John, bp	1:85
Harris	Mary Esther	3 Jan	1836	adm ch; dism 3 Feb 1844 to New Haven	2:95
Harris	Mary Ether [sic]	12 May	1822	ch of Joh [sic], bp	1:84
Harris	Sophia	-	1841	adm ch; dis 1844 to New Haven	3:19
Harris	Sophia	11 Jul	1841	adm ch; [m] Mr. P [faint, erased?]; dism 3 Feb 1844 to New Haven	2:98
Harris	Sophia	Feb	1844	dism to Church St Ch, New Haven	2:48
Harris	Sophia Amanda	2 May	1827	ch of John, bp	1:86
Harrison	Harriet E.	-	1874	adm ch from Wolcott, wife of John T.; dis 1880 Wolcott	3:20
Harrison	Harriet E.	12 Nov	1880	dism to Cong, Wolcott	3:125
Harrison	Herbert Ira	2 May	1880	inf bp; John T.	3:156
Harrison	John T.	-	1874	adm ch from Wolcott; dis 1880 Wolcott	3:20
Harrison	John T.	12 Nov	1880	dism to Cong, Wolcott	3:125
Harrison	Rebecka	14 Dec	1826	of Waterbury, marr James P. Somers	1:153
Harrisson	Harriet E.	5 Jul	1874	w of Jno T., adm fr Cong, Wolcott	3:93
Harrisson	John T.	5 Jul	1874	adm fr Cong, Walcott	3:93
Hart	Henry J.	14 Apr	1881	marr Lydia B. Birdsall, both of Naug	3:213
Hart	Howard Jackson	Nov	1885	bp	3:158
Hart	Ira	2 Dec	1800	Revd Elder attending Consociation at Salem, from Middlebury	1:19
Hart	Ira	29 Sep	1801	Rev. Elder attending consociation in Salem, from Middlebury	1:25
Hart	Luther E.	20 Aug	1887	42 marr Mrs. Emma M. Hallock 34	3:218
Hart	Mary F.	15 Mar	1899	25 marr Frank N. Taylor 37	3:227
Hartley	George Henry	27 Jun	1881	marr Isabelle Jane Noble, both of Naug	3:213
Harvey	Edward William	25 Nov	1897	inf bp; Peter & Fannie [see Hearney]	3:163
Harvey	Sarah Elizebeth	11 Jun	1899	inf bp; Peter & Fannie Loan [see Hearney]	3:164
Hatch	Emmie Ward	30 Mar	1888	dism to Presb, Pullman Ill	3:127
Hatch	Walter	-	-	husband of Emmie E. Ward	3:54
Hatch	Walter P.	20 May	1873	marr Emmie E. Ward, both of Naug	3:210
Hatherly	Ellen	-	1873	adm ch fr City Rd. Baptist, Bristol Eng, w of Joseph;	3:20
-	-	-	-	w'drawn 1885	-
Hatherly	Ellen	6 Jul	1873	w of Joseph, adm fr City Road Baptist, Bristol, Eng.	3:93
Hatherly	Joseph	-	1873	adm ch; Irr 1877 Episcopal	3:20
Hatherly	Joseph	6 Jul	1873	adm ch	3:64
Haus	Eloise Henrietta	2 Jan	1898	inf bp; George & Bertha	3:163
Haus	Geo	30 Sep	1896	29 marr Bertha Rasquin 21	3:224
Haverly	Alice	29 Nov	1888	18 marr Chas M. Hubbell 20	3:219
Haverly	Elmer C.	1 Aug	1897	bp, adult; chapel at Millville	3:162

Haverly	Etta C.	1 Aug	1897	bp, adult; chapel at Millville	3:162
Haverly	Eugene	1 Aug	1897	ch bp; Elmer C. & Etta C.; chapel at Millville	3:162
Haverly	Floyd	1 Aug	1897	ch bp; Elmer C. & Etta C.; chapel at Millville	3:162
Haverly	Ira	1 Aug	1897	ch bp; Elmer C. & Etta C.; chapel at Millville	3:162
Haverly	Miriam	1 Aug	1897	ch bp; Elmer C. & Etta C.; chapel at Millville	3:162
Haverly	Wm	1 Aug	1897	ch bp; Elmer C. & Etta C.; chapel at Millville	3:162
Hawkins	Betsey	-	1828	adm ch; dis 1864	3:18
Hawkins	Betsey	3 Feb	1837	voted to be requested to ask for letter of dism.	2:23
Hawkins	Betsy	4 Jul	1828	adm ch	1:59b
Hawkins	Betsy	6 Jul	1828	adm ch	2:92
Hawkins	Betsy	6 Jul	1828	member	1:94
Hawkins	Betsy	6 Jul	1828	adm ch	1:107
Hawkins	Betsy	25 Mar	1864	voted dism, eligible for letter if asked for [see 3:367]	3:122
Hawkins	Russell	12 Oct	1868	d, 75, dysentery	3:256
Hawley	Susie J.	5 Sep	1888	16 marr Chas H. Bavier 22	3:219
Hayden	Sarah B.	27 Dec	1826	of Salem, marr Horatio Terril	1:153
Hearney	Peter	24 Dec	1895	26 marr Fannie Loan 23 [see Harvey]	3:224
Helm	-	9 Aug	1866	d, 11 ms, dysentery	3:255
Helm	Lewis Henry	26 Nov	1866	ch bp, Mr. & Mrs. Helm -- German	3:154
Henderson	Helen Harriet	25 May	1892	29 marr Thos Harper Fyfe 26	3:222
Hene	Harriet	Aug	1806	d, aged -- [Hine?]	1:157
Henne	Charles	11 Jun	1899	inf bp; Gottleib & Christiane Hosenbein	3:164
Henne	Freda	11 Jun	1899	inf bp; Gottleib & Christiane Hosenbein	3:164
Henne	William	11 Jun	1899	inf bp; Gottleib & Christiane Hosenbein	3:164
Hennigan	Mary	23 Jun	1881	marr John E. Lubitz, both of Naug	3:213
Hepp	John Peter	12 Feb	1898	inf bp; John & Francis	3:163
Hepp	Mary Frances	26 Nov	1899	inf bp; John & Frances	3:164
Hepp	Paulina Eva	24 Dec	1896	inf bp; John & Frances	3:162
Hermanson	John	26 Dec	1885	28 marr Lydia Arandhaltz 24, both of Naug	3:217
Hess	Catharine	8 Jan	1860	(Woodruff), dism to 1st Cong, Waterbury	3:121
Hess	Wm	--	--	husband of Catharine Woodruff	3:54
Heughes	Harriet	14 Apr	1872	dism to East Cong, New Haven [see Hughes]	3:124
Hiccock	Sarah	Jan	1809	Wid, d, 93y	1:159
Hiccox	Esther	14 Dec	1800	adm ch	1:20
Hiccox	Sophia	14 Dec	1800	adm ch	1:20
Hickcox	Jemima	25 Dec	1800	of 1st Waterbury, marr Harvey Judd of this	1:151
Hickey	Margaret	17 Feb	1882	marr Wm Stocks, both of Naug	3:213
Hickock	Sally	5 Aug	1810	bp, ch of Samuel J.	1:175
Hickock	Samuel Hopkins	5 Aug	1810	bp, ch of Samuel J.	1:175
Hickok	Esther	14 Dec	1800	wife of Wm Hine, adm ch; rem 4 May 1827 to Humphryville	2:86
Hickok	Gideon	22 Feb	1781	one of the persons constituting the church	2:79
Hickok	Gideon	22 Feb	1781	adm ch, died 18 Apr 1798	2:81
Hickok	Gideon Jn	22 Feb	1781	one of the persons constituting the church	2:79
Hickok	Gideon Jr.	22 Feb	1781	adm ch; rem 6 Feb 1814 to German, Chen. Co., NY	2:81
Hickok	Hannah	Sep	1784	wife of James, adm ch; died 29 Sep 1838	2:82
Hickok	James	Sep	1784	adm ch; died Nov 1833	2:82
Hickok	James	Nov	1833	died, 88	2:114
Hickok	Laura	5 Aug	1810	wife of Samuel J., adm ch; rem 10 Apr 1848 to Cheshire	2:87
Hickok	Philena	22 Feb	1781	one of the persons constituting the church	2:79
Hickok	Philina	22 Feb	1781	w of Gideon Jr; adm ch; rem 6 Feb 1814 to German, Chen. Co., NY	2:82
Hickok	Samuel	22 Feb	1781	one of the persons constituting the church	2:79
Hickok	Samuel	22 Feb	1781	adm ch; withdrawn to Baptist	2:81
Hickok	Sarah	22 Feb	1781	one of the persons constituting the church	2:79
Hickok	Sarah	22 Feb	1781	wife of Gideon H., adm ch; died 19 Jan 1809	2:81

NAUGATUCK, CONNECTICUT, CONGREGATIONAL CHURCH RECORDS

Hickok	Sophiah	14 Dec	1800	wife of Roger Hitchcock, adm ch; rem to Cheshire	2:86
Hickox	Esther	-	1800	adm ch, wife of Wm Hine; dis 1827 to Humpville	3:17
Hickox	Esther	14 Dec	1800	adm ch	1:56
Hickox	Gideon	-	1781	adm ch; dec 1798	3:17
Hickox	Gideon	22 Feb	1781	original member, dec 18 Apr 1798	1:53
Hickox	Gideon	6 Feb	1814	rec. to ch at German, Chenango Co., NY	1:68
Hickox	Gideon Jr.	-	1781	adm ch; dis 1814 German NY	3:17
Hickox	Gideon Junr	22 Feb	1781	original member, dism 6 Feb 1814	1:53
Hickox	Hanah	Sep	1784	Ja., adm ch	1:53
Hickox	Hannah	-	1784	adm ch; wife of James; dec 1838	3:17
Hickox	Hannah	?	1784	wife of James adm ch	1:7
Hickox	Hannah	-	1822	wife of James, member	1:82
Hickox	James	-	1784	adm ch; dec 1833	3:17
Hickox	James	?	1784	adm ch	1:7
Hickox	James	Sep	1784	adm ch ["died Nov 1833" added]	1:53
Hickox	James	22 Oct	1805	Capt, restored to fellowship	1:39
Hickox	James	-	1822	male, on list of members	1:81
Hickox	Laura	-	1810	adm ch, wife of Saml J.; dis 1848 to Cheshire	3:17
Hickox	Laura	5 Aug	1810	Sa., adm ch	1:56
Hickox	Laura	5 Aug	1810	wife of Samll J. adm ch	1:50
Hickox	Laura	9 Sep	1810	wife of Capt. Samuel J. given certif of membership	1:51
Hickox	Laura	-	1822	wife of Saml, member	1:82
Hickox	Philena	-	1781	adm ch, wife of Gideon Jr.; dis 1814 to German NY	3:17
Hickox	Philena	22 Feb	1781	original member, dism 6 Feb 1814 ["Gideon Jr" added]	1:53
Hickox	Philena	6 Feb	1814	wife of Gideon, rec to ch in German, Chenango Co, NY	1:68
Hickox	Polly	22 Oct	1810	of this place, marr Amy [sic] Hotchkiss of Columbia	1:151
Hickox	Sally	18 Sep	1827	of Salem, marr Merit H. Payne	1:153
Hickox	Saml Jr.	-	1781	adm ch; Irr 1802 Baptist	3:17
Hickox	Samuel	22 Feb	1781	original member, certif	1:53
Hickox	Samuel	29 Apr	1830	d, dropsy, aged almost 91	1:146
Hickox	Sarah	-	1781	adm ch, wife of Gideon; dec 1809	3:17
Hickox	Sarah	22 Feb	1781	original member, d 19 Jan 1809, ["Gideon" added]	1:53
Hickox	Selden	2 Oct	1803	d, ch of Saml J., 2y	1:156
Hickox	Sophia	-	1800	adm ch, wife of R. Hitchcock; dis to Cheshire	3:17
Hickox	Sophia	14 Dec	1800	adm ch, dism	1:56
Hicok	Samuel	6 Aug	1820	wife died, age 84	1:87
Hicox	Gideon	22 Feb	1781	subscribed to Constitution and Covenant	1:5
Hicox	Gideon Junr	22 Feb	1781	subscribed to Constitution and Covenant	1:5
Hicox	Philina	22 Feb	1781	subscribed to Constitution and Covenant	1:5
Hicox	Samuel	22 Feb	1781	subscribed to Constitution and Covenant	1:5
Hicox	Sarah	22 Feb	1781	subscribed to Constitution and Covenant	1:5
Higgins	Cora	1 Jul	1900	inf bp; Horace & Agnes (Church)	3:165
Higgs	Israel	-	1856	adm ch; care withdrawn 1885	3:19
Higgs	Israel	4 May	1856	bp, adult	3:151
Higgs	Israel	4 May	1856	adm ch	3:61
Hill	Amos	15 Jun	1894	Mrs., dism to 2nd Cong, Waterbury	3:128
Hill	Andrew	-	1877	Mrs., adm ch from Episcopal Jacsonvill Ill; erased 1900	3:21
Hill	Andrew	4 Apr	1887	d, 66, congestion lungs	3:259
Hill	Catharine	16 Aug	1866	marr George S. Ward, both of Naug	3:207
Hill	Eliza	4 May	1838	dism to any ch in Ohio	2:32
Hill	Hobart M.	29 Jun	1884	marr Ella D. Fenn, both of Naug	3:216
Hill	Hubert M.	3 Jul	1888	33 marr Hattie Reed 33	3:219
Hill	Jessie E.	15 Oct	1865	d, 9 1/2 ms, Hillside	3:255
Hill	Julius [sic]	-	-	husband of Eliza Porter	3:36

NAUGATUCK, CONNECTICUT, CONGREGATIONAL CHURCH RECORDS

Surname	Given	Date	Notes	Ref
Hill	Junius [sic]	- -	husband of Eliza Porter	2:93
Hill	Sylvia C.	6 Aug 1875	d, 54, typhoid, Hillside	3:257
Hills	Andrew	1866	adm ch from Meth Naug; dec 1887	3:20
Hills	Andrew	7 Jan 1866	adm fr Methodist Naug	3:92
Hills	Andrew	7 Jan 1877	Mrs, adm fr Epis Ch in -- Illinois	3:93
Hills	Lena Francis	9 May 1880	inf bp; Andrew	3:156
Hills	Sylvia C.	1866	adm ch, wife of Andrew; dec 1875	3:20
Hills	Sylvia Cornelia	7 Jan 1866	adm ch, "immersed"	3:63
Hills	Wealthy A.	1869	adm ch, wife of Amos; dis 1894 to Waterbury	3:20
Hills	Wealthy Ann	2 May 1869	adm ch	3:64
Hilman	William	18 Nov 1810	of Black River, marr Rebecca Stevens of Salem	1:151
Hine	-	- -	husband of Margetanny Sperry [see W. Hine]	2:88
Hine	-	- -	see Hene, Hyne	1:157
Hine	A.J.	22 Feb 1881	at centennial exercises; Thomaston Conn	3:300
Hine	Asa	Sep 1808	infant ch d, 9m	1:159
Hine	Bennet	19 Nov 1829	wife d, fever, 27	1:145
Hine	Burr C.	6 Dec 1860	of Naug marr Mary Jane Riggs of Oxford	3:204
Hine	Carrie A.	2 May 1894	33 marr Fredk D. Lattice 33	3:223
Hine	Charles	2 Sep 1866	adm ch	3:63
Hine	Charls	1866	adm ch; dis 1870 [sic] to Congl New Haven	3:20
Hine	Chas	18 Apr 1869	dism to Cong, New Haven	3:124
Hine	Curtice	15 Mar 1818	bp	1:60
Hine	Curtis	15 Mar 1818	adm ch; excomm 9 Nov 1827	2:89
Hine	Curtis	15 Mar 1818	adm ch, ex. 1827	1:58
Hine	Curtis	1822	male, on list of members; excluded 1827	1:81
Hine	Curtis	9 Nov 1827	excluded	1:105
Hine	Curtis	21 Oct 1827	complained against for violating covenants	1:104f
Hine	Curtis	14 Jan 1829	ch d, burnt by its clothes taking fire, 3	1:145
Hine	Curtiss	1818	adm ch; exc 1827	3:18
Hine	Diantha	1817	adm ch, wife of Asa; dec 1854	3:18
Hine	Diantha	16 Nov 1817	wife of Asa, adm ch;	2:87
Hine	Diantha	30 Oct 1854	d, wife of Asa, 81, tumor	3:251
Hine	Dyantha	16 Nov 1817	adm ch, dism abt 1825	1:57
Hine	Dyantha	1822	wife of Asa; member	1:82
Hine	Esther	1822	wife of Wm, member, dism	1:82
Hine	Esther	4 Mar 1827	rec to ch in Humphreyville	1:102
Hine	Esther	4 Sep 1835	adm ch from Humphryville	2:95
Hine	Esther H.	19 Apr 1864	d, 82, Hillside	3:254
Hine	Esther M.	1858	adm ch, wife of Chs; dis 1870 [sic] to Congl, New Haven	3:20
Hine	Esther M.	18 Apr 1869	[wife of] Chas dism to Cong, New Haven	3:124
Hine	Esther Mahelia	7 Mar 1858	bp, adult	3:151
Hine	Esther Mahelia	7 Mar 1858	adm ch	3:61
Hine	Ethel C.	1860	adm ch from Middlebury; dis 1864 to Cong Brooklyn	3:20
Hine	Ethel C.	1 Jul 1860	adm fr Cong Middlebury	3:91
Hine	Ethel C.	3 Jan 1864	dism to Ch of Pilgrims, Brooklyn	3:122
Hine	Eunice	1781	adm ch, wife of Hezek; dec 1813	3:17
Hine	Eunice	27 Mar 1781	wife of Hezekiah, adm ch; died 1 Feb 1813	2:82
Hine	Eunice	27 Mar 1781	Hez., adm ch, d 1 Feb 1813	1:53
Hine	Eunice	27 May 1781	wife of Hezekiah adm ch	1:6
Hine	Eunice	1 Feb 1813	d, Wid	1:160
Hine	Geo	19 Sep 1874	his inf son bur, 6 mon, Hillside	3:257
Hine	George	15 Sep 1828	ch d, dysentery, 1 1/2 y	1:145
Hine	Harlow	10 Feb 1829	ch d, 4 day	1:145
Hine	Hattie Esther	13 Jul 1862	inf bp; Chs & Esther M.	3:152

NAUGATUCK, CONNECTICUT, CONGREGATIONAL CHURCH RECORDS

Hine	Hezekiah	-	1781	adm ch; dec 1807	3:17
Hine	Hezekiah	27 Mar	1781	adm ch; died 13 Sep 1807	2:82
Hine	Hezekiah	27 Mar	1781	adm ch, d 13 Sep 1807	1:53
Hine	Hezekiah	27 May	1781	adm ch	1:6
Hine	Hezekiah	13 Sep	1807	d, 74y	1:158
Hine	Hezekiah	-	1812	son d	1:160
Hine	Ida M.	21 May	1885	21, marr Fred S. Andrew, 24, of Naug	3:216
Hine	Isaac S.	16 Oct	1867	marr Stella D. Granniss, both of Waterbury	3:207
Hine	Julia A.	2 May	1869	adm ch	3:64
Hine	Julia Ann	-	1869	adm ch, wife of Bennett; dec 1877	3:20
Hine	Julia Ann	21 Mar	1877	d, 59, Hillside	3:257
Hine	Lewis	-	-	husband of Nancy Hull	3:18
Hine	Lewis	-	-	husband of Nancy Hull	2:88
Hine	Lewis	19 Nov	1827	of Cairo, NY, marr Nancy Hull of Salem	1:153
Hine	Louisa M.	-	1878	adm ch from Thomaston, wife of A.J.; dis 1880	3:21
Hine	Louisa M.	3 Mar	1878	w of A.J., adm fr Westville Cong.	3:94
Hine	Louisa M.	10 Dec	1880	dism to Cong, Thomaston	3:125
Hine	Mary	-	1812	adm ch from Derby, wife of Thad; dec	3:17
Hine	Mary	3 May	1812	wife of Thadeus, adm ch from Derby; died	2:87
Hine	Mary	3 May	1812	adm ch; dead, dism	1:57
Hine	Mary	3 May	1812	adm ch	1:62
Hine	Mary	15 Apr	1812	wife Thaddeus, cand for memb, from Cong Ch in Derby	1:62
Hine	Mary	5 Sep	1819	ch of William, bp	1:84
Hine	Mary	-	1822	wid, member; dism	1:82
Hine	Mary	-	1841	adm ch; dec 1884	3:19
Hine	Mary	12 Sep	1841	adm ch	2:98
Hine	Mary	20 Apr	1884	d	3:259
Hine	Mary Louisa	-	1878	adm ch from Thomaston; dis 1880	3:21
Hine	Mary Louisa	3 Mar	1878	adm fr Westville Cong	3:94
Hine	Mary Louise	10 Dec	1880	dism to Cong, Thomaston	3:125
Hine	Nancy	20 Mar	1828	formerly Hull, rec to ch in Cairo NY	1:106
Hine	Reuben L.	6 Jul	1874	bur, 77, Gunntown Cem	3:257
Hine	Rufus	17 Nov	1817	bp, ch of Esther wife of Wm	1:176
Hine	Sally	8 Feb	1833	died, 50	2:114
Hine	Samuel Bishop	25 Oct	1807	bp, ch of Wiliam	1:174
Hine	Stiles M.	9 Nov	1854	of Naug marr Harriet Kellogg of Middlebury	3:202
Hine	Thaddeus	-	1812	adm ch from Derby; dec 1816	3:17
Hine	Thaddeus	3 May	1812	adm ch, d Nov 1816	1:57
Hine	Thaddeus	3 May	1812	adm ch	1:62
Hine	Thaddeus	15 Apr	1812	cand for memb, from Cong Ch in Derby	1:62
Hine	Thadeus	3 May	1812	adm ch from Derby; died Nov 1816	2:87
Hine	W.	-	-	husband of Margt Sperry	3:42
Hine	William	5 Aug	1810	his son bp	1:175
Hine	William Edwards	26 May	1822	son of William, bp	1:79
Hine	William Edwards	26 May	1822	ch of William, bp	1:85
Hine	Wm	-	-	husband of Esther Hickox	3:17
Hine	Wm	-	-	husband of Esther Hickok	2:86
Hingst	May Ida	1 Jul	1888	21 marr Max Leonard 23	3:218
Hinman	Elizabeth L.	-	1873	adm ch, wife of E.H. Lewis	3:20
Hinman	Elizabeth L.	6 Jul	1873	bp, adult	3:155
Hinman	Elizabeth L.	6 Jul	1873	adm ch	3:64
Hinman	Shelden	-	1846	adm ch from Pitcher NY; dis 1850	3:19
Hinman	Shelden	20 Nov	1846	adm ch from Pitcher, N.Y.	2:100
Hinman	Shelden	3 May	1850	dism to Cong, Pitcher, Chenango Co, NY	3:120

NAUGATUCK, CONNECTICUT, CONGREGATIONAL CHURCH RECORDS

Hirsch	Anna	1 Jun 1890	21 marr Frank Wuth [Wirth?] 32	3:221
Hitchcock	Annie P.	- 1869	adm ch from Watertown, wife of R.M.; dec 1907	3:20
Hitchcock	Annie P.	2 May 1869	adm fr Watertown	3:92
Hitchcock	Charles Reuben	27 May 1869	ch bp; Reuben M. & Annie O.	3:154
Hitchcock	Chas	- 1885	adm ch; dis 1895 Naug Epis	3:21
Hitchcock	Chas	13 Sep 1885	adm ch	3:68
Hitchcock	Chas R.	24 May 1895	dism to Episcopal, Naug	3:128
Hitchcock	Elihu	26 Mar 1852	d, 54, consumption, Hillside	3:250
Hitchcock	Ella L.	- 1884	adm ch from Plainville Ct	3:21
Hitchcock	Ella L.	2 May 1884	Miss, adm ch fr Cong, Plainville Ct	3:95
Hitchcock	Emeline B.	12 Jan 1865	d, 37, consumption	3:255
Hitchcock	George	24 Mar 1862	d, 27, Hillside	3:253
Hitchcock	Homer E.	17 Feb 1855	d, 27, consumption	3:251
Hitchcock	Mary	25 Oct 1824	of Hartland, marr Vincent Tuttle of Columbia	1:152
Hitchcock	Nancy Eliza	- 1852	adm ch, wife of Mr. Todd; dis 1868 to Arcola Ill	3:19
Hitchcock	Nancy Eliza	4 Jul 1852	bp, profession	3:150
Hitchcock	Nancy Eliza	4 Jul 1852	adm ch	3:60
Hitchcock	Nellie Louisa	3 Jan 1864	inf bp; Oliver & Nancy	3:153
Hitchcock	O.	- -	husband of Nancy Fox	3:13
Hitchcock	Oliver	2 Dec 1800	Revd Elder attending Consociation at Salem, from Columbia	1:19
Hitchcock	Oliver	5 May 1811	Rev, of Columbia, invited to attend installation	1:51
Hitchcock	Oliver	- 1858	adm ch; dec 1864	3:20
Hitchcock	Oliver	4 Jul 1858	bp, adult	3:152
Hitchcock	Oliver	4 Jul 1858	adm ch	3:62
Hitchcock	Oliver	4 Jan 1860	marr Nancy Fox, both of Naug	3:204
Hitchcock	Oliver	1 Jun 1864	d, 32, shot in battle in Va.	3:254
Hitchcock	R.	- -	husband of Sophia Hickox	3:17
Hitchcock	Reuben M.	- 1869	adm ch; dec 1893	3:20
Hitchcock	Reuben M.	2 May 1869	adm ch	3:64
Hitchcock	Reuben M.	12 Jul 1893	d, 66, spasms	3:260
Hitchcock	Roger	- -	husband of Sophia Hickok	2:86
Hitchcock	Sarah E.	24 Dec 1865	of Naug marr William E. Shelton of Huntington	3:207
Hitchcock	Sarah M.	- 1857	adm ch, wife of Amos A.; dis 1862	3:20
Hitchcock	Sarah M.	1 Mar 1857	adm ch, w of Amos A.	3:61
Hitchcock	Sarah M.	18 Apr 1862	dism to Episcopal, Naugatuck	3:122
Hitchcock	Sarah Maria	1 Mar 1857	bp, adult	3:151
Hitchcock	Wilbur Royce	27 May 1869	ch bp; Reuben M. & Annie O.	3:154
Hitchcock	Wm Henry	- 1885	adm ch	3:21
Hitchcock	Wm Henry	5 Jul 1885	bp, adult	3:158
Hitchcock	Wm Henry	5 Jul 1885	adm ch	3:68
Hitchkock	Oliver	8 Jun 1806	Rev, chosen Moderator pro temperary	1:40
Hitchkox	L.	10 Sep 1810	Doctor, infant ch d, 3d	1:160
Hitchkox	Oliver	4 Apr 1799	Revd, of Columbia chosen Moderator	1:14
Hoadley	-	- -	see Hoaly, also --adley	1:9
Hoadley	Albert	30 Sep 1792	bp, ch of Ammi	1:166
Hoadley	Alvan	Sep 1800	bp, ch of Culpepper	1:169
Hoadley	Alvin	21 Sep 1850	d, 52, pulmonary bleeding, Hillside	3:250
Hoadley	Ame	20 Jul 1788	wife of Ammi adm ch	1:11
Hoadley	Ame	30 Aug 1807	wife of Ammi, recomm to 2nd Ch in Woodbridge	1:46
Hoadley	Amy	- 1788	adm ch; wife of Ammi; dis 1807 Woodbridge	3:17
Hoadley	Amy C.	19 Aug 1824	of Salem, marr Elisha M. Stevens	1:152
Hoadley	Asa	9 Aug 1788	bp, ch of Ammi	1:165
Hoadley	Asinetty[sic]	3 May 1818	["Sena" crossed out] wife of Hiel, adm ch. ["D.(?) Beecher" added]	2:89

Hoadley	Augusta	-	1835	adm ch; dis 1844 to Waterbury	3:18
Hoadley	Augusta	5 Jul 1835		adm ch [m] Isac Coe; dism 7 Dec 1844 to Waterbury	2:95
Hoadley	Augusta Ann	3 Sep 1813		bp, ch of Hiel [perhaps 1820]	1:63
Hoadley	Betty	-	1794	adm ch, wife of Chester; dec 1828	3:17
Hoadley	Betty	19 Oct 1794		wife of Chester adm ch	1:13
Hoadley	Betty	94 Oct 1794		C[hester] adm ch, d 23 Aug 1828 [day written "94 Oct"]	1:55
Hoadley	Betty	-	1822	wid of Ch, member; dead	1:82
Hoadley	Betty	23 Aug 1828		wid, d, dysentery, 56	1:144
Hoadley	Calvin	25 Sep 1828		of Salem, marr Betsy Pine [Rine?] of Southbury	1:153
Hoadley	Charles Henry	4 Jul 1828		ch of wid Susan, bp	1:87
Hoadley	Chas W.	21 Dec 1882		marr Emma L. Eggleston, both of Naug	3:215
Hoadley	Chester	-	1811	adm ch; dec 1822	3:17
Hoadley	Chester	18 Jun 1812		brought complaint against Trijah Terril	1:64
Hoadley	Chester	18 Jul 1822		died, aged 51	1:87
Hoadley	Chester	18 Jul 1822		d, consumption, 51	1:161
Hoadley	Culpepper	24 Aug 1800		wife adm ch	1:15
Hoadley	Culpepper	20 May 1857		d, 93, abscess, Hillside	3:251
Hoadley	Deac	20 Dec 1842		to visit and labour with David Hopkins	2:42
Hoadley	Deacon	20 Dec 1842		to visit and labour with Brother Bela Atwater	2:42
Hoadley	Deacon	24 Aug 1843		on comm	2:47
Hoadley	Deacon	9 Oct 1848		on comm	2:58
Hoadley	Eben	-	1840	adm ch; dis 1849	3:19
Hoadley	Eben	12 Jul 1840		adm ch; dism 6 Apr 1848 to Natch[e]z [also says 6 Apr 1849]	2:97
Hoadley	Ebenezer	-	1787	adm ch; dec 1814	3:17
Hoadley	Ebenezer	1 Apr 1787		adm ch	1:10
Hoadley	Ebenezer	12 Jun 1822		ch of Hiel, bp	1:85
Hoadley	Ellen	-	-	see Buckingham	-
Hoadley	Ellen L.	-	1885	adm ch	3:21
Hoadley	Ellen L.	5 Jul 1885		adm ch	3:68
Hoadley	Ellen Lucretia	May 1870		ch bp, Wm B. & Miriam	3:155
Hoadley	Emily N.	-	1873	adm ch, wife of -- Ellis; dis 1884 Middlebury	3:20
Hoadley	Emily N.	6 Jul 1873		adm ch	3:64
Hoadley	Emily N.	4 Jul 1884		(Ellis) dism to Cong Ch, Middlebury Ct	3:126
Hoadley	Emily Naomi	2 Sep 1866		ch bp; Wm B & Mriam [sic] N.	3:154
Hoadley	Erastus W.	13 Oct 1823		marr Abigail Porter of Salem	1:152
Hoadley	Frank	-	1885	adm ch; dis 1896 Denver Col	3:21
Hoadley	Frank	5 Jul 1885		adm ch	3:68
Hoadley	Frank Burr	2 Sep 1866		ch bp; Wm B. & Mriam N.	3:154
Hoadley	Frank L.	21 Feb 1896		dism to 1st Cong, Denver Col [with Samuel Spring]	3:128
Hoadley	George Harvey	4 Jul 1828		ch of wid Susan, bp	1:87
Hoadley	Harry Hine	3 Jan? 1819		ch of Hiel, bp	1:84
Hoadley	Harvey	28 Oct 1825		ch d, 5m[?]	1:163
Hoadley	Harvey	4 Nov 1826		d, consumption, 35	1:144
Hoadley	Hiel	31 May 1824		d, consumption, 33	1:161
Hoadley	Larman	Sep 1800		bp, ch of Culpepper	1:169
Hoadley	Lena	-	1822	wife of Hiel, member	1:82
Hoadley	Leonard	Sep 1800		bp, ch of Culpepper	1:169
Hoadley	Lewis	24 Nov 1826		ch d, fever, 2	1:144
Hoadley	Lewis Hine	21 May 1797		bp, ch of Chester	1:168
Hoadley	Lucretia	-	1835	adm ch, wife of Selden; dec 1874	3:18
Hoadley	Lucretia	4 Jan 1835		wife of Selden, adm ch	2:95
Hoadley	Lucretia	4 Jan 1835		bp, adult	2:104
Hoadley	Lucretia	27 Nov 1874		d, 67, dropsy, Hillside	3:256
Hoadley	Mary Munn	4 Jul 1828		ch of Wid Susan, bp	1:87

Hoadley	Miriam N.	-	1866	adm ch, wife of Wm; dec 1894	3:20
Hoadley	Miriam N.	2 Sep	1866	adm ch	3:63
Hoadley	Molly	-	1800	adm ch, wife of Culpep; dec 1857	3:17
Hoadley	Molly	-	1822	wife of Culpepper, member	1:82
Hoadley	Molly	2 Dec	1857	d, 90, Hillside	3:252
Hoadley	Naomi	19 Feb	1833	died, 38	2:114
Hoadley	Polly Lewis	3 Jan?	1819	ch of Hiel, bp	1:84
Hoadley	Reuben	27 Oct	1852	d, 59, Hillside	3:250
Hoadley	Roxania	Sep	1800	bp, ch of Culpepper	1:169
Hoadley	S.	5 May	1837	Mrs, on comm "to attend to cases of unchristian walk...female members"	2:25
Hoadley	Samll L.	Sep	1800	bp, ch of Culpepper	1:169
Hoadley	Sarah	-	1785	adm ch; dec 1827	3:17
Hoadley	Sarah	-	1787	adm ch, wife of Eben; dec 1827	3:17
Hoadley	Sarah	1 Apr	1787	wife of Ebenezer adm ch	1:10
Hoadley	Sarah	-	1822	wid, member; died 23 Aug 1828	1:82
Hoadley	Sarah	22 Jun	1827	wid, d, 85	1:144
Hoadley	Sarah	-	1843	adm ch, wife of Eben H.; dis 1849 to Waterbury	3:19
Hoadley	Sarah	2 Jul	1843	wife of Eben, adm ch; dism 6 Apr 1849 to Waterbury	2:99
Hoadley	Sarah E.	3 May	1835	bp, ch of Selden, b 5 Dec 1828	2:104
Hoadley	Selden	-	1835	adm ch; dec 1858	3:18
Hoadley	Selden	4 Jan	1835	adm ch	2:95
Hoadley	Selden	5 May	1837	chosen deacon	2:25
Hoadley	Selden	-	1838	appt'd Deacon; removed 1858 Dec	3:1
Hoadley	Selden	1 Apr	1838	Dea, SS Ass. Super.	2:32
Hoadley	Selden	13 Mar	1838	accepted appt. as Deacon	2:31
Hoadley	Selden	24 Feb	1843	on comm	2:46
Hoadley	Selden	7 Oct	1849	Clerk pro tem	2:61
Hoadley	Selden	2 Nov	1956	& Lucretia, guardians to Mary Ellen Buckingham, ch bp	3:151
Hoadley	Seldon	11 Sep	1803	bp, son of Chester	1:172
Hoadley	Seldon	26 Apr	1858	Dea, d, 55, erysipelas, Hillside	3:252
Hoadley	Sena	-	1818	adm ch, wife of D. Beecher; dis 1851 to Waterbury	3:18
Hoadley	Sena	3 May	1818	adm ch; [but see Hoadley, Asinetty; 2:89]	1:59
Hoadley	Silas	9 Aug	1788	bp, ch of Ammi	1:165
Hoadley	Step..	18 Sep	1826	d, fever, 18 [name blotted]	1:163
Hoadley	Stephen	18 Sep	1808	bp, ch of Chester, on right of Bette his wife	1:174
Hoadley	Susan	20 Mar	1828	wid, propounded for adm	1:106
Hoadley	Susan M.	-	1822	female, member adm after 1822	1:83
Hoadley	Susan M.	-	1828	adm ch, wife of L. Baldwin; dis 1830	3:18
Hoadley	Susan M.	4 May	1828	wife of Leonard Baldwin, adm ch; rem 5 Sep 1837	2:92
Hoadley	Susan M.	4 May	1828	wid, adm ch	1:59a
Hoadley	Susan M.	19 Oct	1829	of Salem Bridge, marr Leonard Baldwin of Torrington	1:153
Hoadley	Susan Maria	4 May	1828	adult, bp	1:87
Hoadley	Susan Maria	4 May	1828	wid, adm ch, bp	1:106
Hoadley	Thomson	9 May	1790	bp, ch of Ammi	1:165
Hoadley	William	11 Oct	1817	infant ch d	1:161
Hoadley	William	30 Oct	1824	d, accidently shot at a shooting match [see original], 21	1:162
Hoadley	Wm	17 Apr	1825	ch stillborn	1:162
Hoadley	Wm B.	-	1866	adm ch; dec 1909	3:20
Hoadley	Wm B.	2 Sep	1866	adm ch	3:63
Hoadley	Wm B.	18 Mar	1894	Mrs, d, 62, rheumatism	3:260
Hoadley	Wm Burr	3 May	1835	bp, ch of Selden, b 15 Jun 1830	2:104
Hoadley	Wm Culpepper	11 Jun	1899	inf bp; Wm E. & Bertha Chapman	3:164
Hoadley	Wm E.	7 Apr	1897	25 marr Bertha Chapman 21	3:225

NAUGATUCK, CONNECTICUT, CONGREGATIONAL CHURCH RECORDS

Hoadly	Ame Constant	5 May 1805	bp, dau of Chester, in right of his wife Betty	1:172
Hoadly	Amy	20 Jul 1788	wife of Ammi, adm ch; rem 30 Aug 1807 to Woodbridge	2:84
Hoadly	Amy	20 Jul 1788	Am[mi], adm ch. dism 30 Aug 1807 [to "Woodbury" added]	1:55
Hoadly	Betty	14 Oct 1794	wife of Chester, adm ch; died 23 Aug 1828	2:84
Hoadly	Chester	6 Dec 1811	cand for memb	1:62
Hoadly	Chester	22 Dec 1811	adm ch; died Jul 1822	2:87
Hoadly	Chester	22 Dec 1811	adm ch, d Jul 1822	1:57
Hoadly	Chester	22 Dec 1811	adm ch	1:62
Hoadly	Deacon	1 Jul 1848	on Standing Committee of the Church	2:58
Hoadly	Ebenezer	1 Apr 1787	adm ch; died 23 Sep 1814	2:83
Hoadly	Ebenezer	1 Apr 1787	adm ch; d 23 Sep 1844	1:54
Hoadly	Harriet	7 Dec 1794	bp, ch of Ammi	1:167
Hoadly	Harriet Hine	11 Aug 1811	bp, ch of Betty, wife of Chester	1:175
Hoadly	Hial	2 Nov 1794	bp, ch of Chester	1:167
Hoadly	Molly	24 Aug 1800	wife of Culpepper, adm ch	2:85
Hoadly	Molly	24 Aug 1800	Cu., adm ch	1:56
Hoadly	Ruben	2 Nov 1794	bp, ch of Chester	1:167
Hoadly	Sarah	17 Feb 1785	Wid, adm ch, dead [on 1811 list, "22 Jun 1827" crossed out]	1:53
Hoadly	Sarah	20 Feb 1785	Wd, adm ch; died 22 Jun 1827	2:82
Hoadly	Sarah	1 Apr 1787	wife of Ebenezer, adm ch; died 22 Jun 1827	2:83
Hoadly	Sarah	1 Apr 1787	adm ch, Eb["enezer d 22 Jun 182(7?)" added]	1:54
Hoadly	Sarah Lewis	3 Jan 1802	bp, ch of Chester	1:170
Hoaly	Sarah	20 Feb 1785	widow, adm ch [prob. Hoadley], propounded for memb 17 Feb	1:9
Hodge	Betsy	27 Feb 1803	bp, ch of Chester S.	1:171
Hodge	Hannah	- 1803	adm ch, wife of Chester S.; dec 1803	3:17
Hodge	Hannah	8 Apr 1803	d, wife of Chester, 36y wanting 19d	1:156
Hodge	Hannah	27 Feb 1803	wife of Chester S., adm ch; died 8 Apr 1803	2:86
Hodge	Hannah	27 Feb 1803	Ch., adm ch, d 8 Apr 1803	1:56
Hodge	Hannah	27 Feb 1803	wife of Chester adm ch	1:36
Hodge	Harriot	27 Feb 1803	bp, ch of Chester S.	1:171
Hodge	Julielma	27 Feb 1803	bp, ch of Chester S.	1:171
Hodsell	Hannah	- 1852	adm ch; dis 1864	3:19
Hodsell	Hannah	7 Mar 1852	adm ch	3:60
Hodsell	Hannah	25 Mar 1864	voted dism, eligible for letter if asked for [see 3:367]	3:122
Hokenson	Lewis	21 Sep 1898	25 marr Mrs. Lillian Sultiff Anderson 24	3:226
Holmes	Arthur	2 Nov 1898	22 marr Florence Charlesworth 21	3:226
Holmes	Fred S.	18 Oct 1889	dism to Irving Park Illinois; also wife	3:127
Holmes	Frederick S.	- 1886	adm ch fr Humphrey St. Cong, New Haven; dis 1889 Irving Park Ill	3:21
Holmes	Frederick S.	5 Sep 1886	adm fr Humphrey St. Cong, New Haven; wife also	3:95
Holmes	Henrietta	- 1886	adm ch, wife of Fred. S. [adm & dism as husband]	3:21
Holton	Addie	13 Jun 1853	marr James R. Pitkin, both of Manchester Ct	3:201
Holtz	George	- 1878	adm ch	3:21
Holtz	George	3 Mar 1878	adm ch	3:66
Hooker	Emma M.	15 Nov 1894	38 marr Wm Wood Jr 48	3:223
Hopkins	A.D.	28 Feb 1865	marr Emily C. Mann, both of Naug	3:206
Hopkins	Abbie B.	- 1886	adm ch from Wallingford, wife of Saml E.	3:21
Hopkins	Abiah	- 1818	adm ch, wife of John; dec 1842	3:18
Hopkins	Abiah	4 Jan 1818	wife of John, adm ch; died 25 Oct 1842	2:88
Hopkins	Abiah	4 Jan 1818	wife of John adm ch	1:58
Hopkins	Abiah	- 1822	wife of John, member	1:82
Hopkins	Amelia	3 Jul 1829	ch of John, bp	1:88
Hopkins	Andrew Dwight	5 Sep 1834	bp, ch of David, b 23 Mar 1834	2:104
Hopkins	Betsey	- 1852	adm ch, wife of Willard H.; dis 1854 to Wallingford	3:19
Hopkins	Betsey	4 Jan 1852	adm ch, wife of Willard	3:60

NAUGATUCK, CONNECTICUT, CONGREGATIONAL CHURCH RECORDS

Hopkins	Betsey	16 Apr 1854	w. of Willard dism to Cong, Wallingford	3:120
Hopkins	Betsey	- 1863	adm ch from Wallingford, wife of Willard; dec 1900	3:20
Hopkins	Betsey	5 Jul 1863	adm fr Cong, Wallingford [bracketed with Willard]	3:91
Hopkins	Betsey	22 Apr 1900	Mrs. Willard H, d, 65, dropsy etc	3:261
Hopkins	Catharine	- 1866	adm ch from Prospect, wife of Wm	3:20
Hopkins	Catharine	1 Jul 1866	adm fr Cong, Prospect	3:92
Hopkins	Chas	12 Feb 1874	bur, 55, Hillside	3:257
Hopkins	Clara S.	- 1818	adm ch, wife of David; dec 1879	3:18
Hopkins	Clara S.	4 Jan 1818	["Clarissa" crossed out] wife of David, adm ch	2:88
Hopkins	Clara S.	Jan 1879	d, widow of David H., 78	3:258
Hopkins	Clarissa	- 1841	adm ch, wife of Enos; dec 1845	3:19
Hopkins	Clarissa	- 1841	adm ch; dis 1849 to Prospect	3:19
Hopkins	Clarissa	11 Jul 1841	wife of Enos, adm ch; died 9 Nov 1845	2:97
Hopkins	Clarissa	11 Jul 1841	adm ch; dism 18 Nov 1849 to Prospect	2:97
Hopkins	Clarissa	11 Jul 1841	bp, adult	2:106
Hopkins	Clarissa [sic]	15 Mar 1818	adm ch [but crossed out]	1:59
Hopkins	Clarissa [sic]	- 1822	wife of David, member	1:82
Hopkins	Clarrissa	11 Jul 1841	bp, adult [same name appears twice on same date]	2:106
Hopkins	Classica [sic]	4 Jan 1818	wife of David, adm ch	1:58
Hopkins	D.	2 Nov 1832	on comm.	2:12
Hopkins	David	29 May 1797	bp, ch of David	1:168
Hopkins	David	- 1811	adm ch; dec 1814	3:17
Hopkins	David	13 Oct 1811	adm ch; died 21 Apr 1814	2:87
Hopkins	David	13 Oct 1811	adm ch, d 21 Apr 1814	1:57
Hopkins	David	13 Oct 1811	adm ch	1:62
Hopkins	David	17 Mar 1811	his & Polly's ch d	1:160
Hopkins	David	26 Sep 1811	cand for full communion	1:62
Hopkins	David	3 Jan 1817	decd, bequeathed to ch his share in Rev Dodd's house and lot	1:73
Hopkins	David	- 1818	adm ch; dec 1873	3:18
Hopkins	David	4 Jan 1818	adm ch	2:88
Hopkins	David	4 Jan 1818	adm ch	1:58
Hopkins	David	17 Jun 1821	ch bp [unnamed]	1:63
Hopkins	David	- 1822	male, on list of members	1:81
Hopkins	David	18 Nov 1827	appointed to conf at Monroe	1:105
Hopkins	David	Apr 1833	on committee for SS	2:9
Hopkins	David	Apr 1833	on committee for SS	2:9
Hopkins	David	4 Nov 1836	appt'd delegate to Waterbury	2:20
Hopkins	David	3 Feb 1837	on comm	2:23
Hopkins	David	5 May 1837	SS superintendant	2:25
Hopkins	David	7 Oct 1837	on comm	2:27
Hopkins	David	1 Apr 1839	SS Super.	2:32
Hopkins	David	5 Jan 1838	on comm	2:30
Hopkins	David	20 Dec 1842	to be visited and laboured with	2:42
Hopkins	David	5 Dec 1845	delegate to Waterbury	2:53
Hopkins	David	11 Oct 1846	delegate to Oxford	2:55
Hopkins	David	9 Oct 1848	on comm	2:58
Hopkins	David	24 Jun 1849	on comm to visit Mr. Teele	2:60
Hopkins	David	10 Sep 1873	d, 76, typhoid, Hillside	3:256
Hopkins	David Thompson	20 May 1825	ch of John, bp	1:86
Hopkins	Edson	29 Aug 1858	d, 22, typhus fever, Hillside	3:252
Hopkins	Edward	May 1818	ch of John, bp	1:61
Hopkins	Edwin	24 Mar 1809	bp, ch of David	1:174
Hopkins	Edwin	- 1837	adm ch from Prospect; dis 1864	3:18
Hopkins	Edwin	3 Jull 1837	ch died, 10 days	2:115

NAUGATUCK, CONNECTICUT, CONGREGATIONAL CHURCH RECORDS

Hopkins	Edwin	19 Mar	1837	adm ch from Prospect	2:96
Hopkins	Edwin	19 Mar	1837	adm ch from ch in Prospect	2:24
Hopkins	Edwin	25 Mar	1864	voted dism, eligible for letter if asked for [see 3:367]	3:122
Hopkins	Elisa	16 Jun	1867	ch bp; Wm & Catherine	3:154
Hopkins	Elizabeth	-	1858	adm ch from New Milford, wife of Dwight; dec 1861	3:20
Hopkins	Emely Mabel	11 May	1823	ch of John, bp	1:85
Hopkins	Emily	-	1841	adm ch, wife of W.H. Platt; dis 1849 to Harrison, Penn	3:19
Hopkins	Emily	12 Sep	1841	adm ch; [m] Wm H. Platt; dism 3 Feb 1849 Presb Ch, Harrison Pa	2:98
Hopkins	Emily	2 Sep	1866	ch bp; Wm & Catharine	3:154
Hopkins	Emily	-	1876	adm ch; dis 1886 1st Cong New Britain	3:20
Hopkins	Emily	2 Jul	1876	adm ch	3:65
Hopkins	Emily A.	27 May	1885	23 of Naug marr Wm H. Turton 26 of New Britain	3:216
Hopkins	Emily C.	-	1866	adm ch, wife of Dwight	3:20
Hopkins	Emily C.	4 Nov	1866	adm ch	3:64
Hopkins	Enos	-	1841	adm ch; dis 1883 to Kinton O.	3:19
Hopkins	Enos	11 Jul	1841	adm ch	2:97
Hopkins	Enos	16 Mar	1883	dism to 1st Presb, Kenton O.	3:126
Hopkins	Esther Jane	8 Apr	1827	ch of David, bp	1:86
Hopkins	Fanny	3 Jul	1864	inf bp; John & Susan	3:153
Hopkins	George	20 Dec	1853	d, 27, typhus fever, Hillside	3:250
Hopkins	George	2 Sep	1859	inf bp; John & Susan F.	3:152
Hopkins	George Edward	14 Apr	1854	d, inf son of Willard & Betsey, 1 week, Brot from Wallingford	3:250
Hopkins	George Edwin	21 Sep	1831	ch of John & Abiah, bp	1:89
Hopkins	Harriet	-	1841	adm ch, wife of Wooding; dec 1858	3:19
Hopkins	Harriet	11 Jul	1841	adm ch	2:97
Hopkins	Harriet	2 Sep	1866	ch bp; Wm & Catharine	3:154
Hopkins	Harriet C.	-	1841	adm ch, wife of Saml; dec 1889	3:19
Hopkins	Harriet C.	11 Jul	1841	wife of Samuel, adm ch	2:97
Hopkins	Harriet C.	11 Jul	1841	bp, adult	2:106
Hopkins	Harriet C.	21 Nov	1889	d, 73, cancer	3:259
Hopkins	Harriett	11 Jul	1841	bp, adult	2:106
Hopkins	Harriette	-	1876	adm ch, wife of -- Flint	3:20
Hopkins	Harriette	2 Jul	1876	adm ch	3:65
Hopkins	Hattie L.	9 Jun	1886	marr Wm H. Flint, both of Naug	3:217
Hopkins	Henry B.	14 Mar	1865	d, 22, falling off locomotive in Nashville, bur 28 Mar, Hillside	3:255
Hopkins	Henry Bernett	2 Jul	1843	bp, ch of Enos	2:107
Hopkins	Jane	12 Sep	1841	adm ch; [m] L. Spencer	2:98
Hopkins	Jane C.	-	1843	adm ch, wife of Henry W. ["& Enos" added] dis 1883 Kinton O.	3:19
Hopkins	Jane C.	16 Mar	1883	dism to 1st Presb, Kenton O.	3:126
Hopkins	Jane Caroline	14 May	1842	bp, adult	2:106
Hopkins	Jane Caroline	14 May	1843	wife of Henry, adm ch; [something illegible above his name]	2:99
Hopkins	Jane E.	-	1841	adm ch, wife of L. Spencer; dec 1861	3:19
Hopkins	Jennie E.	11 Dec	1891	(Fairchild), dism to 1st Cong, Meriden Ct	3:127
Hopkins	Jennie Elizabeth	-	1890	adm ch; dis 1891 Meriden	3:21
Hopkins	Jennie Elizabeth	9 Mar	1890	bp, adult	3:159
Hopkins	Jennie Elizabeth	9 Mar	1890	Miss, adm ch	3:70
Hopkins	John	-	1789	adm ch; dec 1802	3:17
Hopkins	John	17 Mar	1789	adm ch, d 12 May 1802	1:55
Hopkins	John	17 May	1789	adm ch; died 12 May 1802	2:84
Hopkins	John	17 May	1789	adm ch	1:12
Hopkins	John	19 Apr	1795	bp, ch of David	1:167
Hopkins	John	12 May	1802	d, 82y 9m 26d	1:155
Hopkins	John	-	1818	adm ch; dec 1859	3:18
Hopkins	John	3 Jul	1818	on committee to est. Sabbath School	1:77

NAUGATUCK, CONNECTICUT, CONGREGATIONAL CHURCH RECORDS

Hopkins	John	4 Jan	1818	adm ch	2:88
Hopkins	John	4 Jan	1818	adm ch	1:58
Hopkins	John	-	1822	male, on list of members	1:81
Hopkins	John	11 Jul	1825	ch d, hooping cough, 5y[?] 4m	1:163
Hopkins	John	7 Oct	1827	on committee	1:103
Hopkins	John	16 Dec	1827	to attend conf at Trumbel	1:105
Hopkins	John	21 Oct	1827	presented complaint against Curtis Hine	1:104
Hopkins	John	6 Nov	1829	voted to attend future conf	1:109
Hopkins	John	17 Dec	1830	on comm	1:112
Hopkins	John	30 Apr	1830	on Sabb School board	1:111
Hopkins	John	Sep	1831	on Visiting Committee	1:115
Hopkins	John	Apr	1833	on committee for SS	2:9
Hopkins	John	7 Sep	1834	bp, ch of John	2:104
Hopkins	John	24 Aug	1843	on comm	2:47
Hopkins	John	5 Mar	1847	appt'd to visit members	2:56
Hopkins	John	-	1858	adm ch; dis 1868 to Centl Congl Brooklyn	3:20
Hopkins	John	4 Jul	1858	adm ch	3:62
Hopkins	John	22 Jun	1859	d, 67, erysipelas, Hillside	3:252
Hopkins	John	25 Oct	1868	dism to Central Cong, Brooklyn NY	3:124
Hopkins	Julia	-	1841	adm ch, wife of Truman; dec 1858	3:19
Hopkins	Julia	11 Jul	1841	wife of Truman, adm ch	2:97
Hopkins	Julia	11 Jul	1841	bp, adult	2:106
Hopkins	Julia	3 Oct	1858	d, w of Truman, 53, typhus, Hillside	3:252
Hopkins	Laura	25 Apr	1802	bp, ch of David	1:170
Hopkins	Lizzie	-	1885	adm ch, wife of Jno Mornoe [sic]; dis 1899 to North NY Congl	3:21
Hopkins	Lizzie	5 Jul	1885	adm ch	3:67
Hopkins	Lizzie M.	26 Dec	1887	21 marr John H. Monroe 23	3:218
Hopkins	Mabel	-	1817	adm ch, wife of A. Stevens; dec	3:18
Hopkins	Mabel	4 May	1817	husband of Alfred Stevens, adm ch; died Apr 18-- [blotted]	2:87
Hopkins	Mabel	4 May	1817	adm ch	1:57
Hopkins	Mabel	8 Apr	1817	cand for memb	1:73
Hopkins	Mary Elisabeth	7 Mar	1858	w of Dwight, adm fr Cong, New Milford Ct	3:91
Hopkins	Mary Eliz[abe]th	16 May	1861	d, w of Dwight, 26, Hillside	3:253
Hopkins	Nancy	-	1841	adm ch, "(Loundsbury) S." [added]; dis 1870 to Bethany	3:19
Hopkins	Nancy	12 Sep	1841	adm ch	2:98
Hopkins	Nancy	12 Sep	1841	bp, adult	2:106
Hopkins	Patience	22 Jul	1802	d, relict of John, 63y & abt 8m	1:155
Hopkins	Polley	5 Apr	1795	wife of David adm ch	1:13
Hopkins	Polley	19 Apr	1795	bp, ch of David	1:167
Hopkins	Polly	-	1795	adm ch, wife of David; dec 1829	3:17
Hopkins	Polly	4 Apr	1795	wife of David, adm ch; died 2 Aug 1829	2:85
Hopkins	Polly	5 Apr	1795	Da[vid], adm ch, d 2 Aug 1829	1:55
Hopkins	Polly	-	1822	Wid, member; d Aug 1829	1:82
Hopkins	Polly	2 Aug	1829	wid, d, lingering, 59	1:145
Hopkins	Polly C.	2 Mar	1851	of Naug marr Julius B. Cook of Cheshire	3:200
Hopkins	Rhoda	-	1788	adm ch, wife of F. Hotchkiss; dis to Prospect	3:17
Hopkins	Rhoda	20 Jul	1788	wife of Frederic Hotchkiss, adm ch; rem to Prospect	2:84
Hopkins	Rhoda	20 Jul	1788	adm ch	1:11
Hopkins	Rhoda	20 Jul	1788	adm ch, dism	1:55
Hopkins	Robert	Sep	1845	bp, ch of Enos	2:107
Hopkins	Saml	-	1841	adm ch; dec 1889	3:19
Hopkins	Saml Mark	1 Nov	1861	inf bp; John & Susan F.	3:152
Hopkins	Samuel	May	1818	ch of John, bp	1:61
Hopkins	Samuel	11 Jul	1841	adm ch	2:97

Hopkins	Samuel	-	1853	Appt'd Deacon; removed 1889 Dec	3:1
Hopkins	Samuel	16 Nov	1889	Dea, d, 73, blood poisoning	3:259
Hopkins	Samuel E.	2 May	1886	Mrs., adm fr Cong, Wallingford Ct	3:95
Hopkins	Samuel Evans	3 Jul	1864	inf bp; Willard & Betsey	3:153
Hopkins	Susan F.	-	1858	adm ch fr Presb Scranton, Pa, w of Dwight; dis 1868 Cent Cong,	3:20
-	-	-	-	Brooklyn	-
Hopkins	Susan F.	25 Oct	1868	dism to Central Cong, Brooklyn	3:124
Hopkins	Susan Frances	4 Jul	1858	adm fr Presb Ch, Scranton Pa.	3:91
Hopkins	Truman	17 Mar	1805	bp, son of David & Polly	1:172
Hopkins	Truman	26 Aug	1824	of Salem, marr Julia Martin of Columbia	1:152
Hopkins	Truman	9 Sep	1858	d, 53, typhus, Hillside	3:252
Hopkins	Willard	12 May	1851	of Naug marr Betsey Adams of Naug	3:200
Hopkins	Willard	-	1852	adm ch; dis 1854 to Wallingford	3:19
Hopkins	Willard	4 Jan	1852	adm ch	3:60
Hopkins	Willard	16 Apr	1854	dism to Cong, Wallingford	3:120
Hopkins	Willard	2 Sep	1861	his & Betsey's inf d, 3 ms, brot from Wallingford, Hillside	3:253
Hopkins	Willard	-	1863	adm ch from Wallingford; dec 1891	3:20
Hopkins	Willard	5 Jul	1863	adm fr Cong, Wallingford	3:91
Hopkins	Willard	-	1881	appt'd Deacon; resigned Jul 1886	3:1
Hopkins	Willard	27 Nov	1891	d, 61, consumption	3:260
Hopkins	William	12 Sep	1841	bp, ch of Samuel	2:106
Hopkins	William	2 Sep	1866	adm ch	3:63
Hopkins	Wm	-	1866	adm ch	3:20
Hopkins	Wm.	11 Jun	1876	a ch, bp	3:155
Horn	August	24 Jul	1889	marr Amelia Zwick	3:220
Horn	John	15 Aug	1869	ch bp; John & Mrs. Horn (German)	3:155
Horn	Lena	16 Nov	1887	20 marr Thomas McKee 22	3:218
Horn	Mattie Lena	15 Aug	1869	ch bp; John & Mrs. Horn (German)	3:155
Horton	Albert	-		husband of Martha Steele Young	3:59
Horton	Amelia	-	1841	adm ch; dis 1887 to Ansonia	3:19
Horton	Amelia	11 Jul	1841	adm ch	2:97
Horton	Amelia	11 Jul	1841	bp, adult	2:106
Horton	Amelia	30 Dec	1887	dism to Ansonia Ct	3:126
Horton	Benjamin	1 Aug	1801	his infant d, 1/2d	1:155
Horton	Ellen Julia	28 Nov	1869	d, 35, consumption, Hillside	3:256
Horton	Emily J.	-	1840	adm ch, wife of R. Coe; dis 1862 to Ansonia	3:19
Horton	Emily J.	12 Jul	1840	adm ch; [m] Robert Coe	2:97
Horton	Emily Jennette	12 Jul	1840	bp	2:106
Horton	Harriet N.	-	1840	adm ch, wife of A.H. Lewis	3:19
Horton	Harriet N.	12 Jul	1840	adm ch; wife of A.H. Lewis	2:97
Horton	Harriet N.	12 Jul	1840	bp	2:106
Horton	John	-	1785	adm ch; dec 1787	3:17
Horton	John	17 Feb	1785	adm ch, d 4 Feb 1787	1:53
Horton	John	20 Feb	1785	adm ch; died 4 Feb 1787	2:82
Horton	John	20 Feb	1785	adm ch	1:9
Horton	John	-	1787	adm ch; dec 1799	3:17
Horton	John	22 Apr	1787	adm ch; died 14 May 1799	2:83
Horton	John	22 Apr	1787	adm ch	1:11
Horton	John	22 Apr	1787	adm ch, d 14 May 1799	1:54
Horton	John	1 Aug	1803	ch d, 2y	1:156
Horton	John	20 Sep	1837	died, 68	2:115
Horton	Julia E.	-	1863	adm ch; wife of --; dec 1869 [see Ellen Julia]	3:20
Horton	Julia E.	3 May	1863	adm ch	3:62
Horton	Laura	-	1840	adm ch, wife of -- Doolittle; dis 1849 to Hamden, Mt. Carmel	3:19

AUGATUCK, CONNECTICUT, CONGREGATIONAL CHURCH RECORDS

Horton	Laura	12 Jul 1840	adm ch; [m] -- Doolittle; dism 7 Aug 1849 to Hamden Mt. C[armel]	2:97
Horton	Laura	12 Jul 1840	bp	2:106
Horton	Mary	- 1787	adm ch, wife of John; dec 1804	3:17
Horton	Mary	22 Apr 1787	wife of John, adm ch; died 20 Dec 1804	2:83
Horton	Mary	22 Apr 1787	wife of John adm ch	1:11
Horton	Mary	22 Apr 1787	Jo. adm ch., d 20 Dec 1804	1:54
Horton	Mary	20 Dec 1804	d, Widow, 64y	1:157
Horton	Miles	28 Oct 1867	d, 73, erysipelas, Hillside	3:255
Horton	Sarah J.	12 Apr 1867	d, (Hamden) 93, Hillside	3:255
Horton	Susanna	20 Feb 1785	wife of John adm ch	1:9
Horton	Susannah	- 1785	adm ch, wife of John; dis to Ridgefield	3:17
Horton	Susannah	17 Feb 1785	Jo., adm ch, dism [to "Prospect" added]	1:53
Horton	Susannah	20 Feb 1785	wife of John, adm ch; rem to Ridgefield	2:82
Hosmer[?]	Francis Lathrop	1 Oct 1883	[Hosmer?] marr Villa Adeline Dencer [?] both of Naug	3:215
Hotchkis	Gideon	Jul 1783	chosen Deacon	1:6
Hotchkis	Julia A.	12 Oct 1823	of Salem, marr Silas Bouton	1:152
Hotchkis	Lucretia	18 Oct 1828	dau of Curtis, d, fever, 12	1:145
Hotchkiss	-	- -	husband of Ella C. Osborne	3:33
Hotchkiss	Abijah	24 Mar 1825	d, ch of August, fever, 1	1:162
Hotchkiss	Abm	- 1801	adm ch from Bethany; dec 1802	3:17
Hotchkiss	Abraham	2 Dec 1800	Delegate at Consociation at Salem, from Columbia	1:19
Hotchkiss	Abraham	1 Nov 1801	adm ch from Bethany; died 24 Nov 1802	2:86
Hotchkiss	Abraham	1 Nov 1801	adm ch, d 24 Nov 1802	1:56
Hotchkiss	Abraham	1 Nov 1801	adm ch	1:32
Hotchkiss	Abraham	15 Oct 1801	and wife of Bethany examined, rec'd as candidates for adm	1:32
Hotchkiss	Abraham	24 Nov 1802	d, 48y 11m [entry crossed out]	1:155
Hotchkiss	Abraham	24 Nov 1802	d, 48y 11m 9d	1:155
Hotchkiss	Abram	7 Apr 1857	d, 59, dropsy, Hillside	3:251
Hotchkiss	Adeline	- 1865	adm ch from Meth Naug, wife of Burrett; dec 1873	3:20
Hotchkiss	Adeline	10 Sep 1865	adm fr Methodist, Naug	3:92
Hotchkiss	Adeline	1 Jul 1873	d (Mrs. B.M.[sic]) 45, inflamation bowles, Hillside	3:256
Hotchkiss	Albert G.	9 Jun 1869	of Torrington marr Ella Osborn of Naug	3:208
Hotchkiss	Alice G.	18 Nov 1882	marr Arthur E. Jones, both of Naug	3:214
Hotchkiss	Amy [sic]	22 Oct 1810	of Columbia, marr Polly Hickox of this place	1:151
Hotchkiss	Angelina	19 Apr 1828	d, Fever, 21	1:144
Hotchkiss	Anna	6 Jan 1788	bp, ch of Eben	1:165
Hotchkiss	Asahel	- 1814	adm ch from Prospect; dis 1833 to Watertown	3:18
Hotchkiss	Asahel	2 Sep 1814	and wife, cand for memb	1:69
Hotchkiss	Asahel	9 Oct 1814	adm ch from Prospect; rem Jun 1833 to Watertown	2:87
Hotchkiss	Asahel	9 Oct 1814	adm ch	1:57
Hotchkiss	Asahel	9 Oct 1814	and wife, adm ch	1:69
Hotchkiss	Asahel	- 1822	male, on list of members	1:81
Hotchkiss	Asahel	2 Dec 1827	to attend eastern conf at Watertown	1:105
Hotchkiss	Asahel	7 Oct 1827	on committee	1:103
Hotchkiss	Asahel	13 Aug 1827	appointed messenger to conference at Southbury	1:103
Hotchkiss	Augustus	- 1818	adm ch; dis to Sharon	3:18
Hotchkiss	Augustus	4 Jan 1818	adm ch; rem to Sharon	2:88
Hotchkiss	Augustus	4 Jan 1818	adm ch	1:58
Hotchkiss	Augustus	- 1822	male, on list of members	1:81
Hotchkiss	B.W.	- -	husband of Emily J. Smith	3:44
Hotchkiss	Betsey	- 1830	adm ch, wife of -- Bishop; dis 1835 to Woodbridge	3:18
Hotchkiss	Betsey	21 Feb 1830	adm ch; rem 7 Jun 1835 to Woodbridge	2:93
Hotchkiss	Betsy	3 May 1829	member	1:94
Hotchkiss	Betsy	3 May 1829	adm ch	1:59b

NAUGATUCK, CONNECTICUT, CONGREGATIONAL CHURCH RECORDS

Hotchkiss	Burrit W.	20 Oct 1874	marr Emily J. Smith, both of Naug	3:210
Hotchkiss	Calvin	23 Dec 1825	marr Asenith Sanford of Columbia	1:152
Hotchkiss	Calvin Austin	1 May 1829	ch of Giles, bp	1:88
Hotchkiss	Chancy	10 Nov 1803	d, 19y, son of Wd Rosette Hotchkiss	1:156
Hotchkiss	Charles	12 Jun 1825	ch of Giles, bp	1:86
Hotchkiss	Charles	Apr 1833	on committee for SS	2:9
Hotchkiss	Charles	- 1835	adm ch; dis 1842 to Torrington	3:18
Hotchkiss	Charles	4 Jan 1835	adm ch from Torington, dism 27 Nov 1842	2:95
Hotchkiss	Charles	4 Jan 1835	bp, adult	2:104
Hotchkiss	Charles	5 Jan 1838	on comm	2:30
Hotchkiss	Charles	6 Nov 1842	and wife, dism to first ch in Torrington	2:42
Hotchkiss	Chauncey Holden	24 Oct 1813	bp, son of Ira	1:176
Hotchkiss	Clarissa	- 1822	wife of G., member, adm since 1822	1:83
Hotchkiss	Clarissa	- 1824	adm ch; Irr 1844 Episcopal	3:18
Hotchkiss	Clarissa	11 Dec 1824	wife of Giles, adm ch; withdrawn to Episcopal	2:91
Hotchkiss	Clarissa	11 Dec 1824	Giles, adm ch	1:59
Hotchkiss	Clarissa	11 Dec 1824	adm ch	1:100
Hotchkiss	Clarissa	24 Nov 1824	wife of Giles propounded for adm	1:100
Hotchkiss	Clarissa	3 Jan 1836	adm ch; withdrawn	2:96
Hotchkiss	Clarissa 2d	- 1836	adm ch; Irr 1844 Episcopal	3:18
Hotchkiss	Clarissa, Mrs.	1 Mar 1844	excomm, having joined Episcopal Ch	2:49n
Hotchkiss	Clarrissa Ann	7 May 1826	ch of Giles, bp	1:86
Hotchkiss	Cloe	8 Jun 1794	bp, ch of Fradrick	1:167
Hotchkiss	Cora I.	- 1885	adm ch; dis 1893 Presbytn NY	3:21
Hotchkiss	Cora I.	5 Jul 1885	adm ch	3:68
Hotchkiss	Cora I.	5 Sep 1889	20 marr Harry A. Bennett 22	3:220
Hotchkiss	Cora Isabel	11 Jun 1876	a ch, bp	3:155
Hotchkiss	Cynthia	2 Apr 1864	Mrs. of Naug marr Ransom Scovill of Watertown	3:205
Hotchkiss	David	29 Sep 1801	Delegate to consociation in Salem, from Woodbridge	1:25
Hotchkiss	David Miles	29 Jan 1798	bp, son of Fradric	1:168
Hotchkiss	Diah	22 Jun 1824	stillborn child	1:161
Hotchkiss	Dyer	21 Jan 1843	called to testify	2:45
Hotchkiss	Dyer	14 Nov 1862	d, 77, Hillside	3:253
Hotchkiss	Easther Frances	Nov 1831	ch of Giles & Clarissa, bp	1:89
Hotchkiss	Eben	3 Jun 1787	adm ch	1:11
Hotchkiss	Ebenezer	- 1787	adm ch; dis Prospect	3:17
Hotchkiss	Ebenezer	3 Jun 1787	adm ch; rem to Prospect	2:83
Hotchkiss	Ebenezer	3 Jun 1787	adm ch, dism [to "Prospect" added]	1:54
Hotchkiss	Edward Charles	3 Jul 1836	bp, ch of Charles, b 22 Nov 1833	2:105
Hotchkiss	Electa	- 1835	adm ch, wife of Chs; dis 1842 to Torrington	3:18
Hotchkiss	Electa	4 Jan 1835	adm ch from Torington, wife of Charles, dism 27 Nov 1842	2:95
Hotchkiss	Eliza Jane	- 1851	adm ch, wife of Wm E. Brown; dis 1861 to Bridgeport	3:19
Hotchkiss	Eliza Jane	6 Jul 1851	adm ch	3:60
Hotchkiss	Eliza Jane	17 Oct 1854	marr Wm E. Brown, both of Naug	3:202
Hotchkiss	Ella A.	3 Jan 1877	of Naug marr Edgar O. Whitney of Meriden	3:211
Hotchkiss	Ella C.	Jan 1870	(Osborn) dism to Wolcottville	3:124
Hotchkiss	Ellen Amelia	5 Sep 1851	bp, 9 yrs, Marcus & Locky L.	3:150
Hotchkiss	Elvira	- 1835	adm ch, wife of L. Baldwin; dis 1863 to Prospect	3:18
Hotchkiss	Elvira	4 Jan 1835	adm ch; [m] Lucius Baldwin	2:95
Hotchkiss	Eunice	14 Nov 1834	died, 52	2:114
Hotchkiss	F.	- -	husband of Rhoda Hopkins	3:17
Hotchkiss	Franklin Augustus	28 Apr 1844	bp, ch of Henry	2:107
Hotchkiss	Frederic	- -	husband of Rhoda Hopkins	2:84
Hotchkiss	Geo	- -	husband of Lydia A. Meramble	3:29

Hotchkiss	Gideon	-	1781	adm ch; dis 1807	3:17
Hotchkiss	Gideon	Mar	1781	adm ch	1:6
Hotchkiss	Gideon	Mar	1781	adm ch, deceased 3 Sep 1807	1:53
Hotchkiss	Gideon	1 Mar	1781	adm ch; rem 3 Sep 1807 ["R" for removed written over "D" for died]	2:82
Hotchkiss	Gideon	-	1783	Deacon, gave book for church records	Pre
Hotchkiss	Gideon	Jul	1783	Deacon, died 3 Sep 1807	2:79
Hotchkiss	Gideon	Jul	1783	Deacon	1:53
Hotchkiss	Gideon	-	1785	Deacon, gave "Bason" for baptism	Pre
Hotchkiss	Gideon	6 Jan	1788	bp, ch of Eben	1:165
Hotchkiss	Gideon	29 Sep	1801	Dn, Delegate to consociation in Salem, from Columbia	1:25
Hotchkiss	Gideon	4 Sep	1807	d, Deacon, of Columbia, 91y wanting 3m	1:158
Hotchkiss	Giles	-	1828	adm ch; Irr 1844 Episcopal	3:18
Hotchkiss	Giles	6 Jul	1828	adm ch; withdrawn	2:92
Hotchkiss	Giles	6 Jul	1828	adm ch	1:59a
Hotchkiss	Giles	6 Jul	1828	member	1:94
Hotchkiss	Giles	6 Jul	1828	adm ch	1:107
Hotchkiss	Giles	20 Mar	1828	propounded for adm	1:106
Hotchkiss	Giles	30 Apr	1830	on Sabb School board	1:111
Hotchkiss	Giles	Sep	1831	on Visiting Committee	1:115
Hotchkiss	Giles	26 Aug	1832	on Board of Managers for SS	2:11
Hotchkiss	Giles	1 Apr	1838	SS Comm	2:32
Hotchkiss	Giles	5 Jan	1838	on comm	2:30
Hotchkiss	Giles	20 Dec	1842	to visit and labour with Mrs. Fanny Fowler	2:42
Hotchkiss	Giles	1 Mar	1844	excomm, having joined Episcopal Ch	2:49n
Hotchkiss	Harry	-	1878	adm ch; dec 1899	3:21
Hotchkiss	Harry S.	6 Feb	1873	marr Mrs Maria Seymour, both of Naug	3:210
Hotchkiss	Harry S.	3 Mar	1878	bp, adult	3:156
Hotchkiss	Harry S.	3 Mar	1878	and wife adm ch	3:66
Hotchkiss	Harry S.	1 Feb	1899	d, 53, heart disease	3:261
Hotchkiss	Helen	15 Jul	1873	d, 31, consumption, Hillside	3:256
Hotchkiss	Helen A.	-	1858	adm ch; dec 1873	3:20
Hotchkiss	Helen Amelia	4 Jul	1858	adm ch	3:62
Hotchkiss	Henry	-	1844	adm ch from Sharon; dis 1849	3:19
Hotchkiss	Henry	5 Jan	1844	adm ch from Sharon; dism 6 Apr 1849	2:99
Hotchkiss	Henry	5 Jan	1844	and wife, adm from Cong Ch in Sharon	2:48
Hotchkiss	Ira	-	1811	adm ch; dec 1816	3:17
Hotchkiss	Ira	13 Oct	1811	adm ch; rem 21 Apr 1816 to Colebrook	2:87
Hotchkiss	Ira	13 Oct	1811	adm ch, dism 21 Apr 1816	1:57
Hotchkiss	Ira	13 Oct	1811	adm ch	1:62
Hotchkiss	Ira	26 Sep	1811	cand for full communion	1:62
Hotchkiss	Isaac G.	18 Apr	1850	inf of Isaac G. & Emiline, d, 1 week	3:250
Hotchkiss	Jacob	2 Dec	1800	Delegate at Consociation at Salem, from Bethany	1:19
Hotchkiss	Jane	24 Sep	1865	of Naug marr James Megin of Hamden	3:207
Hotchkiss	Jane Eliza	29 Jun	1838	bp, ch of Giles	2:105
Hotchkiss	Julia	22 May	1796	bp, ch of Fradrik	1:168
Hotchkiss	Julia Ann	-	1851	adm ch; dis 1857 to Easthamp Mass	3:19
Hotchkiss	Julia Ann	6 Jul	1851	adm ch	3:60
Hotchkiss	Julia Ann	5 Apr	1857	dism to Cong, Easthampton [with Sarah L. Wooster]	3:121
Hotchkiss	Julius	-	1878	adm ch; dec 1879	3:21
Hotchkiss	Julius	3 Mar	1878	bp, adult	3:156
Hotchkiss	Julius	3 Mar	1878	and wife adm ch	3:66
Hotchkiss	Julius	17 Feb	1879	d, 62, paralysis	3:258
Hotchkiss	Julius	8 Oct	1895	Mrs, d, 71, heart disease	3:260

NAUGATUCK, CONNECTICUT, CONGREGATIONAL CHURCH RECORDS

Hotchkiss	Julius Henry	-	1846	bp, ch of Henry	2:107
Hotchkiss	Lockey	-	1822	wife of Marcus, member	1:82
Hotchkiss	Lockey L.	3 Dec	1890	d [date taken fr previous entry]	3:260
Hotchkiss	Locky L.	-	1840	adm ch from Sharon, wife of Marcus; dec 1890	3:19
Hotchkiss	Locky L.	1 Mar	1840	wife of Marcus, adm ch from Sharon	2:97
Hotchkiss	Lucia Electa	3 Jul	1836	bp, ch of Charles, b 22 Nov 1835	2:105
Hotchkiss	Lydia A.	10 Feb	1867	(Meramble) dism to West Meriden	3:123
Hotchkiss	M.	-	-	husband of Locky L. Porter	3:35
Hotchkiss	Marcus	-	-	husband of Locy [sic] L. Porter	2:88
Hotchkiss	Marcus	-	1818	adm ch; dis 1834 to Sharon	3:18
Hotchkiss	Marcus	4 Jan	1818	adm ch; rem 7 Dec 1834 to Sharon	2:88
Hotchkiss	Marcus	4 Jan	1818	adm ch	1:58
Hotchkiss	Marcus	-	1822	male, on list of members	1:81
Hotchkiss	Marcus	Sep	1831	on Visiting Committee	1:115
Hotchkiss	Marcus	7 Dec	1834	and wife, granted letter of rec to ch in Sharon	2:18
Hotchkiss	Marcus	-	1840	adm ch from Sharon; dec 1877	3:19
Hotchkiss	Marcus	1 Mar	1840	adm ch from Sharon	2:97
Hotchkiss	Marcus	18 Apr	1877	d, 76, Old age, Hillside	3:257
Hotchkiss	Maria	-	1822	adm ch; dis 1833 to Watertown	3:18
Hotchkiss	Maria	Sep	1822	adm ch; rem Jun 1833 to Watertown	2:91
Hotchkiss	Maria	Sep	1822	adm ch	1:59
Hotchkiss	Mariah	-	1822	female, member	1:83
Hotchkiss	Mariah	Sep	1822	adm ch	1:96
Hotchkiss	Mariah	10 Sep	1822	cand for memb	1:96
Hotchkiss	Marian	21 Feb	1841	Miss, dism to ch in Benington Vt	2:36
Hotchkiss	Mary A.	-	1847	adm ch from Bennington Vt; dis 1852 to New Haven	3:19
Hotchkiss	Mary A.	-	1856	adm ch from Ridgeville O; dis 1862 to Hamden E. Plains	3:19
Hotchkiss	Mary A.	4 May	1856	adm from Cong, Ridgeville O.	3:90
Hotchkiss	Mary Ann	-	1834	adm ch; dis 1841 to Beningon Vt.	3:18
Hotchkiss	Mary Ann	2 Nov	1834	adm ch, dism to Benington Vt, 21 Feb 184-	2:95
Hotchkiss	Mary Ann	2 Nov	1834	bp, ch[?] of Mark, adult	2:104
Hotchkiss	Mary Ann	29 Feb	1852	dism to College St Ch, New Haven	3:120
Hotchkiss	Mary Ann	10 Nov	1859	of Naug marr Lemuel J. Russel of Hamden	3:204
Hotchkiss	May [sic] A.	16 May	1847	adm ch from Bennington Vt.	2:100
Hotchkiss	Mirilla	22 May	1791	bp, ch of Fraderic	1:166
Hotchkiss	Mrs.	-	1878	adm ch, wife of Julius; dec 1895	3:21
Hotchkiss	Mss. [sic]	-	1878	adm ch, wife of Harry; dec 1904	3:21
Hotchkiss	Orra	20 Nov	1872	Mrs. Diah, d 19 Nov, 89, Hillside	3:257
Hotchkiss	Phebe	-	1796	adm ch, wife of Asahel; dis to Prospect	3:17
Hotchkiss	Phebe	25 Sep	1796	wife of Asahel, adm ch; rem to Prospect	2:85
Hotchkiss	Phebe	25 Sep	1796	Asa[hel], adm ch, dism	1:55
Hotchkiss	Phebe	25 Sep	1796	wife of Asahel adm ch	1:13
Hotchkiss	Phebe	-	1814	adm ch, wife of Asahel; dec 1829	3:18
Hotchkiss	Phebe	9 Oct	1814	wife of Asahel, adm ch; died	2:94
Hotchkiss	Phebe	9 Oct	1814	wife of Asahel, adm ch, d 1829 ["Thankful" crossed out]	1:57
Hotchkiss	Phebe	-	1822	wife of Asahel, member, died 13 Sep 1829	1:82
Hotchkiss	Phebe	13 Sep	1829	wife of Asahel, d, lingering, 71	1:145
Hotchkiss	Polly	26 Jan	1864	d, 71, Hillside	3:254
Hotchkiss	Rachel	-	1818	adm ch; dis to Wolcott	3:18
Hotchkiss	Rachel	15 Mar	1818	adm ch; rem to Woolcut	2:89
Hotchkiss	Rachel	15 Mar	1818	adm ch	1:58
Hotchkiss	Rachel	-	1822	female, on list of members	1:82
Hotchkiss	Rebecca	8 Apr	1836	died, 67	2:115
Hotchkiss	Robert	12 Jun	1825	ch of Giles, bp	1:86

NAUGATUCK, CONNECTICUT, CONGREGATIONAL CHURCH RECORDS

Hotchkiss	Robert	21 Apr 1833	died, 18	2:114
Hotchkiss	Rosett	5 Jan 1844	wife of Henry, adm ch from Sharon; dism 6 Apr 1849	2:99
Hotchkiss	Rosetta	- 1801	adm ch from Bethany, wife of Abm; dec 1841	3:17
Hotchkiss	Rosetta	1 Nov 1801	wife of Abraham, adm ch from Bethany; died Sep 1841	2:86
Hotchkiss	Rosetta	1 Nov 1801	adm ch	1:56
Hotchkiss	Rosetta	1 Nov 1801	wife of Abraham adm ch	1:32
Hotchkiss	Rosetta	- 1822	wid, member	1:82
Hotchkiss	Rosette	- 1844	adm ch, wife of Henry, adm ch from Sharon; dis 1849	3:19
Hotchkiss	Sally	- 1811	adm ch from Waterbury, wife of Ira; dec 1811	3:17
Hotchkiss	Sally	13 Oct 1811	wife of Ira, adm ch from Waterbury; died 6 Nov 1811	2:87
Hotchkiss	Sally	13 Oct 1811	adm ch, d 6 Nov 1811	1:57
Hotchkiss	Sally	13 Oct 1811	adm ch	1:62
Hotchkiss	Sally	26 Sep 1811	wife of Ira, cand. for memb, from Waterbury	1:62
Hotchkiss	Sally Porter	23 Jun 1822	ch of Marus [sic], bp	1:84
Hotchkiss	Sally Porter	23 Jun 1822	ch of Marcus, bp	1:85
Hotchkiss	Sarah	6 Nov 1811	d, wife of Ira	1:160
Hotchkiss	Sarah	1 Mar 1840	adm ch from Sharon; [m] Z. Worster	2:97
Hotchkiss	Sarah E.	- 1840	adm ch, wife of -- Payne; dis 1848 to Prospect	3:19
Hotchkiss	Sarah E.	12 Jul 1840	adm ch; [m] -- Payne	2:97
Hotchkiss	Sarah E.	12 Jul 1840	bp	2:106
Hotchkiss	Sarah L.[sic]	- 1840	adm ch fr Sharon, w of Z. Worcester; dis 1857, Easthampton Mass	3:19
Hotchkiss	Sophia	23 Jul 1815	bp, ch of Ira	1:176
Hotchkiss	Stephen	7 Jun 1827	marr Maria Goodyear of New Haven	1:153
Hotchkiss	Tempe	16 Apr 1797	bp, ch of Asahel	1:168
Hotchkiss	Temperance	- 1817	adm ch, wife of Zina Andrus; dis 1835 to Prospect	3:18
Hotchkiss	Temperance	16 Nov 1817	adm ch; rem Jun 1821 to Prospect	2:94
Hotchkiss	Temperence	16 Nov 1817	adm ch, dism Jun 1821	1:57
Hotchkiss	Wid	27 Dec 1826	d, 89	1:144
Hotchkiss	Wm Henry	5 Sep 1851	bp, 13 yrs, Marcus & Locky L.	3:150
Hotchkiss	Wm Henry	- 1858	adm ch; dec 1865	3:20
Hotchkiss	Wm Henry	4 July 1858	adm ch	3:62
Hotchkiss	Wm Henry	11 Aug 1865	d, 28, fever	3:255
Howland	Howard N.	10 Sep 1897	22 marr Martha Chase 21	3:225
Hoyt	Amanda	26 Feb 1829	of Salem, marr Oliver Albro	1:153
Hoyt	Laura	- 1837	adm ch; dis 1837 to New York	3:18
Hoyt	Laura	5 Mar 1837	adm ch; rem 14 Oct 1837 to New York	2:96
Hoyt	Laura	5 Mar 1837	bp, adult	2:105
Hoyt	Laura	14 Oct 1837	dism to 3rd Presbyterian ch in Rochester NY	2:27
Hubbard	Benjn D.	28 Nov 1860	marr Maria H. Morey, both of Naug	3:204
Hubbel	Alonso F.	23 Nov 1862	dism to Cong, Wallingford	3:122
Hubbel	Alonzo F.	- 1858	adm ch; dis 1862 to Wallingford	3:20
Hubbel	Alonzo Frederick	4 Jul 1858	bp, adult	3:152
Hubbel	Carrie A.	6 Sep 1891	adm ch	3:70
Hubbel	Cornelia Thompson	5 Jul 1856	inf bp; Jerome & Eliza Ann	3:151
Hubbel	Eliza Ann	- 1846	adm ch from So. Britain; dis 1883 to M.E. Beacon Falls Ct	3:19
Hubbel	Eliza Ann	6 Aug 1846	adm ch from S. Britain	2:100
Hubbel	Harold Booth	1 Aug 1897	ch bp; Arthur & Flora H.	3:162
Hubbel	J-- B.	- 1857	adm ch; dis 1883 to M.E. Becon Falls	3:20
Hubbel	Jerome B.	4 Jan 1857	bp, adult	3:151
Hubbel	Jerome B.	4 Jan 1857	adm ch	3:61
Hubbel	Mary L.	- 1866	adm ch; dis 1875 M.E. Beacon Falls	3:20
Hubbel	Mary Louisa	2 Sep 1853	child bp; Jerome & Eliza Ann	3:150
Hubbel	Mary Louisa	7 Jan 1866	adm ch	3:63
Hubbel	William	30 Aug 1861	inf bp; Jerome & Eliza Ann	3:152

NAUGATUCK, CONNECTICUT, CONGREGATIONAL CHURCH RECORDS

Surname	Given Name	Date	Event	Ref
Hubbel	William Charles	2 Sep 1853	child bp; Jerome & Eliza Ann	3:150
Hubbel	Wm Charles	20 Sep 1854	d, son of Jerome & Eliza Ann, 9 y, dysentery, Gunntown	3:251
Hubbell	Alonzo Frederick	4 Jul 1858	adm ch	3:62
Hubbell	Carrie A.	- 1891	adm ch	3:21
Hubbell	Carrie M.	23 Nov 1899	20 marr Arthur Leach 26	3:228
Hubbell	Carrie May	- 1897	adm ch	3:23
Hubbell	Carrie May	4 Jul 1897	adm ch	3:72
Hubbell	Chas M.	29 Nov 1888	20 marr Alice Haverly 18	3:219
Hubbell	Eliza A.	23 Mar 1883	dism to M.E. Ch, Beacon Falls Ct	3:126
Hubbell	Flora E.	- 1880	adm ch, wife of Arthur	3:21
Hubbell	Flora E.	2 May 1880	adm fr Presb, Astoria NY	3:94
Hubbell	Grace Adele	5 Jul 1885	inf bp; Arthur & Flora E.	3:157
Hubbell	Hattee Louise	- 1897	adm ch	3:23
Hubbell	Hattie Louise	4 Jul 1897	adm ch	3:72
Hubbell	J.B.	23 Mar 1883	dism to M.E. Ch, Beacon Falls, Ct	3:126
Hubbell	Lucy E.	20 Feb 1898	20 marr Hiram A. Andrews 20	3:226
Hubbell	Lucy Eva	- 1897	adm ch	3:23
Hubbell	Lucy Eva	4 Jul 1897	adm ch	3:72
Hubbell	Marion E.	19 Oct 1892	17 marr Daniel W.A. Robey 29	3:222
Hubbell	Mary L.	24 Jan 1875	(Culver) dism to M.E. Ch, Beacon Falls	3:124
Hughes	Elizabeth	- 1890	Mrs., adm ch from Wales, England; dis 1890 Cleveland	3:21
Hughes	Elizabeth	5 Jan 1890	Mrs., adm from Wales-- Eng	3:96
Hughes	Elizabeth	- 1897	Mrs., adm ch from Cleveland; dis 1899 Wales	3:21
Hughes	Elizabeth	4 Jul 1897	Mrs, adm fr Jones Ave Cong, Cleveland O.	3:98
Hughes	Elizabeth	17 Nov 1899	Mrs., dism to Any Evan Church in [Scotland crossed out] Wales	3:129
Hughes	Harriet	- 1854	adm ch fr Prospect, w of Reuben; dis 1872 East Cong, New Haven	3:19
Hughes	Harriet	3 Sep 1854	w of R., adm fr Prospect [see Heughes]	3:90
Hughes	Margaretta	- 1897	adm ch	3:23
Hughes	Margretta	8 Sep 1897	23 marr Fredk Arthur Wood 24	3:225
Hughes	Reuben	- 1854	adm ch from Prospect; dis 1873 to Ch of Redeemer, New Haven	3:19
Hughes	Reuben	3 Sep 1854	adm fr Prospect	3:90
Hughs	Elizabeth	5 Sep 1890	Mrs, dism to Cleveland Ohio	3:127
Hughs	Elizabeth	6 Mar 1892	Mrs., adm ch fr Welsh Cong, Cleveland O.	3:97
Hughs	Elizabeth	26 Aug 1892	Mrs., dism to Cleveland O.	3:128
Hughs	James	- 1886	adm ch	3:21
Hughs	James	2 May 1886	Mrs., bp	3:158
Hughs	James	2 May 1886	adm ch	3:69
Hughs	Margaretta	4 Jul 1897	adm ch	3:72
Hughs	Mrs. Elizabeth	- 1892	adm ch from Cleveland O; dis 1892 to Cleveland O.	3:21
Hughs	R.B.	16 Feb 1873	dism to Ch of Redeemer, New Haven	3:124
Hughs	Vina	- 1886	adm ch, wife of James	3:21
Hughs	Vina	2 May 1886	Mrs., adm ch	3:69
Hull	A.G.	- -	husband of Emily M. Porter	3:36
Hull	Ami	18 Sep 1807	d, dau of Doct, 2y	1:158
Hull	Amos G.	- -	husband of Emily Margaret Porter	2:95
Hull	Amos Gift [sic]	4 Sep 1814	bp, inf ch of Amy wife of Doct	1:176
Hull	Amy	- 1800	adm ch, wife of Nimrod; dec 1818	3:17
Hull	Amy	14 Dec 1800	Doct., adm ch, d 1 Jan 1818	1:56
Hull	Amy	14 Dec 1800	wife of Nimrod, adm ch; died 1 Jan 1818	2:85
Hull	Amy	6 Apr 1806	bp, dau of Doctr	1:173
Hull	Anna	14 Dec 1800	wife of Dr. adm ch	1:20
Hull	Betsy	1 Nov 1801	marr Saml Thompson, both of this place	1:151
Hull	Elisabeth	4 Jan 1801	bp, ch of Nimrod	1:169
Hull	Elisabeth	- 1817	adm ch, wife of Ransom Culver; Irr 1844 Episcopal	3:18

NAUGATUCK, CONNECTICUT, CONGREGATIONAL CHURCH RECORDS

Surname	Given Name	Date	Notes	Ref
Hull	Elisebeth	16 Nov 1817	adm ch	1:57
Hull	Elizabeth	16 Nov 1817	wife of Ransom Culver, adm ch; withdrawn to Episcopal	2:88
Hull	Emily M.	14 Jan 1837	wife of Amos G., letter of dism to Cong ch in Danbury	2:20
Hull	Emma	26 Jul 1824	d, sythe cut artery in arm, 12	1:161
Hull	Hanah	19 May 1809	Wd, d	1:159
Hull	Hannah	- 1801	adm ch; dec 1807	3:17
Hull	Hannah	1 Feb 1801	Wd, adm ch; died 7 Aug 1807	2:86
Hull	Hannah	1 Feb 1801	widow, adm ch	1:20
Hull	Hannah	4 Feb 1801	Wid., adm ch, d 7 Aug 1807 [error; should be 1 Feb]	1:56
Hull	Hannah	27 Aug 1807	d, wid, 61y	1:158
Hull	Horace	13 Aug 1826	newborn ch d, 0	1:163
Hull	John Gould	4 Sep 1814	bp, inf ch of Amy wife of Doct	1:176
Hull	Laura	bef Jul 1812	bp, ch of Amy, wife of Doct.	1:175
Hull	Laurance Spencer	6 Nov 1808	bp, son of "Doter" Nimrod	1:174
Hull	Lawrence S.	18 Mar 1830	of Salem, marr Lucetta G. Porter of Middlebury	1:154
Hull	Mary	27 Nov 1823	of Salem, marr Gerry Lewis	1:152
Hull	Nancy	- 1817	adm ch, wife of Lewis Hine; dis 1828 to Cairo NY	3:18
Hull	Nancy	16 Nov 1817	wife of Lewis Hine, adm ch; rem 20 Mar 1828 to Cairo NY	2:88
Hull	Nancy	16 Nov 1817	adm ch, dism abt 1829	1:57
Hull	Nancy	19 Nov 1827	of Salem, marr Lewis Hine of Cairo NY	1:153
Hull	Nancy	20 Mar 1828	now Hine, rec to ch in Cairo NY	1:106
Hull	Nancy	- 1833	adm ch, wife of L.S. Lewis; dec 1881	3:18
Hull	Nancy	6 Jan 1833	wife of Lawrence S. Lewis, adm ch	2:93
Hull	Nancy (Hine)	- 1822	female, on list of members; dism	1:82
Hull	Nancy C.	23 Nov 1853	of Farmington marr Elias F. Merrell of Naug	3:201
Hull	Nimrod	26 Jan 1824	d, Doct. ["Joseph" crossed out], Angnor Pectoris, 51	1:161
Hull	Sally Nancy	17 May 1801	bp, ch of Nimrod	1:170
Hull	Spencer	27 Apr 1833	ch died, 6 mos.	2:114
Hunt	Joann A.	23 Nov 1862	dism to 2d Cong, Waterbury	3:122
Hunt	Joann Adeline	4 Jul 1858	adm ch	3:62
Hunt	Joanna A.	- 1858	adm ch; dis 1862 to 2d ch Waterbury	3:20
Hunter	Cora Della	4 Apr 1898	20 marr Geo Penman Young 22	3:226
Huntington	Abigail	- 1827	adm ch from Haddam; dec 1835	3:18
Huntington	Abigail	13 Aug 1827	w of Jonah ["Josiah"?], adm ch fr Haddam; died 18 Nov 1835	2:91
Huntington	Abigail	13 Aug 1827	adm ch	1:59a
Huntington	Abigail	13 Aug 1827	member, dau of Abigail	1:83
Huntington	Abigail	13 Aug 1827	member	1:83
Huntington	Abigail	13 Aug 1827	had planned to go to Rome; but adm ch from Haddam; w of Josiah	1:103
Huntington	Abigail	13 Aug 1827	had planned to go to Rome; but adm ch fr Haddam, dau of Josiah	1:103
Huntington	Abigail	18 Nov 1835	died, 87	2:115
Huntington	Abigail 2d	- 1827	adm ch from Haddam; dec 1835	3:18
Huntington	Abigail 2nd	13 Aug 1827	adm ch fr Haddam; died 12 May 1835	2:91
Huntington	Abigail 2nd	12 May 1835	died, 51	2:114
Huntington	Abigail Jr	13 Aug 1827	adm ch	1:59a
Huntington	Betsey	- 1836	adm ch, wife of Nathl S.; dis 1840 to New Milford	3:18
Huntington	Betsey	6 Mar 1836	bp, adult	2:105
Huntington	Betsy	6 Mar 1836	wife of Nathaniel, adm ch; dism 20 Jan 1840 to New Milford	2:95
Huntington	Jonah	- 1827	adm ch from Haddam; dec 1835 [name copied wrong from 59a?]	3:18
Huntington	Jonah	13 Aug 1827	adm ch from Haddam; died 29 Mar 1835 [could say "Josiah"]	2:91
Huntington	Josiah	13 Aug 1827	adm ch by letter [looks like Jonah but "i" is dotted]	1:59a
Huntington	Josiah	13 Aug 1827	had planned to go to Rome; but adm ch in Naugatuck from Haddam	1:103
Huntington	Josiah	19 Oct 1827	[sic] on 1822 annotated list of male members	1:81
Huntington	Josiah	29 Mar 1835	died, 88	2:114
Huntington	Maria G.	- 1837	adm ch; dis 1840 to New Milford	3:18

Huntington	Maria G.	5 Mar	1837	adm ch; rem 20 Jan 1840 to New Milford	2:96
Huntington	Mr.	7 Oct	1833	contributed $2 to "the foren M.S."	2:14
Huntington	Nath. G.	9 Oct	1836	appt'd delegate to Hamden	2:20
Huntington	Nathaniel	26 Oct	1834	chosen deacon	2:18
Huntington	Nathaniel G.	26 Oct	1834	Deacon, declined acting	2:79
Huntington	Nathaniel G.	25 Dec	1837	Rev., re dism of Sackett and app't of Lee to Consociat.	2:30
Huntington	Nathl, Mrs.	1 Apr	1838	SS Comm	2:32
Huntinton	G.H.	3 Aug	1834	Mr., appt'd delegate to Bethany	2:17
Hurd	-	13 Aug	1828	ch d, dysentery, 1	1:144
Hyne	Laury	10 Mar	1801	ch of Ziba, d, aged 6m 1d	1:155
Isabel[sic]	Mr.[sic]	21 Jun	1820	died, aged 29	1:87
Isbell	H.	-	-	husband of Lillian Spring	3:46
Isbell	Howard L.	10 Aug	1892	27 marr Lilian Spring 20	3:222
Isbell	Maud	-	-	see Berger	-
Ives	Ellen A.	-	1880	Mrs., adm ch from Newtown Ct; dis 1888 to Cheshire	3:23
Ives	Ellen A.	5 Mar	1880	Mrs, adm fr Cong, Newtown Ct	3:94
Ives	Ellen A.	21 Dec	1888	Mrs., dism to Cong, Cheshire Ct	3:127
Jalabson	Elma	16 Mar	1895	26 marr Emil Sandin 26	3:223
Jenner	Frank E.	2 Aug	1899	21 marr Mattie Mellen 25	3:227
Jenner	Geo Edward	11 Jun	1899	inf bp; Geo A. & Ida Schwartz	3:164
Jenner	Kate E.	4 Sep	1892	adm ch	3:70
Jenner	Kate Elizabeth	-	1892	adm ch; dec 1897	3:22
Jenner	Kate Elizabeth	27 Sep	1897	d, typhoid	3:261
Jenners	Frank Edward	1 Dec	1895	bp, adult	3:161
Jenners	Geo A.	1 Dec	1895	bp, adult	3:161
Jenners	Gladys Mary	1 Dec	1895	inf bp; Geo A. & Ida Swartz ["Ida"written over "Idde"]	3:161
Jenners	Minnie Lettie	1 Dec	1895	bp, adult	3:161
Jennings	-	-	-	husband of Caroline B. Curtiss	3:9
Jennings	Ralph R.	1 Apr	1886	25 marr Carrie B. Curtiss 21, both of Naug	3:217
Jennings	Raymond M.	6 Nov	1887	an inf, bp	3:158
Jewett	Edward	15 Jun	1854	of Newburyport Mass marr Jane A. Dougal of Naug	3:201
Johnson	Adam	-	-	husband of Kissock Locke	3:26
Johnson	Adam	9 Sep	1855	Mrs., adm from Kelton Manse, Scotland (m.n. Kissock Locke)	3:90
Johnson	Adam William	10 Apr	1856	inf bp; Adam & Kissock	3:151
Johnson	Benj	14 Jan	1896	26 marr Venda [sic] C. Bodin 17	3:224
Johnson	Chauncy	15 Nov	1824	ch d, fever, 2	1:162
Johnson	Christine	17 Jun	1893	30 marr Peter Solomonson 35	3:223
Johnson	Edward Hall	1 Aug	1869	ch bp; J.E. & Sarah C.	3:155
Johnson	Emmie Elvira	28 Jun	1893	an inf, bp	3:160
Johnson	Etta	-	1892	Mrs., adm ch from Stettsville Pa; erased 1900	3:22
Johnson	Etta	28 Oct	1892	Mrs., adm fr Pres, Stettsville Pa	3:97
Johnson	Eunice	4 Sep	1825	d, debility, 39	1:163
Johnson	Harriet	24 Nov	1825	of Middlebury, marr Benjamin Grinnels of Litchfield	1:152
Johnson	Herbert Newton	1 Aug	1869	ch bp; J.E. & Sarah C.	3:155
Johnson	J.E.	4 Mar	1877	dism to Waterbury, 2nd Cong	3:125
Johnson	Jesse	23 Sep	1874	bur, 45	3:257
Johnson	John E.	-	1864	adm ch from Waterbury; dis 1877 to 2nd Cong Waterbury	3:22
Johnson	John Edward	4 Sep	1864	adm fr Sec Cong, Waterbury	3:92
Johnson	Julia May	9 May	1897	inf bp; Benjamin & Lena [sic]	3:162
Johnson	Lorien	-	1860	adm ch; dec 1862	3:22
Johnson	Lorien	1 Jan	1860	adm ch	3:62
Johnson	Lorien	2 Apr	1862	d, 28, diphtheria	3:253
Johnson	Louisa E.	-	1857	adm ch; care withdrawn 1885	3:22
Johnson	Louisa E.	1 Mar	1857	adm ch	3:61

NAUGATUCK, CONNECTICUT, CONGREGATIONAL CHURCH RECORDS

Johnson	Louisa Emma Jane	1 Mar	1857	bp, adult	3:151
Johnson	Margarett	-	1885	adm ch, wife of Niels; dis 1889 Swede Naug	3:22
Johnson	Margarett	5 Jul	1885	adm ch	3:68
Johnson	Mary	20 Jan	1802	marr Jehiel Castle, both of Woodbridge	1:151
Johnson	Mary J.	15 Sep	1851	marr George F. Richardson, both of Middlebury	3:200
Johnson	Mary Jane	1 Apr	1858	of Middlebury marr George Camp of New Milford, both colored	3:203
Johnson	Mary Jane	16 Jun	1864	of Seymour marr Obadiah Warner of Naug	3:206
Johnson	Neil	13 Apr	1882	marr Margaret Manyberry [sic], both of Naug	3:214
Johnson	Neils	-	1885	adm ch; dis 1889 to Swede Naug	3:22
Johnson	Neils	5 Jul	1885	adm ch	3:68
Johnson	Neils	29 Nov	1889	and wife to Swedish Ch, Naugatuck	3:127
Johnson	Sarah C.	-	1864	adm ch from Waterbury, wife of John E.; dec 1871	3:22
Johnson	Sarah Cornelia	4 Sep	1864	w of John Edward, adm fr Sec Cong Waterbury	3:92
Johnson	Theodotia	26 Nov	1826	of Salem, marr Silas Gunn	1:153
Johnson	W.S.	1 Nov	1890	24 marr Mary Waldon 23	3:221
Jones	Annie Esther	-	1896	adm ch	3:22
Jones	Annie Esther	1 Mar	1896	adm ch	3:71
Jones	Annie Esther	22 Feb	1896	bp, adult, immersed in Waterbury	3:162
Jones	Annie Jenkins	-	1896	adm ch, wife of James	3:22
Jones	Annie Jenkins	1 Mar	1896	wife of James, adm ch	3:71
Jones	Arthur E.	18 Nov	1882	marr Alice G. Hotchkiss, both of Naug	3:214
Jones	Chas Henry	1 Jul	1900	inf bp; Elbert Henry & Alice (Palmer)	3:165
Jones	Eliza		1822	female, member adm since 1822	1:83
Jones	Eliza	-	1828	adm ch, wife of Henry; exc 1837	3:22
Jones	Eliza	4 May	1828	wife of Henry Judd, adm ch; excomm 3 Feb 1837	2:92
Jones	Eliza	4 May	1828	adm ch	1:59a
Jones	Eliza	4 May	1828	adult, bp	1:87
Jones	Eliza	4 May	1828	adm ch, baptised	1:106
Jones	Eliza	20 Mar	1828	propounded for adm	1:106
Jones	Eliza	3 Feb	1837	now Eliza Judd; disregards covenants, cut off	2:23
Jones	Elvira M.	-	1894	adm ch from W. Winsted; dec 1898	3:22
Jones	Elvira M.	6 May	1894	adm fr 2nd Cong, Winsted	3:97
Jones	Elvira M.	23 Mar	1898	d, 64, cancer	3:261
Jones	Eva	14 Feb	1878	marr Wilson J. Wimple, both of Naug	3:212
Jones	George	9 Jun	1837	ch died, 4 m	2:115
Jones	Isaac V.	30 Oct	1899	29 marr Carrie L. Bradley 29	3:227
Jones	James	-	1896	adm ch	3:22
Jones	James	1 Mar	1896	adm ch	3:71
Jones	James		1897	appt'd Deacon 1897	3:1
Jones	Jane E.	23 Jun	1829	marr Henry Judd, both of Waterbury [see Eliza Jones]	1:153
Jones	Josie	27 Nov	1895	28 marr Geo F. Kreamer 32	3:224
Jones	Laura	-	1828	adm ch; dec 1890 [crossed out?]	3:22
Jones	Laura	4 Jul	1828	adm ch	1:59b
Jones	Laura	6 Jul	1828	adm ch	2:93
Jones	Laura	6 Jul	1828	adult, bp	1:87
Jones	Laura	6 Jul	1828	member	1:94
Jones	Laura	6 Jul	1828	adm ch	1:107
Jones	Laura	Jun	1890	d (in hospital Hartford) [whole entry crossed out]	3:260
Jones	Mark Elbert	1 Jul	1900	inf bp; Elbert Henry & Alice (Palmer)	3:165
Jones	W.	-	-	husband of Jane L. Yale	3:59
Jones	Walter	Apr	1890	Mrs, d, at hospital in Hartford, rheumatism	3:260
Judd	Amer	Jul	1822	"wd" died, aged 87	1:87
Judd	Amer	Jul	1822	d, 87	1:161
Judd	Aner	-	1784	adm ch, wife of Isaac; dec 1822	3:22

NAUGATUCK, CONNECTICUT, CONGREGATIONAL CHURCH RECORDS

Judd	Aner	Sep	1784	wife of Isaac, adm ch; died Jul 1822	2:82
Judd	Anna	-	1876	adm ch, wife of Frank Gunn; dec 1890	3:22
Judd	Anna	7 May	1876	adm ch	3:65
Judd	Anna M.	20 Oct	1886	28 marr Franklin L. Gunn 28, both of Naug	3:217
Judd	Annar	?	1784	wife of Isaac adm ch	1:7
Judd	Anner	Sep	1784	Is., adm ch, d July 1822	1:53
Judd	Betty	-	1786	adm ch, wife of Eben; dis 1806 to Cornwall Vt.	3:22
Judd	Betty	23 Apr	1786	wife of Ebenezer, adm ch; rem 13 Apr 1806 to Cornwall, VT.	2:83
Judd	Betty	23 Apr	1786	wife of Ebenezer adm ch	1:10
Judd	Betty	23 Apr	1786	Eb["enezer" added] adm ch, dism 13 Apr 1806	1:54
Judd	Charlotte A.	16 Jun	1851	of Naug marr Joel Keeler of Bridgeport	3:200
Judd	Chloe	-	1818	adm ch; dec	3:22
Judd	Choncey	24 Feb	1823	d, sudden, 59	1:161
Judd	Cloe	May	1818	bp	1:61
Judd	Cloe	3 May	1818	adm ch; died	2:89
Judd	Cloe	3 May	1818	adm ch	1:59
Judd	Ebenezer	-	1800	adm ch; dis 1806 to Cornwall Vt.	3:22
Judd	Ebenezer	7 Jun	1800	adm ch; rem 13 Apr 1806 to Cornwall VT	2:85
Judd	Ebenezer	7 Jun	1800	adm ch, dism 13 Apr 1806	1:55
Judd	Ebenezer	13 Apr	1806	and wife, letter of rec to ch in Cornwill [sic] VT	1:39
Judd	Ebenr	7 Jun	1800	adm ch	1:15
Judd	Electa	31 Jan	1825	of Salem, marr John W. Bigalow	1:152
Judd	Eliza	3 Feb	1837	formerly Jones; disregards covenants, cut off	2:23
Judd	Eliza	5 Feb	1837	sentence of excommunication publicly read	2:24
Judd	Emily	-	1876	adm ch, wife of Franklin; dec 1881	3:22
Judd	Emily	3 Sep	1876	w of Franklin J., adm fr 2nd Cong, Waterbury	3:93
Judd	Emily	1 Jan	1881	d, Mrs. Franklin, 53, congestion of brain	3:258
Judd	Esther	3 Jan	1802	of Salem, marr Samuel Peck of Woodbridge	1:151
Judd	Eunice	-	1828	adm ch, wife of Larman Lewis; dec 1884	3:22
Judd	Eunice	4 Jul	1828	adm ch	1:59b
Judd	Eunice	6 Jul	1828	adm ch	2:92
Judd	Eunice	6 Jul	1828	adult, bp	1:87
Judd	Eunice	6 Jul	1828	member	1:94
Judd	Eunice	6 Jul	1828	adm ch	1:107
Judd	Harvey	25 Dec	1800	of this, marr Jemima Hickox of 1st Waterbury	1:151
Judd	Harvey	25 Jul	1825	ch d, diabetes, 6	1:163
Judd	Henry	23 Jun	1829	marr Jane E. Jones, both of Waterbury	1:153
Judd	Isaac	-	1785	adm ch; dec 1808	3:22
Judd	Isaac	16 Oct	1785	adm ch; died 9 Jun 1808	2:82
Judd	Isaac	16 Oct	1785	adm ch	1:10
Judd	Isaac	16 Oct	1785	adm ch, d 9 Jun 1808	1:54
Judd	Isaac	14 Sep	1801	on committee	1:24
Judd	Isaac	9 Jun	1808	d, 81y	1:159
Judd	Jemimah	1 Nov	1803	d, wife of Hervey, 25y	1:156
Judd	Larmen[sic]	5 Dec	1827	ch stillborn [not Lucian Judd whose ch was recorded just below]	1:144
Judd	Lois	-	1818	adm ch, wife of B. Candee; Irr 1834 Episcopal	3:22
Judd	Lois	15 Mar	1818	w of Bird Candee, adm ch; withdrawn 19 Dec 1834 to Episcopal	2:89
Judd	Lois	15 Mar	1818	wife of Bird Condee, adm ch	1:59
Judd	Lois	15 Mar	1818	bp	1:60
Judd	Lois	-	1822	female, on list of members [crossed out (out of alph. order)]	1:82
Judd	Lucian	28 Dec	1827	ch d, 6 months	1:144
Judd	Mary E.	8 Jun	1853	of Naug marr James Shaw of Smith Falls (now Easton) Canada	3:201
Judd	Minnie A.	-	1883	adm ch	3:22
Judd	Minnie A.	6 May	1883	adm ch	3:67

NAUGATUCK, CONNECTICUT, CONGREGATIONAL CHURCH RECORDS

Surname	Given	Date	Event	Ref
Judd	Ninnie Alida	6 May 1883	bp, adult; Franklin & Emily J.	3:157
Judd	Walter	2 Apr 1833	died, 74	2:114
Judd	Wid	7 Sep 1827	d, fever, 56	1:144
Judson	Stiles	18 Apr 1864	d, "funeral...Stratford"	3:254
June	Wallace	9 Sep 1872	marr Eliza Keman, both of Naug	3:209
Kahl	Christine Ziegler	4 Dec 1896	dism to 2nd ch, Waterbury	3:128
Kahl	Fred W.	19 Jun 1895	26 marr Christine Zeigler 23	3:224
Kane	S. Louise	- 1893	Mrs, adm ch from Watertown NY; dis 1895 to New Castle	3:24
Kane	S. Louise	5 Nov 1893	Mrs., adm fr Presb, Watertown NY	3:97
Kane	T.F.	- 1894	adm ch; dis 1895 to New Castle	3:24
Kane	T.F.	6 May 1894	adm ch	3:71
Kane	T.F.	20 Sep 1895	dism to New Castle Pa; also wife	3:128
Katick	-	- 1877	see Cerrick	2:258
Kattech	-	- -	see Kohn, Charles	-
Keach	Anna Maria Amelia	22 Feb 1900	41 marr Millard Filmore Mills 36	3:228
Keeler	Joel	16 Jun 1851	of Bridgeport marr Charlotte A. Judd of Naug	3:200
Kellar	Rosa Elizabeth	29 Jul 1888	an inf, bp	3:159
Keller	Eva Elizabeth	24 Jul 1891	an inf, bp	3:160
Keller	Frank Friedrich	24 Jul 1891	an inf, bp	3:160
Keller	Louisa	10 Oct 1886	an inf, bp	3:158
Kellog	Bela	29 Apr 1817	Rev. Elder at Council re Rev. Dodd's removal	1:74
Kellogg	Harriet	9 Nov 1854	of Middlebury marr Stiles M. Hine of Naug	3:202
Kelly	Robert C.	27 Nov 1868	of Meriden marr Henrietta Gunn of Naugatuck	3:208
Keman	Eliza	9 Sep 1872	marr Wallace June, both of Naug	3:209
Kennedy	William	4 Jun 1871	of New York marr Bridget Grenman of Waterbury	3:209
Kenney	Mary E.	6 Apr 1862	her inf dau d, 2 ms, Hillside	3:253
Kenyan	Abbie F.	9 Jan 1868	Mrs, of Westerly RI marr Andrew Warner of Naug	3:208
Kerston	Mattie	15 Oct 1877	marr George Corker, both of Southington	3:212
Kervan	Sarah E.	10 Jun 1868	of Williamsburg NY marr Enos B. Blackman of Middlebury in	3:208
-	-	- -	Middlebury	-
Kilborn	Emelina	- 1851	adm ch fr Litchfield, w of Truman; dis 1855 to 1st ch Waterbury	3:24
Kilborn	Emeline	1 Apr 1855	w of T[ruman] dism to 1st Cong, Waterbury	3:120
Kilborn	Emmeline	6 Jul 1851	w of Truman, adm ch fr 1st ch, Litchfield	3:90
Kilborn	Truman	- 1851	adm ch from Litchfield; dis 1855 to 1st ch Waterbury	3:24
Kilborn	Truman	6 Jul 1851	Deacon, adm ch fr 1st ch, Litchfield	3:90
Kilborn	Truman	1 Apr 1855	dism to 1st Cong, Waterbury	3:120
Killar	Amaria Ida	1 Jun 1891	an inf, bp	3:160
Killer	Jennie Mary	2 Jul 1882	an inf, bp	3:156
Killer	Nellie Lena	1 Jun 1884	an inf, bp	3:157
Kimberly	Widow	16 Nov 1802	d, 88y 6m 6d	1:155
King	James	2 Nov 1869	of Bethany marr Mrs. Sara Pardee of Naug	3:208
Kinney	Mary E.	- 1860	adm ch fr Westville Ct, w of Martin; dis 1885 to Westville	3:24
Kinney	Mary E.	1 Jul 1860	adm fr Cong, Westville Ct.	3:91
Kinney	Mary E.	2 Jan 1885	dism to Cong, Westville Conn	3:126
Kirk	Andrew Briggs	Sep 1885	bp	3:158
Kirk	Bessie May	10 Jun 1900	inf bp; John & Emma (Miller)	3:165
Kirk	Betsy	- 1876	adm ch from Fairfield, wife of John	3:24
Kirk	Betsy	2 Jan 1876	adm fr 1st Cong, Fairfield, Ct	3:93
Kirk	Chas Alexander	3 Jul 1881	inf bp; John & Betsy Kirk	3:156
Kirk	John	- 1876	adm ch from Fairfield	3:24
Kirk	John	2 Jan 1876	adm fr 1st Cong, Fairfield, Ct	3:93
Kirk	Lena Elizabeth	12 Jun 1898	inf bp; John R. & Emma Miller	3:163
Kirk	Louis Ross	23 Dec 1894	bp; John Jr	3:161
Kirk	Mary	11 Jun 1876	ch bp; John	3:155

NAUGATUCK, CONNECTICUT, CONGREGATIONAL CHURCH RECORDS

Surname	Given	Date	Entry	Ref
Kirk	Sarah	2 Jun 1899	21 marr Fred Curtiss 18	3:227
Kirk	Sarah Thompson	29 Dec 1878	inf bp; John	3:156
Kirlkers[?]	Steve	15 Dec 1895	22 marr Clara Sotter 22	
Kleps	Amelia	22 Mar 1897	inf bp; Chas & Amelia (twin)	3:162
Kleps	Charles	4 Jul 1896	inf bp; Charles & Amelia	3:162
Kleps	Edward	8 Mar 1890	an inf, bp	3:159
Kleps	Ferdinand	22 Nov 1888	an inf, bp	3:159
Kleps	Helena Maria	19 Nov 1898	inf bp; Louis W. & Annie Wacker	3:163
Kleps	Martha	4 Jul 1896	inf bp; Charles & Amelia	3:162
Kleps	Rosa Amanda	26 Feb 1898	inf bp; Chas & Amelia	3:163
Kleps	William	22 Mar 1897	inf bp; Chas & Amelia (twin)	3:162
Kling	Charles	17 Dec 1899	21 marr Cndwin [sic] Andrews 23	3:228
Klump	Charles A.	23 Apr 1864	marr Adeline Michael, both of Naugatuck	3:205
Klump	Charles Henry	26 Nov 1866	ch bp; Mr. & Mrs. Klump, German	3:154
Klump	George Albert	19 Oct 1868	ch bp; Mr. & Mrs. Klump (German)	3:154
Klump	Minnie Adeline	26 Nov 1866	ch bp; Mr. & Mrs. Klump, German	3:154
Knoor[?]	Emma	24 Nov 1898	20 marr Harry Lee 21	3:226
Knox	Fred'k E.	23 Jan 1879	watch and care withdrawn; also for wife	3:125
Knox	Frederick E.	- 1876	adm ch from Pres Warsaw NY, with wife; care withdrawn 1879	3:24
Knox	Frederick E.	7 May 1876	adm fr 1st Presb, Warsaw NY; also wife	3:93
Knox	Sarepta [sic]	3 Dec 1880	dism to Cong, Stratford	3:125
Knox	Serepta	- 1876	adm ch fr Northfield Ct, w of Geo W; dis 1880 to Stratford Ct	3:24
Knox	Serepta	7 May 1876	w of Geo W., adm fr Cong, Northfield, Ct	3:93
Kohn	Annie Gertrude	31 Aug 1898	inf bp; Daniel & Katie	3:163
Kohn	Charles	10 Jun 1900	inf bp; Daniel & Kattie (Kattech)	3:165
Kohn	Frederick Wm	13 Jul 1899	inf bp; Daniel & Katie	3:164
Kreamer	Geo F.	27 Nov 1895	32 marr Josie Jones 28	3:224
Kreamer	Hazel Marian	9 May 1897	inf bp; Geo F. & Josephine	3:162
Krell	George	- 1887	adm ch from Mahaney City Pa	3:24
Krell	George	3 Jul 1887	adm fr Reformed Ch, Mahaney City Pa	3:96
Krell	Katie	- 1887	adm ch from Mahaney City Pa	3:24
Krell	Katie	3 Jul 1887	adm fr Reformed Ch, Mahaney City Pa	3:96
Krell	Martha	- 1887	adm ch from Mahaney City Pa	3:24
Krell	Martha	3 Jul 1887	adm fr Reformed Ch, Mahaney City Pa	3:96
Kuchenburg	Emma H.	12 Dec 1883	marr Geo P. Tallmadge, both of Naug	3:216
Kurreck	Antone	23 Mar 1851	of Naug marr Catharine Wirgand of Port Chester NY	3:200
Kurtz	--	19 Feb 1858	d, inf son of Mr. & Mrs, (German), 1 month	3:252
Kurtz	John	20 Sep 1866	ch bp, Mr. & Mrs. Kurtz, German	3:154
Kurtz	Leonart	20 Sep 1866	ch bp, Mr. & Mrs Kurtz, German	3:154
Kutze	Elizabeth	14 Jun 1870	marr Phillip Cwick [sic], both of Naug	3:209
Kydd	George Wright	2 Jan 1887	an inf, bp	3:158
Ladd	Theo S.	28 Oct 1866	dism to Cong, Seymour	3:123
Ladd	Theodore S.	- 1858	adm ch from Rockville; dis 1866 to Seymour	3:26
Ladd	Theodore S.	4 Jul 1858	adm fr 1st Cong, Rockville Ct	3:91
LaFayette	Theo E.	- 1887	adm ch from Boston Mass, erased 1900	3:27
LaFayette	Theo E.	3 Jul 1887	adm fr Park St Ch, Boston Mass	3:96
Lang	Mary Ann	- 1840	adm ch fr Waterbury, w of M. Lines; dis 1849 to Humpeville	3:25
Lang	Mary Ann	12 Jul 1840	adm ch fr Waterbury; w of -- Lines; dism 7 Aug 1849 to Humphrysville	2:97
Langdon	Grace	7 Jul 1882	Miss, adm fr Cong, No. Canaan Ct	3:95
Langdon	Grace	- 1883	adm ch from No. Canaan Ct, wife of F. Payne	3:27
Langdon	Grace	4 Jun 1890	28 marr J. Fred Payne 32	3:221
Langdon	J.P.	- 1851	adm ch; dis 1855 to New Brunswick NJ	3:26
Langdon	James Pierpont	6 Jul 1851	adm ch	3:60

Langdon	Jas P.	1 Apr	1855	dism to 1st Presb, New Brunswick NJ	3:120
Langdon	William H.	2 Oct	1856	d, 5 1/2, scarlet fever, Hillside	3:251
Lanson	Wm A.	22 Feb	1883	marr Marion W. Thompson, both of Naug	3:215
Larsch	Daniel	6 Apr	1889	marr Margarette Becker	3:220
Lates	Clara Belle	3 Mar	1889	an inf, bp	3:159
Lates	Fanny Eliza	3 Mar	1889	an inf, bp	3:159
Lattice	Fredk D.	2 May	1894	33 marr Carrie A. Hine 33	3:223
Lavine	Lottie	May	1895	bp, adult	3:161
Lavine	Lottie H.	-	1895	adm ch, wife of Chas	3:27
Lavine	Lottie H.	6 May	1895	wife of Chas L., adm ch	3:71
Lawrence	Edw A	17 Jul	1853	dism to Cong, Stamford	3:120
Lawrence	Edwd A.	-	1852	adm ch from New Ipswich; dis 1853 to Stamford	3:26
Lawrence	Edwd A.	2 May	1852	adm from 1st Cong, New Ipswich NH	3:90
Lawrence	Joanna P.	-	1852	adm ch fr New Ipswich, w of Edwd A.; dis 1853 to Stamford	3:26
Lawrence	Joanna P.	2 May	1852	w of E.A., adm fr 1st Cong, New Ipswich NH	3:90
Lawrence	Joanna P.	17 Jul	1853	[wife of] Edw A., dism to Cong, Stamford	3:120
Lawrence	Lucy Maria	2 Jul	1852	inf bp, Edwd A. & Joanna P.	3:150
Lawson	Lena	-	1891	adm ch; dis 1892 Swede ch	3:27
Lawson	Lena	1 Mar	1891	Miss, adm ch	3:70
Lawson	Lena	15 Jan	1892	dism to Swede Ch, Naug	3:127
Lawton	J.W.	-	1861	adm ch from Longmeadow; dis 1867 to 1st Pres Syracuse NY	3:26
Lawton	J.W.	3 Nov	1861	adm fr 1st Ch, Longmeadow	3:91
Lawton	J.W.	24 Dec	1867	dism to 1st Presb, Syracuse NY	3:123
Leach	Arthur	1 Aug	1897	bp, adult; [prob. at chapel in Millville]	3:163
Leach	Arthur	23 Nov	1899	26 marr Carrie M. Hubbell 20	3:228
Leavenworth	Mark	22 Feb	1781	supervised organization of ch [see Levenworth]	1:6
Lee	Chauncey G.	10 Dec	1837	voted to be invited to become pastor of this church	2:29
Lee	Chauncey G.	7 Jun	1840	parted with the church in peace, salary overdue, no house	2:34
Lee	Chauncey G.	3 Jan	1841	Rev., letter of recommendation	2:35
Lee	Chauncy G.	10 Jan	1838	Rev., installed Pastor	2:30
Lee	Harry	24 Nov	1898	21 marr Emma Knoor[?] 20	3:226
Lee	Lucia	-	1839	adm ch fr East Windsor, w of Rev. C.G.; dis 1841 to New Haven	3:25
Lee	Lucia	19 May	1839	w of Rev. C.G. adm ch fr East Windsor; dism 12 Dec 184- to	2:97
-	-	-	-	N. Haven	-
Lee	Lucia	12 Dec	1841	Mrs, dism to 3rd ch in New Haven	2:39
Leggett	Alida	-	1876	adm ch; wife of G.M. Allerton; erased 1900	3:26
Leggett	Alida	7 May	1876	adm ch	3:65
Leggett	Anna M.	-	1870	adm ch from Peacedale RI; dec 1878	3:26
Leggett	Anna M.	3 Jul	1870	adm fr Cong, Peacedale RI	3:92
Leggett	Anna Maria Ogden	7 May	1878	d, widow of late Reuben Leggett, 63, paralysis	3:258
Leggett	Anna Ogden	-	1875	adm ch; dec 1876	3:26
Leggett	Anna Ogden	4 Jul	1875	adm ch	3:65
Leggett	Anna Ogden	11 Jul	1876	d, 18, fever at Elizabethport NJ, Hillside	3:257
Leggett	Esther G.	-	1880	adm ch from St. Peters Phoenixville Pa; erased 1900	3:27
Leggett	Esther G.	2 Jan	1880	Miss, adm fr St Peters Episcopal, Phoenixville Pa	3:94
Leggett	Mary Alida	24 Jan	1877	of Naug marr George M. Allerton	3:211
Leggett	Reuben	-	1878	his widow d [see Anna Maria Ogden]	3:258
Lehee	Chas Ernest	28 Oct	1888	an inf, bp	3:159
Lehee	Mary Elizabeth	20 Jan	1891	an inf, bp	3:160
Leineweber[?]	Bessie	6 Mar	1898	Mrs., adm fr Phillips Cong, Boston Mass	3:98
Leinweber	Bessie	-	1898	Mrs., adm ch from Boston; dis 1899 to Middlebury	3:27
Leinweber	Bessie	25 Aug	1899	dism to Cong, Middlebury	3:129
Lemburner	Jennett	11 Jul	1841	bp, adult	2:106
Lent	Catharine	-	1860	adm ch, w of Robert; dis 1875 D. Reform Glasco NY [not rec	3:26

NAUGATUCK, CONNECTICUT, CONGREGATIONAL CHURCH RECORDS

Surname	Given	Date	Note	Ref
-	-	-	under Dismissions]	-
Lent	Catharine	4 Nov 1860	w of --, adm fr Methodist Prot, Matteawan	3:91
Leonard	Helen	1879	Miss, adm ch from Seymour; dis 1884 to Orange Valley NJ	3:26
Leonard	Helen	Nov 1879	Miss, adm fr 1st Cong, Seymour Ct	3:94
Leonard	Helen	16 Nov 1884	Miss, dism to Orange Valley Cong, NJ	3:126
Leonard	Max	1 Jul 1888	23 marr May Ida Kingst 21	3:218
Leonard	S.C.	1879	Mrs, adm ch fr Seymour, w of Rev. S.C.; dis 1884 Orange Valley NY	3:26
Leonard	S.C.	1879	Rev., adm ch from Rushville NY; dis 1884 to Orange Valley NY	3:26
Leonard	S.C.	Nov 1879	Rev., adm fr 1st Cong, Rushville NY	3:94
Leonard	S.C.	Nov 1879	Mrs., adm fr 1st Cong, Seymour Ct	3:94
Leonard	S.C.	1 May 1879	settled as Pastor; dism 1 Sep 1884	3:1
Leonard	S.C.	16 Nov 1884	Rev. and wife dism to Orange Valley Cong, NJ	3:126
Lersch	Harry	24 Jan 1891	an inf, bp	3:160
Lersch	Marguerita	11 Aug 1895	inf bp; Daniel L. & Marguerita	3:161
Levenworth	Mark	22 Feb 1781	one of ministers constituting the church, fr Waterbury	2:79
-	-	-	[see Leavenworth]	-
Lewis	A. Glenford	3 Apr 1896	dism to Cong Ch, Ansonia	3:128
Lewis	A.H.	-	husband of Harriet N. Horton	3:19
Lewis	A.H.	-	husband of Harriet N. Horton	2:97
Lewis	A.H.	3 Oct 1841	delegate to Woodbridge	2:38
Lewis	Abagil	7 Oct 1833	Miss, rec'd by letter from Jefferson, Schoherrie Co., NY	2:14
Lewis	Abigail	-	1822 wife of Saml, member	1:82
Lewis	Abigail	1833	adm ch fr Jefferson NY, w of Saml; dis 1840 to Thompson NY	3:25
Lewis	Abigail	Nov 1833	w of Samuel, adm ch fr Jefferson NY; rem 3 Feb 1840 Thompson NY	2:94
Lewis	Abigail S.	- 1786	adm ch, wife of Saml S.; dec 1841	3:25
Lewis	Abigail S.	30 Jul 1786	wife of Samuel S.L., adm ch; died 28 Oct 1841	2:83
Lewis	Abigail S.	30 Jul 1786	Sam., adm ch	1:54
Lewis	Abigal	30 Jul 1786	wife of Samuel Smith Lewis adm ch	1:10
Lewis	Abraham	- 1789	adm ch; dis to Waterbury	3:25
Lewis	Abraham	19 Sep 1789	adm ch; rem to Waterbury [actually adm 1790, see p. 1:12]	2:84
Lewis	Abraham	29 Sep 1789	adm ch, dism [date copied wrong, should be 19 Sep 1790]	1:55
Lewis	Abram	19 Sep 1790	adm ch	1:12
Lewis	Albert Glenford	- 1891	adm ch from New Britain; dis 1896 to Ansonia	3:27
Lewis	Albert Glenford	6 Sep 1891	adm fr 1st Cong, New Britain Ct	3:97
Lewis	Albert Harris	18 Jun 1826	ch of Seldon & Lockey, bp	1:86
Lewis	Albert N.	- 1866	adm ch; dis 1871 Central Cong, New Britain	3:26
Lewis	Albert N.	2 Sep 1866	adm ch	3:63
Lewis	Albert Newell	- 1848	bp, ch of Ashael	2:108
Lewis	Amelia	- 1843	adm ch, wife of -- Platt; dis 1852 to Waterbury	3:25
Lewis	Amelia	14 May 1843	adm ch; [m] -- Platt	2:99
Lewis	Amelia Maria	18 Jun 1826	ch of Seldon & Lockey, bp	1:86
Lewis	Amzi	9 Jun 1809	Rev, proposed plan to obtain a candidate for trial	1:49
Lewis	Ancil	3 Sep 1819	and wife and dau adm ch	1:59
Lewis	Ann	22 Oct 1860	of Derby marr Frederick A. Allen of Hamden	3:204
Lewis	Anna	- 1813	adm ch, wife of Ezra; dec 1859	3:25
Lewis	Anna	16 May 1813	wife of Ezra, adm ch	2:87
Lewis	Anna	16 May 1813	Ez., adm ch	1:57
Lewis	Anna	16 May 1813	wife of Ezra, adm ch	1:67
Lewis	Anna	30 Apr 1813	wife of Ezra, cand for memb	1:67
Lewis	Anna	- 1822	wife of Ezra, member	1:82
Lewis	Anna	2 Mar 1859	d, 89, Hillside	3:252
Lewis	Ansel	- 1819	adm ch from Waterbury; dis 1840 to Thompson NY	3:25
Lewis	Ansel	3 Sep 1819	adm ch fr Waterbury; rem 3 Feb 1840 to N. Fork, Thompson,	2:91

NAUGATUCK, CONNECTICUT, CONGREGATIONAL CHURCH RECORDS

-	-	-	-	Broom Co.	-
Lewis	Ansel	-	1822	male, on list of members	1:81
Lewis	Asahe [sic] H.	8 Oct	1843	delegate to Bethany	2:47
Lewis	Asahel	5 Oct	1808	d, 36y	1:159
Lewis	Asahel	5 May	1837	SS secretary	2:25
Lewis	Asahel	1 Apr	1838	SS Librarian, Secretary, Treasurer	2:32
Lewis	Asahel H.	-	1836	adm ch; dec 1895 [see Lewiz]	3:25
Lewis	Asahel H.	3 Jan	1836	adm ch	2:95
Lewis	Asahel H.	3 Jan	1836	bp, adult	2:105
Lewis	Asahel H.	7 Oct	1837	on comm	2:27
Lewis	Asahel H.	15 Nov	1840	delegate to North Milford	2:35
Lewis	Asahel H.	1 Nov	1895	d, 88, old age	3:260
Lewis	Asel	10 May	1841	on comm	2:37
Lewis	Ashael	29 Mar	1846	delegate to Hamden Mt. Carmel	2:53
Lewis	Belle L.	22 Feb	1883	marr Geo H. Post, both of Naug	3:215
Lewis	Bethiah Elizabeth	29 Apr	1838	bp, ch of Samuel	2:105
Lewis	Burrit	14 May	1843	adm ch; dism 12 Mar 1849 to Waterby	2:99
Lewis	Burritt	-	1843	adm ch; dis 1849 to Waterbury	3:25
Lewis	Burritt Horton	18 Jun	1826	ch of Seldon & Lockey, bp	1:86
Lewis	Candace	-	1822	female, on list of members	1:82
Lewis	Caroline	31 Oct	1822	ch of Mylo, bp	1:85
Lewis	Catharine	-	1843	adm ch, wife of Wm B.; dec 1888	3:25
Lewis	Catherine E.	21 Nov	1888	Mrs, d, 72	3:259
Lewis	Charles Dwight	12 May	1842	bp, ch of Asahel	2:106
Lewis	Chester	30 Jul	1795	bp, ch of Elisabeth	1:167
Lewis	Clarissa	10 Jun	1828	d, consumption, 19	1:144
Lewis	Clarissa S.	26 Sep	1888	26 marr Homer R. Church 25	3:219
Lewis	David	30 Jul	1795	bp, ch of Elisabeth	1:167
Lewis	David	27 Mar	1803	marr Amica Caulkins, both of this place	1:151
Lewis	Dea.	5 May	1837	Mrs., SS Comm	2:25
Lewis	Deacon	1 Jul	1847	on Standing Committee of the Church	2:58
Lewis	Deacon L.F.	12 Oct	1845	delegate to Middlebury	2:52
Lewis	Dwight W.	11 Jun	1868	marr Mary J. Cutler, both of Naug	3:208
Lewis	Dwight Watson	12 Jun	1840	bp, ch of Lawrence S.	2:106
Lewis	E.H.	-	-	husband of Elizabeth L. Hinman	3:20
Lewis	Edward A.	-	1865	adm ch; Irr 1879 Episcopal	3:26
Lewis	Edward A.	2 Jul	1865	adm ch	3:63
Lewis	Edward Munson	8 Sep	1850	inf bp; Dea. Lucian F.	3:150
Lewis	Edwin A.	23 Jan	1879	Irr dis to Epis Ch	3:125
Lewis	Edwin Augustus	-	1849	bp, ch of Samuel	2:108
Lewis	Edwin H.	-	1877	adm ch	3:26
Lewis	Edwin H.	7 Jan	1877	adm ch	3:65
Lewis	Edwin Horton	2 Jul	1852	inf bp, Asahel H. & Harriet N.	3:150
Lewis	Elisabeth	28 Jun	1795	adm ch	1:13
Lewis	Elisabeth	16 Apr	1802	re confession, breaking 7th command.; restored to fellowship	1:34f
Lewis	Elisabeth	17 Mar	1803	given second admonition	1:36
Lewis	Elisibath	14 Aug	1803	restored to fellowship	1:37
Lewis	Elisth	-	1795	adm ch, wife of David; dis 1811 to Burlington O.	3:25
Lewis	Elizabeth	28 Jun	1795	wife of David, adm ch; rem 11 Aug 1811 to Burlington O.	2:85
Lewis	Elizabeth	28 Jun	1795	adm ch, dism 11 Aug 1811	1:55
Lewis	Elizabeth	11 Aug	1811	certif	1:51
Lewis	Elizabeth 2nd	19 Oct	1796	bp, dau of Elizabeth	1:168
Lewis	Elliott Leighton	-	1848	bp, ch of L.F.	2:108
Lewis	Emeline S.	-	1863	adm ch; dis 1887 Ansonia	3:26

Lewis	Emeline S.	5 Jul 1863	adm ch		3:63
Lewis	Emeline S.	22 Apr 1887	dism to Cong, Ansonia		3:126
Lewis	Emeline Statira	4 Sep 1843	bp, ch of Lawrence S.		2:107
Lewis	Emma F.	- 1863	adm ch, wife of Geo A.; dec 1899		3:26
Lewis	Emma F.	16 May 1867	marr George A. Lewis, both of Naug		3:207
Lewis	Emma F.	2 Mar 1899	Mrs. Geo A., d at DeLand Fla, 51, Brights Disease		3:261
Lewis	Emma Frances	5 Jul 1863	adm ch		3:62
Lewis	Emma Francis	5 Jul 1863	bp, adult		3:153
Lewis	Esqr	27 Sep 1799	brought complaint against Sarah, wife of Austen Smith		1:15
Lewis	Eunice	- 1781	adm ch, wife of Saml; dec 1809		3:25
Lewis	Eunice	22 Feb 1781	one of the persons constituting the church		2:79
Lewis	Eunice	22 Feb 1781	wife of Samuel L., adm ch; died 25 May 1809		2:82
Lewis	Eunice	22 Feb 1781	subscribed to Constitution and Covenant		1:5
Lewis	Eunice	22 Feb 1781	original member, d 25 May 1809 ["Samuel" added]		1:53
Lewis	Eunice	25 May 1809	Wd, d, 71y		1:159
Lewis	Eunice Judd	23 May 1884	d, 76, dropsy		3:259
Lewis	Evan	10 Feb 1872	of Waterbury marr Mary E. Beach of Naug		3:209
Lewis	Frank	6 Sep 1850	d, inf of Thos Lewis, 5 mos, Hillside		3:250
Lewis	Franklin Stern	4 May 1838	bp, ch of Lawrence S.		2:105
Lewis	Geo	24 Apr 1863	Doct, d in Minnesota, 39, consumption, Hillside		3:254
Lewis	Geo A.	- 1878	adm ch		3:26
Lewis	George	2 Jan 1824	ch of Mylo, bp		1:85
Lewis	George A.	16 May 1867	marr Emma F. Lewis, both of Naug		3:207
Lewis	George A.	3 Mar 1878	adm ch		3:66
Lewis	George Albert	- 1849	bp, ch of Samuel		2:108
Lewis	George Lawrence	11 Sep 1842	bp, ch of Lawrence S.		2:106
Lewis	Gerry	27 Nov 1823	marr Mary Hull of Salem		1:152
Lewis	Harriet Amelia	7 Sep 1862	inf bp; Asahel H. & Harriet N.		3:153
Lewis	Helen A.	- 1853	adm ch from Cheshire, wife of Saml J.; dec 1866		3:26
Lewis	Helen A.	6 Nov 1853	w of Saml J, adm fr Cong, Cheshire		3:90
Lewis	Helen A.	18 Jul 1866	d, (Wiscassett, Me.,) 41, consumption, Hillside		3:255
Lewis	Henietta Gennet	31 Aug 1826	of Salem, marr Orange M. Stevens of Stockbridge		1:152
Lewis	Henry Dewitt	11 Jul 1841	bp, ch of Lucian F.		2:106
Lewis	Huldah P.	- 1874	adm ch from Waterbury, w of Wm F; dis 1882 to 2d Cong Waterbury		3:26
Lewis	Huldah P.	3 May 1874	w of Wm F., adm fr 2nd Cong, Waterbury		3:93
Lewis	Huldah P.	15 Dec 1882	dism to 2nd Cong, Waterbury		3:126
Lewis	Isaac	30 Jul 1795	bp, ch of Elisabeth		1:167
Lewis	James S.	- 1869	adm ch		3:26
Lewis	James S.	2 May 1869	adm ch		3:64
Lewis	James Spencer	15 Sep 1827	ch of Seldon, bp		1:87
Lewis	Jane C.	- 1863	adm ch, wife of V. Munger; dis 1872 Ansonia		3:26
Lewis	Jane C.	5 Jul 1863	adm ch		3:63
Lewis	Jane E.	- 1869	adm ch, wife of N.T. Andrew		3:26
Lewis	Jane Elisa	2 May 1869	bp, adult		3:154
Lewis	Jane Eliza	2 May 1869	adm ch		3:64
Lewis	Jane Maria	30 Jun 1826	ch of Milo, bp		1:86
Lewis	Jennie C.	15 Aug 1871	marr Verrenice [sic] Munger, both of Naug		3:209
Lewis	Jennie E.	- 1875	adm ch, wife of Adna Warner; dec 1893		3:26
Lewis	Jennie E.	4 Jul 1875	adm ch		3:65
Lewis	Jennie E.	11 Nov 1875	marr Noyes T. Andrew, both of Naug		3:211
Lewis	John	- 1781	adm ch; dec 1799		3:25
Lewis	John	22 Feb 1781	one of the persons constituting the church		2:79
Lewis	John	22 Feb 1781	adm ch; died 24 Feb 1799		2:81
Lewis	John	22 Feb 1781	subscribed to Constitution and Covenant		1:5

NAUGATUCK, CONNECTICUT, CONGREGATIONAL CHURCH RECORDS

Lewis	John	22 Feb 1781	original member, dec 24 Feb 1799	1:53
Lewis	John	- 1798	adm ch; dec 1812	3:25
Lewis	John	4 Nov 1798	adm ch; died 5 Mar 1812	2:85
Lewis	John	4 Nov 1798	adm ch, d 5 Mar 1812	1:55
Lewis	John	4 Nov 1798	Esqr, adm ch	1:13
Lewis	John	9 Oct 1799	Esqr, on committee	1:15
Lewis	John	4 Sep 1801	complained against by Jared Byington	1:24
Lewis	John	14 Sep 1801	on committee	1:24
Lewis	John	17 Mar 1803	Esqr, on committee	1:36
Lewis	John	27 Jun 1806	Esq, on committee	1:44
Lewis	John	8 Mar 1809	Esq, appointed to rep the ch in Presbetery of Westchester Co NY	1:49
Lewis	John	29 Jun 1810	Esqr, chosen Moderator	1:50
Lewis	John	5 May 1811	Esqr, on committee	1:51
Lewis	John	5 Mar 1812	d, Esqr	1:160
Lewis	John Asahel	6 Sep 1857	inf bp; Asahel H. & Harriet Jr.	3:151
Lewis	John Edward	3 Jul 1835	bp, ch of Selden, b 19 Dec 1834	2:104
Lewis	Joseph	30 Jul 1795	bp, ch of Elisabeth	1:167
Lewis	Josephine L.	24 Apr 1852	d, Wm & Cath, 8, scarlet fever, Hillside	3:250
Lewis	Julia C.	- 1846	adm ch from Woodbury; dis 1850	3:26
Lewis	Julia Caroline	3 May 1846	adm ch from Woodbury; dism Jan 1850	2:100
Lewis	Julia M.	- 1860	adm ch, wife of L.D. Warner; dec 1890	3:26
Lewis	Julia M.	14 Sep 1864	marr Lucian D. Warner, both of Naug	3:206
Lewis	Julia Maria	1 Jul 1860	adm ch	3:62
Lewis	Katharin	2 Jul 1843	wife of Wm B., adm ch	2:99
Lewis	Kittie S.	- 1876	adm ch; dis 1901	3:26
Lewis	Kittie S.	5 Mar 1876	bp, adult	3:155
Lewis	Kittie S.	5 Mar 1876	adm ch	3:65
Lewis	L.F.	5 May 1837	Deacon, SS asst. super.	2:25
Lewis	L.F.	28 Sep 1840	delegate to Milford	2:34
Lewis	L.F.	29 Mar 1850	on comm	2:63
Lewis	L.S.	- -	husband of Nancy Hull	3:18
Lewis	Larman	- -	husband of Eunice Judd	3:22
Lewis	Larman	18 Dec 1877	d, 76, paralysis	3:258
Lewis	Lauren	9 Oct 1848	on comm	2:58
Lewis	Laurence S.	30 Dec 1833	on comm	2:14
Lewis	Lawrence S.	- -	husband of Nancy Hull	2:93
Lewis	Lawrence S.	- 1835	adm ch; dec 1884	3:25
Lewis	Lawrence S.	5 Jul 1835	adm ch	2:95
Lewis	Lawrence S.	5 Jul 1835	bp, adult	2:104
Lewis	Lawrence S.	5 May 1837	SS Librarian	2:25
Lewis	Lawrence S.	30 May 1884	d, 80	3:259
Lewis	Lizzie	21 Aug 1889	Mrs, 40 marr Walter Brooks 43	3:220
Lewis	Lockey	4 Jan 1818	bp	1:60
Lewis	Lockey	- 1822	wife of Sheldon, member	1:82
Lewis	Locky S.	2 Feb 1861	d, 67, Hillside	3:253
Lewis	Louisa C.	22 Nov 1862	d, 21, consumption, Hillside	3:254
Lewis	Lucian F.	- 1833	adm ch; dis 1853 to West Haven	3:25
Lewis	Lucian F.	5 May 1833	adm ch	2:93
Lewis	Lucian F.	- 1834	appt'd Deacon; removed 1853	3:1
Lewis	Lucian F.	19 Dec 1834	chosen deacon	2:18
Lewis	Lucian F.	19 Dec 1834	Deacon	2:79
Lewis	Lucian F.	2 Oct 1837	Dea., substitute for Dea. Spencer	2:27
Lewis	Lucian F.	19 Mar 1837	Deacon, appt'd delegate to Bethany	2:24
Lewis	Lucian F.	1 Apr 1838	Dea., SS Comm	2:32

NAUGATUCK, CONNECTICUT, CONGREGATIONAL CHURCH RECORDS

Lewis	Lucian F.	23 Feb 1843	on comm	2:45
Lewis	Lucian F.	17 Jul 1853	dism to Cong, West Haven	3:120
Lewis	Lucian F.	22 Feb 1881	at centennial exercises	3:300
Lewis	Lucy	16 Mar 1887	wife of Selden, d, 74, pneumonia	3:259
Lewis	Lydia	- 1819	adm ch, wife of Ansel; dec 1820	3:25
Lewis	Lydia	3 Sep 1819	wife of Ansel, adm ch from Waterbury; died 1 Oct 1820	2:91
Lewis	Lydia C.	- 1819	adm ch fr Waterbury, w of E. Bradley; dis 1845 to Bridgeport	3:25
Lewis	Lydia C.	3 Sep 1819	wife of Eldad Bradley, adm ch; rem Apr 1845 to Bridgeport	2:91
Lewis	Lyman	- 1828	adm ch; dis 1840 to Thompson NY	3:25
Lewis	Lyman	6 Jul 1828	adm ch; rem 3 Feb 1840 to Thompson, Broom Co., NY	2:92
Lewis	Lyman	6 Jul 1828	adm ch	1:59a
Lewis	Lyman	6 Jul 1828	member	1:94
Lewis	Lyman	6 Jul 1828	adm ch	1:107
Lewis	Mary	20 Mar 1828	propounded for adm	1:106
Lewis	Mary	- 1869	adm ch, wife of Dwight; dis 1870 Howard Ave., New Haven	3:26
Lewis	Mary	2 May 1869	bp, adult	3:154
Lewis	Mary	2 May 1869	adm ch	3:64
Lewis	Mary	Aug 1870	dism to Howard Ave, New Haven	3:124
Lewis	Mary A.	23 Nov 1828	adm ch	1:59b
Lewis	Mary A.	23 Nov 1828	member	1:94
Lewis	Mary A.	- 1829	adm ch, wife of A. Beecher; Irr 1837 Episcopal	3:25
Lewis	Mary A.	3 Nov 1829	w of Abraham Beecher, adm ch; withdrawn 24 Mar 1837 to Episcopal	2:93
Lewis	Mary A.	3 Feb 1837	voted to be requested to ask for letter of dism.	2:23
Lewis	Mary Antoinitha	28 Jun 1818	ch of Milo, bp	1:61
Lewis	Mary E.	12 Jun 1850	d, wife of Saml J., 32, Hillside Cem	3:250
Lewis	Mary Elisabeth	4 May 1856	inf bp; Saml J. & Helen A.	3:151
Lewis	Mary Jane	3 Jul 1836	bp, ch of Samuel, b 27 Aug 1834	2:105
Lewis	Mary Jane	- 1866	adm ch, wife of James	3:26
Lewis	Mary Jane	4 Nov 1866	adm ch	3:64
Lewis	Milo	- 1818	adm ch; dec 1870	3:25
Lewis	Milo	4 Jan 1818	adm ch	2:88
Lewis	Milo	4 Jan 1818	adm ch	1:58
Lewis	Milo	4 May 1827	on committee	1:102
Lewis	Milo	14 Oct 1827	on committee	1:103
Lewis	Milo	4 May 1828	on comm	1:106
Lewis	Milo	6 Jan 1828	appointed to conf Humphreyville	1:106
Lewis	Milo	6 Nov 1829	voted to attend future conf	1:109
Lewis	Milo	26 Aug 1832	Superintendant of SS	2:11
Lewis	Milo	7 Oct 1837	on comm	2:27
Lewis	Milo	11 Jan 1843	made statement regarding difficulties with Elihu Benham	2:43f
Lewis	Milo	11 Jan 1843	visited Mrs. Fowler with Brother Ransom Culver	2:44
Lewis	Milo	23 Feb 1843	on comm	2:45
Lewis	Milo	24 Aug 1843	on comm	2:46
Lewis	Milo	1 Jul 1848	on Standing Committee of the Church	2:58
Lewis	Milo	29 Mar 1850	on comm	2:63
Lewis	Milo	12 Oct 1870	d, 81, typhoid, Hillside	3:256
Lewis	Minnie E.	22 Sep 1876	d, 21, consumption, Hillside	3:257
Lewis	Mylo	13 Dec 1789	bp, ch of Samll Smith Lewis	1:165
Lewis	Mylo	- 1822	male, on list of members	1:81
Lewis	Mylo	5 Mar 1824	on committee	1:97
Lewis	Nancy Hull	17 Feb 1881	d, wife of Lauren S.	3:258
Lewis	Nettie H.	19 Apr 1869	of Naug marr Bellmont Forrest of Waterbury	3:208
Lewis	Patty	- 1801	adm ch; dis 1812 to Burlington O.	3:25
Lewis	Patty	4 Jan 1801	adm ch; rem 11 Aug 1811 to Burlington O.	2:86

NAUGATUCK, CONNECTICUT, CONGREGATIONAL CHURCH RECORDS

Lewis	Patty	4 Jan 1801	adm ch, dism 11 Aug 1811	1:56
Lewis	Patty	4 Jan 1801	bp & adm ch	1:20
Lewis	Patty	11 Aug 1811	dau of Elizabeth, certif	1:51
Lewis	Phebe	- 1828	adm ch; dis 1829 to Middlebury	3:25
Lewis	Phebe	3 Oct 1828	of Waterbury, marr Jonathan N. --adley of Middlebury	1:153
Lewis	Phebe	4 Jul 1828	adm ch, dism 1829	1:59b
Lewis	Phebe	6 Jul 1828	wife of Nelson Bradley, adm ch; rem 1829 to Middlebury	2:92
Lewis	Phebe	6 Jul 1828	member; dism 1829	1:94
Lewis	Phebe	6 Jul 1828	adm ch	1:107
Lewis	R.J.E.	8 Sep 1875	Mrs. Milo, bur, 61, Hillside	3:257
Lewis	Rachel	- 1828	adm ch, wife of E.A. Smith; dis 1840 to Baptist	3:25
Lewis	Rachel	4 Jul 1828	wife of Edward A. Smith, adm ch; rem 9 Feb 1840 to Baptists	2:94
Lewis	Rachel Cornelia	3 Jul 1836	bp, ch of Samuel, b 2 Oct 1836 [sic]	2:105
Lewis	Robert Selden	6 Sep 1850	inf bp; Lawrence & Nancy	3:150
Lewis	Rocitty[sic]	30 Jul 1795	bp, ch of Elisabeth	1:167
Lewis	Rufus W.	- 1858	adm ch; dis 1860 to Cheshire	3:26
Lewis	Rufus W.	29 Apr? 1860	dism to Cong, Cheshire	3:121
Lewis	Rufus W.	- 1874	adm ch from Cheshire	3:26
Lewis	Rufus W.	4 Jan 1874	adm fr Cong, Cheshire Ct	3:93
Lewis	Rufus W.	- 1899	appt'd Deacon 1899	3:1
Lewis	Rufus Warren	4 Nov 1836	bp, ch of Lawrence S., b 9 Feb 1836	2:105
Lewis	Rufus Warren	7 Mar 1858	adm ch	3:61
Lewis	Ruth	- 1789	adm ch, wife of Abm; dis to Waterbury	3:25
Lewis	Ruth	19 Sep 1789	wife of Abraham, adm ch; rem to Waterbury	2:84
Lewis	Ruth	29 Sep 1789	Ab., adm ch, dism [copied wrong, should be 19 Sep 1790]	1:55
Lewis	Ruth	19 Sep 1790	wife of Abram, adm ch	1:12
Lewis	Ruth	- 1828	adm ch; dis 1840 to Thompson NY	3:25
Lewis	Ruth	4 Jul 1828	adm ch	1:59b
Lewis	Ruth	6 Jul 1828	adm ch; rem 3 Feb 1840 to Thompson, Broom Co, NY	2:92
Lewis	Ruth J.	6 Jul 1828	member	1:94
Lewis	Ruth J.	6 Jul 1828	adm ch	1:107
Lewis	Salle	10 Sep 1786	bp, ch of Samll S.	1:164
Lewis	Sally	10 Sep 1786	ch of Samll Smith Lewis bp [entry crossed out]	1:10
Lewis	Sam'l A.	3 Nov 1878	adm fr North Haven Cong'l	3:94
Lewis	Saml	- 1781	adm ch; dec 1788	3:25
Lewis	Saml	- 1878	adm ch from No Haven; dis 1884 North Haven; same for wife	3:26
Lewis	Saml J.	- 1838	adm ch from Alton Ill; dis 1842 to Sharon	3:25
Lewis	Saml J.	- 1844	adm ch from Sharon; dec 1858	3:25
Lewis	Saml J.	11 Aug 1858	d, 41, consumption, Hillside	3:252
Lewis	Saml Jr.	-	adm ch; dec 1790	3:25
Lewis	Saml M.	30 Aug 1850	d, inf of Saml J., 3 mos 9 da, Hillside	3:250
Lewis	Samuel	Feb 1781	Esqr, chosen Moderator	1:6
Lewis	Samuel	22 Feb 1781	one of the persons constituting the church	2:79
Lewis	Samuel	22 Feb 1781	adm ch; died 11 Apr 1788	2:81
Lewis	Samuel	22 Feb 1781	subscribed to Constitution and Covenant	1:5
Lewis	Samuel	22 Feb 1781	original member, dec 11 Apr 1788	1:53
Lewis	Samuel	Jul 1783	Deacon, died 11 Apr 1788	2:79
Lewis	Samuel	Jul 1783	chosen Deacon	1:6
Lewis	Samuel	Jul 1783	Deacon	1:53
Lewis	Samuel	- 1828	adm ch; dis 1840 to Thompson NY	3:25
Lewis	Samuel	4 May 1828	adm ch; rem 3 Feb 1840 to Tompson, Broom Co, NY	2:92
Lewis	Samuel	4 May 1828	adm ch	1:59a
Lewis	Samuel	4 May 1828	adm ch	1:106
Lewis	Samuel	6 Nov 1829	complained against Ansel Spencer, Jr.	1:108

Lewis	Samuel	1 Apr	1838	SS Asst. Librarian	2:32
Lewis	Samuel A.	28 Mar	1884	dism to Cong, North Haven; also wife	3:126
Lewis	Samuel Ashael	Aug	1846	bp, ch of L.F.	2:107
Lewis	Samuel J.	Feb	1838	adm ch from 1st Presbyterian ch in Alton, Illinois	2:31
Lewis	Samuel J.	4 Feb	1838	adm ch from Alton Illinois; dism 27 Nov 1842 to Sharon	2:97
Lewis	Samuel J.	6 Nov	1842	dism to ch in Sharon	2:42
Lewis	Samuel J.	28 Apr	1844	adm ch from Sharon	2:99
Lewis	Samuel J.	28 Apr	1844	adm from Sharon	2:49
Lewis	Samuel J.	29 Mar	1850	on comm	2:63
Lewis	Samuel John	28 Jun	1818	ch of Milo, bp	1:61
Lewis	Samuel Jr	-	1828	male, on list of members, adm 1828	1:81
Lewis	Samuel Jr	20 Mar	1828	propounded for adm	1:106
Lewis	Samuel Jr.	21 Oct	1787	adm ch; died 19 Aug 1790	2:84
Lewis	Samuel Junior	21 Oct	1787	adm ch	1:11
Lewis	Samuel Junr	21 Oct	1787	adm ch, d 19 Aug 1790	1:54
Lewis	Sarah	-	1833	adm ch; dec 1861	3:25
Lewis	Sarah	5 May	1833	Wd of Asahel, adm ch	2:93
Lewis	Sarah	19 Jan	1861	d, 81, Hillside	3:253
Lewis	Sarah Elizabeth	3 Nov	1843	bp, ch of Lucian F.	2:107
Lewis	Sarah J.	3 Nov	1878	w of Saml A, adm fr North Haven Cong'l	3:94
Lewis	Selden	-	-	husband of Lucy Maria Roberts	3:39
Lewis	Selden	-	-	husband of Locky Spencer	3:42
Lewis	Selden	-	-	husband of Locky Spencer	2:89
Lewis	Selden	28 Oct	1862	marr Lucy M. Roberts, both of Naug	3:205
Lewis	Seldon	23 Feb	1824	wife d, Hydrocephalus, 28	1:161
Lewis	Seldon	13 Mar	1825	marr Lockey Spencer of Salem	1:152
Lewis	Silva	30 Jul	1795	bp, ch of Elisabeth	1:167
Lewis	Susan	-	1818	adm ch, wife of Milo; dec 1858	3:25
Lewis	Susan	4 Jan	1818	wife of Milo, adm ch	2:88
Lewis	Susan	4 Jan	1818	wife of Milo, adm ch	1:58
Lewis	Susan	-	1822	wife of Mylo, member	1:82
Lewis	Susan	-	1837	adm ch fr New York, wife of Lucian F.; dis 1853 to West Haven	3:25
Lewis	Susan	18 Jun	1837	wife of Lucian F. adm ch from New York	2:96
Lewis	Susan	18 Jun	1837	Mrs., adm ch from Central Presbyterian Ch in city of NY	2:26
Lewis	Susan	17 Jul	1853	[wife of] Lucian F., dism to Cong, West Haven	3:120
Lewis	Susan	24 Sep	1858	d, 70, congestion of the brain, Hillside	3:252
Lewis	Tamar	-	1785	adm ch; wife of Elisha; dec	3:25
Lewis	Tamer	18 Sep	1785	wife of Elisha, adm ch; died	2:82
Lewis	Tamer	18 Sep	1785	adm ch	1:10
Lewis	Tamer	18 Sep	1785	adm ch, dead	1:54
Lewis	Thomas	10 Sep	1786	bp, ch of Samll S.	1:164
Lewis	Thomas	10 Sep	1786	ch of Samll Smith Lewis bp [entry crossed out]	1:10
Lewis	Thomas	3 Mar	1804	d, at Sunbury in Georgia, aged 27 y, recorded 5 May	1:156
Lewis	Thomas	28 Jun	1818	ch of Milo, bp	1:61
Lewis	Thomas	26 Nov	1872	bur, 57, Hillside, "stone reads Nov 26, 1871"	3:257
Lewis	Tracey Samuel	Nov	1873?	ch bp; Geo A. & Emma F. [year could be 1875]	3:155
Lewis	Tracy S.	-	1889	adm ch	3:27
Lewis	Tracy S.	6 Jan	1889	adm ch	3:69
Lewis	William	21 Jun	1813	ch of Milo & Susan, bp [perhaps 1820]	1:63
Lewis	William A.	3 Oct	1856	d, 7, croup, Hillside	3:251
Lewis	Wm B.	-	1866	adm ch; dec 1885	3:26
Lewis	Wm B.	2 Sep	1866	adm ch	3:64
Lewis	Wm B.	25 Feb	1885	d, 65, pneumonia	3:259
Lewis	Wm F.	-	1874	adm ch from Waterbury; dis 1882 to 2d Cong Waterbury	3:26

NAUGATUCK, CONNECTICUT, CONGREGATIONAL CHURCH RECORDS

Lewis	Wm F.	3 May 1874	adm fr 2nd Cong, Waterbury	3:93
Lewis	Wm F.	15 Dec 1882	dism to 2nd Cong, Waterbury	3:126
Lewiz [sic]	Asahel H.	12 Jun 1843	chosen delegate to Prospect	2:46
Limburner	Jennett	- 1841	adm ch, wife of -- Wooding; dis 1859 to Cheshire	3:25
Limburner	Jennett	11 Jul 1841	adm ch; wife of -- Wooding	2:98
Lines	-	- -	husband of Mary Ann Lang	2:97
Lines	-	11 Dec 1828	ch d, 1	1:145
Lines	Cordelia	- 1858	adm ch; dis 1872 to Park St., Bridgeport	3:26
Lines	Cordelia	7 Mar 1858	bp, adult	3:151
Lines	Cordelia	7 Mar 1858	adm ch	3:61
Lines	Cordelia	Mar 1872	dism to Park St Cong, Bridgeport	3:124
Lines	Eliza	- 1844	adm ch; dis 1862 to South Britain	3:25
Lines	Eliza	28 Apr 1844	bp, adult	2:107
Lines	Eliza	28 Apr 1844	adm ch; dism to South Brtain [sic][see Smith, Eliza (Lines)]	2:99
Lines	Harriet	- 1854	adm ch, wife of Henry; dec 1898	3:26
Lines	Harriet	5 Mar 1854	adm ch	3:61
Lines	Harriet	24 Feb 1898	d, 82, cancer	3:261
Lines	Henry W.	30 Jan 1863	d, 50, consumption, Hillside	3:254
Lines	M.	- -	husband of Mary Ann Lang	3:25
Lines	Mary Elisabeth	- 1845	adm ch from Waterbury; dec 1863	3:25
Lines	Mary Elisabeth	10 Aug 1845	adm ch from Waterbury	2:99
Lines	Mary Eliza	7 Feb 1879	d, dau of late Henry W., 23, consumption	3:258
Lines	Mary Elizabeth	10 Aug 1845	Miss, adm from ch in Waterbury	2:51
Lines	Mary Elizabeth Lin	31 Mar? 1863	d [day not given, follows entry for 31 Mar]	3:254
Lines	Rebecca	18 Feb 1850	marr Hial S. Stevens, both of Naug	3:200
Linz	Gussie	23 Apr 1898	24 marr Adolph N. David 37	3:226
Loan [sic]	Fannie	24 Dec 1895	23 marr Peter Hearney 26 [see Harvey]	3:224
Locke	Kissock	- 1855	adm ch fr Kelton Manse Scotland, w of Adam Johnson; Erased 1866	3:26
Locke	Kissock	9 Sep 1855	(Mrs. Adam Johnson), adm from Kelton Manse, Scotland	3:90
Locke	Kissock (Johnson)	30 Mar 1866	voted dismissed, eligible for letter if asked [see 3:369]	3:123
Lockwood	C.H.	22 Feb 1881	Mrs., at centennial exercises	3:300
Lockwood	Emma	22 Feb 1881	Miss, at centennial exercises	3:300
Lockwood	Libbie O.	9 Oct 1879	marr Theodore B. Beach, both of Seymour	3:212
Logan	John	- 1897	and wife adm ch from Stamford Ct; dis 1897 to any church	3:27
Logan	John	3 Jan 1897	and wife adm fr Presb, Stamford Ct	3:98
Logan	John	23 Jul 1897	and wife dism, General letter	3:129
Longfellow	C.D.	15 Jun 1864	marr Mary C. Street, both of Naug	3:205
Longfellow	Mary C. (Street)	13 Aug 1865	d, 26, consumption, Hillside	3:255
Loomis	Maud M.	10 Feb 1883	marr Frank Reed, both of Naug	3:215
Loomis	Robert R.	20 Oct 1889	20 marr Florence M. Megin 17	3:220
Loomis	Sarah F.	- 1856	adm ch from Wolcottville; dis 1859 to Ansonia	3:26
Loomis	Sarah F.	4 May 1856	adm from Cong, Wolcottville	3:90
Loomis	Sarah F.	2 Oct 1859	dism to Cong, Ansonia Ct	3:121
Loomis	Sarah F.	- 1860	adm ch, "(Letter retd)"; dis 1868 to Wolcottville	3:26
Loomis	Sarah F.	6 May 1860	Letter to Ansonia retd by her	3:91
Loomis	Sarah F.	1 Nov 1868	dism to Cong, Wolcottville	3:124
Loser[?]	Wm	22 Feb 1881	Mrs., at centennial exercises	3:300
Louin	Augusta	27 Jan 1884	marr Martin Schlennsin[?], both of Naug	3:216
Loundsbury	Nancy	10 Apr 1870	(Hopkins) dism to Bethany	3:124
Loundsbury	S.	- -	husband of Nancy Hopkins?	3:19
Louwin	Bertha	25 Aug 1883	marr David Yost, both of Naug	3:215
Lowe	Ellen	24 Jun 1853	d, 23, pulmonary bleeding	3:250
Lowes	Lillie F.	10 Feb 1881	marr George Warren, both of Naug	3:213
Lownsbury	--	7 Apr 1836	(stranger) died, 48	2:115

NAUGATUCK, CONNECTICUT, CONGREGATIONAL CHURCH RECORDS

Lubitz	John E.	23 Jun 1881	marr Mary Hennigan, both of Naug	3:213
Lunway	Elnora	26 Jun 1899	27 marr John Shortell 37	3:227
Lutz	Georgi	8 Dec 1873	marr Anna Singstacken, both of Naug	3:210
Lyman	Asa	2 Dec 1800	Revd Elder attending Consociation at Salem, from Hamden	1:19
Lyon	Anna F.	- 1879	adm ch; dis 1882 to M.E. Plattsville Ct	3:26
Lyon	Anna F.	5 Jan 1879	bp, adult	3:156
Lyon	Anna F.	5 Jan 1879	adm ch	3:67
Lyon	Anna F.	10 Nov 1882	dism to M.E. Ch, Plattsville Ct	3:126
M'Donald	Polly	3 Jan 1802	marr Charles Williams, both of Columbia	1:151
Magiuris	Estella Noble	5 Jul 1891	an inf, bp	3:160
Magiuris	Inez Jane	5 Jul 1891	an inf, bp	3:160
Magiuris	Rollin Daniel	5 Jul 1891	an inf, bp	3:160
Mahon	Esther	17 Mar 1855	marr William Pinder, both of Naug	3:202
Mai	Annie Bella	- 1892	an inf, bp	3:160
Mai	Willie Grover	- 1892	an inf, bp	3:160
Maine	Sylvester S.	8 Jan 1875	marr Mary L. Sweet, both of Naug	3:210
Maldenhower	Augs H.	17 Oct 1856	d, 6ys, scarlet fever, Hillside	3:251
Mallory	Mr.	20 Apr 1864	d, "funeral...Middlebury"	3:254
Mann	Emily C.	28 Feb 1865	marr A.D. Hopkins, both of Naug	3:206
Mansfield	-	24 Jun 1828	ch d, dysentery, 1	1:144
Mansfield	Ida J.	2 Jul 1876	dism to 1st Presb, Windham NY	3:124
Mansfield	Ida Jane	- 1876	adm ch; dis 1876 to 1 Presby Windham	3:29
Mansfield	Ida Jane	5 Mar 1876	bp, adult	3:155
Mansfield	Ida Jane	5 Mar 1876	adm ch	3:65
Manville	Charles	- 1896	Mrs., adm ch	3:29
Manville	Chas	1 Nov 1896	Mrs., adm ch	3:71
Manville	Chas Theodore	13 Jun 1897	an inf, bp	3:162
Manville	Eleanor Margaret	13 Jun 1897	an inf, bp	3:162
Manyberry	Margaret	13 Apr 1882	marr Neil Johnson, both of Naug	3:214
Marsh	Alice	- 1890	adm ch from Waterbury; dis 1897	3:29
Marsh	Alice	9 Mar 1890	bp, adult	3:159
Marsh	Alice	27 Mar 1897	dism to Trinity Ch, Waterbury	3:129
Marsh	Allice	9 Mar 1890	Miss, adm ch	3:70
Marsh	Emily	- 1890	adm ch from New Britain	3:29
Marsh	Emily	9 Mar 1890	Miss, adm fr South Cong, New Britain Ct	3:96
Marshall	-	12 Dec 1872	marr --, both of Naug	3:209
Marshall	Samuel E.	19 Jan 1882	marr Jennie M. Zellar, both of Naug	3:213
Marsland	Alice	5 Jul 1891	an inf, bp	3:160
Marsland	Carrie	- 1891	Mrs, adm ch	3:29
Marsland	Carrie	1 Mar 1891	Mrs., adm ch [see Cowles, Carrie]	3:70
Marsland	Chas Leroy	5 Jul 1891	an inf, bp	3:160
Marsland	Harry Eugene	5 Jul 1891	an inf, bp	3:160
Marsland	Jessie	5 Jul 1891	an inf, bp	3:160
Martin	Albert Hillman	3 Sep 1813	ch of Granvil, bp [perhaps 1820]	1:63
Martin	Anna M.	- 1900	adm ch	3:29
Martin	Anna M.	6 May 1900	bp, adult	3:165
Martin	Anna M.	6 May 1900	adm ch	3:72
Martin	G.	- -	husband of Minerva Stevens	3:42
Martin	Geo B.	- 1885	Mrs, voted to be erased	3:409
Martin	Granville	7 Nov 1826	d, fever, at Columbia, 33	1:144
Martin	Gronville	- -	husband of Minerva Stevens	2:89
Martin	Julia	26 Aug 1824	of Columbia, marr Truman Hopkins of Salem	1:152
Martin	Louis J.	- 1885	colored, adm ch; dis 1887 Medford Mass	3:29

NAUGATUCK, CONNECTICUT, CONGREGATIONAL CHURCH RECORDS

Martin	Louis J.	5 Jul 1885	adm ch, "colored"	3:68
Martin	Louis J.	21 Oct 1887	dism to Mystic Ch, Medford, Mass.	3:126
Martin	Manerva	- 1822	wife of Granvil, member	1:82
Martin	Polly	22 Jan 1857	d, 87	3:251
Martin	Wm Dunham	14 Feb 1899	23 marr Bessie Conkling 19	3:227
Mason	Emery	28 Apr 1828	marr Lucinda Atwater of Salem	1:153
Mason	Geo W.	- 1882	adm ch; erased 1900	3:29
Mason	Geo W.	30 Jan 1883	marr Carrie Griswold, both of Naug	3:215
Mason	George William	5 Mar 1882	adm ch	3:67
Mather	Emma L.	29 May 1882	marr Chas E. Turner, both of Naug	3:214
Matthews	Mary	20 Sep 1826	of Cheshire, marr Charles Thrall	1:152
Matz	George	7 Feb 1900	33 marr Anna Rehm[?] 26	3:228
Maving	-	-	see Stahl	-
May	Austin E.	5 May 1880	of Naug marr Grace Anna Spencer of Middletown	3:212
McCarrick	Maggie	31 Dec 1874	of Naug marr W.H. Murfield of Waterbury	3:210
McCollum	Donald Louis	13 Jun 1897	inf bp; Louis &	3:162
McCollum	Louis T.	- 1897	adm ch from New Haven, also wife	3:29
McCollum	Louis T.	2 May 1897	adm fr Grand Ave Cong, New Haven; also wife	3:98
McConnel	Abbe E.	9 Jan 1864	d, 51, congestion of lungs	3:254
McCornish	Margaret	29 Nov 1855	marr James Pilkington, both of Manchester at Manchester	3:202
McCrumb[?]	Lilly	5 Apr 1884	marr Fred Dennen, both of Naug	3:216
McDonald	-	- 1902	see M'Donald	1:151
McGinnis	Angie	24 Nov 1878	marr William Waite, both of Naug	3:212
McGinnis	Lillian Noble	- 1891	adm ch, wife of Daniel	3:29
McGinnis	Lillian Noble	5 Jul 1891	Mrs, adm ch	3:70
McKee	Otto John	13 Jan 1889	an inf, bp	3:159
McKee	Thomas	16 Nov 1887	22 marr Lena Horn 20	3:218
McKinney	Clarence E.	12 Dec 1898	21 marr Mattie Wooster 20	3:227
McKinney	Ida	1 Oct 1885	21 marr Arthur Freeman 22, both of Naug	3:217
McKinney	M.J.	25 Oct 1882	marr Henry B. Richmond, both of Naug	3:214
McNaughton	Jane	- 1850	adm ch from Dundboe, Ireland; care withdrawn 1885	3:29
McNaughton	Jane	5 May 1850	adm ch from 1st Presb, Dunboe, Ireland	3:90
McSwets[?]	Anne	9 Jun 1896	inf bp; Andrew & Mary	3:162
McSwets[?]	Martha	9 Jun 1896	inf bp; Andrew & Mary	3:162
Mead	March	29 Apr 1817	Rev. Elder at Council re Rev. Dodd's removal	1:74
Mead	Mark	5 May 1811	Rev, of Middlebury, invited to attend installation	1:51
Mead	Mary	- 1814	adm ch from Carmel NY, wife of Ashbel Stevens; dis 1830	3:29
Mead	Mary	28 Apr 1814	w of Ashbel Stevens, adm ch fr Carmel NY; rem 22 Aug 1830 to NY	2:87
Mead	Mary	28 Apr 1814	adm ch	1:57
Mead	Mary	28 Apr 1814	adm ch by letter from Carmel, NY	1:68
Mead	Sylvester	9 Sep 1873	marr Nettie V. Newton, both of Waterbury	3:210
Meeker	M.H.	3 Mar 1878	adm ch	3:66
Meeker	M.H.	3 Mar 1878	bp, adult	3:156
Meeker	Melvin H.	- 1878	adm ch; dec 1884; reported died in Denver Col.	3:29
Megin	Florence M.	20 Oct 1889	17 marr Robert R. Loomis 20	3:220
Megin	James	24 Sep 1865	of Hamden marr Jane Hotchkiss of Naug	3:207
Melbourn	Thomas	5 Sep 1883	marr Ellen Wilton, both of Middlebury	3:215
Mellen	Mattie	2 Aug 1899	25 marr Frank E. Jenner 21	3:227
Meramble	Belle E.	2 May 1886	bp, adult	3:158
Meramble	Belle Elizabeth	- 1886	adm ch	3:29
Meramble	Belle Elizabeth	2 May 1886	adm ch	3:69
Meramble	Clarence E.	- 1885	adm ch	3:29
Meramble	Clarence E.	5 Jul 1885	bp, adult	3:157
Meramble	Clarence E.	5 Jul 1885	adm ch	3:67

NAUGATUCK, CONNECTICUT, CONGREGATIONAL CHURCH RECORDS

Surname	Given	Date	Event	Ref
Meramble	Lydia	1 Mar 1863	adm fr Cong, Roxbury	3:91
Meramble	Lydia A.	- 1863	adm ch from Roxbury, wife of Geo Hotchkiss; dis 1867	3:29
Merrell	-	9 Oct 1825	ch d, 4	1:163
Merrell	Elias F.	23 Nov 1853	of Naug marr Nancy C. Hull of Farmington	3:201
Merrell	Nathanl	6 Jul 1851	of Naug marr Susan Hall of Waterbury	3:200
Merrells	Melissa D.	5 Nov 1855	of Naug marr Miner C. Wedge of Warren Ct	3:202
Merrill	-	Aug 1825	ch d, 0	1:163
Merrill	Grant U.	- 1885	adm ch; 1891 "Irr Dis. Bap. Pattersn"	3:29
Merrill	Grant U.	5 Jul 1885	bp, adult	3:157
Merrill	Grant U.	5 Jul 1885	adm ch	3:68
Merrill	Grant U.	7 Aug 1891	Irr Dism Paterson NJ Baptist	3:127
Merrills	Mary C.	1 Oct 1862	d, 6, diphtheria	3:253
Mersey	Jacob	14 Jun 1894	33 marr Carrie Biland 26	3:223
Mersey	Lorenz Jacob	16 Oct 1898	inf bp; Jacob & Carrie	3:163
Mersy	Lena Elizabeth	24 Nov 1895	inf bp; Jacob & Caroline Beland	3:161
Messner	Henry	7 Aug 1875	marr Louisa Schultz, both of Naug	3:211
Meyers	Elizabeth	-	see Birdsall	-
Meyers	Frederick Henry	21 Feb 1889	29 marr Jennie E. Sanford 16	3:220
Michael	Adeline	23 Apr 1864	marr Charles A. Klump, both of Naugatuck	3:205
Middlebury	Ellis	1 Oct 1850	dau d, 7 ys, canker	3:250
Milberg[?]	Lima	20 Nov 1896	[Nulberg?] 20 marr Yugue Ciderholm 25	3:225
Miles	-	-	husband of Alma Porter	2:95
Miles	Benjn F.	14 Apr 1850	of Cheshire marr Sarah M. Stevens of Naug	3:200
Miller	Addie L.	- 1901	adm ch, wife of Wm H., from M.E. ch, Naug	3:29
Miller	Addie L.	3 Mar 1901	Mrs., adm fr M.E. Ch, Naugatuck	3:99
Miller	Anna	6 Mar 1892	adm ch	3:70
Miller	Anna L.C.	- 1892	adm ch, wife of Geo W. Goodrich	3:29
Miller	Annie L.C.	2 May 1896	19 marr Geo W. Goodrich 28	3:224
Miller	Bessie May	-	see Kirk	-
Miller	Edward T.	21 Oct 1868	marr Mary E. Whitney, both of Naug	3:208
Miller	Geo Andrew	- 1897	adm ch	3:29
Miller	George Andrew	2 May 1897	adm ch	3:71
Miller	Gertrude Schenck	10 Mar 1892	Mrs, 35 marr David Shannon 39	3:221
Miller	Leonard	16 Oct 1834	died, 27	2:114
Miller	Lillian Marguerite	9 Jun 1901	ch bp; George A. & Marguerite (Weaving)	3:165
Miller	Mary J.	22 Nov 1898	24 marr Hermann A. Ringe 28	3:226
Miller	Mary Jane	- 1897	adm ch	3:29
Miller	Mary Jane	2 May 1897	adm ch	3:71
Miller	Smith	5 Oct 1825	of Annsvill, Oneida Co, NY, marr Lydia Bracket of Waterbury	1:152
Miller	Wm H.	- 1901	adm ch	3:29
Miller	Wm H.	3 Mar 1901	adm ch	3:72
Miller	Zalmon	6 Nov 1826	of Cornwall, marr Elizabeth F. Terrel of Salem	1:152
Mills	A.	-	husband of Anna Baldwin	3:4
Mills	Amasa	-	husband of Anna Baldwin	2:83
Mills	George A.	23 Aug 1866	of Copake NY marr Sarah W. Sherman of Naug	3:207
Mills	George Sherman	28 Jun 1868	ch bp; Geo. A. & Sarah W. (of Copahe)	3:154
Mills	Mary	1 Sep 1888	19 marr George Tafft 28	3:219
Mills	Millard Filmore	22 Feb 1900	36 marr Anna Maria Amelia Keach 41	3:228
Mills	Sarah W.	17 Nov 1867	dism to Reformed Dutch, Copahe NY	3:123
Mills	Wm S.	- 1885	adm ch [crossed out]	3:29
Mills	Wm S.	5 Jul 1885	adm ch	3:68
Milson	Mary Jane	- 1851	adm ch, wife of Franklin Beecher; dec 1889	3:29
Milson	Mary Jane	6 Jul 1851	bp, profession	3:150
Milson	Mary Jane	6 Jul 1851	adm ch	3:60

NAUGATUCK, CONNECTICUT, CONGREGATIONAL CHURCH RECORDS

Surname	Given	Date	Note	Ref
Milson	Mary Jane	2 Jan 1853	dism to Methodist, Naug	3:120
Miner	Solomon C.	7 Mar 1875	dism to 1st Cong, Waterbury [see Minor]	3:124
Minkewitz	Barbara	- 1897	Mrs, adm ch from New Britain	3:29
Minkewitz	Paul Herman	- 1897	adm ch	3:29
Minkwitz	Agnes O.	10 Jun 1894	bp; Paul Harman & Barbara	3:161
Minkwitz	Barbara	4 Jul 1897	Mrs., adm fr 1st Cong, New Britain Ct	3:98
Minkwitz	Barbara Katherine	10 Jun 1894	bp; Paul Harman & Barbara	3:161
Minkwitz	Paul	13 Jun 1897	inf bp; Paul Herman	3:162
Minkwitz	Paul Herman	4 Jul 1897	adm ch	3:72
Minkwitz	Rosalia Blanch	7 Sep 1890	an inf, bp	3:159
Minor	Solomon C.	- 1873	adm ch from Yale College; dis 1875 to 1st ch Waterbury	3:29
Minor	Solomon C.	2 Nov 1873	adm fr Ch of Yale College [see Miner]	3:93
Mirfield	Wm H.	21 Dec 1888	dism to Cong, Malden, Mass; also wife [see Murfield]	3:127
Monroe	John H.	26 Dec 1887	23 marr Lizzie M. Hopkins 21 [see Mornoe, Munroe]	3:218
Monroe	Lizzie Hopkins	20 Jan 1899	dism to North Cong, NY City	3:129
Morehead	Cora B.	18 Apr 1883	marr Chas F. Silvernail, both of Naug	3:215
Morehouse	Elijah P.	13 Apr 1886	60 marr Emily E. Taylor 43, both of Naug	3:217
Morey	Maria H.	28 Nov 1860	marr Benjn D. Hubbard, both of Naug	3:204
Morey	Mrs.	12 Sep 1866	d	3:255
Morgan	Chas F.	4 Feb 1898	27 marr Emma Wilson 32	3:225
Morgan	Eliza Jane	- 1851	adm ch; erased 1866	3:29
Morgan	Eliza Jane	6 Jul 1851	adm ch	3:60
Morgan	Eliza Jane	30 Mar 1866	voted dismissed, eligible for letter if asked [see 3:369]	3:123
Morgan	Laura	- 1818	adm ch, wife of A. Payne; dis 1840 to Prospect	3:29
Morgan	Laura	4 Jan 1818	wife of A. Payne, adm ch; rem 25 Feb 1840 to Prospect	2:89
Morgan	Laura	4 Jan 1818	adm ch	1:58
Morgan	Laura	- 1822	female, on list of members	1:82
Moris [sic]	Lois	12 May 1799	wife of David, adm ch; died	2:85
Mornoe [sic]	-	- -	husband of Lizzie Hopkins [see Monroe]	3:21
Morris	Alanson	12 May 1799	bp, ch of David	1:169
Morris	David	12 May 1799	bp, ch of David	1:169
Morris	Julious	12 May 1799	bp, ch of David	1:169
Morris	Lois	- 1799	adm ch, wife of David; dec	3:29
Morris	Lois	10 May 1799	Da., adm ch; dead	1:55
Morris	Lois	12 May 1799	wife of David bp & adm ch	1:14
Morris	Marcus	12 May 1799	bp, ch of David	1:169
Morris	Poley	12 May 1799	bp, ch of David	1:169
Morse	Jeremiah	- 1856	adm ch from East Avon; dis 1857 to Platteville Wisconsin	3:29
Morse	Jeremiah	6 Jan 1856	adm fr Cong, E. Avon	3:90
Morse	Jeremiah	3 May 1857	dism to Cong, Platteville, Wis.	3:121
Moulthrop	John T.	19 Mar 1861	of Bridgeport marr Ophelia Chittenden of Waterbury	3:205
Moulton	Rosa B.	- 1876	adm ch; dis 1881 Cong Sidney Plains NY	3:29
Moulton	Rosa B.	5 Mar 1876	bp, adult	3:155
Moulton	Rosa B.	5 Mar 1876	adm ch	3:65
Moulton	Rosa B.	24 Jun 1881	(Thompson), dism to Cong, Sidney Plains NY	3:125
Mudge	Frank M.	29 Jun 1893	23 marr Augusta V. Blansfield 20	3:223
Mudge	Leland Hiram	29 Dec 1895	inf bp; Frank M. & Augusta B.	3:161
Munger	Rufus E.	17 Jun 1883	marr Mary A. Blake, both of Naug	3:215
Munger	V.	- -	husband of Jane C. Lewis	3:26
Munger	Verennis	- 1868	adm ch from Woodbury; dis 1872 to Ansonia [no entry under "Dismissions"]	3:29
Munger	Verennis	8 Nov 1868	adm fr 1st Congl, Woodbury	3:92
Munger	Verrenice[sic]	15 Aug 1871	marr Jennie C. Lewis, both of Naug	3:209

NAUGATUCK, CONNECTICUT, CONGREGATIONAL CHURCH RECORDS

Surname	Given name	Date	Year	Notes	Ref
Munroe	Rheta May	11 Jun	1899	inf bp; John H. & Lizzie Hopkins [see Monroe]	3:164
Munson	Mary	-	1785	adm ch; dec 1802	3:29
Munson	Mary	17 Feb	1785	wid, adm ch, d 23 May 1802	1:53
Munson	Mary	20 Feb	1785	Wd, adm ch; died 23 May 1802	2:82
Munson	Mary	20 Feb	1785	widow, adm ch	1:9
Munson	Mary	23 May	1802	Wd, d, 87y 11m 13d	1:155
Munson	Mary G.	1 Mar	1835	adm ch; dism 4 Sep 1836	2:95
Munson	Mary G.	4 Sep	1836	letter of dism to any ch	2:20
Munson	Mary S.	-	1835	adm ch; dis 1836	3:29
Murfield	W.H.	31 Dec	1874	of Waterbury marr Maggie McCarrick of Naug	3:210
Murfield	Wm	-	1878	and wife adm ch from Meth Ch, Naug, dis 1888 to Malden Mass	3:29
Murfield	Wm	3 Mar	1878	and wife adm fr M.E. Ch, Naugatuck [see Mirfield]	3:94
Murray	Silas H.	-	1866	adm ch; dis 1870 to Northl Cong Woodbury	3:29
Murray	Silas H.	Mar	1870	dism to North Cong, Woodbury	3:124
Murray	Silas Hayes	1 Jul	1866	bp, adult	3:153
Murray	Silas Hayes	1 Jul	1866	adm ch	3:63
Murray	Silvia Ann	Mar	1870	[wife of] Silas H. dism to North Cong, Woodbury	3:124
Murray	Sylvia Ann	-	1866	adm ch, wife of Silas; dis 1870 to North Cong Woodbury	3:29
Murray	Sylvia Ann	2 Sep	1866	adm fr Cong, Oxford	3:92
Mussner	Anna Marie	21 Feb	1882	marr Robert Wagner, both of Naug	3:214
Neal	Alonzo	23 Aug	1827	of Southington, marr Polly Beecher of Salem	1:153
Neal	Polly	-	1834	adm ch from Lebanon O, wife of Alonzo; dis 1842	3:31
Neal	Polly	8 Sep	1834?	wife of Alonzo, adm ch from Lebanon O.; rem 27 Nov 1842	2:93
Neal	Polly	30 Nov	1842	wife of Alonzo H., dism to ch in Southington	2:42
Needham	Anice F.	13 Dec	1888	21 marr Samuel Whiteley Jr 29	3:220
Neilson	Carrie	27 Jun	1889	marr Louis Hakenson	3:220
Nelson	Hedvig	17 Sep	1898	inf bp; Emil & Amanda	3:163
Nettleton	-	-	-	see Smith, Brainard Andrew	-
Nettleton	Clark	17 Nov	1858	d, 49, bur in Middlebury	3:252
Nettleton	Geo W.	-	1876	and wife adm ch; she dec 1896	3:31
Nettleton	Geo W.	7 May	1876	and wife adm ch	3:65
Nettleton	Laura Ann	-	1858	adm ch, wife of Clark N.	3:31
Nettleton	Laura Ann	7 Mar	1858	bp, adult	3:151
Nettleton	Laura Ann	7 Mar	1858	adm ch, bapt as adult	3:61
Nettleton	Mary	-	1876	Mrs., widow, adm ch from Middlebury; dec 1893	3:31
Nettleton	Mary	7 May	1876	Mrs., adm fr Cong, Middlebury	3:93
Nettleton	Mary	16 Jan	1893	Mrs, d, 94, old age	3:260
Newcomb	Nancy M.	27 Jun	1853	of Plymouth marr David K. Douglass of Naug	3:201
Newman	Henry	31 Mar	1898	21 marr Grace Warner 23	3:226
Newman	James H.	17 Mar	1865	of New Haven marr Susan P. Tuller of Naug	3:206
Newton	Elizabeth	3 Jul	1894	marr John A. Crich	3:223
Newton	Enoch	15 Jun	1823	ch of John, bp	1:85
Newton	Enoch	-	1869	adm ch	3:31
Newton	Enoch	2 May	1869	adm ch	3:64
Newton	Hannah	-	1833	adm ch, wife of Ansel Spencer; dec 1900	3:31
Newton	Hannah	6 Jan	1833	adm ch	2:93
Newton	Harriet M.	-	1861	adm ch	3:31
Newton	Harriet M.	3 Nov	1861	adm ch	3:62
Newton	Harriet Maria	4 Jan	1833	bp, ch of John	2:104
Newton	John	2 Sep	1813	ch of John, bp [perhaps 1820]	1:63
Newton	John	-	1818	adm ch; dec 1866	3:31
Newton	John	3 Jul	1818	on committee to est. Sabbath School	1:77
Newton	John	4 Jan	1818	adm ch	2:88
Newton	John	4 Jan	1818	adm ch	1:58

NAUGATUCK, CONNECTICUT, CONGREGATIONAL CHURCH RECORDS

Newton	John	-	1822	male, on list of members	1:81
Newton	John	23 Jul	1866	d, 78, found dead in bed, Hillside	3:255
Newton	Nettie V.	9 Sep	1873	marr Sylvester Mead, both of Waterbury	3:210
Newton	Sybel	-	1818	adm ch, wife of John; dec 1867	3:31
Newton	Sybel	4 Jan	1818	wife of John, adm ch	2:88
Newton	Sybel	4 Jan	1818	wife of John, adm ch	1:58
Newton	Sybel	-	1822	wife of John, member	1:82
Newton	Sybel	1 Nov	1867	d, 78, cancer, Hillside	3:255
Newton	Thomas H.	-	1889	adm ch from Thomaston	3:31
Newton	Thos H.	6 Jan	1889	adm fr Cong, Thomaston Ct	3:96
Nichols	Alfred Judson	8 Mar	1892	29 marr Julia M. Cable 19	3:221
Nichols	Amanda	-	1851	adm ch; dis 1854 Middlebury	3:31
Nichols	Amanda	6 Jul	1851	adm ch	3:60
Nichols	Amanda	22 Oct	1854	dism to Cong, Middlebury	3:120
Nichols	David K.	1 Dec	1851	of Waterbury marr Harriet D. Williams of Naug	3:201
Nichols	Derwood Orson	9 Jun	1901	ch bp; Frank R. & Lena (Wedge) [sic]	3:165
Nichols	E.H.	-	1893	Mrs., adm ch	3:31
Nichols	E.H.	2 Jul	1893	Mrs, adm ch	3:70
Nichols	Frank R.	26 Apr	1893	21 marr Lena P. Widge 21	3:223
Nichols	Maude Gertrude	-	1890	adm ch	3:31
Nichols	Maude Gertrude	9 Mar	1890	bp, adult	3:159
Nichols	Maude Gertrude	9 Mar	1890	Miss, adm ch	3:70
Nichols	Melecent A.	-	1885	adm ch	3:31
Nichols	Melecent A.	5 Jul	1885	adm ch	3:68
Nichols	Melicent A.	5 Jul	1885	bp, adult	3:158
Nichols	Melicent A.	8 Oct	1889	24 marr Ferdinand Fredk Schaffer 36	3:220
Nichols	Muriel	13 Jun	1897	an inf, bp	3:162
Nichols	Rebecca	-	1836	adm ch; dis 1840	3:31
Nichols	Rebecca	3 Jan	1836	adm ch; [m] -- Platt; dism 25 Feb 1840 to Prospect	2:96
Nielson	Anna Mary F.	3 Sep	1897	dism to 1st Pres, Patterson NJ [with Carl Trautviller]	3:129
Nillson	Anna Mary F.	-	1897	adm ch; dis 1897	3:31
Nillson	Anna Mary Friderik	2 May	1897	adm ch	3:71
Noble	Chas	-	1876	adm ch from No. Manchester; dis 1892 to Mason City Iowa	3:31
Noble	Chas	-	1876	Mrs., adm ch from No. Manchester; dec 1882	3:31
Noble	Chas	7 May	1876	and wife adm fr Cong, No Manchester Ct	3:93
Noble	Chas	18 Dec	1882	d, Mrs., 47, cancer on liver	3:258
Noble	Chas	12 Aug	1892	dism to M.E. Ch, Mason City Iowa	3:127
Noble	Eliza	-	1887	Mrs, adm ch from Pittsfield Mass; dec 1899	3:31
Noble	Eliza	1 May	1887	Mrs, adm fr 1st Baptist, Pittsfield Mass	3:95
Noble	Eliza	22 Aug?	1899	Mrs, d [day taken fr previous entry]	3:261
Noble	Emma	-	1887	Miss, adm ch fr Pittsfield Mass; dec 1893 [see Davis, Emma]	3:31
Noble	Emma	1 May	1887	Miss, adm fr 1st Baptist, Pittsfield Mass	3:95
Noble	Henry W.	-	1878	adm ch	3:31
Noble	Henry W.	3 Mar	1878	bp, adult	3:156
Noble	Henry W.	3 Mar	1878	adm ch	3:66
Noble	Isabelle J.	-	1876	adm ch from No. Manchester; Dis Irr. 1884	3:31
Noble	Isabelle J.	7 May	1876	Miss, adm fr Cong, No Manchester Ct	3:93
Noble	Isabelle J.	18 May	1884	(Hartley) dism to United Episcopal Ch	3:126
Noble	Isabelle Jane	27 Jun	1881	marr George Henry Hartley, both of Naug	3:213
Noble	John W.	26 Sep	1888	21 marr Lena Maud Snyder 17	3:219
Noble	Lottie L.	28 Oct	1874	of Naug marr Edward Shipman of Glastenbury	3:210
Noble	Minnie E.	3 May	1875	bur, 11 mos, Hillside	3:257
Nolt	Anson	5 Apr	1857	d, 15 ms, scarlet fever & measles	3:251
North	Louise	-	1900	(Garrison), adm ch, wife of Tracy W., from Naug Episcopal	3:31

NAUGATUCK, CONNECTICUT, CONGREGATIONAL CHURCH RECORDS

North	Louise Garrison	6 May	1900	Mrs., adm fr St. Michaels Episcopal [Naug]	3:99
North	Margaret Louise	9 Jun	1901	ch bp; Tracy W. & Louise (Garrison)	3:165
North	Tracey William	9 Mar	1890	adm ch	3:70
North	Tracey Wm	-	1890	adm ch	3:31
North	Tracy William	9 Mar	1890	bp, adult	3:159
Norton	-	9 May	1873	bur, 58 [just below Mary Norton, ditto mark only under surname]	3:257
Norton	Cyrus	-	1788	adm ch; dis 1804 to Wolcott	3:31
Norton	Cyrus	20 Jul	1788	adm ch; rem 7 Oct 1804 to Wolcott	2:84
Norton	Cyrus	20 Jul	1788	adm ch	1:11
Norton	Cyrus	20 Jul	1788	adm ch, dism 7 Oct 1804	1:55
Norton	Cyrus	7 Oct	1804	given letter of rec	1:38
Norton	David	-	1788	adm ch; dec	3:31
Norton	David	20 Jul	1788	adm ch; died	2:84
Norton	David	20 Jul	1788	adm ch	1:11
Norton	David	20 Jul	1788	adm ch; dead	1:55
Norton	Eben	12 Jun	1864	d, 25, consumption, Hillside	3:254
Norton	Elihu H.	20 May	1855	of Litchfield marr Jane E. Haigh of Naug	3:202
Norton	H.A.	9 Sep	1877	d, 78, Heart disease	3:258
Norton	Horatio A.	-	1868	adm ch from Thomaston; dis Aug 1870 to Cheshire	3:31
Norton	Horatio A.	5 Jan	1868	adm fr Thomaston	3:92
Norton	Horatio A.	28 Aug	1870	dism to Cong, Cheshire	3:124
Norton	Ida F.	2 Nov	1882	marr James H. Burbank, both of Naug	3:214
Norton	Jabez Simons	4 Jan	1801	bp, ch of Cyrus	1:169
Norton	Jerusha	-	1788	adm ch, wife of Cyrus; dis 1804 to Wolcott	3:31
Norton	Jerusha	20 Jul	1788	wife of Cyrus, adm ch; rem 7 Oct 1804 to Wolcott	2:84
Norton	Jerusha	20 Jul	1788	wife of Cyrus adm ch	1:11
Norton	Jerusha	20 Jul	1788	C., adm ch, dism 7 Oct 1804	1:55
Norton	Jerusha	7 Oct	1804	wife of Cyrus given letter of rec	1:38
Norton	Jerusha Johnson	2 Nov	1798	bp, ch of Cyrus	1:168
Norton	Lois	27 Apr	1862	d, 59, dropsy	3:253
Norton	Lowman Green	2 Jun	1793	bp, ch of Cyrus	1:166
Norton	Mary	10 Feb	1873	bur, 2 wks	3:257
Norton	Rachel	-	1801	adm ch; dis 1804 to Wolcott	3:31
Norton	Rachel	22 Feb	1801	adm ch; rem 7 Oct 1804 to Wolcott	2:86
Norton	Rachel	22 Feb	1801	adm ch, dism 7 Oct 1804	1:56
Norton	Rachel	22 Feb	1801	adm ch	1:21
Norton	Rachel	7 Oct	1804	dau of Cyrus and Jerusha given letter of rec	1:38
Norton	Roxcillane	21 Feb	1796	bp, ch of Cyrus	1:167
Norton	Submit Bouton	8 Aug	1790	bp, ch of Cyrus	1:165
Norton	Urania B.	9 Mar	1878	Mrs, marr Benjamin Fowler, both of Naug	3:212
Nulberg	-	-	-	see Milberg	-
O'Donnell	Harry A.	16 Sep	1896	34 marr Lizzie Schumacher 26	3:224
Olson	Matilda	24 Apr	1886	28 marr Gustave E. Anderson 28, both of Naug	3:217
Orsbon	Elizabeth	22 Feb	1781	one of the persons constituting the church	2:79
Orsborn	Amos	22 Feb	1781	adm ch; died 1 Nov 1790	2:81
Orsborn	Elizabeth	22 Feb	1781	wife of Amos O., adm ch; rem	2:82
Orsborn	Molly	31 May	1795	wife of Asahel, adm ch; rem 9 Sep 1810 to Columbia O.	2:85
Orsborn	Sarah	12 Jun	1814	wife of Samuel, adm ch; died 1817	2:87
Orsbron	Charlotte	27 Nov	1842	wife of Samuel, adm ch	2:98
Orsbron	Charlotte	27 Nov	1842	w of Samuel C., adm fr First Ch in Harwinton[?]	2:42
Orsbron	Norman Wilson	1 Sep	1843	bp, ch of Samuel C.	2:107
Orsbron	Sally M.	15 Aug	1842	dism to ch in Munroe	2:41
Orsbron	Samuel C.	27 Nov	1842	adm ch	2:98
Orsbron	Samuel C.	27 Nov	1842	adm from first Ch in Harwinton[?]	2:42

NAUGATUCK, CONNECTICUT, CONGREGATIONAL CHURCH RECORDS

Osbon	Clarisa Marshal	8 Feb	1801	bp, ch of Asahel	1:169
Osborn	Aaron	8 Dec	1852	of Naug marr Polly M. Bishop of Woodbury	3:201
Osborn	Alma	29 May	1796	bp, ch of Asahel	1:168
Osborn	Amelia	29 Apr	1798	bp, ch of Asahel	1:168
Osborn	Amos	22 Feb	1781	one of the persons constituting the church	2:79
Osborn	Amos	22 Feb	1781	subscribed to Constitution and Covenant	1:5
Osborn	Amos	22 Feb	1781	original member, dec 1 Nov 1790	1:53
Osborn	Asahel Benham	14 Aug	1803	bp, ch of Asahel	1:171
Osborn	Asahel Benham	4 May	1810	d, son of Asahel, 6y	1:160
Osborn	Charlotte	-	1842	adm ch, wife of Saml; dec 1886	3:33
Osborn	Charlotte	22 Nov	1886	Mrs S.C., d, 65, peritonitis	3:259
Osborn	Daniel	25 Jul	1801	d, 62y 2m 12d	1:155
Osborn	Elijah	2 Oct	1803	wife d, 56y	1:156
Osborn	Elisabeth	22 Feb	1781	subscribed to Constitution and Covenant	1:5
Osborn	Elizabeth	22 Feb	1781	original member, dism, ["Amos" added]	1:53
Osborn	Ella	9 Jun	1869	of Naug marr Albert G. Hotchkiss of Torrington	3:208
Osborn	Ella Charlotte	-	1848	bp, ch of Samuel	2:108
Osborn	Emma	7 May	1876	adm ch	3:65
Osborn	Eunice	-	1849	adm ch from HumpVille; dis 1850 Oxford	3:33
Osborn	Eunice	May	1849	adm ch from Humphriesville	2:100
Osborn	Experience	Feb	1813	d	1:160
Osborn	Ezra	-	-	husband of Louisa Gunn	3:15
Osborn	Ezra	5 Jun	1854	marr Harriet Louisa Gunn, both of Naug	3:201
Osborn	Frank Ely	1 Nov	1850	inf bp, Saml C. & Charlotte	3:150
Osborn	Frank Ely	5 Oct	1854	d, son of Saml C. & Charlotte, 5 y, dysentery, Hillside	3:251
Osborn	George	18 Oct	1864	of Naug marr Martha Pierpont of Plymouth	3:206
Osborn	Hattie J.	2 Jul	1876	adm ch	3:65
Osborn	Hershall	22 Jun	1795	bp, ch of Asahel	1:167
Osborn	Lottie E.	-	1885	adm ch; dis 1887 Hudson NY	3:33
Osborn	Lottie E.	5 Jul	1885	bp, adult	3:157
Osborn	Lottie E.	5 Jul	1885	adm ch	3:68
Osborn	Lottie E.	27 May	1887	dism to Dutch R., Hudson NY	3:126
Osborn	Louisa	18 Mar	1866	dism to Sugar Grove Chris. Un. Church	3:123
Osborn	Maggie P.	27 May	1887	dism to Dutch R., Hudson NY	3:126
Osborn	Mariette	16 Jul	1807	bp, dau of Asahel	1:173
Osborn	Martha A.	12 Oct	1880	marr Walter W. Donnan[?], both of Seymour	3:213
Osborn	Menervia	16 Jul	1807	bp, dau of Asahel	1:173
Osborn	Miss [sic]	19 Dec	1825	ch d, fever, 5	1:163
Osborn	Molley	22 Jun	1795	bp, ch of Asahel	1:167
Osborn	Molly	-	1795	adm ch, wife of Asahel; dis 1810 to Columbia O.	3:33
Osborn	Molly	31 May	1795	Asa[hel], adm ch, dism 9 Sep 1810	1:55
Osborn	Molly	31 May	1795	wife of Asahel bp & adm ch	1:13
Osborn	Molly	9 Sep	1810	wife of Asahel given cert of membership	1:51
Osborn	Mrs.	18 May	1814	speech impediment, written narrative of her conversion	1:68
Osborn	Polly	-	1822	wife of Saml, member, died 29 May 1826	1:82
Osborn	Sally M.	-	1837	adm ch from Munroe; dis 1842	3:33
Osborn	Sally Maria	5 Mar	1837	adm ch; rem May 1842 to Munro	2:96
Osborn	Sam	Dec	1823	committee appointed to visit him due to neglect of covenant	1:97f
-	-	-	-	commitments	
Osborn	Saml	-	1818	adm ch; dec 1824	3:33
Osborn	Saml	19 Feb	1823	ch stillborn	1:161
Osborn	Saml C.	-	1842	adm ch from Harwinton; dec 1863	3:33
Osborn	Samuel	6 Sep	1818	adm ch; excomm 1 Aug 1824	2:91
Osborn	Samuel	6 Sep	1818	adm ch, dism	1:59

NAUGATUCK, CONNECTICUT, CONGREGATIONAL CHURCH RECORDS

Osborn	Samuel	-	1822	male, on list of members; excluded	1:81
Osborn	Samuel	1 Aug	1824	excluded [by his own desire]	1:99
Osborn	Samuel	29 May	1826	wife d, childbed, 42	1:163
Osborn	Samuel	2 Jul	1829	d, sudden at Harwinton, 63	1:145
Osborn	Sarah	3 Apr	1803	d, wife of Andrew, abt 85y wanting 17d	1:156
Osborn	Sarah	-	1814	adm ch, wife of Saml; dec 1817	3:33
Osborn	Sarah	12 Jun	1814	Sam., adm ch, d 29 Oct 1817	1:57
Osborn	Sarah	12 Jun	1814	adm ch	1:68
Osborn	Sarah	28 Apr	1814	Mrs., prop to join ch but due to ill health her case was postponed	1:68
Osborn	Temperance	-	1827	adm from Brick Ch NY, wife of Saml; dec 1850	3:33
Osborn	Temperance	13 Aug	1827	w of Samuel, adm ch fr New York Brick Ch; died 12 Dec 1850	2:91
Osborn	Temperance	13 Aug	1827	Wid, adm ch	1:59a
Osborn	Temperance	29 Oct	1827	wife of Samuel, adm on rec from Brick Ch New York	1:104
Osborn	Temperance	-	1829	wife of Samuel, member adm	1:83
Osborn	Temperance	12 Dec	1850	d, 73, Inflam, Hillside	3:250
Osborn	Walter Samuel	Aug	1846	bp, ch of Samuel	2:107
Osborn	Wilson N.	27 May	1887	dism to Dutch R., Hudson NY	3:126
Osborne	Amos	-	1781	adm ch; dec 1790	3:33
Osborne	Amos	5 Mar	1865	ch bp; Ezra & Louisa	3:153
Osborne	Elisabeth	-	1781	adm ch, wife of Amos; dis	3:33
Osborne	Ella C.	-	1869	adm ch, wife of -- Hotchkiss; dis 1869 to Wolcottville	3:33
Osborne	Ella C.	2 May	1869	adm ch	3:64
Osborne	Emily Louisa	5 Mar	1856	d, ch of Ezra & Emily, 8 ms, dropsy, Gunntown	3:251
Osborne	Emma	-	1876	adm ch; dec 1879	3:33
Osborne	Emma	4 Oct	1876	marr Ralph Tolles, both of Naug	3:211
Osborne	Eunice	26 May	1850	dism to Cong, Oxford Ct	3:128
Osborne	George Skinner	4 Nov	1853	ch bp; Saml & Charlotte	3:150
Osborne	George Skinner	27 Sep	1854	d, Saml C. & Charlotte, 2 yr, dysentery, Hillside	3:251
Osborne	Harriet Joann	2 Mar	1863	inf bp; S.C. & Charlotte	3:153
Osborne	Hattie J.	-	1876	adm ch, wife of E. Spencer	3:33
Osborne	Margaret P.	-	1869	adm ch from Waterbury, wife of W.N.; dis 1887 to Hudson NY	3:33
Osborne	Margaret P.	3 Jan	1869	adm fr 1st Cong, Waterbury	3:92
Osborne	Mary Emma	5 Sep	1858	ch bp; Saml C. & Charlotte	3:152
Osborne	Saml C.	28 Feb	1863	d, 42, falling of a limb, Hillside	3:254
Osborne	William	5 Mar	1865	ch bp; Ezra & Louisa	3:153
Osborne	Wilson N.	-	1865	adm ch; dis 1887 Hudson NY	3:33
Osborne	Wilson N.	7 May	1865	adm ch	3:63
Osbron	Samuel C.	29 Mar	1850	on comm	2:63
Owen	Mary Jones	-	1899	adm ch, wife of Rich E.	3:33
Owen	Mary Jones	2 Jul	1899	Mrs., adm fr Memorial Pres, Utica NY	3:98
Owen	Richard Edwd	-	1897	adm ch	3:33
Owens	Richard Edwards	4 Jul	1897	adm ch	3:72
Oxby	William	5 Jul	1865	marr Elizabeth Draper, both of Naug	3:206
Page	Mary	-	1852	adm ch; erased 1866	3:36
Page	Mary	4 Jul	1852	bp, profession	3:150
Page	Mary	4 Jul	1852	adm ch	3:60
Page	Mary	30 Mar	1866	voted dismissed, eligible for letter if asked [see 3:369]	3:123
Painter	A.A.	23 Feb	1889	19 marr Addie Gay 31	3:220
Painter	C.C.	28 Nov	1869	settled as Pastor; dism May 1872	3:1
Painter	Chas C.	22 Feb	1881	at centennial exercises	3:300
Pallman	August P.	23 Oct	1883	marr Christina Wicke, both of Naug	3:216
Palmer	Alice S.	-	1894	adm ch	3:37
Palmer	Alice S.	7 Jan	1894	adm ch [see Jones, Chas Henry & Mark Elbert]	3:71

NAUGATUCK, CONNECTICUT, CONGREGATIONAL CHURCH RECORDS

Palmer	George	10 Dec 1826	of New Haven, marr Hannah O. Alling of Salem	1:153
Palmer	Liberty	16 May 1864	ch d, "funeral, Middleb[ur]y" 1 1/2, scarlet fever	3:254
Pardee	Asa	20 Oct 1791	bp, ch of widow Tryphina	1:166
Pardee	Esther	20 Oct 1791	bp, ch of widow Tryphina	1:166
Pardee	Isaac	30 Oct 1791	bp, ch of the widow ["Pardee" smudged out]	1:166
Pardee	Lucy	20 Oct 1791	bp, ch of widow Tryphina	1:166
Pardee	Meliscent	- 1828	adm ch, dism 1829	1:59a
Pardee	Millissent	- 1828	adm ch fr Waterbury, w of T. Baldwin; dis 1829 to Middlebury	3:35
Pardee	Milliscent	6 Jan 1828	adm ch; rec by ch of Waterbury	1:106
Pardee	Milliscent	- 1829	female, member; dism	1:83
Pardee	Millissent	6 Jan 1828	wife of Theo. Baldwin, adm ch from Waterbury; rem to Middlebury	2:91
Pardee	Phebe	20 Oct 1791	bp, ch of Widow Tryphine	1:166
Pardee	Sara	2 Nov 1869	Mrs, of Naug marr James King of Bethany	3:208
Pardee	Triphena	17 Jul 1791	Wd. of Isaac, adm ch; rem [husb "Theopha" & "to Middlebury"	2:84
-	-	- -	crossed out]	
Pardee	Triphena	17 Jul 1791	Wid. adm ch, dism	1:55
Pardee	Triphina	20 Oct 1791	bp, ch of widow Tryphina	1:166
Pardee	Tryphena	- 1791	adm ch, wife of Isaac; dis	3:35
Pardee	Tryphina	20 Oct 1791	children bp ["widow of Jonathan, Revolutionary soldier" added]	1:166
Pardee	Tryphina	17 Jul 1791	widow, adm ch	1:12
Parker	Mattie	21 Aug 1899	19 marr Wallace A. Rowland 29	3:227
Parker	Robt V.	- 1887	Mrs., adm ch from Woodbury	3:37
Parker	Robt V.	1 May 1887	Mrs., adm fr 1st Cong, Woodbury, Conn	3:95
Parkington	Geo A.	1 Jan 1860	dism to Methodist Ch, Naug	3:121
Parkington	George A.	- 1858	adm ch; dis 1860 Methodist Naug	3:36
Parkington	George Amasa	4 July 1858	adm ch	3:62
Parmalee	Hattie A.	7 Aug 1887	marr Chas V. Wheeler of Seymour 23	3:218
Partree	John	- 1843	adm ch; dis 1844 Waterbury	3:36
Partree	John	5 Nov 1843	delegate to Woodbridge	2:48
Partree	John	14 May 1843	adm ch; dism 8 Apr 1844	2:99
Partree	John	7 Apr 1844	dism to ch in Watertown	2:49
Paterson	Henry	9 Jan 1842	adm ch from HumphreyVill; dism 19 Nov 1843 to HumphrusVille	2:98
Paterson	Henry	19 Nov 1843	dism to ch in Humphries Ville	2:48
Patterson	Celestia	27 Nov 1850	of Naug marr William W. Smith of Bridgeport	3:200
Patterson	Chs M.	- 1852	adm ch; dec 1856	3:36
Patterson	Chs M.	23 Nov 1856	d, 25, "shot while in pursuit of game," Hillside	3:251
Patterson	Chs. Moses	2 May 1852	bp, profession	3:150
Patterson	Chs. Moses	2 May 1852	adm ch	3:60
Patterson	Ellen Rebecca	- 1876	adm ch, wife of H.D.	3:37
Patterson	Ellen Rebecca	2 Jan 1876	bp, adult	3:155
Patterson	Ellen Rebecca	2 Jan 1876	wife of H.D.P., adm ch	3:65
Patterson	Emily	- 1852	adm ch from Plymouth, wife of Chs Spencer	3:36
Patterson	Emily	21 Mar 1852	w of Charles P[atterson?], adm fr Plymouth Center Cong.	3:90
Patterson	Emily A.	24 Nov 1859	marr Charles Spencer, both of Naug	3:204
Patterson	Harry	- 1845	adm ch from Humpevill; dec 1890	3:36
Patterson	Henry	- 1842	adm ch from Hump,Ville; dis 1843 Hump,eville	3:36
Patterson	Henry	19 Jan 1842	adm ch from HumphreysVille	2:40
Patterson	Henry	11 May 1845	adm ch, from HumphriesVille	2:99
Patterson	Henry	11 May 1845	adm from ch in Humphries Ville	2:50
Patterson	Henry	- 1887	Mrs, adm ch; dec 1891	3:37
Patterson	Henry	4 Sep 1887	bp, adult, "Mrs"	3:158
Patterson	Henry	4 Sep 1887	Mrs, adm ch	3:69
Patterson	Henry	29 Nov 1890	d, 81, pneumonia	3:260
Patterson	Henry	26 Dec 1891	Mrs, d, 80, La Grippe	3:260

NAUGATUCK, CONNECTICUT, CONGREGATIONAL CHURCH RECORDS

Patterson	Hiram	-	1866	adm ch; dis 1890 1st Cong Meriden	3:36
Patterson	Hiram	2 Sep	1866	adm ch	3:63
Patterson	Hiram	24 Oct	1890	dism to 1st Cong, Meriden Conn	3:127
Patterson	John G.	4 Jan	1860	marr Lucy A. Fox, both of Naug	3:204
Patterson	Lena M.	22 Apr	1896	23 marr Nelson J. Peck 21	3:224
Patterson	Lena May	7 May	1886	youth, bp; H. Dewitt & Ellen	3:158
Patterson	Lena May	27 May	1898	dism to 1 Presb, Willoughby Ohio	3:129
Patterson	Lina May	-	1886	adm ch; dis 1898	3:37
Patterson	Lina May	7 Nov	1886	adm ch	3:69
Patterson	M. Lizzie E.	19 Sep	1877	["E." crossed out] of Naug marr Alvin D. Ayers of Syracuse NY	3:211
Patterson	Mary Elisabeth	4 May	1856	inf bp; Chs M. & Emily	3:151
Patterson	Nellie L.	-	1885	adm ch; dec 1890	3:37
Patterson	Nellie L.	5 Jul	1885	bp, adult	3:157
Patterson	Nellie L.	5 Jul	1885	adm ch	3:68
Patterson	Nellie L.	2 Mar	1890	d, 20, scarlet fever	3:260
Payne	-	-	-	husband of Sarah E. Hotchkiss	3:19
Payne	-	-	-	husband of Sarah E. Hotchkiss	2:97
Payne	A.	-	-	husband of Laura Morgan	3:29
Payne	A.	-	-	husband of Laura Morgan	2:89
Payne	Carrie E.	-	1885	adm ch	3:37
Payne	Carrie E.	5 Jul	1885	bp, adult	3:157
Payne	Carrie E.	5 Jul	1885	adm ch	3:68
Payne	Catharine	13 Jun	1897	inf bp; Walter & Mabel	3:162
Payne	Cora Allie	13 Aug	1899	ch bp; Willis Edwd & Pattie Jones, 6 yr.	3:164
Payne	F.	-	-	husband of Grace Langdon	3:27
Payne	Harry Van D.	13 Aug	1899	ch bp; Willis Edwd & Pattie Jones, 9 yr.	3:164
Payne	J. Fred	4 Jun	1890	32 marr Grace Langdon 28	3:221
Payne	Joseph M.	16 Mar	1826	of Waterbury, marr Abigail Doolittle of Cheshire	1:152
Payne	Juliette A.	-	1866	adm ch, wife of Geo B. Twitchell	3:36
Payne	Juliette A.	2 Sep	1866	adm ch	3:63
Payne	Maria	-	1865	adm ch, husband of -- Cook; dis 1894 to Epis-Wallingford	3:36
Payne	Maria	2 Jul	1865	adm ch	3:63
Payne	Maria	5 Oct	1870	of Naug marr William R. Cook of Wallingford	3:209
Payne	Maria (Cook)	13 Apr	1894	dism to Episcopal, Wallingford	3:128
Payne	Marjorie	23 Jun	1895	inf bp; Walter & Mabel Johnson	3:161
Payne	Mary E.	-	1893	adm ch	3:37
Payne	Mary E.	7 May	1893	adm ch	3:70
Payne	Mary Imogene	3 May	1885	ch bp; Sheldon F. & Mrs.	3:157
Payne	Merit	8 Nov	1829	ch d, lung fever, 14 m	1:145
Payne	Merit H.	18 Sep	1827	marr Sally Hickox of Salem	1:153
Payne	Orrie A.	11 Jan	1864	d, 14, typhoid, Hillside	3:254
Payne	Sally	-	1837	adm ch, wife of Edwd M.; dis 1858 Waterbury	3:36
Payne	Sally	5 Mar	1837	wife of Edward M., adm ch	2:96
Payne	Sally	20 Jun	1858	dism to 2d Cong, Waterbury	3:121
Payne	Sarah	-	1866	adm ch from Prospect, wife of Harman[?] P. ["P" crossed out]	3:36
Payne	Sarah	7 Jan	1866	adm fr Cong, Prospect	3:92
Payne	Shelden F.	-	1886	appt'd Deacon	3:1
Payne	Sheldon F.	-	1885	adm ch, with wife, from Geneva O.	3:37
Payne	Sheldon F.	3 May	1885	and wife adm fr 1st Cong, Geneva Ohio	3:95
Payne	Theodore L.	-	1852	adm ch; dis 1858 to Waterbury	3:36
Payne	Theodore L.	7 Mar	1852	adm ch	3:60
Payne	Theodore L.	21 Mar	1858	dism to 1st Cong, Waterbury	3:121
Payne	Theodore Luzerne	7 Mar	1852	bp, profession	3:150
Payne	Willis Edwd	13 Aug	1899	bp, adult	3:164

NAUGATUCK, CONNECTICUT, CONGREGATIONAL CHURCH RECORDS

Pease	Harriet L.	20 Jun	1892	27 marr Frederick A. Fitts 36	3:222
Peck	-	9 Sep	1798	adm ch, dism 4 Jan 1801	1:55
Peck	Dorcas	-	1798	adm ch, wife of Ward; dis 1801 Waterbury	3:35
Peck	Dorcas	9 Apr	1798	["Lucy" crossed out] w of Ward, adm ch; rem 4 Jan 1801 Waterbury	2:85
Peck	Elisabeth	16 Sep	1798	bp, ch of Ward	1:168
Peck	Erwin	12 Nov	1857	marr Jane Gilbert, both of Naug	3:203
Peck	Franklin	19 Mar	1859	d, 4 1/2, conges. of the brain, Hillside	3:252
Peck	Harriet	12 Nov	1857	of Naug marr Edward Tuttle of Woodbury	3:203
Peck	Hermon	16 Sep	1798	bp, ch of Ward	1:168
Peck	Libbie	25 Dec	1899	23 marr Erwin W. Cable 22	3:228
Peck	Lyman	16 Sep	1798	bp, ch of Ward	1:168
Peck	Nelson J.	22 Apr	1896	21 marr Lena M. Patterson 23	3:224
Peck	Roxy	16 Sep	1798	bp, ch of Ward	1:168
Peck	Samuel	3 Jan	1802	of Woodbridge, marr Esther Judd, of Salem	1:151
Peck	Sherman	16 Sep	1798	bp, ch of Ward	1:168
Peck	So--	16 Sep	1798	bp, ch of Ward	1:168
Peck	Ward	9 Sep	1798	wife adm ch	1:13
Peck	Ward	-	1799	bp, son of Ward	1:169
Peck	Ward	4 Jan	1801	wife rec to ch in Waterbury	1:20
Penley[sic]	W.D.	Sep	1831	on Visiting Committee, [see Benley]	1:115
Perkins	F.T.	Jul	1872	settled as Pastor; dism May 1875	3:1
Perkins	F.T.	-	1873	Rev., adm ch from 1st Cong Hartford; dis 1875 Tilton NH	3:36
Perkins	F.T.	5 Jan	1873	Rev., adm fr 1st Cong, Hartford, Ct., wife also	3:92
Perkins	F.T.	15 Aug	1875	Rev., dism to Cong, Tilton NH; also wife	3:124
Perkins	Fred T.	-	1873	Mrs., adm ch from 1st Cong Hartford; dis 1875 Tilton NH	3:36
Perkins	Rev. Mr.	17 Aug	1806	addressed Thomas Porter re his sin	1:45
Peterson	Chas C.	29 Jun	1887	marr Lizzie S. Shindler	3:218
Peterson	Florence A.	4 Jan	1860	d, inf of Mr. (col[ore]d), 4 m, Hillside	3:252
Pettengill	Amos	23 Jun	1822	Rev, chosen Moderator	1:80
Pettengill	Amos	26 May	1822	Rev, invited to be Minister	1:80
Pettengill	Hannah	-	1822	female, member, adm since 1822	1:83
Pettengill	Hannah	-	1823	adm ch from So. Farms, wife of Amos; dis 1840 to Wellfleet	3:35
Pettengill	Hannah	30 Aug	1840	Mrs., dism to 1st ch in Wellfleet M.S. [sic]	2:34
Petter	Cordelia	5 Jun	1900	Mrs., 34 marr Louis A. Raymond 37	3:228
Pettibone	Stephen H.	15 Apr	1855	marr Mrs. Corinthia Skinner both of Harwinton	3:202
Pettingill	Amos	-	1823	Rev., installed; died 19 [sic] Aug 1830	2:2
Pettingill	Amos	1 Jan	1823	Pastor, died 19 [sic] Aug 1830	2:79
Pettingill	Amos	20 Aug	1830	Rev, d, 50 10 days	1:146
Pettingill	H.	5 May	1837	Mrs., on comm "to attend to cases of unchristian walk...female members"	2:25
-	-	-	-		
Pettingill	Hannah	7 Jul	1822	adm ch	1:59
Pettingill	Hannah	5 Sep	1823	w of Amos, adm ch fr South Farms; rem 30 Aug 1840 Wellfleet, MS.	2:91
Pettingill	Hannah	5 Sep	1823	wife of Amos, adm, from ch in Litchfield South Farms	1:97
Pettingill	Hannah Elizabeth	13 Aug	1826	ch of Amos, Pastor, bp	1:86
Pettingill	Mary Ann	20 Mar	1828	propounded for adm	1:106
Pettingill	Mary Ann	23 Nov	1828	adm ch	1:59b
Pettingill	Mary Ann	23 Nov	1828	member	1:94
Pettingill	Mary Ann	-	1829	adm ch; dis 1842	3:35
Pettingill	Mary Ann	3 Nov	1829	[date is as written] adm ch; rem 1842	2:93
Pettingill	Mr.	28 Nov	1822	voted to be installed as Pastor	1:96
Pettingill	Mr.	1 Jan	1823	installed	1:96
Pettingill	Samuel Martyn	4 May	1823	ch of A., Pastor, bp	1:85
Phelps	Catharine J.	17 Nov	1826	of Salem, marr Garry Arnts	1:153
Phelps	Frederick A.	25 May	1887	22 marr Sadie A. Bristol 22	3:218

NAUGATUCK, CONNECTICUT, CONGREGATIONAL CHURCH RECORDS

Phelps	Lucinda A.	-	1866	adm ch, wife of Henry; dis 1873 1st Cong Waterbury	3:36
Phelps	Lucinda A.	18 May	1873	dism to 1st Cong, Waterbury	3:124
Phelps	Lucinda Ann	1 Jul	1866	bp, adult	3:153
Phelps	Lucinda Ann	1 Jul	1866	adm ch	3:63
Phelps	Sadie Bristol	1 Sep	1892	Mrs, 27 marr Frederick Allison Smith 29	3:222
Picket	Nancy E.	10 Jan	1875	dism to Presb, Darien Ct	3:124
Picket	Nancy E.	-	1890	Mrs., adm ch from Watertown; dec 1890	3:37
Picket	Nancy E.	3 Dec	1890	d, 72, congestion of spine	3:260
Picket	Nancy E.	7 Sep	1890	Mrs., adm fr Cong, Watertown Ct	3:96
Pickett	Julia B.	22 Sep	1869	marr Stephen C. Bartlett, both of Naug	3:208
Pickett	Nancy E.	-	1866	adm ch from Morris Ct, wife of --; dis 1875 to Darien	3:36
Pickett	Nancy E.	1 Jul	1866	adm fr Cong, Morris Ct.	3:92
Pierce	Robert	29 Oct	1892	24 marr Bridget Splan 24	3:222
Pierpoint	Fanny	-	1877	adm ch; dis 1880 Fair Haven	3:37
Pierpont	Fanny	20 Feb	1880	dism to Cong, Fair Haven	3:125
Pierpont	Henry	22 Feb	1881	at centennial exercises; 264 York St, New Haven	3:300
Pierpont	Martha	18 Oct	1864	of Plymouth marr George Osborn of Naug	3:206
Pierrpont	Fanny	7 Jan	1877	adm ch	3:65
Pilkington	James	29 Nov	1855	marr Margaret McCornish, b of Manchester at Manchester	3:202
Pinder	William	17 Mar	1855	marr Esther Mahon of Naug	3:202
Pine [Rine?]	Betsy	25 Sep	1828	of Southbury, marr Calvin Hoadley of Salem	1:153
Pinneo	Bezabel	29 Sep	1801	Rev. Elder attending consociation in Salem, from 1st Milford	1:25
Pitkin	Frederick Wells	30 Aug	1868	ch bp [at] Manchester; Jas. R. & Adelaide	3:154
Pitkin	James R.	13 Jun	1853	marr Addie Holton, both of Manchester Ct	3:201
Platt	-	-	-	husband of Amelia Lewis	3:25
Platt	-	-	-	husband of Rebecca Nichols	2:96
Platt	-	-	-	husband of Amelia Lewis	2:99
Platt	-	10 Aug	1874	bur 72 Hillside [from stone "1801 Jul 16 1872 Sep 18 Fanny F."]	3:257
Platt	Adeline E.	29 Sep	1872	marr Miles S. Clark, both of Waterbury	3:209
Platt	Alfred	19 Jun	1864	of Waterbury marr Mrs. Lola Russell of Prospect	3:206
Platt	Amelia (Lewis)	22 Aug	1852	dism to 2d Cong, Waterbury	3:120
Platt	Amelia M.	-	1860	adm ch from Waterbury, wife of Clark; dis 1867 to 2d Cong Waterb	3:36
Platt	Amelia M.	2 Sep	1860	w of Clark, adm fr 2 Cong, Waterbury	3:91
Platt	Amelia M.	29 Dec	1867	dism to 2d Cong, Waterbury	3:123
Platt	Annie	-	-	see Brownlow	-
Platt	Bertha L.	-	1866	adm ch; dis 1867 to 2d Cong Waterb	3:36
Platt	Bertha L.	29 Dec	1867	dism to 2d Cong, Waterbury	3:123
Platt	Bertha Louisa	2 Sep	1866	bp, adult	3:153
Platt	Bertha Louisa	2 Sep	1866	adm ch	3:64
Platt	Charles H.	11 Apr	1862	d, 8 y, consumption	3:253
Platt	David M.	30 Sep	1824	marr Ann Chittendon of Columbia	1:152
Platt	David M.	30 Sep	1825	"& Ann Chittendon"; [this is faintly among deaths, poss.	1:162
-	-	-	-	smudged out]	
Platt	Diantha	4 May	1873	w of Luther S., adm fr 1st Cong, Middlebury Ct.	3:92
Platt	Diantha	4 May	1873	adm ch from Middlebury Ct, wife of Luther S.	3:36
Platt	Edward L.	29 Dec	1862	d, 6, diphtheria	3:254
Platt	Elihu	6 Jun	1866	d (Prospect) 76	3:255
Platt	Gideon	29 Apr	1817	Deacon, from Waterbury, at Council re Rev. Dodd's removal	1:74
Platt	Henry	-	1845	adm ch from Fair Haven; dis 1849 to Harrison Penn.	3:36
Platt	Henry	12 Oct	1845	adm from ch in Fair Haven, Conn.	2:52
Platt	Luther S.	4 May	1873	adm fr 1st Cong, Middlebury, Ct	3:92
Platt	Luther S.	4 May	1873	adm ch from Middlebury Ct; dec 1900	3:36
Platt	Luther S.	28 Oct	1900	d, 80, 24 hrs illness, neuralgia stomach	3:261
Platt	Maggie C.	2 Apr	1870	dism to Cong, Middlefield Ct	3:124

NAUGATUCK, CONNECTICUT, CONGREGATIONAL CHURCH RECORDS

Platt	Margaret C.	-	1863	adm ch from Middlefield Ct.; dis 1871 to Middlefield	3:36
Platt	Margaret C.	6 Sep	1863	adm fr Middlefield Conn.	3:92
Platt	Margaret C.	-	1880	adm ch from Middletown	3:37
Platt	Margaret C.	31 Dec	1880	adm fr 1st Cong, Middletown Ct	3:94
Platt	W.H.	-	-	husband of Emily Hopkins	3:19
Platt	Wm	-	1845	adm ch from Fair Haven; dis 1849	3:36
Platt	Wm	11 May	1845	adm ch from Fair Haven; dism 3 Mar 1849	2:99
Platt	Wm	7 May	1859	d, 27, lung fever	3:252
Platt	Wm H	-	-	husband of Emily Hopkins	2:98
Platts	Henry	9 Nov	1845	adm ch from Fair Haven; dism 3 Feb 1849 to Harrison, Pa.	2:100
Plumb	Wheaton S.	10 Oct	1853	of Wallingford marr Maria A. Douglass of Naug	3:201
Pond	Wm L.	1 May	1880	marr Cora E. Bailey, both of Naug	3:216
Pope	Eva	-	1877	adm ch; erased 1900	3:37
Pope	Eva	4 Mar	1877	adm ch	3:65
Pope	Ida	-	1877	adm ch; erased 1900	3:37
Pope	Ida	4 Mar	1877	adm ch	3:65
Porter	Abi	10 Sep	1822	rec to ch in Columbia	1:96
Porter	Abigail	13 Oct	1823	of Salem, marr Erastus W. Hoadley	1:152
Porter	Abigail Baldwin[?]	15 Mar	1818	ch of Wd Sally, bp, [could be 2 children]	1:60
Porter	Albert	12 May	1822	ch of Julius, bp	1:84
Porter	Albert	12 May	1822	ch of Julius, bp	1:85
Porter	Albert	25 Mar	1860	d, 38, consumption, Hillside	3:252
Porter	Albert	-	1886	adm ch; dis 1894 Jamestown NY	3:37
Porter	Albert	2 May	1886	adm ch	3:69
Porter	Albert R.	2 May	1886	bp, adult	3:158
Porter	Albert R.	15 Apr	1887	25 marr Mary L. Scott 25	3:218
Porter	Albert R.	1 Jun	1894	dism to Cong, Jamestown NY; also wife	3:128
Porter	Alma	19 Apr	1795	bp, ch of Truman	1:167
Porter	Alma	-	1835	adm ch; dis 1838 to Oxford	3:36
Porter	Alma	5 Jul	1835	adm ch; [m] -- Miles; dism 7 Oct 1838 to Oxfd or Covtry C.	2:95
-	-	-	-	[sic] Co. NY	
Porter	Anna	2 Jun	1807	d, 5y	1:158
Porter	Anna Amanda	15 Mar	1818	ch of Wd Sally, bp [could be 2 children]	1:60
Porter	Arba	3 Apr	1785	bp, ch of Jo.	1:164
Porter	Arba	3 Apr	1785	bp	1:9
Porter	Arbi	-	-	husband of Alanta [sic] Scott	3:41
Porter	Arbi	-	-	husband of Atlanta Scott	2:88
Porter	Arbi	-	1818	adm ch; dis 1822 to Prospect	3:35
Porter	Arbi	6 Sep	1818	adm ch; rem 10 Sep 1822 to Prospect	2:91
Porter	Arbi	6 Sep	1818	adm ch	1:59
Porter	Arbi	-	1822	male, on list of members; dism	1:81
Porter	Asa	7 Oct	1787	bp, ch of Ebenezer	1:164
Porter	Asa	27 Aug	1815	bp, ch of Widow Sarah	1:176
Porter	Asahel	1 Jan	1809	infant ch d, 4m	1:159
Porter	Asahel	3 Jan	1817	had sold house and lot to David Hopkins	1:73
Porter	Ashbel	-	1781	adm ch; exc	3:35
Porter	Ashbel	22 Feb	1781	one of the persons constituting the church	2:79
Porter	Ashbel	22 Feb	1781	adm ch; excomm	2:81
Porter	Ashbel	22 Feb	1781	subscribed to Constitution and Covenant	1:5
Porter	Ashbel	22 Feb	1781	original member, excommunicated	1:53
Porter	Atlanta	-	1822	wife of Arbi, member; dism	1:82
Porter	Atlanta	10 Sep	1822	wife of Abi [sic], dism to ch in Columbia	1:96
Porter	Beacher	5 Jun	1791	bp, son of Ezekiel	1:166
Porter	Benjamin	14 May	1843	adm ch	2:99

NAUGATUCK, CONNECTICUT, CONGREGATIONAL CHURCH RECORDS

Porter	Benjn	-	1843	adm ch; dec	3:36
Porter	Betty	-	1789	adm ch, wife of Ezekl; dis	3:35
Porter	Betty	17 Mar	1789	Ez ["Ebenezer" written over later] adm ch, dism	1:55
Porter	Betty	17 May	1789	wife of Ezekiel, adm ch; rem	2:84
Porter	Betty	17 May	1789	wife of Ezekiel adm ch	1:12
Porter	Charlotte	21 Jun	1789	bp, dau of Ezekiel	1:165
Porter	Chs H.	1 Oct	1854	marr Isabell T. Carter, both of Naug	3:202
Porter	Clarinda	10 Oct	1824	ch of Julius & Mabel, bp	1:85
Porter	Clarissa	-	1798	adm ch, wife of D. Beecher; dec 1840	3:35
Porter	Clarissa	26 Aug	1798	wife of Daniel Beecher, adm ch; died 1 Nov 1840	2:85
Porter	Clarissa	26 Aug	1798	["Daniel Beecher" added], adm ch	1:55
Porter	Clarissa	26 Aug	1798	adm ch	1:13
Porter	Cornelius H.	5 Feb	1855	of Naug marr Priscilla Ayres of Poughkeepsie NY	3:202
Porter	Danil	7 Oct	1787	bp, ch of Ebenezer	1:164
Porter	Dea	10 Apr	1825	on committee	1:101
Porter	Dea	19 Feb	1826	appointed substitute delegate to consociation at North Milford	1:101
Porter	Dea	4 May	1827	on committee	1:102
Porter	Dea	23 Sep	1827	appointed to attend conference at Derby	1:103
Porter	Dea	6 Nov	1829	on comm	1:109
Porter	Dea	6 Nov	1829	voted to attend future conf	1:109
Porter	Dea	13 Dec	1829	appointed delegate to Consociation at North Milford	1:110
Porter	Dea	14 Mar	1830	to attend Consociation at Middlebury	1:110
Porter	Dea	30 Apr	1830	on Sabb School board, Moderator	1:111
Porter	Dea T.	Sep	1831	on Visiting Committee	1:115
Porter	Deacon	26 Aug	1832	on Board of Managers for SS	2:11
Porter	Ebenezer	-	1787	adm ch; dec 1810	3:35
Porter	Ebenezer	30 Sep	1787	adm ch; died 22 Aug 1810	2:83
Porter	Ebenezer	30 Sep	1787	adm ch	1:11
Porter	Ebenezer	30 Sep	1787	adm ch, d 22 Aug 1810	1:54
Porter	Ebenezer	22 Aug	1810	Capt, d, 60y	1:160
Porter	Elisabeth Agustia	15 Mar	1818	ch of Wd Sally, bp [could be 2 children]	1:60
Porter	Eliza	-	1833	adm ch, wife of Julius Hill; dis 1838	3:36
Porter	Eliza	5 May	1833	wife of Junius Hill, adm ch; rem 4 May 1838 to any Ch	2:93
Porter	Emily M.	-	1835	adm ch, wife of A.G. Hull; dis 1837 Danbury	3:36
Porter	Emily Margaret	4 Jan	1835	adm ch, [m] Amos G. Hull, dism 14 Jan 1837 to Danbury	2:95
Porter	Esther	-	1840	adm ch; dec 1841	3:36
Porter	Esther	12 Jul	1840	adm ch; died 23 Mar 1841	2:97
Porter	Esther Minerva	8 Sep	1822	ch of Thomas, bp	1:85
Porter	Eunice	18 May	1788	bp, dau of Jos	1:165
Porter	Evadene M.	22 Jun	1873	of New Haven marr Sidney A. Wilson of Naug	3:210
Porter	Ezra	7 Oct	1787	bp, ch of Ebenezer	1:164
Porter	Ezra	31 Aug	1794	bp, ch of Jos	1:167
Porter	Ezra	29 May	1802	d, 76y and abt 10 m	1:155
Porter	Ezra	16 Feb	1830	d, lungfever, 36	1:146
Porter	Fanni [sic]	4 Oct	1789	bp, ch of Nathan	1:165
Porter	Fanny	-	1822	Wid, member adm since 1822	1:83
Porter	Fanny	1 Dec	1824	widow, propounded for adm [perhaps also from Baptist ch in Plymouth]	1:100
Porter	Fanny	11 Dec	1824	Wd. of Ezra, adm ch; rem 2 Sep 1837 to Alton Ill.	2:91
Porter	Fanny	11 Dec	1824	Wid, adm ch	1:59
Porter	Fanny	11 Dec	1824	wid, adm ch	1:100
Porter	Fanny	30 Apr	1830	wid, on Sabb School board	1:111
Porter	Fanny	Apr	1833	Miss, on committee for SS	2:9
Porter	Fanny Abiah	11 Dec	1824	ch of Wid Fanny, bp	1:85

NAUGATUCK, CONNECTICUT, CONGREGATIONAL CHURCH RECORDS

Porter	Frances A.	-	1835	adm ch; dis 1838 to Alton Ill	3:36
Porter	Frances A.	1 Mar	1835	adm ch; dism 18 Mar 1838 to Alton Illinois	2:95
Porter	Frances A.	18 Mar	1838	Miss, dism to 1st Presbyterian Ch in Alton, Illinois	2:32
Porter	George Egbert	5 Sep	1824	ch of Sally & Thomas, bp	1:85
Porter	Hactor	Apr	1833	Superintendant for Sabbath School	2:9
Porter	Hactor [sic]	6 Oct	1805	bp, son of Truman	1:173
Porter	Hannah	-	1781	adm ch, wife of Ashbel; dis	3:35
Porter	Hannah	22 Feb	1781	one of the persons constituting the church	2:79
Porter	Hannah	22 Feb	1781	wife of Ashbel P., adm ch; rem	2:82
Porter	Hannah	22 Feb	1781	subscribed to Constitution and Covenant	1:5
Porter	Hannah	22 Feb	1781	original member, dead [as of 1811, "Ashbel" added]	1:53
Porter	Hariet A.	23 Feb	1826	of Salem, marr Daniel Sacket of Milford	1:152
Porter	Harriet	27 Aug	1815	bp, ch of Widow Sarah	1:176
Porter	Hector	-	1828	adm ch; dis 1837 to Coventry NY	3:35
Porter	Hector	-	1828	male, on list of members, adm 1828	1:81
Porter	Hector	4 May	1828	adm ch; rem 26 Feb 1837	2:92
Porter	Hector	4 May	1828	adm ch, [see Porter, Hactor]	1:59a
Porter	Hector	4 May	1828	adm ch	1:106
Porter	Hector	20 Mar	1828	propounded for adm	1:106
Porter	Hector	23 Oct	1828	marr Isabel Upson of Salem	1:153
Porter	Hector	14 Oct	1832	Secretary of Missionary Society	2:12
Porter	Hector	26 Aug	1832	Secretary for SS	2:11
Porter	Hector	30 Dec	1833	on comm	2:14
Porter	Hector	3 Feb	1837	voted to be requested to ask for letter of dism.	2:23
Porter	Hector	26 Feb	1837	dism to 2nd Cong ch in Coventry NY	2:24
Porter	Henrietta	27 Aug	1815	bp, ch of Widow Sarah	1:176
Porter	Henry	27 Aug	1815	bp, ch of Widow Sarah	1:176
Porter	Henry Handel	15 Mar	1818	ch of Wd Sally, bp [could be 2 children]	1:60
Porter	Hirva [sic]	22 May	1796	bp, ch of Ezekl	1:168
Porter	Horace Virgil	15 Mar	1818	ch of Wd Sally, bp [could be 2 children]	1:60
Porter	Isabel	-	1829	adm ch, wife of Hector; dis 1837 to Coventry NY	3:36
Porter	Isabel	3 May	1829	wife of H., member	1:94
Porter	Isabel	3 May	1829	Hector, adm ch	1:59b
Porter	Isabel	3 May	1829	wife of Hector, adm ch; rem 26 Feb 1837 to Coventry NY	2:93
Porter	Isabel	3 Feb	1837	voted to be requested to ask for letter of dism.	2:23
Porter	Isabel	26 Feb	1837	dism to 2nd Cong ch in Coventry NY, wife of Hector	2:24
Porter	James	1 Aug	1790	bp, ch of Joseph	1:165
Porter	James	-	1840	adm ch; dis 1840 Binghampton NY	3:36
Porter	James	12 Jul	1840	adm ch; dism 20 Dec 1840 to Binghamton	2:97
Porter	James E.	20 Dec	1840	dism to ch in Binghamton NY	2:35
Porter	Joseph	-	1785	adm ch; dec 1820	3:35
Porter	Joseph	17 Feb	1785	adm ch, d Jun 1820	1:53
Porter	Joseph	20 Feb	1785	adm ch; died Jun 1820	2:82
Porter	Joseph	20 Feb	1785	[sic, voted on 17 Feb] bp & adm ch	1:9
Porter	Joseph	-	1799	his ch bp	1:169
Porter	Joseph	6 Sep	1807	infant ch bp	1:174
Porter	Joseph	27 Jun	1820	died in a sudden maner in 63 y of age	1:87
Porter	Joseph Edward	20 May	1827	ch of Julius, bp	1:87
Porter	Joseph Jr.	1 Jul	1792	bp, ch of Joseph	1:166
Porter	Julius	17 ???	1790	bp, ch of Truman [month is after Aug]	1:166
Porter	Julius	19 Sep	1831	bp, ch of Wd Mabel	1:88
Porter	Laura B.	-	1835	adm ch; dis 1837 to Alton Ill	3:36
Porter	Laura B.	1 Mar	1835	adm ch; dism 19 Mar 1837 to Alton Illinois	2:95
Porter	Laura B.	3 Feb	1837	voted to be requested to ask for letter of dism.	2:23

NAUGATUCK, CONNECTICUT, CONGREGATIONAL CHURCH RECORDS

Porter	Laura B.	19 Mar	1837	dism to Presbyterian ch in Alton, Illinois	2:24
Porter	Laura Beecher	11 Dec	1824	ch of Wid Fanny, bp	1:85
Porter	Leonard	19 Sep	1802	bp, son of Saml	1:171
Porter	Locky L.	-	1818	adm ch, wife of M. Hotchkiss; dis 1834 Sharon	3:35
Porter	Locy L. [sic]	4 Jan	1818	wife of Marcus Hotchkiss, adm ch; rem 7 Dec 183- to Sharon	2:88
Porter	Lucetta G.	18 Mar	1830	of Middlebury, marr Lawrence S. Hull of Salem	1:154
Porter	Lucy	21 Apr	1786	bp, ch of Joseph ["Joseph" poss smudged out]	1:164
Porter	Lucy	21 May	1786	bp [entry crossed out]	1:10
Porter	Lucy	28 Oct	1787	bp, ch of Samuel Jr.	1:164
Porter	Lucy	-	1797	adm ch, wife of Saml; dis 1808 to Coventry NY	3:35
Porter	Lucy	26 Feb	1797	2nd wife of Samuel, adm ch; rem 3 Apr 1808 to Coventry NY	2:85
Porter	Lucy	26 Feb	1797	Sa., adm ch, dism 31 Apr 1808	1:55
Porter	Lucy	26 Feb	1797	wife of Samll adm ch	1:13
Porter	Lucy	3 Apr	1808	wife of Samuel, rec to ch at Coventry NY	1:48
Porter	Lucy L.	4 Jan	1818	adm ch	1:58
Porter	Mabel	-	1816	adm ch, wife of Julius; dec 1842	3:35
Porter	Mabel	5 Dec	1816	wife of Julius, cand for memb	1:73
Porter	Mabel	22 Dec	1816	wife of Julius, adm ch; died Apr 1842	2:87
Porter	Mabel	22 Dec	1816	adm ch	1:57
Porter	Mabel	22 Dec	1816	adm ch	1:73
Porter	Mabel	-	1822	wife of Julius, member	1:82
Porter	Mahitable [sic]	-	1786	adm ch, wife of Thos; dec 1837	3:35
Porter	Margret	14 Oct	1787	bp, ch of Truman	1:164
Porter	Marshal	13 Jul	1788	bp, ch of Samuel Jr.	1:165
Porter	Martha Hine	31 Oct	1828	ch of Thomas, bp	1:88
Porter	Mehitabel	30 Jul	1786	wife of Thomas, adm ch; died 1 Jun 1837	2:83
Porter	Mehitabel	30 Jul	1786	Tho., adm ch [d "Jan 1817" crossed out]	1:54
Porter	Mehitabel	1 Jun	1837	Wid, died, 98	2:115
Porter	Mehitable	30 Jul	1786	wife of Thomas, adm ch	1:10
Porter	Mehitable	-	1822	Wid., member	1:82
Porter	Milissent	-	1802	adm ch, wife of Joseph; dec 1823	3:35
Porter	Millesent	17 Oct	1802	wife of Joseph adm ch	1:34
Porter	Milliscent	19 Mar	1823	d, wid, consumption, 60	1:161
Porter	Millisent	17 Oct	1802	wife of Joseph, adm ch; died 1823	2:86
Porter	Millisent	17 Oct	1802	Jo., adm ch, d 1823	1:56
Porter	Milly	-	1823	Wid, member; dead 1823	1:82
Porter	Minerva	21 Dec	1788	bp, ch of Truman	1:165
Porter	Myretta	-	1828	adm ch; wife of Edwin Birge[?]; dis 1833 to Coventry NY	3:35
Porter	Myretta	4 Jul	1828	adm ch	1:59b
Porter	Myretta	6 Jul	1828	wife of Edwin Birge[?], adm ch; rem 5 May 1833 to Coventry NY	2:92
Porter	Myretta	6 Jul	1828	member	1:94
Porter	Myretta	6 Jul	1828	adm ch	1:107
Porter	Nancy Woodruff	12 Oct	1817	ch of Julius, bp	1:60
Porter	Obediah	28 Oct	1787	bp, ch of Samuel Jr.	1:164
Porter	Polly	14 Jun	1801	marr Lewis Williams, both of this place	1:151
Porter	Pru	4 Jun	1797	wife of Nathan adm ch	1:13
Porter	Prue	-	1797	adm ch, wife of Nathan; dec 1806	3:35
Porter	Prue	4 Jun	1797	wife of Nathan, adm ch; died 8 Jul 1806	2:85
Porter	Prue	4 Jun	1797	["Nathan?" added], adm ch, d 8 Jul 1806	1:55
Porter	Prue	8 Jul	1806	d, wife of Nathan, 47y	1:157
Porter	Robert	7 Apr	1817	bp, ch of Mabel wife of Julius	1:176
Porter	Robert	8 Oct	1836	died, 24	2:115
Porter	Ruel Sperry	3 Apr	1785	bp, ch of Jos. Porter	1:164
Porter	Ruel Spery	3 Apr	1785	bp	1:9

NAUGATUCK, CONNECTICUT, CONGREGATIONAL CHURCH RECORDS

Porter	Sally	15 Nov	1801	bp, ch of Truman	1:170
Porter	Sally	-	1817	adm ch, wife of Henry; dec 1864	3:35
Porter	Sally	16 Nov	1817	wife of Henry, adm ch	2:88
Porter	Sally	16 Nov	1817	adm ch	1:57
Porter	Sally	-	1818	adm ch, wife of Thos; dis 1843 to Binghampton	3:35
Porter	Sally	6 Sep	1818	wife of Thomas, adm ch; rem 29 May 184- to Binghampton NY	2:91
Porter	Sally	6 Sep	1818	adm ch	1:59
Porter	Sally	-	1822	Wid of Asa, member	1:82
Porter	Sally	-	1822	Wid of Henry, member	1:82
Porter	Sally	-	1822	wife of Thomas, member	1:82
Porter	Sally	-	1828	adm ch; dis 1837 to Coventry NY	3:35
Porter	Sally	4 Jul	1828	adm ch	1:59b
Porter	Sally	6 Jul	1828	adm ch; rem 26 Feb 1837 to Coventry NY	2:92
Porter	Sally	6 Jul	1828	member	1:94
Porter	Sally	6 Jul	1828	adm ch	1:107
Porter	Sally	3 Feb	1837	voted to be requested to ask for letter of dism.	2:23
Porter	Sally	26 Feb	1837	dism to 2nd Con ch in Coventry NY	2:24
Porter	Sally	27 Apr	1864	d, 83, smallpox, Grove cemetery	3:254
Porter	Saml 2d	-	1787	adm ch; dis 1808 Coventry NY	3:35
Porter	Saml E.	-	1801	adm ch; dis 1806 Rutland NY	3:35
Porter	Samll Ebenezer	7 Oct	1787	bp, ch of Ebenezer	1:164
Porter	Samuel	-	1781	adm ch; dec 1793	3:35
Porter	Samuel	22 Feb	1781	one of the persons constituting the church	2:79
Porter	Samuel	22 Feb	1781	adm ch; died 8 Jan 1793	2:81
Porter	Samuel	22 Feb	1781	subscribed to Constitution and Covenant	1:5
Porter	Samuel	22 Feb	1781	original member, dec 8 Jan 1793	1:53
Porter	Samuel	21 Oct	1787	adm ch	1:11
Porter	Samuel	3 Apr	1808	rec to ch at Coventry NY	1:48
Porter	Samuel 2	21 Oct	1787	adm ch; rem 3 Apr 1808 to Coventry NY	2:83
Porter	Samuel E.	22 Feb	1801	adm ch; rem 26 May 1806 to Rutland, Jefferson Co., NY	2:86
Porter	Samuel E.	22 Feb	1801	adm ch, dism 26 May 1806	1:56
Porter	Samuel E.	26 May	1806	letter of rec to ch in Rutland, Jefferson Co., NY	1:40
Porter	Samuel Ebenezer	22 Feb	1801	adm ch	1:21
Porter	Samuel Junr	21 Oct	1787	adm ch, dism 31 Apr 1808 [to "Camden NY" prob. ref. to previous entry]	1:54
Porter	Samuel Munson	11 Jul	1790	bp, ch of Samuel Jr.	1:165
Porter	Samuel S. Lewis	15 Mar	1818	ch of Wd Sally, bp [could be 2 children, but see Lewis entries.]	1:60
Porter	Sarah	-	1787	adm ch, wife of Eben; dis to Camden NY	3:35
Porter	Sarah	-	1787	adm ch, wife of Truman; dec 1837	3:35
Porter	Sarah	30 Sep	1787	wife of Ebenezer, adm ch; to Camden NY	2:83
Porter	Sarah	30 Sep	1787	wife of Truman, adm ch; died 29 Aug 1837	2:83
Porter	Sarah	30 Sep	1787	wife of Ebenezer adm ch	1:11
Porter	Sarah	30 Sep	1787	wife of Truman adm ch	1:11
Porter	Sarah	30 Sep	1787	Eb, adm ch., ["rec" added later, unclear]	1:54
Porter	Sarah	30 Sep	1787	Tr., adm ch	1:54
Porter	Sarah	-	1802	adm ch; dis 1806 Milford	3:35
Porter	Sarah	17 Oct	1802	Wd, adm ch; rem Mar 1806 to Milford	2:86
Porter	Sarah	17 Oct	1802	Wid., adm ch, dism Mar 1806	1:56
Porter	Sarah	17 Oct	1802	wd, adm ch	1:34
Porter	Sarah	Mar	1806	widow, letter of rec to ch at Milton	1:39
Porter	Sarah	-	1815	adm ch; dis 1834 Bethany	3:35
Porter	Sarah	23 Jul	1815	Wd, adm ch; rem 7 Mar 1834 to Bethany	2:87
Porter	Sarah	23 Jul	1815	Widow, adm ch	1:57
Porter	Sarah	23 Jul	1815	Wid, adm ch	1:69

NAUGATUCK, CONNECTICUT, CONGREGATIONAL CHURCH RECORDS

Porter	Sarah	27 Aug	1815	bp, ch of Widow Sarah	1:176
Porter	Sarah	30 Jun	1815	Wid, cand for memb	1:69
Porter	Sarah	-	1822	wid of Eben, member	1:82
Porter	Sarah	-	1822	wife of Truman, member	1:82
Porter	Sarah	5 Jan	1826	d, gangrene of the mouth & fever, 13 [poss 10]	1:163
Porter	Sarah	29 Aug	1837	Mrs., wife of Truman Jr., died, 75y 9m	2:115
Porter	Sarah Mariah	Nov	1831	ch of Hictor, bp	1:89
Porter	Selden	3 Jun	1792	bp, ch of Samll Junr	1:166
Porter	Sereno [sic]	11 Dec	1824	ch of Wid Fanny, bp	1:85
Porter	Sibbel	22 Apr	1787	wife of Samuel Jr, adm ch; died	2:83
Porter	Sibbel	22 Apr	1787	wife of Samll adm ch	1:11
Porter	Sibbel	22 Apr	1787	Sa Junr, adm ch; dead	1:54
Porter	Stephen	28 Oct	1787	bp, ch of Samuel Jr.	1:164
Porter	Stephen	-	1801	adm ch; dis	3:35
Porter	Stephen	22 Feb	1801	adm ch; a minister of the gospel; rem	2:86
Porter	Stephen	22 Feb	1801	adm ch, a settled Minister	1:56
Porter	Stephen	22 Feb	1801	adm ch	1:21
Porter	Sybel	-	1787	adm ch, wife of Saml Jr.; dec	3:35
Porter	Thomas	-	1786	adm ch; exc 1806	3:35
Porter	Thomas	30 Jul	1786	adm ch; excomm 17 Aug 1806	2:83
Porter	Thomas	30 Jul	1786	adm ch	1:10
Porter	Thomas	30 Jul	1786	adm ch, [d "Jan 1818" crossed out] excommunicated 17 Aug 1806	1:54
Porter	Thomas	17 Mar	1793	bp, ch of Truman	1:166
Porter	Thomas	8 Jun	1806	complained against for drunkenness	1:40f
Porter	Thomas	17 Aug	1806	excommunicated	1:45
Porter	Thomas	-	1818	adm ch; dis 1843 to Binghampton	3:35
Porter	Thomas	6 Sep	1818	adm ch; rem 23 May 1843	2:91
Porter	Thomas	6 Sep	1818	adm ch	1:59
Porter	Thomas	-	1822	male, on list of members	1:81
Porter	Thomas	6 Nov	1829	voted to attend future conf	1:109
Porter	Thomas	30 Apr	1830	on Sabb School board	1:111
Porter	Thomas	28 May	1843	and wife, dism to ch in Binghampton, NY	2:46
Porter	Thomas Edwards	4 Sep	1835	bp, ch of Thomas, b 17 Nov 1832 [twin, surname hard to read]	2:104
Porter	Truman	-	1787	adm ch, dec 1838	3:35
Porter	Truman	30 Sep	1787	adm ch; died 28 Sep 1838	2:83
Porter	Truman	30 Sep	1787	adm ch	1:11
Porter	Truman	30 Sep	1787	adm ch	1:54
Porter	Truman	7 Jul	1803	ch bp	1:171
Porter	Truman	13 Jun	1806	referred to in testimony	1:42
Porter	Truman	17 Jun	1806	his wife testified against Thomas Porter	1:43
Porter	Truman	5 May	1811	a delegate to Westchester Presbytery, on committee	1:51
Porter	Truman	9 Apr	1813	Deacon; died 28 Sep 1838	2:79
Porter	Truman	9 Apr	1813	chosen Deacon	1:67
Porter	Truman	3 Jan	1817	Deacon, on committee	1:73
Porter	Truman	8 Apr	1817	Deacon, on committee	1:74
Porter	Truman	12 Aug	1818	chosen Clerk	1:78
Porter	Truman	3 Jul	1818	on committee to est. Sabbath School	1:77
Porter	Truman	-	1822	male, on list of members; dea	1:81
Porter	Truman	3 Oct	1830	delegate to Consociation at Middlebury	1:112
Porter	Truman	7 Jan	1831	Deacon, chosen Moderator	1:113
Porter	Truman Edson	4 Sep	1835	bp, ch of Thomas, b 17 Nov 1832 [twin, surname hard to read]	2:104
Porter	Wiliam [sic]	10 Jan	1808	bp, ch of Truman	1:174
Porter	Willard	21 Sep	1831	ch of Thomas & Esther [sic], bp	1:89
Porter	William	7 May	1797	bp, ch of Joseph	1:168

NAUGATUCK, CONNECTICUT, CONGREGATIONAL CHURCH RECORDS

Porter	William	30 Mar 1809	d, ch of Truman, 1y 6m	1:159
Porter	William Egbert	7 Apr 1817	bp, ch of Mabel wife of Julius	1:176
Porter	Zubah	28 Oct 1787	bp, ch of Samuel Jr.	1:164
Post	Geo H.	22 Feb 1883	marr Belle L. Lewis, both of Naug	3:215
Potter	Aaron	20 Jun 1803	ch d, 2y	1:156
Potter	Adah Jane	4 Jul 1858	ch bp; D.G. & B.E.	3:152
Potter	Anne	3 Sep 1786	bp, ch of Lemuel	1:164
Potter	Anne	3 Sep 1786	ch of Lemll bp [entry crossed out]	1:10
Potter	Betsey	16 Jun 1866	dism to Cong, Plainville	3:123
Potter	Betsey E.	- 1858	adm ch, wife of D.G.; dis 1866 to Plainville	3:36
Potter	Betsey Elmina	4 Jul 1858	bp, adult	3:152
Potter	Betsey Elmina	4 July 1858	adm ch	3:61
Potter	D.G.	16 Jun 1866	dism to Cong, Plainville	3:123
Potter	Frances Ella	4 Jul 1858	cp bp; D.G. & B.E.	3:152
Potter	G.	- 1847	Doctor, adm ch from Bristol; dis 1866 to Plainville	3:36
Potter	G.	16 May 1847	Doctor, adm ch from Bristol	2:100
Potter	G.	23 Mar 1851	Doctor, dism to Cong, Prospect	3:120
Potter	G.	1 Jan 1854	Doctor, retd letter from this ch'h n't used	3:90
Potter	Lanson	Jul 1800	bp, son of Thos	1:169
Potter	Laura	11 Apr 1863	d, dau of D.G. & B.E., 3, congestion lungs	3:254
Potter	Laura Jennett	13 Jul 1862	inf bp; D.G. & B.E.	3:152
Potter	Liman	Jul 1800	bp, son of Thos	1:169
Potter	Lucy	- 1799	adm ch, wife of Thos; dis 1808 Coventry NY	3:35
Potter	Lucy	28 Jul 1799	wife of Thomas, adm ch; rem 11 Apr 1808 to Coventry NY	2:94
Potter	Lucy	28 Jul 1799	wife of Thos adm ch	1:14
Potter	Lucy	26 Aug 1804	bp, ch of Thomas	1:172
Potter	Lucy	11 Aug 1808	wife of Thomas rec to ch at Coventry NY	1:48
Potter	M.E.	1 Sep 1882	see Stoddard, Wm B., Mrs.	3:125
Potter	Mary	- 1868	adm ch from Sharon, wid, erased 1900, died 7 Jan 1901	3:36
Potter	Mary	5 Jul 1868	adm fr Cong, Sharon, Ct.	3:92
Potter	Mary	7 Jan 1901	Mrs, d in Waterbury	3:261
Potter	Mary E.	- 1882	adm ch from New Britain; dis 1882	3:37
Potter	Mary E.	10 Feb 1882	Miss, adm fr So. Cong, New Britain Ct	3:95
Potter	Mary E.	30 Apr 1882	marr Wm B. Stoddard, both of Naug	3:214
Potter	Mary W.	- 1863	adm ch, wife of E.S. Williams; dis 1867 to Easthampton, Mass.	3:36
Potter	Mary Ward	1 Nov 1863	adm ch	3:63
Potter	Rachel	- 1786	adm ch, wife of Leml; Irr Baptist	3:35
Potter	Rachel	9 Mar 1786	wife of Lemuel, adm ch; withdrawn to Baptist	2:83
Potter	Rachel	9 Mar 1786	wife of Lemuel, adm ch	1:10
Potter	Rachel	9 Mar 1786	adm ch ["Baptist" added] certificated	1:54
Potter	Rachellana	14 Dec 1800	bp, ch of Thomas	1:169
Potter	Ransom	17 Jun 1826	newborn ch d, 0	1:163
Potter	Richard Thomason	27 Aug 1813	ch of Jules, bp [perhaps 1820]	1:63
Potter	Samll	26 Jun 1803	child d, 4y	1:156
Potter	Samuel	9 Mar 1835	ch died, 1y 5m 20d	2:114
Potter	Sarah E.	1 Nov 1863	bp, adult	3:153
Potter	Sarah Ellen	- 1863	adm ch, wife of -- Candee; erased 1900	3:36
Potter	Sarah Ellen	1 Nov 1863	adm ch	3:63
Potter	Sibel	12 Sep 1803	bp, ch of Thomas	1:171
Potter	Wid	26 Nov 1827	d, old society of Waterbury, 85 [written over "84"?]	1:144
Potter	Zenas	Nov 1833	ch died, 5 days	2:114
Power	Margaret E.	- 1852	adm ch; dis 1853 New York	3:36
Power	Margaret E.	6 Nov 1853	dism to Allen St Presb, New York	3:120
Power	Margaret Ellenor	2 May 1852	adm ch	3:60

NAUGATUCK, CONNECTICUT, CONGREGATIONAL CHURCH RECORDS

Power	Margaret Ellinor	2 Mar	1852	bp, profession	3:150
Pratt	Abigel Mary	18 Jan	1818	"family of Mr. Pratt," bp [could be 2 children]	1:60
Pratt	Caroline A.	-	1895	adm ch; dec 1897	3:37
Pratt	Caroline A.	6 Jan	1895	Mrs., adm ch	3:71
Pratt	Caroline A.	6 Jun	1897	d	3:261
Pratt	Danl	-	-	husband of Nancy Beardsley	3:5
Pratt	Frances Hall	18 Jan	1818	"family of Mr. Pratt," bp [could be 2 children]	1:60
Pratt	George	-	1818	adm ch; dis to Waterbury	3:35
Pratt	George	4 Jan	1818	adm ch; rem to Waterbury	2:89
Pratt	George	4 Jan	1818	adm ch, recommend	1:58
Pratt	George	4 Jan	1818	bp	1:60
Pratt	Hannah	-	1817	adm ch; dis 1827 Waterbury	3:35
Pratt	Hannah	16 Nov	1817	adm ch; rem 4 May 1827 to Waterbury	2:87
Pratt	Hannah	16 Nov	1817	adm ch, dism abt 1825	1:57
Pratt	Hannah	-	1822	wife of Roswell, member	1:83
Pratt	Hannah	-	1827	rec to ch in Waterbury	1:102
Pratt	Hannah Meriah	18 Jan	1818	"family of Mr. Pratt," bp [could be two children]	1:60
Pratt	Henry James	18 Jan	1818	"family of Mr. Pratt," bp [could be two children]	1:60
Pratt	Julia At--[?]	18 Jan	1818	"family of Mr. Pratt," bp [could be two children]	1:60
Pratt	Mr.	-	-	husband of Nancy Beardsley	2:98
Presbry	Bertha J.	16 Dec	1892	dism to Cong, Brookville Kan	3:128
Presbry	Bertha Juline	-	1890	adm ch; dis 1892 to Brookville Kan	3:37
Presbry	Bertha Juline	9 Mar	1890	bp, adult	3:159
Presbry	Bertha Juline	9 Mar	1890	Miss, adm ch	3:70
Prior	Frederick H.	26 Mar	1884	marr Minnie E. Rogers, both of Naug	3:216
Quinn	Peter J.	10 Nov	1897	24 marr Cassie Baumer 21	3:225
Racke	Eleanor Viola	28 May	1899	inf bp; Philip Frederick & Bertha Maria S.	3:164
Racke	Elizabeth Frederic	28 May	1899	inf bp; Philip Frederick & Bertha Maria S.	3:164
Racke	Martha Elizabeth	28 May	1899	inf bp; Philip Frederick & Bertha Maria S.	3:164
Radford	Eliza	26 Apr	1835	died, 21	2:114
Randall	Abbie A.	21 Aug	1882	marr Wm A. Tiltey [Titley?], both of Naug	3:214
Randall	Ann E.	7 Apr	1857	d, 19 ys, convulsions	3:251
Rasquin	-	-	-	see Rosquin	-
Rasquin	Bertha	30 Sep	1896	21 marr Geo Haus 29	3:224
Rasquin	Chas	21 Sep	1887	35 marr Henrietta Schwabie 27	3:218
Rasquin	Winand	25 Nov	1896	35 marr Mrs. Lena Eggert 41	3:225
Raymond	Louis A.	5 Jun	1900	37 marr Mrs. Cordelia Petter 34	3:228
Reed	Frank	10 Feb	1883	marr Maud M. Loomis, both of Naug	3:215
Reed	Hattie	3 Jul	1888	33 marr Hubert M. Hill 33	3:219
Reed	Martin	12 Apr	1865	marr Emma J. Curtiss, both of Newtown	3:206
Reffelt	Adaline E.	28 Nov	1900	20 marr Ellis C. Curry 22 at Beacon Falls	3:228
Rehm[?]	Anna	7 Feb	1900	26 marr George Matz 33 [see Reihm]	3:228
Reihm	Herman Henry	18 Nov	1883	inf bp; Frederick & Mrs. [see Rehm]	3:157
Rempfen	-	-	-	see Rumpfen	-
Renz[?]	Andrew	-	-	husband of Harriet A. Wooding	3:55
Rexford	-	-	-	see 4 entries under Bristol	-
Rexford	Kate Burwell	22 Feb	1881	at centennial exercises, Mrs.	3:300
Rice	Geo M.	7 Jun	1890	32 marr Lillie J. Blake 25	3:221
Richards	-	20 Jan	1832	ch d, measles, 5, now residing at New Haven	1:147
Richards	Dorothy Mary	10 Jun	1900	inf bp; Henry & Pauline (Gibbud)	3:165
Richardson	George F.	15 Sep	1851	marr Mary J. Johnson, both of Middlebury	3:200
Richardson	J.B.	14 Oct	1832	President of Missionary Society	2:12
Richardson	J.B.	26 Aug	1832	Moderator recording church business	2:11
Richarson	John B.	10 Jun	1832	appointed Moderator	1:119

NAUGATUCK, CONNECTICUT, CONGREGATIONAL CHURCH RECORDS

Richmond	Henry B.	25 Oct 1882	marr M.J. McKinney, both of Naug	3:214
Riggs	Fred	- 1899	adm ch	3:39
Riggs	Fred	5 Mar 1899	adm ch	3:72
Riggs	Mary A.	- 1900	adm ch from Oxford Ct.	3:39
Riggs	Mary A.	6 May 1900	Mrs., adm fr Cong, Oxford Ct	3:99
Riggs	Mary C.	- 1899	Mrs, adm ch	3:39
Riggs	Mary C.	7 May 1899	Mrs, adm ch	3:72
Riggs	Mary Jane	6 Dec 1860	of Oxford marr Burr C. Hine of Naug	3:204
Riggs	Robert	21 Jul 1834	ch died, 6m	2:114
Riggs	Sarah	15 Jan 1869	d, 76, Gunntown	3:256
Rine	see Pine	- 1828	-	1:153
Ringe	Ethel May	10 Jun 1900	inf bp; Herman & Mary (Miller)	3:165
Ringe	Hermann A.	22 Nov 1898	28 marr Mary J. Miller 24	3:226
Risley	Hannah Jay	- 1894	adm ch	3:39
Risley	Hannah Jay	1 Jul 1894	Miss, adm ch	3:71
Robberts	Joseph	30 Sep 1787	adm ch [see Roberts, Roberds]	1:11
Robberts	Joseph	30 Sep 1787	adm ch, dism	1:54
Robbins	Myrtie	- 1892	adm ch from New Boston, Mass, wife of Dr. Robbins	3:39
Robbins	Myrtie	26 Aug 1892	Mrs, adm ch fr Cong, New Boston, Mass	3:97
Roberds	Moses	20 Dec 1789	bp, ch of Joseph	1:165
Roberts	Albert Wm	18 Dec 1900	bp, adult; an Englishman, d in Jan 1901, bur 17 Jan 1901	3:165
Roberts	Amos	- 1845	adm ch from Waterbury; dis 1848 to Cheshire	3:39
Roberts	Amos	31 Oct 1845	adm ch from Waterbury; dism Sep 1848 to Cheshire	2:99
Roberts	Catharine E.	- 1866	adm ch, wife of Canfield Booth	3:39
Roberts	Catharine E.	2 Sep 1866	adm ch	3:64
Roberts	David	Jun 1827	d, fever occasioned by intemperance, 30	1:144
Roberts	Emily	- 1845	adm ch from New Haven, wife of Geo F.; dec 1880	3:39
Roberts	Emily	31 Oct 1845	wife of George F., adm ch from Waterbury	2:99
Roberts	Emily	24 Mar 1880	d, Mrs. Geo F., cancer	3:258
Roberts	Geo F.	7 Jul 1883	d, palsey	3:259
Roberts	George F.	- 1845	adm ch from Waterbury; dec 1888	3:39
Roberts	George F.	31 Oct 1845	adm ch from Waterbury	2:99
Roberts	Ida Mary Jane	3 Mar 1889	an inf, bp	3:159
Roberts	Joseph	30 Sep 1787	adm ch; rem [see Robberts]	2:83
Roberts	Joseph R.	9 Nov 1871	of Naug marr Helen Sawyer of Hartford	3:209
Roberts	Lucy A.	- 1866	adm ch, wife of -- Candee; dec 1873	3:39
Roberts	Lucy A.	2 Sep 1866	adm ch	3:64
Roberts	Lucy M.	28 Oct 1862	marr Selden Lewis, both of Naug	3:205
Roberts	Lucy Maria	- 1838	adm ch from Waterbury, wife of Selden Lewis; dec 1887	3:39
Roberts	Lucy Maria	8 Apr 1838	adm ch from Waterbury	2:97
Roberts	Lucy Maria	8 Apr 1838	Miss, adm ch from ch in Waterbury	2:32
Roberts	Martha Adeline	- 1878	adm ch, wife of Henry	3:39
Roberts	Martha Adeline	14 Jul 1878	bp, adult	3:156
Roberts	Martha Adeline	14 Jul 1878	wife of Henry, adm ch	3:67
Robey	Daniel W.A.	19 Oct 1892	29 marr Marion E. Hubbell 17	3:222
Robinson	Chas A.	27 Sep 1887	25 marr Ida I. Birch 18	3:218
Robinson	Chester	29 Nov 1860	marr Elisabeth Stevens, both of North Haven	3:204
Robinson	Mary C.	20 Feb 1873	Mrs, marr Isaac Scott, both of Naug	3:210
Rockefellow	Mary H.	5 Jul 1899	58 marr Wm K. Wight 66	3:227
Rogers	Abijah H.	17 May 1825	of Branford, marr Hariet Chidacy of East Haven	1:152
Rogers	Daisey Emma	- 1897	adm ch	3:39
Rogers	Daisey Emma	4 Jul 1897	adm ch	3:72
Rogers	Minnie E.	26 Mar 1884	marr Frederick H. Prior, both of Naug	3:216
Rollasen	Harriet Maria	3 May 1863	bp, adult	3:153

NAUGATUCK, CONNECTICUT, CONGREGATIONAL CHURCH RECORDS

Rollason	Cora[?] Louisa	3 May	1863	inf bp; Harriet M.	3:153
Rollason	Harriet M.	-	1863	adm ch, wife of --, withdrawn 1885	3:39
Rollason	Harriet Maria	3 May	1863	adm ch	3:62
Rollinson	Addie A.	-	1900	adm ch	3:39
Rollinson	Addie A.	6 May	1900	bp, adult	3:164
Rollinson	Addie A.	6 May	1900	adm ch	3:72
Rollinson	Clara L.	-	1900	adm ch	3:39
Rollinson	Clara L.	6 May	1900	bp, adult	3:164
Rollinson	Clara L.	6 May	1900	adm ch	3:72
Rollinson	Lizzie	-	1900	adm ch	3:39
Rollinson	Lizzie	6 May	1900	bp, adult	3:164
Rollinson	Lizzie	6 May	1900	adm ch	3:72
Root	Chloe Jane	6 Jul	1851	bp, profession	3:150
Root	Chloe Jane	-	1851	adm ch; dec 1901	3:39
Root	Chloe Jane	6 Jul	1851	adm ch; also baptized	3:60
Root	Chloe Jane	-	1885	voted to be erased	3:409
Root	Chloe Jane	30 Jan	1901	d in Meriden, 70	3:261
Root	John	7 Dec	1785	bp, ch of Jo. [prob says "Jos"]	1:164
Root	John	7 Dec	1785	bp [entry crossed out, see p. 1:164]	1:10
Root	Joseph Junr	2 Jul	1786	bp, ch of Jos	1:164
Root	Joseph Junr	2 Jul	1786	bp [entry crossed out]	1:10
Root	Loyal Lockwood	8 Jan	1804	bp, son of Joseph	1:172
Root	Lucy	7 Dec	1785	bp, ch of Jo.	1:164
Root	Lucy	7 Dec	1785	bp [entry crossed out]	1:10
Root	Lyman	7 Dec	1785	bp, ch of Jo. [prob says "Jos"]	1:164
Root	Lyman	7 Dec	1785	bp [entry crossed out]	1:10
Root	Mary	-	1785	adm ch, wife of Joseph; Irr Baptist	3:39
Root	Mary	20 Nov	1785	wife of Joseph, adm ch; withdrawn to Baptist	2:83
Root	Mary	20 Nov	1785	wife of Jo. adm ch	1:10
Root	Mary	20 Nov	1785	adm ch ["Joseph - Baptist" added] certificated	1:54
Root	Roxanna S.	-	1852	adm ch; dis 1864	3:39
Root	Roxanna S.	4 Jan	1852	adm ch	3:60
Root	Roxanna S.	25 Mar	1864	voted dism, eligible for letter if asked for [see 3:367]	3:122
Root	Salmon	7 Dec	1785	bp, ch of Jo. [prob says "Jos"]	1:164
Root	Salmon	7 Dec	1785	bp [entry crossed out]	1:10
Roots	Joseph	Nov	1798	ch bp	1:169
Roots	Polly	16 Jun	1793	bp, ch of Joseph	1:166
Roots	Russel	10 Apr	1791	bp, ch of Joseph	1:166
Roots	Sally	29 May	1796	bp, ch of Jos	1:168
Rosquin	-	-		see Rasquin	-
Rosquin	Albrecht	-	1892	an inf, bp	3:160
Rosquin	Hattie Schwabie	-	1890	Mrs, adm fr Terryville Ct	3:39
Rosquin	Hattie Schwabie	9 Mar	1890	Mrs., adm fr Terryville Cong	3:96
Rosquin	Karl	-	1892	an inf, bp	3:160
Roswell	Abbie E.	-	1877	adm ch; dis 1878 to College St., N. Haven	3:39
Roswell	Abbie E.	9 Jul	1877	adm ch	3:66
Roswell	Abbie E.	12 Apr	1878	dism to New Haven	3:125
Roswell	Emeline	-	1852	adm ch; dec 1876	3:39
Roswell	Emeline	4 Jul	1852	bp, profession	3:150
Roswell	Emeline	4 Jul	1852	adm ch	3:60
Roswell	Emeline	12 Dec	1876	d, 43, typhoid, Hillside	3:257
Roswell	Samantha	23 Jul	1874	bur, 48, Hillside	3:257
Roswell	Sarah S.	-	1852	adm ch; dec 1874	3:39
Roswell	Sarah S.	7 Mar	1852	bp, profession	3:150

Surname	Given	Date	Event	Ref
Roswell	Sarah S.	7 Mar 1852	adm ch	3:60
Rowe	Dencey F.	2 May 1827	of Columbia, marr Warren Wilson of Harwinton	1:153
Rowland	Wallace A.	21 Aug 1899	29 marr Mattie Parker 19	3:227
Rowley	Zelia	19 May 1864	of Naug marr James Ford of New Haven	3:205
Roys	Louisa H.	- 1854	adm ch, wife of -- Spencer; dis 1863 to Binghampton	3:39
Roys	Louisa H.	5 Mar 1854	adm ch	3:61
Runpfen[?]	Henry	1 Jan 1890	20 marr Rosa Zwick 21 [Rempfen?]	3:221
Russel	Aaron	- -	husband of Ether Spencer	2:88
Russel	Aaron	7 Dec 1826	from Boston, marr Esther Spencer of Salem	1:153
Russel	Charles A.	1 Jan 1825	marr Lockey Beebe of Waterbury	1:152
Russel	Delia	14 Mar 1864	marr Lucius Cwick, both of Naug [see Zwick]	3:205
Russel	Emma	16 Sep 1866	d, inf dau of Chs & Martha, Wolcottville, 6 ms, dysentery,	3:255
Russel	Jane G.	- 1869	adm ch, wife of Clifford; erased 1900	3:39
Russel	Jane Gray	3 Jan 1869	bp, adult	3:154
Russel	Jane Gray	3 Jan 1869	adm ch	3:64
Russel	Jennie E.	21 Apr 1856	d, ch of Edwin, Hamden, 4 y, convulsion fits, Hillside	3:251
Russel	Lemuel J.	10 Nov 1859	of Hamden marr Mary Ann Hotchkiss of Naugatuck	3:204
Russel	Mary Ann	7 Sep 1862	(Hotchkiss) dism to Methodist, Hamden E. Plains	3:122
Russell	A.	- -	husband of Esther Spencer	3:41
Russell	Cora	- -	see Bristol, Franklin Benjamin	-
Russell	Eliza	3 May 1850	dism to Meth, Buckland, Mass.	3:120
Russell	Eliza A.	- 1847	adm ch; dis 1850 to Buckland	3:39
Russell	Eliza A.	5 Sep 1847	adm ch from N. Haven Methodist	2:100
Russell	George S.	20 May 1879	marr Addie S. Squires, both of Naug	3:212
Russell	Lola	19 Jun 1864	Mrs, of Prospect marr Alfred Platt of Waterbury	3:206
Rust	Nellie E.	- 1886	adm ch from Easthampton, Payson Cong Ch, Mass.	3:39
Rust	Nellie E.	5 Sep 1886	adm fr Payson Cong, Easthampton Mass	3:95
Sabin	Henry	- 1856	adm ch from Amherst College; dis 1860 to Middle[tow]n Pt NJ	3:44
Sabin	Henry	2 Nov 1856	adm from ch Amherst College	3:90
Sabin	Henry	1 Jul 1860	dism to Presb, Middletown Point NJ	3:121
Sacket	Daniel	23 Feb 1826	of Milford, marr Hariet A. Porter, of Salem	1:152
Sacket	Mr.	21 Sep 1834	voted to settle here	2:17
Sacket	Seth	- 1834	began recording adm to ch during his ministry until Jun 1837	2:95
Sacket	Seth	16 Oct 1834	Rev, installed as Pastor	2:18
Sackett	Edward G.	23 Jul 1837	bp, ch of Seth, b 27 Feb 1836 [sic, but prob 1837]	2:105
Sackett	Frances Sophia	1 Sep 1837	bp, ch of Daniel, b 29 Mar 1836	2:105
Sackett	Hariet G.	1 Mar 1835	wife of Seth, adm ch, from Berlin; dism to Berlin 11 Mar 1838	2:95
Sackett	Hariet G.	11 Mar 1838	Mrs., dism to ch in Berlin	2:31
Sackett	Harriet A.	- 1835	adm ch, wife of Danl; dis 1864	3:43
Sackett	Harriet A.	1 Mar 1835	wife of Daniel, adm ch	2:95
Sackett	Harriet A.	25 Mar 1864	voted dism, eligible for letter if asked for [see 3:367]	3:122
Sackett	Harriet Cornelia	1 Jan 1836	bp, ch of Daniel, b 7 Oct 1832	2:105
Sackett	Harriet G.	- 1835	adm ch from Berlin, wife of Seth; dis 1838 to Berlin	3:43
Sackett	Julia Maria	2 Oct 1836	bp, ch of Seth, b 20 Jun 1836 [sic]	2:105
Sackett	Mrs.	3 Oct 1841	letter of rec. reconsidered, "her conduct...with certain Brethren"	2:38
Sackett	Mrs.	12 Sep 1841	letter of recommendation	2:38
Sackett	Sarah Amelia	1 Jan 1836	bp, ch of Daniel, b 19 Jan 1828	2:105
Sackett	Seth	16 Oct 1834	Pastor	2:79
Sackett	Seth	9 Nov 1837	Pastor, "left the chair," voted letter of rec. and $10	2:29
Sanberg	Walter Theo	20 Aug 1888	an inf, bp	3:159
Sanders	Russell J.	16 Mar 1872	marr Fannie E. Gunn, both of Naugatuck	3:209
Sandford	Jared	24 Aug 1800	adm ch, dism 14 May 1804	1:56
Sandin	Emil	16 Mar 1895	26 marr Elma Jalabson 26	3:223

NAUGATUCK, CONNECTICUT, CONGREGATIONAL CHURCH RECORDS

Surname	Given	Date	Event	Ref
Sandland	Henry	3 Apr 1828	of Birmingham, Eng., marr Mary L. Atwood of Watertown	1:153
Sanford	Adelia	30 Jun 1855	of Oxford marr Bennett Scovill of Oxford	3:202
Sanford	Asa	- 1828	adm ch; dis 1836 to Litchfield	3:42
Sanford	Asa	- 1828	male, on list of members, adm 1828	1:81
Sanford	Asa	4 May 1828	adm ch; rem 4 Mar 1836 to Litchfield	2:92
Sanford	Asa	4 May 1828	adm ch	1:59a
Sanford	Asa	4 May 1828	adm ch	1:106
Sanford	Asa	20 Mar 1828	propounded for adm	1:106
Sanford	Asa	4 Mar 1836	letter of dism to ch in Litchfield	2:19
Sanford	Asenith	23 Dec 1825	of Columbia, marr Calvin Hotchkiss	1:152
Sanford	Brother	4 May 1849	to be visited	2:59
Sanford	Charles	1 Dec 1859	d, 23, fever	3:252
Sanford	Dorcas	- 1828	Dism to Little falls, NY	1:143
Sanford	Dorcas	4 Jul 1828	adm ch, dism 1828	1:59b
Sanford	Dorcas T.	- 1828	adm ch, w of W. Hammel; dis 1828 to Little Falls NY	3:42
Sanford	Dorcas T.	4 Jul 1828	w of Wm. Hammell, adm ch; rem 4 [May?] 1828 Little Falls NY	2:94
Sanford	Dorcas T.	6 Jul 1828	member, dism	1:94
Sanford	Dorcas T.	6 Jul 1828	adm ch	1:107
Sanford	Dorcas Thomas	8 Jul 1828	of Salem, marr Wm Hammill of Little Fall, NY	1:153
Sanford	Dorcus Thomas	6 Jul 1828	adult, bp	1:87
Sanford	Eliada	2 Dec 1800	Dea, Delegate at Consociation at Salem, from North Haven	1:19
Sanford	Eliza	- 1836	adm ch from Methodist, wife of John; withdrawn 1885	3:43
Sanford	Eliza	14 Feb 1836	wife of John, adm ch from Epis. Meth.	2:95
Sanford	George	27 May 1860	marr Ann Collins, both of Naug	3:204
Sanford	Isaac S.	14 Apr 1865	marr Delia J. Ford, both of Waterbury	3:206
Sanford	Jared	- 1800	adm ch; dis 1804 to Prospect	3:41
Sanford	Jared	24 Aug 1800	adm ch; rem 14 May 1804 to Prospect	2:85
Sanford	Jared	24 Aug 1800	bp & adm ch	1:15
Sanford	Jared	14 May 1804	rec to ch in Columbia	1:37
Sanford	Jennie E.	21 Feb 1889	16 marr Frederick Henry Meyers 29	3:220
Sanford	John	- 1836	adm ch; exc 1857	3:43
Sanford	John	3 Jan 1836	adm ch	2:95
Sanford	Julia	4 Mar 1836	wife of Asa, letter of dism to ch in Litchfield	2:19
Sanford	Marvin	6 Apr 1857	of Naug marr Mrs. Betsey H. Scoville of Oxford	3:203
Sanford	Mary	- 1841	adm ch; dis to Hump.ville	3:43
Sanford	Mary	11 Jul 1841	adm ch; dism to Humphries Ville	2:98
Sanford	Mary	28 Apr 1844	dism to Methedist ch in Humphries ville	2:49
Sanford	Polly L.	4 Aug 1850	of Oxford marr Egbert R. Burnham of Naug	3:200
Sanford	Susan	- 1822	wife of Asa, member adm since 1822	1:83
Sanford	Susan	- 1828	adm ch, wife of Asa; dis 1836 to Litchfield	3:42
Sanford	Susan	4 May 1828	wife of Asa, adm ch; rem 4 Mar 1836 to Litchfield	2:92
Sanford	Susan	4 May 1828	Asa, adm ch	1:59a
Sanford	Susan	4 May 1828	wife of Asa, adm ch	1:106
Sanford	Susan	20 Mar 1828	wife of Asa, propounded for adm	1:106
Sauger	Annie B.	- 1896	adm ch from Wauregan	3:46
Sauger	Annie B.	6 Sep 1896	w of Geo T., adm fr Cong, Wauregan Ct	3:98
Sauger	Geo T.	- 1896	adm ch from Wauregan	3:46
Sauger	Geo T.	6 Sep 1896	adm fr Cong, Wauregan Ct	3:98
Saunders	E.A.	- 1882	adm ch from Geneseo, Ill, erased 1900	3:45
Saunders	Emmet A.	3 Mar 1882	Mr., adm fr 1st Cong, Geneseo, Ill	3:95
Saunders	Grace	6 Mar 1868	d, inf of Merit & Carrie, 6 wks, Hillside	3:256
Saunders	Grace P.	23 Feb 1857	d, 5 1/2y, Scarlet fever, Hillside	3:251
Saunders	J.R.	- -	husband of Lydia Bannister Birdsall	3:6
Saunders	M.C.	- -	husband of Carrie L. Budrow	3:6

NAUGATUCK, CONNECTICUT, CONGREGATIONAL CHURCH RECORDS

Surname	Given	Date	Event	Ref
Saunders	M.C.	29 Apr 1881	Mrs., dism to Cong, Ansonia	3:125
Saunders	M.C.	- 1884	Mrs, adm ch from Ansonia Ct	3:45
Saunders	M.C.	29 Feb 1884	Mrs., adm ch fr Cong, Ansonia Ct	3:95
Saunders	Merrett C.	3 Nov 1864	marr Carrie Budrow, both of Naug	3:206
Saunders	Orra P.	- 1863	adm ch, wife of J. Webster	3:44
Saunders	Orra P.	1 Nov 1863	bp, adult	3:153
Saunders	Orra P.	25 Dec 1867	marr Joel F. Webster, both of Naug	3:207
Saunders	Orra Parthena	1 Nov 1863	adm ch	3:63
Saunders	William	10 Jan 1893	23 marr Rose Bartlemas 23	3:222
Saunders	Wm	- -	husband of Rose M. Bartlemas	3:7
Sawyer	Helen	9 Nov 1871	of Hartford marr Joseph R. Roberts of Naug	3:209
Saylor	Lottie	5 Nov 1897	23 marr Walter Ellis 24	3:225
Scappa	Adam	8 Sep 1850	of Naug marr Sarah Jane Thompson of Naug	3:200
Schaffer	Ferdinand Fredk	8 Oct 1889	36 marr Melicent A. Nichols 24	3:220
Schaffer	Josephine	- 1887	adm ch	3:46
Schaffer	Josephine	3 Jul 1887	adm ch	3:69
Schandrew	Ella F.	- 1899	adm ch from St. Paul Min [see Shandrew]	3:46
Schatchman	-	- -	see Schthman	-
Schatchman	Frederic William	Jul 1871	ch bp; Mr. & Mrs. D. (German)	3:155
Schatzman	Daniel Herman	4 Jul 1880	inf bp; Daniel	3:156
Schatzman	Emma Theresa	2 Jul 1882	inf bp; Daniel & Mrs.	3:156
Schatzman	Geo Washington	4 Jul 1880	inf bp; Daniel	3:156
Schatzman	Lena Josephina	2 Jul 1882	inf bp; Daniel & Mrs.	3:156
Schatzman	Lizzie	31 Dec 1885	19 marr Henry W. Dethlefson 28, both of Naug	3:217
Schatzman	Louis Victor	4 Jul 1880	inf bp; Daniel	3:156
Schatzman	Terressa Eliza	18 Nov 1883	inf bp; Daniel & Mrs.	3:157
Scheiblen	Rosa	20 Aug 1870	d, 9 mos, cholera infantum	3:256
Schlennsin[?]	Martin	27 Jan 1884	marr Augusta Louin, both of Naugatuck [Schlennsin?]	3:216
Schlesenger	Anna	4 Jul 1858	ch bp; Augs D. & Jerusha C.	3:152
Schlesenger	Augs D.	- 1851	adm ch; dis 1872 to College Point LI	3:43
Schlesenger	Ellen	7 Aug 1862	ch bp at College Point; A.D. & J.C.	3:153
Schlesenger	Frank Samuel	2 Mar 1855	inf bp; A.D. & J.C.	3:151
Schlesenger	Jerusha C.	- 1845	adm ch fr E. Hartford, w of Augs D.; dis 1872 College Point LI	3:43
Schlesenger	Mary	6 Nov 1859	inf bp; A.D. & J.C.	3:152
Schlesinger	Augs D.	14 Apr 1972	dism to 1st Reformed Ch, College Point LI	3:124
Schlesinger	Augt D.	6 Jul 1851	adm ch	3:60
Schlesinger	Auguste Felix	29 Aug 1867	ch bp at College Point; A.D. & J.C.	3:154
Schlesinger	Bertha E.	6 Feb 1870	ch bp; A.D. & J.C.	3:155
Schlesinger	Jerusha C.	1 Jan 1854	w of Augs adm ch fr Cong, East Hartd	3:90
Schlesinger	Jerusha C.	14 Apr 1872	dism to First Reformed Ch, College Point LI	3:124
Schmidt	Alfred Wm	2 Jul 1893	an inf, bp; Mr. & Mrs. Wm	3:160
Schmidt	Charlotte Bernarda	5 Jul 1891	an inf, bp	3:160
Schmidtz	Wm	- 1892	adm ch, with wife	3:46
Schmidtz	Wm	3 Jul 1892	and wife adm ch	3:70
Schofield	Annie (Gyde)	- 1899	adm ch	3:46
Schofield	Annie (Gyde)	5 Mar 1899	bp, adult	3:164
Schofield	Annie Gyde	5 Mar 1899	Mrs, adm ch	3:72
Schofield	Fairwell	4 Jun 1890	24 marr Annie E. Gyde 19	3:221
Schthman	-	- -	see Schatchman	-
Schthman	Minnie	15 Aug 1869	ch bp; John & Mrs. Schthman (German)	3:155
Schubert	Max	2 Jul 1888	23 marr Emma Grieder 19	3:219
Schultz	Louisa	7 Aug 1875	marr Henry Messner, both of Naug	3:211
Schumacher	Lizzie	16 Sep 1896	26 marr Harry A. O'Donnell 34	3:224
Schumake	John	17 Sep 1857	d, 20, dysentery, Hillside, (from Ireland)	3:252

Surname	Given Name	Date		Event	Ref
Schumann	John Henry	24 Dec	1898	inf bp; Emil & Matilda	3:163
Schumann	Julia	24 Nov	1897	inf bp; Emil & Matilda	3:163
Schwabie	Emma	-	1876	adm ch	3:45
Schwabie	Emma	5 Mar	1876	adm ch	3:65
Schwabie	Hattie	-	1877	adm ch; dis 1882 to Cong., Terryville Ct	3:45
Schwabie	Hattie	10 Nov	1882	dism to Cong, Terryville Ct	3:126
Schwabie	Hattie L.	6 May	1877	adm ch	3:66
Schwabie	Henrietta	21 Sep	1887	27 marr Chas Rasquin 35	3:218
Schwenk	Elfrida Dora	5 Jul	1891	an inf, bp	3:160
Schwitz	Viola Annie	10 Jun	1900	inf bp; Wm V. & Mary (Geisler)	3:165
Scott	Abm	-	1787	adm ch; dis to Watertown	3:41
Scott	Abner	-	1800	adm ch; dec 1812	3:41
Scott	Abner	24 Aug	1800	adm ch; died 13 Mar 1812	2:85
Scott	Abner	24 Aug	1800	adm ch, d 13 Mar 1812	1:56
Scott	Abner	24 Aug	1800	adm ch	1:15
Scott	Abner	27 Jun	1806	on committee	1:44
Scott	Abner	13 Mar	1812	d	1:160
Scott	Abraham	22 Oct	1797	adm ch; rem to Watertown	2:85
Scott	Abraham	22 Oct	1797	adm ch, dism	1:55
Scott	Abraham	22 Oct	1797	adm ch	1:13
Scott	Alanta [sic]	-	1817	adm ch, wife of Arbi Porter; dis 1822 to Prospect	3:41
Scott	Alathea	-	1813	adm ch, wife of Abner; dec	3:41
Scott	Alethea	Sep	1800	bp, ch of Abner	1:169
Scott	Aletheah	5 Feb	1813	wid., cand for memb [perhaps 1820][see Eletheah, Althea]	1:63
Scott	Aletheah	5 Feb	1813	adm ch [perhaps 1820]	1:63
Scott	Alethiah	21 Feb	1813	wife of Abner, adm ch; died	2:94
Scott	Alpheus	11 Dec	1785	bp, ch of Uri	1:164
Scott	Alpheus	11 Dec	1785	bp [entry crossed out]	1:10
Scott	Alpheus	-	1818	adm ch; dis to Vermont	3:42
Scott	Alpheus	4 Jan	1818	adm ch; rem to Vt.	2:88
Scott	Alpheus	4 Jan	1818	adm ch, recomended	1:58
Scott	Alpheus	-	1822	male, on list of members; dism	1:81
Scott	Althea	-	1818	adm ch; dis 1834 to Ohio [see Alethea, Eletheah]	3:42
Scott	Althea	4 Jan	1818	adm ch; rem 8 Sep 1834 to O.	2:88
Scott	Althea	4 Jan	1818	adm ch	1:58
Scott	Alvin	18 Jan	1818	ch of Alpheus, bp	1:60
Scott	Anne	12 Sep	1789	bp, ch of Thad	1:165
Scott	Anne	29 Jun	1802	dau Thadde, d, 14y 4m 28d	1:155
Scott	Appalina	3 Nov	1830	relict of Enoch, d at Oxford	1:146
Scott	Appelina	-	1801	adm ch, wife of Enoch; dec 1830	3:41
Scott	Appelina	1 Nov	1801	wife of Enoch, adm ch; died	2:86
Scott	Appelina	1 Nov	1801	En, adm ch	1:56
Scott	Appelina	1 Nov	1801	wife of Enoch adm ch	1:32
Scott	Appelina	-	1822	wife of Enoch, member	1:83
Scott	Asahel	6 Dec	1801	bp, ch of Enoch	1:170
Scott	Asahel	-	1812	his ch d	1:160
Scott	Asahel	2 Nov	1837	died, 54	2:115
Scott	Atlanta	16 Nov	1817	wife of Arbi Porter, adm ch; rem 10 Sep 1822 to Prospect	2:88
Scott	Atlanta	16 Nov	1817	adm ch, dism [see Scott, Alanta]	1:57
Scott	B.	3 May	1829	his wife a member [see Bezuliel 1:94]	1:94
Scott	Bezaleel	11 Apr	1827	marr Sally Clark of Waterbury	1:153
Scott	Bezaleel	-	1829	adm ch; dec 1889	3:43
Scott	Bezaleel	May	1829	adm ch	1:108
Scott	Bezaleel	3 May	1829	adm ch	2:93

NAUGATUCK, CONNECTICUT, CONGREGATIONAL CHURCH RECORDS

Scott	Bezaleel	3 May 1829	adm ch	1:59b
Scott	Bezaleel	17 Apr 1829	propounded for adm	1:108
Scott	Bezaleel	9 Nov 1837	on comm	2:28
Scott	Bezaleel	30 Oct 1889	d, 86, old age	3:259
Scott	Bezeleel	1 Jun 1803	bp, ch of Thadda	1:171
Scott	Bezuliel	3 May 1829	member	1:94
Scott	Charles Eliott	13 Dec 1828	ch of Moses, bp	1:88
Scott	Clara	Sep 1800	bp, ch of Abner	1:169
Scott	Clarence Wood	19 Jul 1899	inf bp; Frank E. & Beatrice Wood	3:164
Scott	Clarisa	4 Jan 1818	wife of Alpheus adm ch, recommended	1:58
Scott	Clarissa	- 1818	adm ch, wife of Alpheus; dis to Vermont	3:42
Scott	Clarissa	4 Jan 1818	wife of Alpheus, adm ch; rem to Vt.	2:88
Scott	Clarissa	- 1822	wife of Alpheus, member; dism	1:83
Scott	Clark	- 1818	adm ch; dis 1834 to Berlin O.	3:41
Scott	Clark	4 Jan 1818	adm ch; rem 22 Jun 1834 to Berlin O.	2:88
Scott	Clark	4 Jan 1818	adm ch	1:58
Scott	Clark	4 Jan 1818	bp	1:60
Scott	Clark	- 1822	male, on list of members	1:81
Scott	Clark	2 Oct 1825	ch d, a fit, 1y 6m[?]	1:163
Scott	Clark	2 Dec 1827	to attend western conf at Bethel	1:105
Scott	Clark	14 Oct 1827	on committee	1:103
Scott	Clarke	5 Mar 1833	made confession, "unchristian conduct...with a neighbor"	2:13
Scott	Clerke	22 Jun 1834	about to remove to Ohio, with wife requested letter	2:16
Scott	Cornelia	- 1860	adm ch from Middlebury, wife of Thos	3:44
Scott	Cornelia	1 Jul 1860	adm fr Cong Middlebury	3:91
Scott	Daniel Bukley	14 Nov 1824	ch of Clark & Flora	1:85
Scott	David Caulkins	6 Dec 1801	bp, ch of Enoch	1:170
Scott	Dea	1 Dec 1822	on committee	1:96
Scott	Dea	5 Mar 1824	on committee	1:97
Scott	Dea	30 Sep 1827	appointed to attend conference at Huntington	1:103
Scott	Dea	6 Nov 1829	voted to attend future conf	1:109
Scott	Deborah	Sep 1800	bp, ch of Abner	1:169
Scott	Edward Moses	13 Dec 1828	ch of Moses, bp	1:88
Scott	Edwin	4 May 1817	child of Eldred, bp	1:60
Scott	Edwin	- 1841	adm ch	3:43
Scott	Edwin	11 Jul 1841	adm ch	2:98
Scott	Edwin	11 Jul 1841	bp, adult	2:106
Scott	Eldad	Sep 1800	bp, ch of Abner	1:169
Scott	Eldad	4 Jan 1826	ch d, canker, 2	1:163
Scott	Elethea	- 1822	Wid, member [see Alethea, Althea]	1:83
Scott	Elethea	5 Jul 1830	Wid, d, 67	1:146
Scott	Elethea, Jr	- 1822	female, on list of members	1:83
Scott	Elisabeth	17 Mar 1858	marr Guy Beecher, both of Naug	3:203
Scott	Elisha	23 Apr 1826	ch of Eldad, bp	1:86
Scott	Eliza Jane	1 May 1829	ch of Clark, bp	1:88
Scott	Elizebeth Hull	13 Dec 1828	ch of Moses, bp	1:88
Scott	Ellen A.	8 Oct 1856	marr Nelson T. Scott, both of Oxford	3:203
Scott	Ellen A.	- 1860	adm ch from Oxford; wife of Nelson T.; dec 1881	3:44
Scott	Ellen A.	6 May 1860	adm fr Cong, Oxford Ct	3:91
Scott	Ellen A.	Nov? 1881	d [month taken fr previous entry]	3:258
Scott	Ellen Elisa	- 1859	adm ch	3:44
Scott	Ellen Eliza	6 Jul 1851	ch bp, Edwin & --	3:150
Scott	Ellen Eliza	3 Jul 1859	adm ch, age 15	3:62
Scott	Emerit[?]	18 Jan 1818	ch of Alpheus, bp	1:60

NAUGATUCK, CONNECTICUT, CONGREGATIONAL CHURCH RECORDS

Scott	Emila [sic]	4 Mar	1825	ch of Alpheus, bp	1:86
Scott	Enoch	-	1781	adm ch; dec	3:41
Scott	Enoch	22 Feb	1781	one of the persons constituting the church	2:79
Scott	Enoch	22 Feb	1781	adm ch; died	2:81
Scott	Enoch	22 Feb	1781	subscribed to Constitution and Covenant	1:5
Scott	Enoch	22 Feb	1781	original member, dead [on 1811 list]	1:53
Scott	Enoch	19 Jul	1795	bp, ch of Uri	1:167
Scott	Enoch	15 Oct	1801	his w[ife] examined and rec'd as candidate for adm	1:32
Scott	Enoch	29 Aug	1830	d, 76	1:146
Scott	Enos	27 Aug	1813	ch of Alpheas, bp [perhaps 1820]	1:63
Scott	Ester	13 Nov	1785	wife of Uri adm ch	1:10
Scott	Esther	-	1785	adm ch, wife of Uri; dis Oxford 1803	3:41
Scott	Esther	13 Nov	1785	wife of Uri, adm ch; rem to Oxford 1 May 1803	2:82
Scott	Esther	13 Nov	1785	U. ["Uri" added] adm ch, dism 1 May 1803 [to "Oxford" added]	1:54
Scott	Esther	-	1801	adm ch, wife of Mark; dis 1808 to Coventry NY [see "Tenty"]	3:41
Scott	Esther	1 Feb	1801	wife of Mark, adm ch; rem 11 Aug 1808 to Coventry NY	2:86
Scott	Esther	1 Feb	1801	wife of Mark bp & adm ch	1:20
Scott	Esther	4 Feb	1801	Ma., adm ch, dism [error in book, should be 1 Feb]	1:56
Scott	Esther	5 Apr	1801	bp, ch of Mark	1:170
Scott	Esther	1 May	1803	wife Uri rec to ch in Oxford	1:37
Scott	Esther Robberts	29 Aug	1790	bp, ch of Uri	1:165
Scott	Eunice	4 Nov	1792	bp, ch of Uri	1:166
Scott	Eunice	-	1814	adm ch from Oxford, wife of Eldad; dis to Watertown	3:41
Scott	Eunice	18 Jul	1814	wife of Eldad, adm ch from Oxford; rem	2:87
Scott	Eunice	18 Jul	1814	adm ch, dism	1:57
Scott	Eunice	18 Jul	1814	wife of Eldad, adm ch from ch in Oxford	1:68
Scott	Eunice	-	1818	adm ch, wife of Leveret; dis 1822 to Torrington	3:42
Scott	Eunice	4 Jan	1818	wife of Leveret, adm ch; rem 10 Sep 1822 to Torrington	2:88
Scott	Eunice	4 Jan	1818	wife of Liverit, adm ch, Recommend	1:58
Scott	Eunice	-	1822	wife of Eldad, member	1:83
Scott	Eunice	-	1822	wife of Leveret, member; dism	1:83
Scott	Eunice	10 Sep	1822	wife of Leveret, rec to ch in Torington	1:96
Scott	Fannie L.	-	1885	adm ch	3:45
Scott	Fannie L.	5 Jul	1885	adm ch	3:67
Scott	Fannie Louise	27 May	1869	ch bp; Thomas & Cornelia Scott	3:154
Scott	Flora	-	1818	adm ch, wife of Clark; dis 1834 to Berlin O.	3:41
Scott	Flora	4 Jan	1818	wife of Clark, adm ch; rem 22 Jun 1834 to Berlin, O.	2:88
Scott	Flora	-	1822	wife of Clark, member	1:83
Scott	Flory	4 Jan	1818	wife of Clark, adm ch	1:58
Scott	Frank E.	15 Feb	1856	d, son of Edwin & Hannah, 4, complicated disease, Hillside	3:251
Scott	Frank E.	-	1885	adm ch	3:45
Scott	Frank E.	5 Jul	1885	adm ch	3:67
Scott	Frank Ellsworth	27 May	1869	ch bp; Thomas & Cornelia Scott	3:154
Scott	Garravan [sic]	5 Apr	1801	bp, ch of Mark	1:170
Scott	Gerret	15 Sep	1827	ch of Clark, bp	1:87
Scott	Hannah	21 Oct	1872	Mrs. Isaac d 20 Oct, 65, Hillside	3:257
Scott	Harriet	-	1856	adm ch; dec 1862	3:44
Scott	Harriet	2 Nov	1856	bp, adult	3:151
Scott	Harriet	2 Nov	1856	adm ch	3:61
Scott	Harriet	20 Jan	1862	d, 22, Hillside	3:253
Scott	Harriot	14 Nov	1802	bp, dau of Mark	1:171
Scott	Harris	May	1818	ch of Alpheas, bp	1:61
Scott	Hattie	18 Mar	1858	d, inf of Edwin, 2 mos, congestion of lungs, Hillside	3:252
Scott	Ira	18 Jan	1818	ch of Alpheus, bp	1:60

NAUGATUCK, CONNECTICUT, CONGREGATIONAL CHURCH RECORDS

Scott	Isaac	-	1784	adm ch; dec	3:41
Scott	Isaac	Sep	1784	adm ch; died	2:82
Scott	Isaac	Sep	1784	adm ch	1:7
Scott	Isaac	Sep	1784	adm ch, dead [as of 1811]	1:53
Scott	Isaac	28 Jun	1801	bp, ch of Thadde	1:170
Scott	Isaac	-	1822	male, on list of members, adm since 1822	1:81
Scott	Isaac	-	1824	adm ch from Plymouth; dec 1881	3:42
Scott	Isaac	1 Dec	1824	presented letter from Plymouth ch	1:100
Scott	Isaac	1 Dec	1824	wife propounded for adm from Baptist ch in Plymouth	1:100
Scott	Isaac	11 Dec	1824	adm ch from Plymoth	2:91
Scott	Isaac	11 Dec	1824	adm ch	1:59
Scott	Isaac	11 Dec	1824	adm ch	1:100
Scott	Isaac	20 Feb	1873	marr Mrs. Mary C. Robinson, both of Naug	3:210
Scott	Isaac	16 Feb	1881	d, apoplexy	3:258
Scott	Isabel	-	1800	adm ch, wife of Sanfd [sic]; dec 1827	3:41
Scott	Isabel	14 Dec	1800	wife of Samuel [sic], adm ch; died 19 Sep 1827	2:85
Scott	Isabel	14 Dec	1800	Sam., adm ch, d 19 Sep 1827	1:56
Scott	Isabel	14 Dec	1800	wife of Samuel [sic] adm ch	1:20
Scott	Isabell	-	1822	Wid, member	1:83
Scott	Isablel [sic]	19 Sep	1827	Wid, d, dropsy, 78	1:144
Scott	Jacob	12 Sep	1789	bp, ch of Thad	1:165
Scott	James M.	-	1876	adm ch; care withdrawn 1885	3:45
Scott	James M.	5 Mar	1876	adm ch	3:65
Scott	John	15 Aug	1824	child d, scalded, water poured out of the winder on its head, age 1 1/2	1:162
Scott	John	-	1856	adm ch; dis 1890 to Baptist ch, Cromwell Ct	3:44
Scott	John	2 Nov	1856	bp, adult	3:151
Scott	John	2 Nov	1856	adm ch	3:61
Scott	John	28 Feb	1890	Rev, dism to Bap Ch, Cromwell Ct	3:127
Scott	Julia	6 Dec	1801	bp, ch of Enoch	1:170
Scott	Julia Daisy	-	1878	adm ch	3:45
Scott	Julia Daisy	3 Mar	1878	bp, adult; Edwin	3:156
Scott	Julia Daisy	3 Mar	1878	adm ch	3:66
Scott	Julia E.	-	1885	adm ch	3:45
Scott	Julia E.	5 Jul	1885	adm ch	3:67
Scott	Julia Elisa	27 May	1869	ch bp; Thomas & Cornelia Scott	3:154
Scott	Lauren	9 Oct	1829	son of Clark, d, complaint of bowels after fall, 11	1:145
Scott	Lauren Clark	20 Jun	1819	ch of Clark, bp	1:84
Scott	Laury	5 Apr	1801	bp, ch of Mark	1:170
Scott	Leena	-	1822	wife of I., member, adm after 1822	1:83
Scott	Leena	-	1824	adm ch from Plymouth, wife of Isaac; dec 1833	3:42
Scott	Leena	11 Dec	1824	wife of Isaac, adm ch from Plymoth Baptist; died 1 Mar 1833	2:91
Scott	Leena	11 Dec	1824	wife of Isaac, adm ch, dead	1:59
Scott	Leena	11 Dec	1824	wife of Isaac, adm ch	1:100
Scott	Leena	1 Mar	1833	died, 28	2:114
Scott	Leroy Ellsworth	19 Jul	1899	inf bp; Frank E. & Beatrice Wood	3:164
Scott	Leva	14 Nov	1824	ch of Clark & Flora, bp	1:85
Scott	Leveret	-	1818	adm ch; dis 1822 to Torrington	3:42
Scott	Leveret	4 Jan	1818	adm ch; rem 10 Sep 1822 to Torrington	2:88
Scott	Leveret	10 Sep	1822	rec to ch in Torington	1:96
Scott	Levi	12 Sep	1789	bp, ch of Thad	1:165
Scott	Levrit	4 Jan	1818	bp	1:60
Scott	Lewis Munro	3 Jan	1819	ch of Leverit, bp	1:84
Scott	Liverit	4 Jan	1818	adm ch, Recommend	1:58

Scott	Lois	-	1789	adm ch, wife of Isaac; dec	3:41
Scott	Lois	19 Sep	1789	wife of Isaac, adm ch; died	2:84
Scott	Lois	29 Sep	1789	Is. adm ch, dead [19 Sep 1790, copying errors in book]	1:55
Scott	Lois	19 Sep	1790	[date is correct] wife of Isaac adm ch	1:12
Scott	Lonson Lewis	28 Jun	1918	ch of Clerk, bp	1:61
Scott	Loues	1 Nov?	1807	bp, ch of Mark	1:174
Scott	Lucretia	-	1822	wife of Moses, member adm since 1822	1:83
Scott	Lucretia	-	1828	adm ch, wife of Moses; dec 1862	3:42
Scott	Lucretia	4 May	1828	wife of Moses, adm ch	2:92
Scott	Lucretia	4 May	1828	Moses, adm ch	1:59a
Scott	Lucretia	4 May	1828	adult, bp	1:87
Scott	Lucretia	4 May	1828	wife of Moses, adm ch (Bapti...	1:106
Scott	Lucretia	20 Mar	1828	wife of Moses, propounded for adm	1:106
Scott	Lucretia	25 May	1862	d, 66, Hillside	3:253
Scott	Lucy	Sep	1800	bp, ch of Abner	1:169
Scott	Lucy	6 Dec	1801	bp, ch of Enoch	1:170
Scott	Lucy A.	-	1860	adm ch from Oxford; dec 1873	3:44
Scott	Lucy A.	6 May	1860	adm fr Cong, Oxford Ct.	3:91
Scott	Luious[sic] Sidney	3 Jan	1819	ch of Leverit, bp	1:84
Scott	Mabel	19 Aug	1792	bp, ch of Thadeus	1:166
Scott	Mabel	24 Oct	1803	d, dau of Thadda, 11y	1:156
Scott	Marcus Bradley	25 Oct	1807	bp, ch of Abner	1:174
Scott	Mary	-	1797	adm ch, wife of Abm; dis to Watertown	3:41
Scott	Mary	22 Oct	1797	wife of Abraham, adm ch; rem to Watertown	2:85
Scott	Mary	22 Oct	1797	Ab., adm ch, dism	1:55
Scott	Mary	22 Oct	1797	wife of Abraham adm ch	1:13
Scott	Mary Ann	19 Jun	1825	ch of Isaac, bp	1:86
Scott	Mary Ann	9 Mar	1869	d, 44, dropsy, Hillside	3:256
Scott	Mary L.	15 Apr	1887	25 marr Albert R. Porter 25	3:218
Scott	Mary Lines	-	1878	adm ch; dis 1894 to Jamestown NY	3:45
Scott	Mary Lines	3 Mar	1878	bp, adult; Edwin	3:156
Scott	Mary Lines	3 Mar	1878	adm ch	3:66
Scott	Moses	7 Apr	1795	bp, ch of Thadeus	1:167
Scott	Moses	-	1828	adm ch; dec 1829	3:42
Scott	Moses	-	1828	male, on list of members, adm 1828, died 3 Jan 1829	1:81
Scott	Moses	4 May	1828	adm ch; died 3 Jan 1829	2:92
Scott	Moses	4 May	1828	adm ch, d 1829 [name is starred]	1:59a
Scott	Moses	4 May	1828	adm ch	1:106
Scott	Moses	20 Mar	1828	propounded for adm	1:106
Scott	Moses	3 Jan	1829	d, consumption, 34	1:145
Scott	Nellie Elisa	7 Sep	1862	inf bp; Nelson T. & Ellen A.	3:153
Scott	Nelson T.	8 Oct	1856	marr Ellen A. Scott, both of Oxford	3:203
Scott	Nelson T.	-	1860	adm ch from Oxford Ct; erased 1900	3:44
Scott	Nelson T.	6 May	1860	adm fr Cong, Oxford Ct	3:91
Scott	Orange	-	1799	adm ch; wife of Thad; dec	3:41
Scott	Orange	28 Jul	1799	["Oring" crossed out], wife of Thadeus, adm ch; died	2:85
Scott	Orange	-	1822	wife of Thadda, member; died 4 Mar 1826	1:83
Scott	Orange	21 Mar	1826	d, wife of Dea Scott, diabetes, 66	1:163
Scott	Oring	28 Jul	1799	Th., adm ch	1:55
Scott	Oring	28 Jul	1799	wife of Thade, adm ch	1:14
Scott	Phebe	21 Jun	1801	bp, ch of Abner	1:170
Scott	Phebe	4 Oct	1805	d, dau of Abner, 5y	1:157
Scott	Phebe Elmina	27 Oct	1805	bp, dau of Abner	1:173
Scott	Philo	30 Jan	1791	bp, ch of Thadeus	1:166

Scott	Polly	5 Apr	1801	bp, ch of Mark	1:170
Scott	Ransom	6 Dec	1801	bp, ch of Enoch	1:170
Scott	Robert	26 Jun	1814	bp, ch of Eunice wife of Eldad	1:176
Scott	Roxana Jane	23 May	1824	ch of Eldad & Eunice, bp	1:85
Scott	Rusha	11 Dec	1785	bp, ch of Uri	1:164
Scott	Rusha	11 Dec	1785	bp [entry crossed out]	1:10
Scott	Sally	-	1822	female, on list of members	1:83
Scott	Sally	-	1829	adm ch, wife of Bezaleel; dec 1871	3:43
Scott	Sally	3 May	1829	wife of Bezaleel, adm ch	2:93
Scott	Sally	3 May	1829	Bezaleel, adm ch	1:59b
Scott	Saml	-	1781	adm ch; Irr 1802	3:41
Scott	Saml	29 Sep	1801	confession	1:30
Scott	Saml	1 Jan	1802	proposed to leave the ch	1:32
Scott	Saml Jr.	-	1818	adm ch; exc 1837	3:42
Scott	Samll Jur	15 Mar	1818	adm ch, R[ecommend]	1:58
Scott	Samuel	22 Feb	1781	one of the persons constituting the church	2:79
Scott	Samuel	22 Feb	1781	adm ch; withdrawn 1 Jan 1802	2:81
Scott	Samuel	22 Feb	1781	subscribed to Constitution and Covenant	1:5
Scott	Samuel	22 Feb	1781	original member, certif 1 Jan 1802	1:53
Scott	Samuel	12 Feb	1801	complained against by Jared Byington for slander	1:21f
Scott	Samuel	-	1822	male, on list of members	1:81
Scott	Samuel Jr.	15 Mar	1818	adm ch; excomm 3 Feb 1837	2:89
Scott	Samuel Jr.	3 Feb	1837	disregards covenants, cut off	2:22
Scott	Samuel Jr.	5 Feb	1837	sentence of excommunication publicly read	2:24
Scott	Samuel Junr	15 Mar	1818	bp	1:60
Scott	Sara Ann	6 Jul	1828	member	1:94
Scott	Sara Ann	6 Jul	1828	adm ch	1:107
Scott	Sarah	-	1791	adm ch, wife of Enoch; dec	3:41
Scott	Sarah	7 Aug	1791	wife of Enoch, adm ch; died	2:84
Scott	Sarah	7 Aug	1791	wife of Enoch, adm ch	1:12
Scott	Sarah	7 Aug	1791	En[och], adm ch; dead	1:55
Scott	Sarah	-	1818	adm ch, wife of A. Beecher; dec 1879	3:42
Scott	Sarah	4 Jan	1818	adm ch	2:89
Scott	Sarah	4 Jan	1818	adm ch	1:58
Scott	Sarah	-	1835	adm ch; dis 1852	3:43
Scott	Sarah	4 Jan	1835	adm ch	2:95
Scott	Sarah	4 Jan	1835	bp, adult	2:104
Scott	Sarah	18 Jan	1852	dism to Cong, Oxford	3:120
Scott	Sarah	13 Aug	1879	d, wid Argus Beecher, 92 Old age	3:258
Scott	Sarah Ann	28 Jun	1818	ch of Clerk, bp	1:61
Scott	Sarah Ann	-	1828	adm ch; dis 1835 to Berlin O.	3:42
Scott	Sarah Ann	4 Jul	1828	adm ch	1:59b
Scott	Sarah Ann	6 Jul	1828	adm ch; rem 11 Oct 1835 to Berlin O.	2:92
Scott	Sarah Ann	11 Oct	1835	letter of dism to Presbyterian in Berlin, Ohio	2:19
Scott	Sarrah	30 Mar	1788	bp, ch of Uri	1:165
Scott	Sary[?] Clarisica	5 Sep	1819	ch of Eldad, bp	1:84
Scott	Seth	30 Apr	1800	bp, son of Uri	1:169
Scott	Silas	11 Dec	1785	bp, ch of Uri	1:164
Scott	Silas	11 Dec	1785	bp [entry crossed out]	1:10
Scott	Susan	4 Jun	1825	d, Wid, apoplexy, 64	1:162
Scott	T.	Sep	1831	Dea, on Visiting Committee	1:115
Scott	Tenty [sic]	11 Aug	1808	wife of Mark, rec to ch at Coventry NY [definitely not "Esther",	1:48
-	-	-	-	see Esther]	
Scott	Thada	27 Jun	1806	on committee	1:44

NAUGATUCK, CONNECTICUT, CONGREGATIONAL CHURCH RECORDS

Scott	Thada	3 Jul	1818	on committee to est. Sabbath School	1:77
Scott	Thadd	-	1822	male, on list of members, dea	1:81
Scott	Thadde	3 Jan	1817	Deacon, on committee	1:73
Scott	Thadde	8 Apr	1817	Deacon, on committee	1:74
Scott	Thaddeus	-	1789	adm ch; dec 1832	3:41
Scott	Thaddeus	22 Feb	1789	adm ch, d 25 Aug 1832	1:55
Scott	Thaddeus	9 Apr	1813	chosen Deacon	1:67
Scott	Thade	Dec	1799	on committee	1:16
Scott	Thadeus	22 Feb	1789	adm ch; died 25 Aug 1832	2:84
Scott	Thadeus	22 Feb	1789	adm ch	1:12
Scott	Thadeus	22 Oct	1797	bp, son of Thadeus	1:168
Scott	Thadeus	9 Apr	1813	Deacon, died 25 Aug 1832	2:79
Scott	Thadeus	25 Aug	1832	died, age 75	2:114
Scott	Thalia	-	1864	adm ch fr Waterbury, w of Wm C.; dis 1865 to Waterbury 1st ch	3:44
Scott	Thalia	3 Jul	1864	w of W.C., adm fr 1st Cong, Waterbury	3:92
Scott	Thalia	10 Sep	1865	dism to 1st Cong, Waterbury	3:123
Scott	Thomas	19 Sep	1831	ch of Beguil, bp	1:88
Scott	Thomas	-	1869	adm ch	3:45
Scott	Thomas	2 May	1869	adm ch	3:64
Scott	Truman	30 Dec	1798	bp, ch of Thadeus	1:169
Scott	Truman	18 Oct	1803	d, son of Mr. Thadda, 5y	1:156
Scott	Uri	-	1787	adm ch; dis 1803 Oxford	3:41
Scott	Uri	30 Sep	1787	adm ch; rem 1 May 1803 to Oxford	2:83
Scott	Uri	30 Sep	1787	adm ch	1:11
Scott	Uri	30 Sep	1787	adm ch., dism 1 May 1803 [to "Oxford" added]	1:54
Scott	Uri	1 May	1803	rec to ch in Oxford	1:37
Scott	Uribial	12 Nov	1797	bp, ch of Uri	1:168
Scott	Wealthy	-	1818	adm ch; exc	3:42
Scott	Wealthy	-	1822	female, on list of members	1:83
Scott	Wealthy	15 Jan	1829	complained against for intoxication	1:1074
Scott	Welthey	4 Jan	1818	adm ch	1:58
Scott	Welthy	Sep	1800	bp, ch of Abner	1:169
Scott	Welthy	4 Jan	1818	adm ch; excomm	2:89
Scott	Welthy	17 Dec	1830	restored on promise to abstain	1:113
Scott	William C.	3 Jul	1864	adm fr 1st Cong, Waterbury	3:92
Scott	William C.	22 Feb	1881	at centennial exercises	3:300
Scott	William Clark	3 Jul	1829	ch of Bezaleel, bp	1:88
Scott	William Ira	1 May	1829	ch of Isaac, bp	1:88
Scott	Wm	-	1841	adm ch; dis 1851	3:43
Scott	Wm	12 Sep	1841	adm ch	2:98
Scott	Wm C.	10 Mar	1850	of Naug marr Thalia J. Boughton of Naug	3:200
Scott	Wm C.	16 Mar	1851	dism to Cong, Waterbury	3:120
Scott	Wm C.	-	1864	adm ch from Waterbury; dis 1865 to Waterbury 1st ch	3:44
Scott	Wm C.	10 Sep	1865	dism to 1st Cong, Waterbury	3:123
Scott	Wm Ira	11 Dec	1829	ch of Isaac, d, Burnt by falling into the fire, 1 1/2	1:146
Scott	Zeruiah[?]	28 Jun	1818	3 children bp, unnamed [looks like "Spenrah," doesn't resemble given name of any church member surnamed Scott]	1:61
-	-	-	-		-

NAUGATUCK, CONNECTICUT, CONGREGATIONAL CHURCH RECORDS

Scoval	Wid	16 Dec	1828	son d, croup, 4	1:145
Scovill	Bennett	30 Jun	1855	of Oxford marr Adelia Sanford of Oxford	3:202
Scovill	Ransom	2 Apr	1864	of Watertown marr Mrs. Cynthia Hotchkiss of Naug	3:205
Scoville	Betsey H.	6 Apr	1857	Mrs, of Oxford, marr Marvin Sanford of Naug	3:203
Scribner	Edwd J.	1 Jan	1882	marr Helen J. Widge, both of Naug	3:213
Scusceur	Barbara	21 Sep	1881	marr Louis Dettuel, both of Naug	3:216
Seeley	Edford C.	18 Aug	1891	marr Hattie A. Basham	3:221
Seeley	Edford C.	10 Jun	1894	bp; Eldridge Elliot & Alice Ella	3:161
Seeley	Hattie Basham	10 Jun	1894	bp, Eldridge Elliot & Alice Ella	3:161
Seeley	Thos N.	3 Nov	1869	of Derby marr Cynthia E. Terry of Ansonia	3:209
Selback	Elizabeth Annie	19 Nov	1898	inf bp; Henry & Annie	3:163
Senior	Ann	-	1878	adm ch from Cong, Rockville	3:45
Senior	Ann	3 Mar	1878	adm fr Rockville Cong	3:94
Settler	Peter	16 Aug	1882	marr Anne Dunder [?], both of Naug	3:214
Seymour	Elisa H.	-	1858	adm ch	3:44
Seymour	Elisa Humphrey	4 July	1858	adm ch	3:62
Seymour	Grace	-	1882	adm ch, wife of Geo Ham	3:45
Seymour	Grace	5 Mar	1882	bp, adult	3:156
Seymour	Grace	5 Mar	1882	adm ch	3:67
Seymour	Grace	9 Jun	1892	27 marr George C. Ham 25	3:222
Seymour	Harry	Jul?	1870	d, 3, drowned, Hillside [Jul written over Jan?]	3:256
Seymour	Isabella Rockwell	4 Jul	1858	ch bp; Ruby M.	3:152
Seymour	Jeannette P.	24 Oct	1888	marr Howard B. Tuttle	3:219
Seymour	Maria	6 Feb	1873	Mrs, marr Harry S. Hotchkiss, both of Naug	3:210
Seymour	Minerva A.	5 May	1868	d, 30, pleurisy, Hillside	3:256
Seymour	Nettie Phelps	-	1882	adm ch, wife of H.B. Tuttle	3:45
Seymour	Nettie Phelps	1 Jan	1882	bp, adult	3:156
Seymour	Nettie Phelps	1 Jan	1882	adm ch	3:67
Seymour	Ruby M.	-	1858	Wid, adm ch; dec 1900	3:44
Seymour	Ruby M.	5 Dec	1900	d, 89, old age	3:261
Seymour	Ruby Maria	4 July	1858	adm ch	3:62
Seymour	S. Zera	17 Dec	1872	d, 34, kidney trouble, Hillside	3:256
Seymour	Saml Z.	-	1858	adm ch; dec 1872	3:44
Seymour	Saml. Zera	4 July	1858	adm ch	3:62
Shandrew	Ella F.	5 Nov	1899	Mrs., adm fr Olivet Cong, St. Paul Min [see Schandrew]	3:98
Shannon	David	10 Mar	1892	39 marr Mrs. Gertrude Schenck Miller 35	3:221
Sharer	Henry	28 Jun	1899	40 marr Anna Winslow 30	3:227
Shaw	James	8 Jun	1853	of Smith Falls (now Easton) Canada marr Mary E. Judd of Naug	3:201
Sheldon	Alban J.	-	1878	adm ch	3:45
Sheldon	Alban J.	5 May	1878	adm ch	3:67
Sheldon	Albert J.	-	1885	adm ch; dis 1896 Boston	3:45
Sheldon	Albert J.	5 Jul	1885	bp, adult	3:157
Sheldon	Albert J.	5 Jul	1885	adm ch	3:67
Sheldon	Albert J.	3 Apr	1896	dism to New Old South, Boston	3:128
Sheldon	Eliza Denton	-	1878	adm ch, wife of Alban J.; dec 1900	3:45
Sheldon	Eliza Denton	5 May	1878	wife of Alban J., adm ch	3:67
Sheldon	Eliza Denton	16 Mar	1900	d in Boston	3:261
Sheldon	Frank A.	-	1885	adm ch; dis 1897 Boston	3:45
Sheldon	Frank A.	5 Jul	1885	bp, adult	3:157
Sheldon	Frank A.	5 Jul	1885	adm ch	3:67
Sheldon	Frank A.	15 Oct	1897	dism to Old South, Boston	3:129
Sheldon	Hattie C.	-	1885	adm ch; dis 1897 Boston	3:45
Sheldon	Hattie C.	5 Jul	1885	bp, adult	3:157
Sheldon	Hattie C.	5 Jul	1885	adm ch	3:67

NAUGATUCK, CONNECTICUT, CONGREGATIONAL CHURCH RECORDS

Surname	Given	Date	Event	Ref
Sheldon	Hattie C.	15 Oct 1897	dism to Old South, Boston	3:129
Shelton	William E.	24 Dec 1865	of Huntington marr Sarah E. Hitchcock of Naugatuck	3:207
Shepherd	Ellenor C.	- 1854	adm ch; erased 1866	3:43
Shepherd	Ellenor C.	30 Mar 1866	voted dismissed, eligible for letter if asked [see 3:369]	3:123
Shepherd	Ellenor Chloe	5 Mar 1854	bp, profession	3:150
Shepherd	Ellinor C.	5 Mar 1854	adm ch	3:60
Sherman	-	27 Nov 1826	ch d, croup 5	1:144
Sherman	C.S.	4 Nov 1849	Rev., accepted call as pastor	2:61
Sherman	C.S.	22 Feb 1881	at centennial exercises; Nassau, Renss Co, NY	3:300
Sherman	Charles S.	21 Nov 1849	Rev., installed as Pastor of this Church	2:62
Sherman	Chs Selden	21 Nov 1849	settled as Pastor; dism 25 May 1869	3:1
Sherman	Delia	30 Sep 1810	d, ch of James, 1y 7m	1:160
Sherman	Edward Crosby	4 Jul 1852	inf bp, Chs S. & E.W.	3:150
Sherman	Emily Pitkin	22 Feb 1857	inf bp; C.S. & E.W.	3:151
Sherman	Esther W.	- 1850	adm ch fr Manchester, w of Rev C.S.; dis 1871 Presb, Nassau NY	3:43
Sherman	Esther W.	3 Mar 1850	wife of C.S. adm ch from Cong, Manchester Ct	3:90
Sherman	Esther W.	- 1871	dism to Nassau NY	3:124
Sherman	Loruhama	- 1799	adm ch; dis 1809 to Tyringham Mass	3:41
Sherman	Loruhama	28 Jul 1799	adm ch; rem Dec 1809 to Tyringham, Mass.	2:94
Sherman	Richd P.	26 Jun 1853	d, C.S. & E.W., 4, scarlet fever	3:250
Sherman	Sarah W.	- 1860	adm ch, wife of G.A. Mills; dis 1867 to Ref.D.Ch, Copahe NY	3:44
Sherman	Sarah W.	23 Aug 1866	of Naug marr George A. Mills of Copake NY	3:207
Sherman	Sarah Williams	1 Jul 1860	adm ch	3:62
Shermon	Miss	Dec 1809	rec to ch at Tyringham MA	1:50
Shindler	Lizzie S.	29 Jun 1887	marr Chas C. Peterson	3:218
Shipman	Edward	28 Oct 1874	of Glastenbury marr Lottie L. Noble of Naug	3:210
Shortell	John	26 Jun 1899	37 marr Elnora Lunway 27	3:227
Shultz	August	28 Oct 1879	marr Annie Flor, both of Beacon Falls	3:212
Shumway	George H.	- 1878	adm ch; suspended 1879; Vide--"Dismission"	3:45
Shumway	George H.	- 1878	Mrs., adm ch; care withdrawn 1885	3:45
Shumway	George H.	3 Mar 1878	bp, adult	3:156
Shumway	George H.	3 Mar 1878	and wife adm ch	3:66
Shumway	George H.	23 Jan 1879	suspended, to become exc Apr 23, 1879 unless reason to contrary.	3:125
Silvermail	Chas F.	18 Apr 1883	marr Cora B. Morehead, both of Naug	3:215
Simmons	Charles	22 Feb 1895	Mrs., dism to Cong, Canaan	3:128
Simmons	Chas	7 May 1893	Mrs, adm fr Claverack NY	3:97
Simmons	Chas.	- 1893	Mrs., adm ch; dis 1895	3:46
Simons	Clarissa	11 Feb 1801	wife of Joseph, d, age 19 y 24d	1:155
Simpson	Daniel W.	23 Jun 1880	marr Mary E. Spencer, both of Seymour	3:212
Singstacken	Anna	8 Dec 1873	marr Georgi Lutz, both of Naug	3:210
Skinner	Corinthia	15 Apr 1855	Mrs. marr Stephen H. Pettibone, both of Harwinton	3:202
Sloan	Margaret J.	27 Mar 1869	of Bethany marr Theodore Decker of Watertown	3:208
Slon[?]	John	spring 1818	invited to return and labour	1:77
Small	Thos K.	2 Jan 1853	of Truro, Mass marr Jerusha M. Baldwin of Naug	3:201
Smf [sic]	Chas H.	16 Jan 1896	25 marr Addie M. Carter 19 [see Zumpf, Sumpf]	3:224
Smith	Abner	2 Dec 1800	Revd Elder attending Consociation at Salem, from Great Hill	1:19
Smith	Addie E.	2 Apr 1862	marr Billeous C. Hall, both of Naug	3:205
Smith	Adelaide	- 1858	adm ch, wife of B.C. Hall; dec 1899	3:44
Smith	Adelaide	4 Jul 1858	bp, adult	3:152
Smith	Adelaide	4 July 1858	adm ch	3:61
Smith	Adelia	3 Feb 1837	wife of William, comm to inquire into her "Christian walk"	2:21
Smith	Adelia	9 Nov 1837	w of William, united with Episcopal ch without dism fr this	2:28
Smith	Adelia	5 Jan 1838	wife of William, letter to Episcopal Ch	2:30
Smith	Agnes Elizabeth	31 Aug 1884	ch bp; Edwin F. & Hattie	3:157

NAUGATUCK, CONNECTICUT, CONGREGATIONAL CHURCH RECORDS

Smith	Alonzo Perry	31 Jul	1825	ch of Harry, bp	1:86
Smith	Amanda	16 Aug	1812	bp, ch of Sally wife of Anson	1:175
Smith	Amee	30 Sep	1787	adm ch	1:11
Smith	Amy	-	1787	adm ch, wife of Jonah Frisbie; dis 1805 Solon NY	3:41
Smith	Amy	30 Sep	1787	wife of Jonah Frisbie, adm ch; rem 27 Jan 1805 to Solon NY	2:83
Smith	Amy	30 Sep	1787	adm ch, dism	1:54
Smith	Anson	12 Dec	1828	d, lung fever, 53	1:145
Smith	Anthony	-	1822	male, on list of members	1:81
Smith	Anthony	-	1828	adm ch; dec 1838	3:42
Smith	Anthony	4 Jul	1828	adm ch; died 3 Mar 1838	2:94
Smith	Anthony	3 Mar	1838	died, 86	2:115
Smith	Asahael	-	1888	adm ch; dec 1888	3:46
Smith	Asahael	6 May	1888	adm ch	3:69
Smith	Asahel	12 Nov	1829	marr Elizebeth Thomas of Salem	1:153
Smith	Asahel	11 May	1888	d, 84, cancer	3:259
Smith	Asel	9 Apr	1805	bp, ch of Ansel, [sic] in right of the wife	1:172
Smith	Austain [sic]	4 Jan	1807	had left; given cert of membership	1:46
Smith	Austin	-	1784	adm ch; dec 1797	3:41
Smith	Austin	?	1784	adm ch	1:7
Smith	Austin	Sep	1784	adm ch; died 8 Feb 1797	2:82
Smith	Austin	Sep	1784	adm ch, d 8 Feb 1797	1:53
Smith	Austin Jr.	-	1787	adm ch; dec 1807	3:41
Smith	Austin Jr.	18 Nov	1787	adm ch; rem 4 Jan 1807 to Gorman NY	2:84
Smith	Austin Junior	18 Nov	1787	adm ch	1:11
Smith	Austin Junr	18 Nov	1787	adm ch, dism 4 Jan 1807	1:54
Smith	Bennet	15 Mar	1818	ch of Calvin, bp	1:60
Smith	Betsey	-	1818	adm ch, wife of Calvin; irr 1837	3:42
Smith	Betsey	4 Jan	1818	wife of Calvin, adm ch; withdrawn 3 Feb 1837	2:88
Smith	Betsey	3 Feb	1837	wife of Calvin, connected with Methodist ch in Ohio; dism	2:21
Smith	Betsy	4 Jan	1818	adm ch	1:58
Smith	Bolare	-	1822	female, member adm since 1822	1:83
Smith	Bolare	6 Mar	1825	wife of Harry, adm ch from Waterbury	1:101
Smith	Bolary	10 Dec	1824	Harry. Adm ch [date prob wrong]	1:59a
Smith	Bolary	-	1825	adm ch from Waterbury, wife of Harry; dec 1863	3:42
Smith	Bolary	6 Mar	1825	wife of Harry, adm ch from Waterbury	2:91
Smith	Bolary	31 Mar	1863	d, w of Harry, Southport, born 1799 Jan 30, Hillside	3:254
Smith	Brainerd Andrew	9 Jun	1901	youth bp; Charles H. & Ella (Andrew) Nettleton	3:165
Smith	Calvin	Nov	1806	ch d, aged --	1:157
Smith	Caroline	25 Aug	1816	bp, ch of Sarah wife of Anson	1:176
Smith	Catharine Sophia	31 Jul	1825	ch of Harry, bp	1:86
Smith	Charls Nelson	5 Sep	1819	ch of Roswel, bp	1:84
Smith	Cohiliad	4 Jul	1813	bp, ch of Phebe wife of Roswell	1:176
Smith	D.	-	-	husband of Polly G. Wheeler	3:54
Smith	David	2 Dec	1787	bp, ch of Austin Jr	1:164
Smith	David	25 Dec	1856	marr Grace B. Wheeler, both of Naug	3:203
Smith	E.A.	-	-	husband of Rachel Lewis	3:25
Smith	Edw.	18 Feb	1854	son d, 4 1/2, dropsy	3:250
Smith	Edward	28 Nov	1823	d, carbuncle on his back which appeared at first like a bile, 28	1:161
Smith	Edward	Sep	1845	bp, ch of Ralph	2:107
Smith	Edward A.	-	-	husband of Rachel Lewis	2:94
Smith	Edward Arnold	4 Jul	1828	ch of wid Sally, bp	1:87
Smith	Edwin	-	-	husband of Harriet E. Spencer	3:44
Smith	Edwin	18 Apr	1866	marr Hattie E. Spencer, both of Naug	3:207
Smith	Eldridge	4 Jul	1828	ch of wid Sally, bp	1:87

NAUGATUCK, CONNECTICUT, CONGREGATIONAL CHURCH RECORDS

Smith	Eliot	4 Jul	1828	ch of wid Sally, bp	1:87
Smith	Eliza (Lines)	10 Aug	1862	dism to Cong, So. Britain	3:122
Smith	Elizabeth	--	1858	adm ch, wife of Asahel; dec 1892	3:44
Smith	Elizabeth	4 Jul	1858	adm ch, bapt as adult (years since immersed)	3:61
Smith	Elizabeth	5 Jun	1892	d, widow of Asahel, 78, heart failure	3:260
Smith	Emeline	--	1865	adm ch from Waterbury, wife of Wm H.	3:44
Smith	Emeline	2 Jul	1865	w of W.H., adm fr 2d Cong, Waterbury	3:92
Smith	Emeline A.	9 Nov	1855	d, dau of Augustin, 13, fever, d in Fair Haven	3:251
Smith	Emily A.	--	1865	adm ch fr Waterbury, w of Rufus Hall; dis Jan 1874 E Bridgeport	3:44
Smith	Emily A.	2 Jul	1865	adm fr 2d Cong, Waterbury	3:92
Smith	Emily A.	18 Oct	1869	of Naug marr Rufus W. Hall of Bridgeport	3:208
Smith	Emily A. (Hall)	4 Jan	1874	dism to Cong, East Bridgeport	3:124
Smith	Emily J.	--	1858	adm ch, w of B.W. Hotchkiss, Geo D. Back	3:44
Smith	Emily J.	20 Oct	1874	marr Burrit W. Hotchkiss, both of Naug	3:210
Smith	Emily Josephine	4 Jul	1858	bp, adult	3:152
Smith	Emily Josephine	4 Jul	1858	adm ch	3:61
Smith	Esther	--	1822	wife of Anthony, member ["1827" appears next to her name]	1:83
Smith	Esther	--	1828	adm ch from Prospect, wife of Anthony; dec 1845	2:42
Smith	Esther	4 Jul	1828	wife of Anthony, adm ch from Prospect; died 3 Apr 1845	2:94
Smith	Esther Hotchkiss	4 Jul	1828	ch of wid Sally, bp	1:87
Smith	Fanna	19 Sep	1802	bp, dau of Anson	1:171
Smith	Frank A.	--	1886	adm ch	3:45
Smith	Frank A.	7 Nov	1886	adm ch	3:69
Smith	Frank Asahel	27 May	1869	ch bp; Edwin & Harriet E. [Spencer crossed out]	3:155
Smith	Fred A.	--	1897	att'd Deacon; resigned 1899	3:1
Smith	Frederick	5 Jul	1885	adm ch	3:68
Smith	Frederick Allison	1 Sep	1892	29 marr Mrs. Sadie Bristol Phelps 27	3:222
Smith	Fredrick	--	1885	adm ch	3:45
Smith	Friend	7 Sep	1823	ch of Anson & Sally, bp	1:85
Smith	Friend	15 Feb	1825	d, ch of Anson, 2	1:162
Smith	George	16 Aug	1812	bp, ch of Sally wife of Anson	1:175
Smith	Gerusha Hatch	15 Mar	1818	ch of Calvin, bp	1:60
Smith	Ginott	13 Aug	1831	d, age 22, belonged to Gunntown [also written "Jennett" later]	1:146
Smith	Guy Carleton	5 Jul	1812	bp, ch of Phebe wife of Roswell	1:175
Smith	Hanaford	--	--	husband of Henrietta Beers	3:126
Smith	Hardy Massam	14 Jun	1900	35 marr Gertrude Jane Widge 26	3:228
Smith	Harry	28 Jun	1801	bp, ch of Anson	1:170
Smith	Hattie E.	3 May	1885	25, marr Chas R. Clark, 30, of Waterbury	3:216
Smith	Henry E.	1 Nov	1892	37 marr Carrie G. Spencer 25	3:222
Smith	Horace	28 Jun	1801	bp, ch of Anson	1:170
Smith	Ira	29 Apr	1817	Deacon, from Columbia, at Council re Rev. Dodd's removal	1:74
Smith	James	--	1875	adm ch from Cong, Middlebury; dec 1896	3:45
Smith	James	3 Jan	1875	adm fr Cong, Middlebury	3:93
Smith	James	Apr	1877	appt'd Deacon; Removed Dec 1896	3:1
Smith	James	15 Jun	1896	Dea, d, paralysis	3:261
Smith	John	29 Sep	1828	ch d, dysentery, 8 m	1:145
Smith	John Augustine	9 Jan	1879	d, 67, dyspepsia	3:258
Smith	Julia M.	--	1875	adm ch from Cong, Middlebury	3:45
Smith	Julia M.	3 Jan	1875	adm fr Cong, Middlebury	3:93
Smith	Laura	2 Sep	1828	d, dysentery, 19	1:144
Smith	Lockwood	5 Jul	1812	bp, ch of Phebe wife of Roswell	1:175
Smith	Lucy	23 Dec	1894	bp; Frederic A. & Sadie	3:161
Smith	M. Eugenia	7 Aug	1865	of W. Haven marr Thomas H. Wallace of West Haven (Orange) at W. Haven	3:207

NAUGATUCK, CONNECTICUT, CONGREGATIONAL CHURCH RECORDS

Smith	Madeline	31 Aug 1884	inf bp; C.H. & Ella	3:157
Smith	Margaret	- 1784	adm ch, wife of Austin; dec 1803	3:41
Smith	Margaret	Sep 1784	wife of Austin S., adm ch; died 26 Mar 1803	2:82
Smith	Margaret	Sep 1784	adm ch, d 26 Mar 1803 [date is clear]	1:53
Smith	Marget [sic]	27 Mar 1803	d, abt 91y 10m [date is clear]	1:155
Smith	Margret	Sep 1784	adm ch	1:7
Smith	Maria	4 Sep 1843	[end of given name blotted] dism to ch in Washington	2:47
Smith	Maria	- 1845	adm ch from Washington, wife of Ralph; dis 1851 to New Haven	3:43
Smith	Maria	11 May 1845	wife of Ralph, adm ch from Washington	2:99
Smith	Maria	11 May 1845	adm from Washington	2:50
Smith	Maria (Ward)	16 Mar 1851	dism to Chapel Str. Ch, New Haven	3:120
Smith	Maria W.	- 1888	adm ch from N. Haven, w of Ralph	3:46
Smith	Mary E.	- 1896	adm ch from Waterbury	3:46
Smith	Mary E.	5 Jan 1896	Miss, adm fr 2nd Cong, Waterbury	3:98
Smith	Mary Loesa	27 Sep 1829	ch of Harry, bp	1:88
Smith	Mary W.	- 1875	adm ch from Middlebury, w of James	3:45
Smith	Mary W.	3 Jan 1875	adm fr Cong, Middlebury	3:93
Smith	Minnie	29 Aug 1883	Gideon F. Bray	3:215
Smith	Nancy	16 Aug 1812	bp, ch of Sally wife of Anson	1:175
Smith	Nancy Lucretia	5 Sep 1819	adopted ch of Roswel, bp	1:84
Smith	Nehemiah	2 Dec 1800	Delegate at Consociation at Salem, from West Haven	1:19
Smith	Obedience	30 Sep 1826	d, wid, 87	1:163
Smith	Phebe	- 1810	adm ch, wife of Roswell; dis 1842 to New Haven	3:41
Smith	Phebe	5 Aug 1810	wife of Roswell, adm ch; rem 12 Jan 1842 to New Haven	2:86
Smith	Phebe	5 Aug 1810	Ros., adm ch	1:56
Smith	Phebe	5 Aug 1810	wife of Roswell adm ch	1:50
Smith	Phebe	- 1822	wife of Roswell, member	1:83
Smith	Phebe	3 Feb 1837	voted to be requested to ask for letter of dism.	2:23
Smith	Phebe	25 Jul 1841	Mrs., dism to Church Street Ch, New Haven	2:38
Smith	Phebe Dodd	5 Sep 1819	ch of Roswel, bp	1:84
Smith	Polly G.	6 Jan 1899	(Wheeler) Mrs. David, d	3:261
Smith	Ralph	- -	husband of Maria Ward	3:54
Smith	Ralph	- -	husband of Maria Ward	2:95
Smith	Ralph	- 1888	adm ch from New Haven; dec 1889	3:46
Smith	Ralph	21 Dec 1888	and wife adm fr Dwight Place Ch, New Haven Ct	3:96
Smith	Ralph	11 Apr 1889	d, 71, paralysis	3:259
Smith	Ralph	7 May 1893	adm ch	3:70
Smith	Ralph E.	- 1893	adm ch	3:46
Smith	Ralph Edwin	31 Aug 1884	ch bp; Edwin F. & Hattie	3:157
Smith	Rhoda A.	- 1854	adm ch from Waterbury, wife of John A.; dec 1881	3:44
Smith	Rhoda A.	2 Jul 1854	w of John A. adm fr 1st Cong, Waterbury	3:90
Smith	Rhoda A.	Nov 1881	d, cancer	3:258
Smith	Robert M.	7 Jun 1876	of Naug marr Susie [Carrie crossed out] Baldwin	3:211
Smith	Roswell	27 Jun 1807	infant ch d soon after birth	1:158
Smith	Sally	- 1800	adm ch, wife of Anson; dec	3:41
Smith	Sally	14 Dec 1800	wife of Anson, adm ch;	2:85
Smith	Sally	14 Dec 1800	An., adm ch	1:56
Smith	Sally	14 Dec 1800	wife of Anson bp & adm ch	1:20
Smith	Sally	- 1822	wife of Anson, member	1:83
Smith	Sally	- 1822	Wid, member adm since 1822	1:83
Smith	Sally	- 1828	adm ch, wife of Edw; dis 1837 [sic] to Ridgeville O.	3:42
Smith	Sally	4 May 1828	Wd of Edward, adm ch; rem 26 Feb 1837 [prob 1843] to Ridge	2:92
-	-	- -	Ville, Ohio	-
Smith	Sally	4 May 1828	wid, adm ch	1:59a

NAUGATUCK, CONNECTICUT, CONGREGATIONAL CHURCH RECORDS

Smith	Sally	4 May	1828	wid, adm ch	1:106
Smith	Sally	20 Mar	1828	wid, propounded for adm	1:106
Smith	Sally	3 Feb	1837	Wid., her case to be reported on in subsequent meeting	2:23
Smith	Sally	31 Mar	1837	Mrs., wid of Anson, "improper use of ardent spirits"	2:25
Smith	Sally	20 Feb	1838	Wid., confessed...ardent spirits...bodily infirmity	2:30
Smith	Sally	26 Feb	1843	Wd., dism to Ridge Ville, Ohio [year transcribed correctly]	2:46
Smith	Sarah	-	1781	adm ch, wife of Austin Jr.; exc 1800	3:41
Smith	Sarah	22 Feb	1781	one of the persons constituting the church	2:79
Smith	Sarah	22 Feb	1781	wife of Austin S. Jn., adm ch; excomm 25 Jun 1800	2:82
Smith	Sarah	22 Feb	1781	subscribed to Constitution and Covenant	1:5
Smith	Sarah	22 Feb	1781	original member, dead [as of 1811, "Austin Jr." added]	1:53
Smith	Sarah	27 Sep	1799	wife of Austen, complained against	1:15
Smith	Sarah	12 Feb	1800	wife of Austen complained against for stealing	1:16
Smith	Sarah	4 Oct	1807	wife of Austin, confession	1:47
Smith	Sarah D.	-	1875	adm ch from Cong, Middlebury	3:45
Smith	Sarah D.	3 Jan	1875	adm fr Cong, Middlebury	3:93
Smith	Stanley	5 Jul	1812	bp, ch of Phebe wife of Roswell	1:175
Smith	Susan B.	-	1877	adm ch fr 1st Cong, Waterbury, w of Robt M; dis 1895 Darien Ct	3:45
Smith	Susan B.	4 Jan	1895	Mrs. R.M.S., Cong, Darien	3:128
Smith	Susan E. [sic]	2 Sep	1877	w of Robt M, adm fr Waterbury Ct 1st Cong	3:94
Smith	Walton Bronson	11 Jun	1899	inf bp; Wm H. & Jennie Malone	3:164
Smith	Warren A.	24 Jul	1873	d, son of E.F. & Hattie, 23 mon, cholera infantum, Hillside	3:256
Smith	William Henry	25 May	1865	d, 2y	3:255
Smith	William W.	27 Nov	1850	of Bridgeport marr Celestia Patterson of Naug	3:200
Smith	Willis R.R.	25 Aug	1887	23 marr Gertrude R. Barlow 21, both of Watertown	3:218
Smith	Wm	-	-	husband of Adelia Boughton	2:92
Smith	Wm H.	-	1865	adm ch from Waterbury; dec 1872	3:44
Smith	Wm H.	2 Jul	1865	adm fr 2d Cong, Waterbury	3:92
Smith	Wm H.	19 Nov	1872	bur, 80 [Hillside crossed out]	3:257
Snath	H.R.	22 Feb	1881	at centennial exercises; Hartford	3:300
Snath	Henry R.	-	1858	adm ch; withdrawn 1885 [5/14/83 faintly in entry]	3:44
Snath	Henry R.	5 Sep	1858	adm ch	3:62
Snyder	Lena Maud	26 Sep	1888	17 marr John W. Noble 21	3:219
Solomonson	Peter	17 Jun	1893	35 marr Christine Johnson 30	3:223
Somers	James P.	14 Dec	1826	marr Rebecka Harrison of Waterbury	1:153
Somers	Joseph H.	30 Jul	1861	of Waterbury marr Frances D. Woolworth of Naug	3:205
Soper	Ada Bingham	-	1900	Mrs, adm ch	3:46
Soper	Ada Bingham	2 Sep	1900	adm ch	3:72
Soper	Harry A.	-	1886	adm ch from Central Brooklyn NY	3:45
Soper	Harry A.	2 May	1886	adm fr Central Cong, Brooklyn NY	3:95
Soper	Harry Arthur	12 Oct	1892	26 marr Ada Francis Bingham 23	3:222
Sotter	Clara	15 Dec	1895	22 marr Steve Kirlkers[?] 22	3:224
Soule	Caroline L.	-	1892	adm ch from Beverly Mass	3:46
Soule	Caroline L.	1 May	1892	adm fr Dane St Cong, Beverly Mass	3:97
Soule	George	1 May	1898	inf bp; Sherrod & Mary Haines	3:163
Soule	Mary C.	-	1892	adm ch from Beverly Mass	3:46
Soule	Mary C.	1 May	1892	adm fr Dane St Cong, Beverly Mass	3:97
Soule	Mary C.H.	-	1894	Mrs. Sherrod, adm ch	3:46
Soule	Mary C.H.	2 Sep	1894	Mrs., adm fr Episcopal, Dover NH	3:97
Soule	Sherrod	-	1892	Rev, adm ch from Beverly Mass	3:46
Soule	Sherrod	1 Feb	1892	settled as Pastor	3:1
Soule	Sherrod	1 May	1892	Rev, adm ch from Dane St Cong, Beverly Mass	3:97
Soule	Sherrod Jr.	9 Jun	1895	inf bp, Sherrod & Mary C.H.	3:161
Southworth	Esther S.	7 Sep	1862	(Beardsley) dism to Baptist, Deep River	3:122

NAUGATUCK, CONNECTICUT, CONGREGATIONAL CHURCH RECORDS

Spachman	Rose	4 Nov	1897	22 marr Geo Webber 28	3:225
Spackman	Joseph	24 Jan	1883	marr Rosa Veil, both of Naug	3:215
Spencer	-	-	-	husband of Louisa H. Roys	3:39
Spencer	Abbie J.	16 Nov	1895	24 marr Alzamora Strong 25	3:224
Spencer	Albert	4 Sep	1835	bp, ch of Francis, b 28 Jun 1834	2:104
Spencer	Ancel	6 Sep	1818	ch of Abel, bp [looks like Abl, possibly Acel]	1:61
Spencer	Ancel	15 Mar	1818	adm ch	1:58
Spencer	Ancel	6 Jul	1828	member, [note says "excluded 7 Jan 1831"]	1:94
Spencer	Ancel Jr.	7 Jan	1831	excluded	1:114
Spencer	Ansel	-	-	husband of Hannah Newton	3:31
Spencer	Ansel	-	1818	adm ch; dec 1850	3:42
Spencer	Ansel	15 Mar	1818	adm ch	2:89
Spencer	Ansel	-	1822	male, on list of members	1:81
Spencer	Ansel	7 Sep	1850	d, 87, Hillside	3:250
Spencer	Ansel G. Jr.,	7 Aug	1868	d 64, affec of the liver, Hillside	3:256
Spencer	Ansel Jn.	6 Jul	1828	adm ch; excomm 7 Jan 1831	2:92
Spencer	Ansel Jr	6 Jul	1828	adm ch	1:107
Spencer	Ansel Jr	6 Nov	1829	complained against for several reasons	1:108f
Spencer	Ansel Jr.	-	1828	adm ch; dec 1868	3:42
Spencer	Ansel Jr.	6 Jul	1828	adm ch	1:59a
Spencer	Calvin	-	1787	adm ch; dec 1846	3:41
Spencer	Calvin	18 Nov	1787	adm ch; died 8 Mar 1846	2:84
Spencer	Calvin	18 Nov	1787	adm ch	1:11
Spencer	Calvin	18 Nov	1787	adm ch	1:54
Spencer	Calvin	6 May	1791	Deacon	2:79
Spencer	Calvin	6 May	1791	chosen Deacon	1:11
Spencer	Calvin	1 Jan	1801	Deac, appointed ruling elder	1:33
Spencer	Calvin	14 Sep	1801	Deac, on committee	1:24
Spencer	Calvin	15 Oct	1801	Deacon, on committee	1:32
Spencer	Calvin	16 Aug	1801	bp, ch of Deacon Calvin	1:170
Spencer	Calvin	8 Apr	1803	Deacon, chosen Clerk of the Church	1:36
Spencer	Calvin	17 Mar	1803	Deac, on committee	1:36
Spencer	Calvin	17 Mar	1803	Deacon, reappointed ruling elder	1:36
Spencer	Calvin	1 Jun	1804	reappointed ruling elder	1:37
Spencer	Calvin	11 Oct	1805	on committee	1:39
Spencer	Calvin	8 Jun	1806	complained against Thomas Porter for drunkenness	1:40
Spencer	Calvin	5 May	1811	Deacon, on committee	1:51
Spencer	Calvin	2 May	1817	Deacon, chosen Clerk [has terrible handwriting]	1:76
Spencer	Calvin	3 Jan	1817	Deacon, on committee	1:73
Spencer	Calvin	8 Apr	1817	Deacon, on committee	1:74
Spencer	Calvin	3 Jul	1818	on committee to est. Sabbath School	1:77
Spencer	Calvin	12 Aug	1818	chosen Moderator	1:78
Spencer	Calvin	-	1822	male, on list of members; dea	1:81
Spencer	Calvin	1 Oct	1837	Dea., delegate to Prospect	2:27
Spencer	Calvin	28 May	1837	Dea., delegate to Oxford	2:26
Spencer	Calvin Jnr.	20 Jun	1832	ch died, 11 d	2:114
Spencer	Carrie G.	1 Nov	1892	25 marr Henry E. Smith 37	3:222
Spencer	Catharine	6 Sep	1818	ch of Abel, bp [looks like "Abl," possibly "Acel"]	1:61
Spencer	Charles	24 Nov	1859	marr Emily A. Patterson, both of Naug	3:204
Spencer	Charlotte	20 Apr	1857	d, w of Charles, 28	3:251
Spencer	Chs	-	-	husband of Emily Patterson	3:36
Spencer	Clara Hopkins	18 Jul	1852	inf bp; Lawrence & Jane	3:150
Spencer	Dea	1 Dec	1822	on committee	1:96
Spencer	Dea	5 Mar	1824	on committee	1:97

NAUGATUCK, CONNECTICUT, CONGREGATIONAL CHURCH RECORDS

Spencer	Dea	10 Apr 1825	on committee	1:101
Spencer	Dea	19 Feb 1826	appointed delegate to consociation at North Milford	1:101
Spencer	Dea	4 May 1827	on committee	1:102
Spencer	Dea	23 Dec 1827	to attend conf at Oxford	1:105
Spencer	Dea	28 Oct 1827	appointed delegate to conference at Waterbury	1:104
Spencer	Dea	4 May 1828	on comm	1:106
Spencer	Dea	12 Mar 1828	on comm	1:106
Spencer	Dea	6 Nov 1829	on comm	1:109
Spencer	Dea	6 Nov 1829	voted to attend future conf	1:109
Spencer	Dea	11 Oct 1829	appointed delegate to Consociation at Bethany	1:108
Spencer	Dea C.	Sep 1831	on Visiting Committee	1:115
Spencer	Deacon	26 Aug 1832	on Board of Managers for SS	2:11
Spencer	Dr. L.	26 Apr 1836	ch died, 1y 6m	2:115
Spencer	E.	- -	husband of Hattie J. Osborne	3:33
Spencer	Edward	4 Sep 1835	bp, ch of Francis, b 17 Dec 1832	2:104
Spencer	Elihu	- 1836	adm ch; dec 1840	3:43
Spencer	Elihu	2 Oct 1836	adm ch; died 30 Aug 1840	2:96
Spencer	Elisa	- 1833	adm ch; dec 1887	3:43
Spencer	Eliza	5 May 1833	adm ch	2:93
Spencer	Eliza	1 May 1835	bp, ch of Thomas, b 28 Sep 1817	2:104
Spencer	Eliza	29 May 1887	d, 81, broken hip	3:259
Spencer	Ellen	- 1858	adm ch	3:44
Spencer	Ellen	7 Mar 1858	bp, adult	3:152
Spencer	Ellen	7 Mar 1858	adm ch	3:61
Spencer	Ellen	21 Dec 1870	marr Henry Sykes, both of Naug	3:209
Spencer	Ellen E.	- 1863	adm ch, wife of Henry Sykes	3:44
Spencer	Ellen Elizabeth	5 Jul 1863	adm ch	3:62
Spencer	Esther	19 Nov 1797	bp, ch of Dea. Calvin	1:168
Spencer	Esther	- 1799	adm ch, wife of Calvin; dec 1840	3:41
Spencer	Esther	17 Jul 1799	wife of Calvin, adm ch; died 7 Aug 1840	2:85
Spencer	Esther	17 Jul 1799	Cal, adm ch	1:55
Spencer	Esther	17 Jul 1799	wife of Decn adm ch	1:14
Spencer	Esther	- 1817	adm ch, wife of A. Russel; dis 1827 to Boston	3:41
Spencer	Esther	16 Nov 1817	wife of Aaron Russel, adm ch; rem 1827 to Boston, Mass.	2:88
Spencer	Esther	16 Nov 1817	adm ch, dism abt 1827	1:57
Spencer	Esther	- 1822	wife of Calvin, member	1:83
Spencer	Esther	7 Dec 1826	of Salem, marr Aaron Russel from Boston	1:153
Spencer	Esther	1 May 1835	bp, ch of Thomas, b 11 Oct 1832	2:104
Spencer	Esther Jr.	- 1822	female, on list of members	1:83
Spencer	Eunice	- 1841	adm ch; dis 1843 to Hump.ville	3:43
Spencer	Eunice	11 Jul 1841	adm ch; dism 10 Sep 1843 to HumphreysVille	2:98
Spencer	Eunice	11 Jul 1841	bp, adult	2:106
Spencer	Eunice	4 Sep 1843	Miss, dism to ch in Humphries Ville	2:47
Spencer	Francis	31 Jan 1841	on comm	2:36
Spencer	Francis	- 1866	adm ch; dec 1880	3:45
Spencer	Francis	2 Sep 1866	bp, adult	3:153
Spencer	Francis	2 Sep 1866	adm ch	3:64
Spencer	Francis	20 Oct 1880	d, 81, dysentery	3:258
Spencer	Francis Willard	28 Apr 1844	bp, ch of Wid Harriet	2:107
Spencer	G.	- -	husband of Julia Ann Beecher	3:5
Spencer	G.	22 Feb 1881	at centennial exercises	3:300
Spencer	George Beecher	4 Sep 1835	bp, ch of Lawrence S.	2:105
Spencer	Grace Anna	5 May 1880	of Middletown marr Austin E. May of Naug	3:212
Spencer	Gustavus	- -	husband of Julia Ann Beecher	2:93

NAUGATUCK, CONNECTICUT, CONGREGATIONAL CHURCH RECORDS

Spencer	Gustavus	26 Jun 1808	bp, ch of Calvin & Esther	1:174
Spencer	Gustavus	- 1849	adm ch from Yale College; dis 1867 to Stratford	3:43
Spencer	Gustavus	May 1849	adm ch from Yale College	2:100
Spencer	Gustavus	24 Mar 1850	on comm	2:63
Spencer	Gustavus	10 Jun 1867	dism to Stratford	3:123
Spencer	H.W.	- -	husband of Eliza H. Beecher	3:5
Spencer	H.W.	- -	husband of Eliza H. Beecher	2:96
Spencer	Hannah	16 Jan 1835	died, 31	2:114
Spencer	Hannah Newton	18 Apr 1900	Mrs. Ansel, d, 83, paralysis	3:261
Spencer	Hariet	7 Jan 1830	member, recd by letter [probably 1831]	1:94
Spencer	Hariet	7 Jan 1831	.. of Doct Lucien, received by letter	1:114
Spencer	Hariet	15 Aug 1842	dism to ch in Bethany	2:41
Spencer	Harriet	- 1831	adm ch from Bethany, wife of Lucian; dis 1842 to Bethany	3:43
Spencer	Harriet	7 Jan 1831	wife of Lucian, adm ch from Bethany; rem 15 Aug 1842	2:93
Spencer	Harriet	1 May 1835	bp, ch of Thomas, b 16 Jul 1830	2:104
Spencer	Harriet	- 1858	adm ch	3:44
Spencer	Harriet	7 Mar 1858	adm ch	3:61
Spencer	Harriet C.	- 1845	adm ch from Bethany, wife of Francis; dec 1866	3:43
Spencer	Harriet E.	10 Aug 1845	wife of Fr---, adm ch from Bethany	2:99
Spencer	Harriet E.	10 Aug 1845	Mrs., adm from ch in Bethany	2:51
Spencer	Harriet E.	- 1860	adm ch, wife of Edwin Smith	3:44
Spencer	Harriet E.	11 Nov 1866	d, 59, dropsy	3:255
Spencer	Harriet Emily	28 Apr 1844	bp, ch of Wid Harriet	2:107
Spencer	Harriet Emily	1 Jul 1860	adm ch	3:62
Spencer	Harris	9 Oct 1791	bp, ch of Calvin	1:166
Spencer	Harris	1 Sep 1861	d, 70, Hillside	3:253
Spencer	Harris	2 Jan 1887	Mrs, d, 78, pneumonia	3:259
Spencer	Hattie E.	18 Apr 1866	marr Edwin Smith, both of Naug	3:207
Spencer	Hellen Mary	4 Sep 1835	bp, ch of Lawrence S.	2:105
Spencer	Henry	6 Sep 1818	ch of Abel, bp [looks like "Abl," possibly "Acel"]	1:61
Spencer	James	1 Feb 1806	d, son of Ancel, 7y	1:157
Spencer	James	6 Sep 1818	ch of Abel, bp [looks like "Abl," possibly "Acel"]	1:61
Spencer	James Elihu	28 Apr 1844	bp, ch of Ansil Jun	2:107
Spencer	James L.	- 1857	adm ch from Seymour; dis 1860 to Seymour	3:44
Spencer	James L.	5 Jul 1857	adm fr Cong Seymour Ct	3:91
Spencer	James L.	4 Nov 1860	dism to Cong, Seymour Ct	3:121
Spencer	James L.	22 Feb 1881	at centennial exercises, "chair"[?]	3:300
Spencer	James L.	22 Feb 1881	at centennial exercises; Mrs.	3:300
Spencer	James Willard	5 Jul 1857	ch bp; James L. & Marion E.	3:151
Spencer	Jane Atwater	28 Apr 1844	bp, ch of Ansil Jun	2:107
Spencer	Jane E.	14 Dec 1861	d, 35, Hillside	3:253
Spencer	Jennie	16 Jan 1870	d, 18, fever, Hillside	3:256
Spencer	John Calvin	31 Aug 1832	bp, ch of Lucian, b 20 Jun 1830	2:104
Spencer	John Newton	4 Jan 1850	inf bp, Ansel Jr. & Hannah	3:150
Spencer	Julia	- 1858	adm ch, wife of J.H. Whittemore	3:44
Spencer	Julia	4 Jul 1858	bp, adult	3:152
Spencer	Julia	4 July 1858	adm ch	3:62
Spencer	Julia A.	10 Jun 1863	marr John H. Whittemore, both of Naug	3:205
Spencer	L.	- -	husband of Jane E. Hopkins	3:19
Spencer	L.	- -	husband of Jane Hopkins	2:98
Spencer	L.	30 Nov 1861	d, inf of Mrs, 2ds	3:253
Spencer	Laura	1 May 1835	bp, ch of Thomas, b 1 Feb 1825	2:104
Spencer	Laurence S.	11 Apr 1827	marr Maria Beecher, Salem [see Stern Spencer]	1:153
Spencer	Lawrence	24 Mar 1850	Mrs., on comm	2:63

NAUGATUCK, CONNECTICUT, CONGREGATIONAL CHURCH RECORDS

Spencer	Lawrence S.	26 Jan	1864	marr Amanda Wood, both of Naugatuck	3:205
Spencer	Leonard	7 Apr	1865	d, 69, Hillside	3:255
Spencer	Lockey	-	1822	female, on list of members [crossed out]	1:83
Spencer	Lockey	13 Mar	1825	of Salem, marr Seldon Lewis	1:152
Spencer	Locky	2 Feb	1794	bp, ch of Deacon	1:166
Spencer	Locky	-	1818	adm ch, wife of Selden Lewis; dec 1861	3:42
Spencer	Locky	15 Mar	1818	wife of Selden Lewis, adm ch	2:89
Spencer	Locky	15 Mar	1818	adm ch ["Lewis" added]	1:58
Spencer	Loly	-	1818	adm ch, wife of Ansel; dec 1860	3:42
Spencer	Loly	15 Mar	1818	wife of Ansel, adm ch	2:89
Spencer	Loly	15 Mar	1818	wife of Ancel, adm ch	1:58
Spencer	Loly	-	1822	wife of Ansel, member	1:83
Spencer	Loly	15 Oct	1860	d, 87, Hillside	3:253
Spencer	Louisa H.	27 Sep	1863	(Roys) dism to Cong, Binghampton	3:122
Spencer	Louisa Maria	-	1850	adm ch; dec 1897	3:43
Spencer	Louisa Maria	6 Jan	1850	adm ch	3:60
Spencer	Louisa Maria	15 Feb	1897	d	3:261
Spencer	Louiza Maria	4 Sep	1835	bp, ch of Lawrence S.	2:105
Spencer	Lucian	28 Apr	1844	bp, ch of Wid Harriet	2:107
Spencer	Lucium	24 Jan	1790	bp, ch of Calvin	1:165
Spencer	Lutium	6 Nov	1795	bp, ch of Dea. Calvin	1:167
Spencer	M.C.	22 Feb	1881	Mr. or Mrs. [?] at centennial exercises	3:300
Spencer	Maria	-	1833	adm ch, wife of Lawrence; dec 1844	3:43
Spencer	Maria	5 May	1833	wife of L. Stern, adm ch; died Apr 1844	2:93
Spencer	Marion E.	-	1857	adm ch from Seymour, wife of Jas; dis 1860 to Seymour	3:44
Spencer	Marion E.	5 Jul	1857	w of J.L., adm fr Cong, Seymour Ct	3:91
Spencer	Marion E.	4 Nov	1860	[wife of] James L. dism to Cong, Seymour Ct	3:121
Spencer	Mary	Apr	1833	Miss, on committee for SS	2:9
Spencer	Mary C.	-	1818	adm ch, wife of J. Street; dis 1836 to Prospect	3:42
Spencer	Mary C.	4 Jan	1818	wife of James Street, adm ch; rem 14 Feb 1836	2:88
Spencer	Mary C.	4 Jan	1818	adm ch	1:58
Spencer	Mary C.	4 Jan	1818	bp [name is very hard to read but matches with her adm]	1:60
Spencer	Mary C.	-	1822	female, on list of members	1:83
Spencer	Mary C.	-	1849	adm ch from Stratford; dis 1867 to Stratford	3:43
Spencer	Mary C.	May	1849	wife of Gustavus, adm ch from Stratford	2:100
Spencer	Mary C.	10 Jun	1867	[wife of] Gustavus dism to Stratford	3:123
Spencer	Mary Caroline	11 Sep	1842	bp, ch of Henry W.	2:106
Spencer	Mary E.	23 Jun	1880	marr Daniel W. Simpson, both of Seymour	3:212
Spencer	Mary Judson	16 Sep	1860	ch bp; Gustavus & Mary C.	3:152
Spencer	May Parker	7 Apr	1897	26 marr Frank M. Twitchell 41	3:225
Spencer	Nelson Stanley	2 May	1858	ch bp; Gustavus & Mary C.	3:152
Spencer	Polly	-	1817	adm ch; dis 1820 to Prospect	3:41
Spencer	Polly	16 Nov	1817	adm ch; rem 4 Mar 1820 to Prospect	2:88
Spencer	Polly	16 Nov	1817	adm ch	1:57
Spencer	Ruth	14 Oct	1855	d, 81, Hillside	3:251
Spencer	S. Louie	3 Apr	1878	d, son of Mr. & Mrs. L.S. Spencer, 10, diphtheria	3:258
Spencer	Sarah	-	1835	adm ch, wife of Francis; dec 1844	3:43
Spencer	Sarah	1 Mar	1835	wife of Francis, adm ch	2:95
Spencer	Sarah C.	-	1866	adm ch	3:45
Spencer	Sarah C.	2 Sep	1866	adm ch	3:63
Spencer	Sarah Clarissa	28 Apr	1844	bp, ch of Wid Harriet	2:107
Spencer	Sarah G.	-	1859	adm ch, wife of C. Walker; dec 1866	3:44
Spencer	Sarah G.	2 Jul	1859	bp, youth	3:152
Spencer	Sarah G.	3 Jul	1859	adm ch, age 17	3:62

NAUGATUCK, CONNECTICUT, CONGREGATIONAL CHURCH RECORDS

Surname	Given	Date	Event	Ref
Spencer	Sarah G.	14 Sep 1864	of Naug marr Charles F. Walker	3:206
Spencer	Sarah L.	- 1859	adm ch, wife of Leonard; dec 1897	3:44
Spencer	Sarah L.	2 Jan 1859	adm ch	3:62
Spencer	Sarah L.	21 Nov 1897	d, 96, paralysis	3:261
Spencer	Shandy	6 Sep 1818	ch of Abel, bp [looks like "Abi" possibly "Ace"]	1:61
Spencer	Shundy Bela	28 Apr 1844	bp of Ansil Jun	2:107
Spencer	Stern	Nov 1833	ch died [see Lawrence S. Spencer]	2:114
Spencer	Temparance	9 Feb 1807	d, 82y	1:158
Spencer	Thomas	6 Jul 1788	bp, son of Calvin	1:165
Spencer	Thomas	15 Jul 1829	son d, black canker, 7	1:145
Spencer	Thomas	Apr 1833	on committee for SS	2:9
Spencer	Thomas	6 Jan 1833	adm ch	2:93
Spencer	Thomas	27 May 1868	d, 80, old age, Hillside	3:256
Spencer	Thos	- 1833	adm ch; dec 1868	3:43
Spencer	Tirza	- 1835	adm ch, wife of Harris; dec 1887	3:43
Spencer	Tirza	4 Jan 1835	wife of Harris, adm ch	2:95
Spencer	Tirza	4 Jan 1835	bp, adult	2:104
Sperry	-	Aug 1835	died	2:115
Sperry	Abel	4 Sep 1808	bp, ch of Ruel	1:174
Sperry	Clarissia	4 Sep 1808	bp, ch of Ruel	1:174
Sperry	Cornelia	25 Nov 1851	of Waterbury marr Harvey Crane of Bethlehem Ct	3:201
Sperry	Earl	28 May 1823	marr Anna Balwin of Woodbridge	1:152
Sperry	Lucy	- 1807	adm ch, wife of Ruel; dec 1852	3:41
Sperry	Lucy	4 Aug 1807	Ri [sic], adm ch	1:56
Sperry	Lucy	4 Aug 1808	wife of Ruel, adm ch	2:86
Sperry	Lucy	4 Aug 1808	wife of Ruel, ill, bp & adm ch	1:48
Sperry	Lucy	4 Sep 1808	bp, wife of Ruel	1:174
Sperry	Lucy	4 Sep 1808	bp, ch of Ruel	1:174
Sperry	Margetanny	4 Jan 1818	wife of -- Hine, adm ch; died	2:88
Sperry	Margetany	4 Jan 1818	adm ch	1:58
Sperry	Margittania	4 Sep 1808	bp, ch of Ruel	1:174
Sperry	Margrettana	- 1822	female, on list of members	1:83
Sperry	Margt	- 1818	adm ch, wife of W. Hine; dec	3:42
Sperry	Ruel	9 Sep 1860	d, 87, apoplexy, Hillside	3:253
Sperry	Sally L.	2 Jan 1852	d, w. of Ruel S., 74, Hillside	3:250
Sperry	Sally [sic]	- 1822	wife of Ruel, member	1:83
Splan	Bridget	29 Oct 1892	24 marr Robert Pierce 24	3:222
Splitstone	John	- 1878	adm ch	3:45
Splitstone	John	3 Mar 1878	bp, adult	3:156
Splitstone	John	3 Mar 1878	adm ch	3:66
Spring	Elizabeth Payton	12 Jun 1892	an inf, bp	3:160
Spring	Frederic	- 1887	Dr, adm ch from Bergen Pt. NJ	3:45
Spring	Frederic	2 Jan 1887	adm fr Dutch Reform, Bergen Pt NJ	3:95
Spring	Gladys	17 Jun 1888	an inf, bp	3:158
Spring	Isabelle B.	- 1887	Mrs., adm ch from Bergen Pt. NJ	3:45
Spring	Isabelle B.	2 Jan 1887	Mrs, adm fr Dutch Reform Bergen Pt, NJ	3:95
Spring	Justine Brockway	13 Jun 1897	inf bp; Dr. Frederic & Isabelle	3:162
Spring	L. Louis	- 1901	adm ch from Bergen Point NJ	3:46
Spring	L. Louis	5 May 1901	adm fr Dutch Reform, Bergen Point NJ	3:99
Spring	Lilian	10 Aug 1892	20 marr Howard L. Isbell 27	3:222
Spring	Lillian	- 1889	adm ch from Bergen Point NJ; wife of H. Isbell	3:46
Spring	Lillian	5 May 1889	Miss, adm fr Reformed, Bergen Point NJ	3:96
Spring	Nathalie	9 Jun 1895	inf bp; Dr Fred & Isabelle Brockway	3:161
Spring	Samuel	- 1888	adm ch from Bergen Point NJ; dis 1896	3:46

NAUGATUCK, CONNECTICUT, CONGREGATIONAL CHURCH RECORDS

Surname	Given	Date	Event	Ref
Spring	Samuel	4 Nov 1888	adm fr Reformed Ch, Bergen Pt, NJ	3:96
Spring	Samuel	21 Feb 1896	dism to 1st Cong, Denver Col [with Frank L. Hoadley]	3:128
Squire	Chas T.	14 May 1891	marr Maggie Casey	3:221
Squires	Addie S.	20 May 1879	marr George S. Russell, both of Naug	3:212
Squires	Isabelle R.	- 1885	adm ch; dec 1892	3:45
Squires	Isabelle R.	5 Jul 1885	Mrs., adm ch	3:68
Squires	Isabelle R.	13 Jun 1892	d; 43, accident	3:260
Stacey	Margaret	24 Dec 1864	marr George Brooks, both of Naug	3:206
Stahl	Chas H.	3 Nov 1886	20 marr Lizzie W. Maving 24, both of Naug	3:217
Stahl	Elizabeth Waltham	30 Sep 1896	inf bp [entry crossed out]	3:162
Stahl	Hazel Jaennette	30 Sep 1896	inf bp; Chas Henry & Elizabeth	3:162
Stahl	Henry James	17 Jun 1888	an inf, bp	3:158
Stahl	Raymond Arthur	20 May 1900	ch bp; Chas & Elizabeth (Maving)	3:165
Stahl	Theodore Erasmus	11 Jun 1899	inf bp; Erasmus & Ellen Casey	3:164
Staples	Mary	3 Oct 1888	36 marr Aaron Yerks 33	3:219
Steeber	Emma	- 1891	adm ch	3:46
Steeber	Mattie	- 1891	adm ch, Mrs. Young	3:46
Steeber	Mattie	1 Mar 1891	Miss, adm ch	3:70
Steele	Katie F.	19 Jan 1887	marr Nelson D. Clark	3:218
Steele	Lilian Browning	- 1890	adm ch	3:46
Steele	Lilian Browning	9 Mar 1890	bp, adult	3:159
Steele	Lillian Browning	9 Mar 1890	Miss, adm ch	3:70
Steele	Rebecca B.	- 1885	adm ch, wife of E. J.	3:45
Steele	Rebecca B.	5 Jul 1885	Mrs., adm ch	3:68
Steiber	Emma	1 Mar 1891	Miss, adm ch	3:70
Steiber	Emma	15 Nov 1898	23 marr Michael J. Bruce 23	3:226
Steiber	Martha	11 Jan 1894	20 marr William E. Young 23	3:223
Steinholtz	Henry M.	3 Jun 1896	27 marr Katherine Young 23	3:224
Steinholtz	Robert Earl	12 Jun 1898	inf bp; Henry M. & Catharine Young	3:163
Stelle	Florence Mackey	2 Jul 1900	26 marr Harry B. Wright 24	3:228
Stelle	Margaurite	2 Sep 1900	adm ch	3:72
Stelle	Marguerite	- 1900	adm ch	3:46
Stelle	Martha A.	- 1900	Mrs., adm ch from New Brunswick NJ	3:46
Stelle	Martha A.	2 Sep 1900	Mrs., adm fr 1st Baptist, New Brunswick NJ	3:99
Stephens	A.	13 Mar 1838	Miss, on comm	2:31
Stephens	Agnes	17 May 1789	wife of Elisha, adm ch; died 29 Apr 1837	2:84
Stephens	Alford [sic]	31 Apr 1819	appointed Sabbath School teacher	1:78
Stephens	Bekkah	6 Mar 1785	bp	1:9
Stephens	David	4 Jan 1818	adm ch; died 8 Nov 1822	2:89
Stephens	David	10 Aug 1845	dism to Chapel St. Cong. Ch in New Haven	2:51
Stephens	Elisha	fall 1781	adm ch	1:6
Stephens	Elisha Miller	29 Apr 1804	bp, son of David	1:172
Stephens	Elisha, Deacon	15 Oct 1801	on committee	1:32
Stephens	Harvey	5 Mar 1801	ch of David, d, aged 1 m 18d, ["Hillside Cemetry CHH" added]	1:155
Stephens	Harvey	5 Mar 1801	bp, ch of David	1:169
Stephens	James	1 Jul 1821	ch of Alford, bp	1:63
Stephens	Lauren Lewis	14 Sep 1817	ch of David, bp	1:60
Stephens	Mable	31 Apr 1819	wife Alford, appointed Sabbath School teacher	1:78
Stephens	Martin	- -	husband of Tirza Tyrell	2:83
Stephens	Olive	28 Dec 1800	marr Seth Castle, both of this place	1:151
Stevens	A.	- -	husband of Mabel Hopkins	3:18
Stevens	Agnas	- 1822	Wid, member	1:83
Stevens	Agnes	- 1789	adm ch, wife of Elisha; dec 1837	3:41
Stevens	Agnes	17 Mar 1789	Eli[sha], adm ch	1:55

NAUGATUCK, CONNECTICUT, CONGREGATIONAL CHURCH RECORDS

Stevens	Agnes	17 May 1789	wife of Deacon Elisha adm ch	1:12
Stevens	Agnes	28 Apr 1837	died, 81	2:115
Stevens	Alford [sic]	18 Sep 1796	bp, ch of Deacon E.	1:168
Stevens	Alfred	- -	husband of Mabel	2:87
Stevens	Alfred	- 1818	adm ch; dis 1836	3:42
Stevens	Alfred	15 Mar 1818	adm ch; rem 1 Jan 1836	2:89
Stevens	Alfred	15 Mar 1818	adm ch	1:58
Stevens	Alfred	- 1822	male, on list of members	1:81
Stevens	Alfred	22 Feb 1823	wife d, consumption, 23	1:161
Stevens	Alfred	16 Sep 1824	wife adm on rec from Columbia	1:99
Stevens	Alfred	18 Feb 1825	ch d, 3m	1:162
Stevens	Alfred	3 Nov? 1830	ch d	1:146
Stevens	Alfred	12 Nov 1832	ch died, 9 mos.	2:114
Stevens	Alfred	1 Jan 1836	letter of rec to any ch	2:19
Stevens	Alfred	- 1844	adm ch; dis 1857 to Cheshire	3:43
Stevens	Alfred	1 Mar 1844	adm ch	2:99
Stevens	Alfred	1 Mar 1844	adm from Presbyterian ch at Lowville NY	2:49
Stevens	Alfred	22 Feb 1857	dism to Cong, Cheshire	3:121
Stevens	Alida Elvira	4 Jul 1858	ch bp; David R. & Angeline	3:152
Stevens	Alvira	30 Apr 1800	bp, dau of David	1:169
Stevens	Amanda	- 1828	adm ch; dec 1891	3:42
Stevens	Amanda	4 Jul 1828	adm ch	1:59b
Stevens	Amanda	6 Jul 1828	adm ch	2:92
Stevens	Amanda	6 Jul 1828	member	1:94
Stevens	Amanda	6 Jul 1828	adm ch	1:107
Stevens	Amanda	1 Dec 1891	d, 84, heart failure	3:260
Stevens	Amasa	16 Feb 1825	ch of Hershal, bp a few hours before its death	1:86
Stevens	Amy	- 1828	adm ch, wife of Elisha; dec 1830	3:42
Stevens	Amy	6 Jul 1828	wife of Elisha M, adm ch; died 7 Oct 1830	2:92
Stevens	Amy	6 Jul 1828	Elisha, adm ch	1:59a
Stevens	Amy	6 Jul 1828	member	1:94
Stevens	Amy	6 Jul 1828	wife of Elisha M., adm ch	1:106
Stevens	Amy	7 Oct 1830	wife of Elisha, d, 25	1:146
Stevens	Angeline	- 1856	adm ch from Coventry NY, wife of David; dec 1863	3:44
Stevens	Angeline	6 Jan 1856	w of David, adm fr Coventry NY	3:90
Stevens	Angeline	29 Dec 1863	d, 38, consumption	3:254
Stevens	Anson Leroy	4 Sep 1829	ch of Linus, bp	1:88
Stevens	Arthur	4 Sep 1861	d, 4 y	3:253
Stevens	Ashbel	- -	husband of Mary Mead	3:29
Stevens	Ashbel	18 Feb 1826	d, apoplexy, shock of palsy a yr ago, 42	1:163
Stevens	Ashbel Mead	5 May 1824	ch of Ashbel, bp	1:85
Stevens	Augusta A.	8 Mar 1867	marr Francis L. Hall, both of Naug	3:207
Stevens	Barzillai	29 Aug 1812	bp, ch of Hopy L. wife of Ashbel	1:175
Stevens	Barzillia	15 Mar 1789	bp, ch of Elisha	1:165
Stevens	Barzilly	24 Oct 1804	d, son Deac Elisha, 16y	1:157
Stevens	Bekkah	6 Mar 1785	bp, ch of Elisha	1:164
Stevens	Calvin	22 Aug 1830	chosen Clark	1:111
Stevens	Clarissa	10 Mar 1793	bp, dau of Dea Elisha	1:166
Stevens	David	- 1818	adm ch; dec 1823	3:42
Stevens	David	4 Jan 1818	adm ch, d 1822	1:58
Stevens	David	- 1822	male, on list of members; dead 8 Nov 1822	1:81
Stevens	David	8 Nov 1822	d, typhus fever & consumption, 44	1:161
Stevens	David	- 1843	adm ch; dis 1845 to New Haven	3:43
Stevens	David	14 May 1843	adm ch; dism 10 Aug 1845 to N. Haven	2:99

NAUGATUCK, CONNECTICUT, CONGREGATIONAL CHURCH RECORDS

Stevens	David	25 Jun	1855	his & Angeline's inf dau d, 15 ms, whooping cough	3:251
Stevens	David R.	-	1854	adm ch from West Town NY; dis 1864	3:44
Stevens	David R.	12 Mar	1854	adm fr Presbn, West Town NY [Wat Town?]	3:90
Stevens	David R.	-	1858	Appt'd Deacon; removed 1863	3:1
Stevens	David R.	26 Jun	1864	dism to College St Ch, N. Haven	3:122
Stevens	David R?ush	1 Jan	1830	ch of Elisha, bp	1:88
Stevens	Deacon	8 Mar	1813	d	1:160
Stevens	Decn	12 Feb	1800	brought complain against Sarah the wife of Austen Smith	1:16
Stevens	E.	5 May	1837	Mrs., on comm "to attend to cases of unchristian walk...female members"	2:25
Stevens	Easther Genet	7 May	1809	bp, dau of David on the right of Esther his wife	1:175
Stevens	Eddie H.	30 May	1875	bur, 21, drowned in Mch, Hillside	3:257
Stevens	Elisa A.	3 Nov	1861	adm fr 1st Cong, Waterbury	3:91
Stevens	Elisabeth	29 Nov	1860	marr Chester Robinson, both of North Haven	3:204
Stevens	Elisha	-	1781	adm ch; dec 1813	3:41
Stevens	Elisha	fall	1781	adm ch; died 8 Mar 1813	2:82
Stevens	Elisha	fall	1781	adm ch, d 8 Mar 1813	1:53
Stevens	Elisha	8 Jul	1788	Deacon, died 8 Mar 1818 [sic]	2:79
Stevens	Elisha	8 Jul	1788	chosen Deacon	1:11
Stevens	Elisha	1 Jan	1801	Deac, appointed ruling elder	1:33
Stevens	Elisha	17 Mar	1803	Deacon, reappointed ruling elder	1:36
Stevens	Elisha	1 Jun	1804	reappointed ruling elder	1:37
Stevens	Elisha	8 Mar	1813	Deacon, died about 4 am, served ch 24y 8m	1:67
Stevens	Elisha	6 Jul	1828	adm ch	1:59a
Stevens	Elisha	Apr	1833	Secretery for SS	2:9
Stevens	Elisha M.	19 Aug	1824	marr Amy C. Hoadley of Salem	1:152
Stevens	Elisha M.	-	1828	adm ch; dis 1838 to Darien Ala. [sic, but prob wrong]	3:42
Stevens	Elisha M.	6 Jul	1828	adm ch; rem 31 Aug 1838 to Marion Ma. [sic, but "Ma" looks like "Ala"]	2:92
Stevens	Elisha M.	6 Jul	1828	member	1:94
Stevens	Elisha M.	6 Jul	1828	adm ch	1:106
Stevens	Eliza	20 Aug	1815	bp, ch of Mary wife of Ashbel	1:176
Stevens	Eliza A.	-	1861	adm ch from Waterbury; dec 1864	3:44
Stevens	Eliza A.	28 Feb	1864	d, 24, consumption, Hillside	3:254
Stevens	Ellen	29 May	1836	bp, ch of Linus, b Aug 1831	2:105
Stevens	Emma F.	8 Apr	1873	marr Fremont W. Tolles, both of Naug	3:210
Stevens	Esther	-	1799	adm ch, wife of David; dec 1842	3:41
Stevens	Esther	17 Jul	1799	wife of David, adm ch; died 6 Sep 1842	2:85
Stevens	Esther	17 Jul	1799	Da., adm ch	1:55
Stevens	Esther	17 Jul	1799	wife of David adm ch	1:14
Stevens	Esther	-	1822	wife of David, member; wid	1:83
Stevens	Esther	6 Nov	1829	wid, on comm	1:109
Stevens	Fanny	-	1822	wife of L, member adm since 1822	1:83
Stevens	Fanny	-	1824	adm ch, wife of Linus; dis 1836 to Auburn NY	3:42
Stevens	Fanny	11 Dec	1824	w of Linus, adm ch; rem 30 Oct 1836 to Auburn NY	2:91
Stevens	Fanny	11 Dec	1824	Linus, adm ch	1:59
Stevens	Fanny	11 Dec	1824	adm ch	1:100
Stevens	Fanny	24 Nov	1824	wife of Linus, propounded for adm	1:100
Stevens	Fanny	-	1830	adm ch, wife of W. Bateman; dis 1838 to Blackwoodtown NJ	3:43
Stevens	Fanny	2 Jan	1830	wife of Wm Bateman, adm ch; rem 14 Sep 1838	2:93
Stevens	Fanny	2 Jan	1830	adm ch	1:59c
Stevens	Fanny	29 May	1836	w of Linus, letter to ch in Hornisbury [Homes- Harrisbury?], NY	2:20
Stevens	Fanny	30 Oct	1836	Mrs., not having taken letter given letter to ch in Auburn NY	2:20
Stevens	Fernando D.	29 May	1836	bp, ch of Linus, b Dec 1834	2:105

NAUGATUCK, CONNECTICUT, CONGREGATIONAL CHURCH RECORDS

Stevens	Geo A.	11 Oct 1888	21 marr Clara B. Goodspeed 18	3:219
Stevens	George	12 Mar 1861	d, brought fr Waterbury, 46	3:253
Stevens	George Spencer	29 Aug 1812	bp, ch of Hopy L. wife of Ashbel	1:175
Stevens	Hariel [sic]	15 Mar 1818	adm ch	1:58
Stevens	Harriet	2 May 1802	bp, dau of David	1:170
Stevens	Harriet	- 1818	adm ch, wife of J.W. Harris; dis 1844 to New Haven	3:42
Stevens	Harriet	15 Mar 1818	wife of John Harris, adm ch; rem 4 Feb 1844 to New Haven	2:89
Stevens	Harry	1 Jan 1830	ch of Elisha, bp	1:88
Stevens	Harry	- 1854	adm ch from Amesbury Mass; dis 1865 to Col. Str. N Haven	3:43
Stevens	Harry	5 Mar 1854	adm fr 2nd ch Amesbury Mass	3:90
Stevens	Harry	11 Jun 1858	his & Joanna R.'s inf son d, 7 weeks	3:252
Stevens	Harry	5 Nov 1865	dism to Col. Str. New Haven	3:123
Stevens	Harry	22 Feb 1881	at centennial exercises; 522 Howard Ave, New Haven	3:300
Stevens	Harvy	16 Nov 1794	bp, ch of Da	1:167
Stevens	Hattie	24 Jun 1864	d, inf of David, 15 mo, catar fever	3:254
Stevens	Hershal	16 Nov 1794	bp, ch of Da	1:167
Stevens	Hershal	15 Mar 1818	adm ch; excomm 3 Feb 1837	2:89
Stevens	Hershal	15 Mar 1818	adm ch	1:58
Stevens	Hershal	-- 1822	male, on list of members	1:81
Stevens	Hershal	16 Feb 1825	ch d, 11m	1:162
Stevens	Hershel	- 1818	adm ch; exc 1837	3:42
Stevens	Hershel	3 Feb 1837	disregards covenants, cut off	2:22
Stevens	Hershel	5 Feb 1837	sentence of excommunication publicly read	2:24
Stevens	Hial	1 Dec 1874	Mrs, d, 54, consumption bowels, Hillside	3:256
Stevens	Hial S.	18 Feb 1850	of Naug marr Rebecca Lines of Naug	3:200
Stevens	Hopkins	8 Jan 1804	bp, son of Martin	1:172
Stevens	Hopy L.	- 1812	adm ch, wife of Ashbel; dec 1813	3:41
Stevens	Hopy L.	24 Aug 1813	d	1:160
Stevens	Hopy Lord	23 Aug 1812	wife of Ashbel, adm ch; died 24 Aug 1813	2:87
Stevens	Hopy Lord	23 Aug 1812	wife of Ashbel, bp, adm ch	1:62
Stevens	Hopy Lord	23 Aug 1813	Ash., adm ch, d 24 Aug 1813	1:57
Stevens	James	- 1840	adm ch from Lowville NY; dis 1848	3:43
Stevens	James	8 Nov 1840	adm ch from Loville NY; dism 1848	2:97
Stevens	James	8 Nov 1840	adm ch from Presbyterian Ch in Lowville NY	2:35
Stevens	Jennie E.	- 1866	adm ch, w of Geo. B. Martin; withdrawn 1885	3:45
Stevens	Jennie Eliza	2 Sep 1866	bp, adult	3:153
Stevens	Jennie Eliza	2 Sep 1866	adm ch	3:63
Stevens	Joanna R.	- 1854	adm ch fr Amesbury Ma, w of Harry; dis 1865 Col. Str. N. Haven	3:43
Stevens	Joanna R.	5 Mar 1854	w of Harry, adm fr 2nd ch, Amesbury Mass.	3:90
Stevens	Joanna R.	5 Nov 1865	[wife of] Harry dism to Col. Str. New Haven	3:123
Stevens	Joseph Beecher	4 Sep 1829	ch of Alfred, bp	1:88
Stevens	Julia	- 1822	wife of A.S., member	1:83
Stevens	Julia	- 1822	wife of Alfred, member adm after 1822	1:83
Stevens	Julia	- 1824	adm ch from Prospect, wife of Alfred; dis 1836	3:42
Stevens	Julia	10 Dec 1824	Alfred. Adm ch [day prob wrong]	1:59a
Stevens	Julia	16 Sep 1824	2nd wife of Alfred, adm ch from Prospect; rem 1 Jan 1836	2:91
Stevens	Julia	1 Jan 1836	wife of Alfred, letter of rec to any ch	2:19
Stevens	Julia	- 1844	adm ch from Lowville NY; dis 1857 to Cheshire	3:43
Stevens	Julia	1 Mar 1844	adm ch from Lowville NY	2:99
Stevens	Julia	1 Mar 1844	wife of Alfred, adm from Presbyterian Ch at Lowville NY	2:49
Stevens	Julia	22 Feb 1857	w. of A[lfred] dism to Cong. Cheshire	3:121
Stevens	Laura Elmina	7 Nov 1811	bp, ch of Tirzah, wife of Martin	1:175
Stevens	Lillie A.	28 Dec 1876	marr Charles H. Andrews, both of Naug	3:211
Stevens	Loren L.	- 1861	adm ch from Waterbury; dis 1869 to East Bridgeport	3:44

Stevens	Loren L.	3 Nov 1861	adm fr 1st Cong, Waterbury	3:91
Stevens	Mabel	- 1822	wife of Alfred, member; died 22 Feb 1823	1:83
Stevens	Mabel Hopkins	7 May 1826	ch of Alfred, bp	1:86
Stevens	Magrettia	4 May 1817	adm ch, dism Nov 1828	1:57
Stevens	Margaretta	8 Apr 1817	cand for memb	1:73
Stevens	Margarette	4 May 1817	wife of Hezekiah Thomas, adm ch; rem 13 Mar 1828 to Bethany	2:87
Stevens	Margt	- 1817	adm ch, wife of H. Thomas; dis 1828 to Bethany	3:41
Stevens	Martin	- -	husband of Tirza Tirrell	3:48
Stevens	Martin	30 Sep 1787	husband of Tirzah Terril	1:54
Stevens	Martin	Jan 1807	bp, son of Martin, bp in right of Thersia his wife	1:173
Stevens	Mary	13 Nov 1791	bp, ch of Martin	1:166
Stevens	Mary	- 1822	wife of Ashbel, member; wid	1:83
Stevens	Mary	- 1830	dism to State of NY	1:143
Stevens	Mary	22 Aug 1830	rec; moving to state of NY [surely "Mary"]	1:111
Stevens	Milton	9 Jan 1791	bp, ch of Deacon Elisha	1:166
Stevens	Milton	11 Oct 1828	wife d, dysentery, 37	1:143
Stevens	Milton	3 Mar 1829	d, consumption, intemperate, 37	1:145
Stevens	Minerva	20 Jan 1799	bp, ch of Deacon Elisha	1:169
Stevens	Minerva	- 1818	adm ch, wife of G. Martin; dec 1831	3:42
Stevens	Minerva	15 Mar 1818	wife of Gronville Martin, adm ch; died 1 Jan 1831	2:89
Stevens	Minerva	15 Mar 1818	Martin, adm ch	1:58
Stevens	Minnie Louise	7 Sep 1862	inf bp; Harry & Joanna R.	3:153
Stevens	Nelson	7 Oct 1827	ch of Linus, bp	1:87
Stevens	Orange M.	31 Aug 1826	of Stockbridge, marr Henietta Gennet Lewis of Salem	1:152
Stevens	Orpha	6 Sep 1818	ch of Ashbel	1:61
Stevens	Parnel[sic]	24 Mar 1809	bp, infant ch of Martin	1:174
Stevens	Ransom	24 Dec 1786	bp, ch of Elisha	1:164
Stevens	Ransom	24 Dec 1786	bp [entry crossed out]	1:10
Stevens	Rebecca	18 Nov 1810	of Salem, marr William Hilman of Black River	1:151
Stevens	Robert	29 Jun 1823	ch of Hershel, bp	1:85
Stevens	Roxanna	- 1861	adm ch from Waterbury, wife of Loren L.; dec 1867	3:44
Stevens	Roxanna	3 Nov 1861	adm fr 1st Cong, Waterbury	3:91
Stevens	Roxanna	11 Dec 1867	d, 57, consumption, Hillside	3:255
Stevens	Samuel	5 Dec 1827	son of Milton, d, bowel complaint, 15	1:144
Stevens	Sarah	- 1844	adm ch from Lowville NY; erased 1866	3:43
Stevens	Sarah	1 Mar 1844	adm ch from Lowville NY	2:99
Stevens	Sarah	30 Mar 1866	voted dismissed, eligible for letter if asked [see 3:369]	3:123
Stevens	Sarah M.	14 Apr 1850	of Naug marr Benjn F. Miles of Cheshire	3:200
Stevens	Sarah Maria	Jul 1828	ch of Alfred, bp	1:88
Stevens	Stearn	7 Aug 1825	ch of Linus, bp	1:86
Stevens	Tirza	- 1828	adm ch; dis 1835 to Camden NY	3:42
Stevens	Tirza	4 Jul 1828	adm ch	1:59b
Stevens	Tirza	6 Jul 1828	adm ch; rem 7 Jun 1835 to Camden NY	2:92
Stevens	Tirza	6 Jul 1828	member	1:94
Stevens	Tirza	6 Jul 1828	adm ch	1:107
Stevens	Tirza	7 Jun 1835	Mrs., letter of rec to ch in Camden, NY	2:18
Stevens	Tirza	7 Jun 1835	Miss, letter of rec to ch in Camden, NY	2:18
Stevens	Tirzah	29 Aug 1813	bp, ch of Tirzah wife of Martin	1:176
Stevens	Tirzah	- 1822	wife of Martin, member	1:83
Stevens	Tirzah	25 Feb 1852	d, 82, Lung fever, Hillside	3:250
Stevens	Zerua	- 1818	adm ch; dis 1821 to Prospect	3:42
Stevens	Zerua	15 Mar 1818	adm ch; rem 30 Apr 1821 to Prospect	2:89
Stevens	Zervia	15 Mar 1818	adm ch	1:58
Stevenson	Elizabeth Murray	- 1895	adm ch	3:46

NAUGATUCK, CONNECTICUT, CONGREGATIONAL CHURCH RECORDS

Surname	Given	Date	Event	Ref
Stevenson	Elizabeth Murray	Sep 1895	bp, adult	3:161
Stevenson	Elizabeth Murray	1 Sep 1895	adm ch	3:71
Stillson	Mary	4 Mar 1896	28 marr Chas C. Booth 26	3:224
Stocks	Wm	17 Feb 1882	marr Margaret Hickey, both of Naug	3:213
Stodard	David Eli	10 Jul 1842	bp, adult [day sic]	2:106
Stodard	David Eli	10 May 1842	adm ch; dism 22 Sep 1844 to Avon	2:98
Stodard	Esther	12 Sep 1841	adm ch; wife of Abiga[?]; died Aug 1847	2:98
Stodard	Esther	12 Sep 1841	bp, adult	2:106
Stodard	Mary Ann	10 Jul 1842	bp, adult [day sic]	2:106
Stodard	Mary Ann	10 May 1842	adm ch; died 2 Jan 1850	2:98
Stoddard	Abijah C.	13 Dec 1858	d, 76, d in Westfield Mass, Hillside	3:252
Stoddard	David E.	- 1842	adm ch; dis 1844 to Avon	3:43
Stoddard	David E.	22 Sep 1844	dism to ch in Avon	2:49
Stoddard	Esther	19 Oct 1826	d, Fever, 17	1:144
Stoddard	Esther	- 1841	adm ch, wife of Abijah; dec 1847	3:43
Stoddard	Mary Ann	- 1842	adm ch; dec 1850	3:43
Stoddard	Mary Ann	2 Jan 1850	d 38, Hillside Cemetry	3:250
Stoddard	Wm B.	1 Sep 1882	Mrs. (M.E. Potter) dism by General Letter	3:125
Stoddard	Wm B.	30 Apr 1882	marr Mary E. Potter, both of Naug	3:214
Stone	Francis Leander	7 Mar 1858	ch bp; Chs & Esther M.	3:152
Stone	Henry F.	- 1900	adm ch from Branford Ct	3:46
Stone	Henry F.	6 May 1900	adm fr Cong, Branford, Ct	3:99
Stone	J.B.	22 Feb 1881	at centennial exercises; Hartford	3:300
Stone	James B.	- 1860	adm ch; dis 1865 to Asylum Hill Cong, Hartford	3:44
Stone	James B.	9 Apr 1865	dism to Asylum Hill Cong, Hartd	3:123
Stone	James Burrel	1 Jan 1860	bp, adult	3:152
Stone	James Burrell	1 Jan 1860	adm ch	3:62
Stone	Julia A.	- 1860	adm ch fr Warwick, w of Jas. B; dis 1865 to Asylum Hill Cong, Hartford	3:44
Stone	Julia A.	4 Mar 1860	adm fr Warwick F.W. Baptist	3:91
Stone	Julia A.	9 Apr 1865	dism to Asylum Hill Cong, Hartd	3:123
Stone	Nancy	- 1847	adm ch, wife of W.J. Baldwin; dis 1850 to Kent	3:43
Stone	Nancy	31 Dec 1847	adm ch; [m] Wm J. Baldwin; dism 3 Feb 1850 to Kent	2:100
Stone	S.M.	20 Apr 1888	Mrs., dism to Ch of Strangers NY	3:127
Stone	Samuel M.	- 1886	Mrs., adm ch from 1st Waterbury; dis 1888 to Ch Strangers NY	3:45
Stone	Samuel M.	2 May 1886	Mrs, adm fr 1st Waterbury	3:95
Storm[?]	Salina Ella Joseph	28 Jan 1895	"Infants" bp; Alfred & Ida Olivia [3 ch?]	3:161
Street	Fredk F.	- 1854	adm ch; dis 1864, 1st Presn Harris[bur]g	3:43
Street	Fredk F.	5 Mar 1854	adm ch	3:61
Street	Fredk F.	3 Apr 1864	dism to 1st Presb, Harrisburg Pa.	3:122
Street	J.	-	husband of Mary C. Spencer	3:42
Street	James	-	husband of Mary C. Spencer	2:88
Street	Martha	- 1850	adm ch; dis 1851 to Prospect	3:43
Street	Martha	6 Jan 1850	adm ch	3:60
Street	Martha	9 Mar 1851	dism to Cong, Prospect	3:120
Street	Mary C.	14 Feb 1836	Mrs, letter of dism to sister ch in Prospect	2:19
Street	Mary C.	- 1856	adm ch; dec 1865	3:44
Street	Mary C.	2 Nov 1856	adm ch	3:61
Street	Mary C.	15 Jun 1864	marr C.D. Longfellow, both of Naug	3:205
Strong	Alzamora	16 Nov 1895	25 marr Abbie J. Spencer 24	3:224
Summers	Jerusha	28 Mar 1802	of Milford, marr Amzi Bebee	1:151
Sumpf	Alice Lilly	- 1897	Mrs, adm ch [see Zumpf, Smf]	3:46
Sumpf	Alice Lilly	4 Jul 1897	Mrs., adm ch	3:72
Sumpf	Geo McInentyre[?]	11 Jun 1899	inf bp; Wm & Alice Lilly [McImntyre?]	3:164

Swan	James, Mrs.	22 Feb	1881	at centennial exercises	3:300
Sweet	John B.	-	1866	adm ch; dis 1868 to Trin Cong, Matan [sic], Mass.	3:45
Sweet	John Baylies	2 Sep	1866	bp, adult	3:153
Sweet	John Baylies	2 Sep	1866	adm ch	3:63
Sweet	John Baylies	19 Jan	1868	dism to 1st Trin Cong, Malden, Mass.	3:123
Sweet	Mary L.	8 Jan	1875	marr Sylvester S. Maine, both of Naug	3:210
Sweetlove	Rebecca	12 May	1851	d, 73	3:250
Swift	Zepeneh	Sep	1831	Rev., preached	1:116
Swift	Zephaniah	29 Apr	1817	Rev. Elder at Council re Rev. Dodd's removal	1:74
Sykes	Fannie May	-	1897	adm ch	3:46
Sykes	Fannie May	2 May	1897	bp, adult	3:162
Sykes	Fannie May	2 May	1897	adm ch	3:71
Sykes	Henry	-	-	husband of Ellen E. Spencer	3:44
Sykes	Henry	21 Dec	1870	marr Ellen Spencer, both of Naug	3:209
Symons	Noah J., Rev.	9 Oct	1799	agreed with to preach for one year	1:15
Szabo	Matilda Olga	30 Nov	1900	inf bp; Peter & Olga	3:165
Tafft	George	1 Sep	1888	28 marr Mary Mills 19	3:219
Tallmadge	Geo P.	12 Dec	1883	marr Emma H. Kuchenburg, both of Naug	3:216
Talmadge	Olive	-	1810	adm ch; dis 1818 Southington	3:48
Talmadge	Olive	5 Aug	1810	adm ch; dism [crossed out]	2:94
Talmadge	Sarah E.	18 Nov	1889	marr Chas E. Taylor	3:220
Talmage	Charles (Fenton)	3 May	1885	ch bp; James & Elizabeth	3:157
Talmage	Olive	5 Aug	1810	adm ch; rem 6 Sep 1818 to Southington	2:87
Talmage	Olive	5 Aug	1810	adm ch, dism 6 Sep 1819	1:56
Talmage	Sarah (Fenton)	3 May	1885	ch bp; James & Elizabeth	3:157
Taylor	Chas E.	18 Nov	1889	marr Sarah E. Talmadge	3:220
Taylor	Emily E.	13 Apr	1886	43 marr Elijah P. Morehouse 60, both of Naug	3:217
Taylor	Frank	-	1896	adm ch from Prospect	3:49
Taylor	Frank	5 Jan	1896	adm fr Cong, Prospect Ct	3:98
Taylor	Frank N.	15 Mar	1899	37 marr Mary F. Hart 25	3:227
Taylor	H.A.	10 Dec	1840	Rev, voted as Moderator & clerk [dism abt Jun 1841?]	2:35
Taylor	Helen E.	-	1894	adm ch	3:49
Taylor	Helen E.	6 May	1894	Mrs., adm ch	3:71
Teale	Cornelia	18 Nov	1849	Mrs., dism to any Ch	2:62
Teale	Cornelia C.	-	1845	adm ch from Stratford, wife of Albert K.; dis 1849	3:48
Teator	Elizabeth A.	3 Jan	1900	Mrs, 50, marr Robert Campbell 45	3:228
Teele	A.K.	10 Jun	1849	wants to leave, salary not paid	2:59
Teele	Albert K.	10 Aug	1845	Attests to record for first time as Pastor	2:51
Teele	Cornelia C.	31 Oct	1845	wife of Albert K., adm ch from Stratford; dism 18 Nov 1849	2:100
Teele	Rev. Mr.	2 Mar	1845	voted to be invited to settle over this Church	2:50
Terell	Susannah	8 Jul	1781	Wd, adm ch; died 3 Apr 1794	2:82
Terrel	-	-	-	see Tirrel, Tyrell	-
Terrel	Aaron	21 Aug	1808	bp, son of Mr. Joseph G., in right of his wife	1:174
Terrel	Beulah Smith	16 Jan	1803	bp, dau of Elias	1:171
Terrel	Elizebeth F.	6 Nov	1826	of Salem, marr Zalmon Miller of Cornwall	1:152
Terrel	Esth--	1 Feb	1801	wife of Jared adm ch	1:20
Terrel	Henrietta Susanna	14 Dec	1800	bp, ch of Irijah	1:169
Terrel	Henry	6 Jul	1828	adm ch	1:59a
Terrel	Horace	17 May	1801	bp, ch of Jared	1:170
Terrel	Irijah	2 Dec	1800	Consociation held at his house in Salem	1:19
Terrel	Irijah	29 Sep	1801	consociation held at his house in Salem	1:25
Terrel	Irijah	11 Oct	1805	on committee	1:39
Terrel	Israel	1 Jan	1801	appointed ruling elder	1:33
Terrel	Israel	14 Sep	1801	on committee	1:24

Terrel	Israel	17 Mar	1803	reappointed ruling elder	1:36
Terrel	Israel	17 Mar	1803	on committee	1:36
Terrel	Israel	11 Oct	1805	on committee	1:39
Terrel	Joel	12 Apr	1805	his dau, Polly Worster, wife of Levi, d, 20y	1:157
Terrel	Julia Marcia	3 May	1801	bp, ch of Elias	1:170
Terrel	Letsom	25 May	1863	d, 72	3:254
Terrel	Letsom D.	2 Sep	1866	adm ch	3:63
Terrel	Letsom [sic]	17 May	1801	bp, ch of Jared	1:170
Terrel	Loly	22 Feb	1801	wife of Joseph Goodwin Terrel adm ch	1:21
Terrel	Major	2 May	1824	ch d, lived about 2 hrs.	1:161
Terrel	Martin	3 May	1801	bp, ch of Joseph Goodwin Terrel	1:170
Terrel	Mary	5 Sep	1852	adm ch, w. of Monroe	3:60
Terrel	Molly	Mar	1863	d, Cornwall	3:254
Terrel	Monroe	-	1856	adm ch; dec 1900	3:48
Terrel	Monroe	4 May	1856	bp, profession	3:151
Terrel	Monroe	4 May	1856	adm ch	3:61
Terrel	Moses	25 Apr	1802	bp, ch of Joseph	1:170
Terrel	Nathanael	13 Mar	1803	bp, son of Irijah	1:171
Terrel	Nelson	3 May	1801	bp, ch of Joseph Goodwin Terrel	1:170
Terrel	Polly M.	30 Mar	1865	d, 58	3:255
Terrel	Rollin M.	27 Sep	1867	d, 20, typhoid	3:255
Terrel	Susan	12 Aug	1804	bp, ch of Elias	1:172
Terrell	Ansel	14 Aug	1855	d, 85, Erysipelas, Hillside	3:251
Terrell	Etta	26 Sep	1890	Mrs. Harry A. Dalby dism to Cong, So Norwalk Conn.	3:127
Terrell	Josiah	28 Nov	1852	d, 85,	3:250
Terrell	Lester E.	13 Mar	1878	marr Mary Barlow, both of Naug	3:212
Terrell	Letsom D.	-	1866	adm ch; dis 1875 to Waterbury Ct	3:49
Terrell	Letsom David	3 May	1857	ch bp; Monroe & Mary	3:151
Terrell	Mary	Jun	1875	d (Mrs. Monroe) 54, consumption, Hillside	3:256
Terrell	Mary Sevier	3 May	1857	ch bp; Monroe & Mary	3:151
Terrell	Monroe	4 Jan	1900	d in Waterbury	3:261
Terrell	Rollin M.	-	1865	adm ch; dec 1867	3:49
Terrell	Rollin M.	7 May	1865	adm ch	3:63
Terrell	Rollin Monroe	3 May	1857	ch bp; Monroe & Mary	3:151
Terrell	Sally	20 Aug	1869	d, 82, Hillside	3:256
Terrell	Sarah	8 Jul	1781	adm ch, rem to Oxford	2:82
Terril	Aaron	1 Jan	1810	d, ch of Joseph G., 1y 7m	1:160
Terril	Abijah Buckingham	2 Dec	1787	bp, ch of I..j.h [blotted, prob Irijah]	1:164
Terril	Alfred	26 Nov	1829	d, "the gravel," 38	1:145
Terril	Alma	2 Dec	1787	bp, ch of I..j.h [blotted, prob Irijah]	1:164
Terril	Alma	14 Jun	1795	bp, ch of Irijah	1:167
Terril	Alma	5 May	1833	adm ch; rem 24 Feb 1850 to Waterbury	2:93
Terril	Amalo[?] Grace	4 Sep	1818	ch of Alben, bp [could be 2 children, but record says 3 were bp]	1:61
Terril	Ancel	18 Jun	1812	abused by Irijah Terril on 11 May	1:64
Terril	Ancel	23 Nov	1828	adm ch	1:59b
Terril	Ancel	23 Nov	1828	member	1:94
Terril	Anne Maria	6 Apr	1806	bp, dau of Joseph G.	1:173
Terril	Ansel	14 Sep	1828	a Baptist, requested adm	1:107
Terril	Ansel	3 Nov	1829	adm ch fr Baptist [error in record; yr actually 1828]	1:107
Terril	Brother	15 Oct	1801	re his expenses in providing for Council	1:32
Terril	Damaras	26 Sep	1789	wife of Oliver, adm ch; died	2:84
Terril	Damaras	26 Sep	1789	Ol[iver] adm ch; dead [actually adm 1790]	1:55
Terril	Damaras	26 Sep	1790	wife of Oliver adm ch	1:12
Terril	Elias Green	2 Jun	1811	bp, ch of Hannah, wife of Elias	1:175

NAUGATUCK, CONNECTICUT, CONGREGATIONAL CHURCH RECORDS

Terril	Esther	1 Feb	1801	wife of Jared, adm ch, died Aug 1839	2:86
Terril	Esther	4 Feb	1801	Ja, adm ch [copied wrong in book, date was 1 Feb]	1:56
Terril	Esther	-	1822	wife of Jared, member	1:83
Terril	Fowler	25 Feb	1787	bp, ch of Israel	1:164
Terril	Fowler	25 Feb	1787	bp [entry crossed out]	1:10
Terril	George Buckingham	12 Jul	1829	ch of Horatio, bp	1:88
Terril	Hannah	Apr	1800	E., adm ch, dism 6 Feb 1814	1:55
Terril	Hannah	Apr	1800	wife of Elias adm ch	1:15
Terril	Hannah	1 Apr	1800	w of Elias, adm ch; rem 6 Feb 1814 to German, Chenango Co., NY	2:85
Terril	Hannah Buckingham	2 Dec	1787	bp, ch of T..j.h [blotted, prob. Irijah]	1:164
Terril	Hanna[h]	2 Mar	1800	wife of Elias adm ch	1:16
Terril	Heman	5 Jun	1791	bp, son of Israil	1:166
Terril	Henrietta Susannah	27 Nov	1803	d, dau of Irijah, 3y	1:156
Terril	Henry	6 Jul	1828	adm ch	1:107
Terril	Henry	6 Nov	1829	voted to attend future conf	1:109
Terril	Henry L.	6 Jul	1828	member	1:94
Terril	Henry Laurence	6 Jul	1828	adult, bp	1:87
Terril	Horatio	26 Nov	1797	bp, ch of Irijah	1:168
Terril	Horatio	27 Dec	1826	marr Sarah B. Hayden, of Salem	1:153
Terril	Horatio	2 Sep	1828	ch d, dysentery, -- months	1:144
Terril	Irenia	May	1800	bp, dau of Elias	1:169
Terril	Irijah	18 Nov	1787	adm ch	1:11
Terril	Irijah	18 Nov	1787	adm ch, excommunicated	1:54
Terril	Irijah	18 Jun	1812	complained against, dealt with by church	1:64f
Terril	Irijah	Jan	1813	wife d	1:160
Terril	Irijah	21 Jan	1816	excommunicated	1:72
Terril	Irijah Leverit	11 Nov	1792	bp, ch of Irijah	1:166
Terril	Israel	May	1784	adm ch, d 8 Jan 1811	1:53
Terril	Israel	9 Oct	1799	on committee	1:15
Terril	Israel	1 Jun	1804	reappointed ruling elder	1:37
Terril	Israel	8 Jan	1811	d, a member of this ch, aged 74y	1:160
Terril	Joel	4 Sep	1818	ch of Alben, bp	1:61
Terril	Joseph G.	13 Jun	1806	testimony against Thomas Porter	1:42
Terril	Joseph G.	29 May	1814	wife given letter of rec, to state of NY	1:68
Terril	Leonora	30 Apr	1809	bp, ch of Elias, on right of Hannah his wife	1:175
Terril	Leveret	6 Nov	1829	d, consumption, 37	1:145
Terril	Lois	20 May	1789	wife of Israel, adm ch from Southington; rem 20 Oct 1816	2:93
Terril	Lois	20 Sep	1789	wife of Israel adm ch	1:12
Terril	Lois	20 Oct	1816	Wid, certificate voted	1:73
Terril	Loly	22 Feb	1801	wife of Joseph G.T., adm ch; rem 29 May 1814 to Columbia O.	2:86
Terril	Loly	22 Feb	1801	Jo., adm ch, dism 12 Jun 1814	1:56
Terril	Major	19 Jun	1823	marr Amanda Adams, "Waty" [she of Wat(erbur)y?]	1:152
Terril	Major	6 Oct	1827	ch d, 2 days	1:144
Terril	Meason [sic]	19 Aug	1804	bp, ch of Joseph G.	1:172
Terril	Melinda	23 Aug	1812	bp, ch of Molly wife of Josiah	1:175
Terril	Molley	5 Aug	1810	wife of Josiah adm ch	1:50
Terril	Molly	5 Aug	1810	wife of Josiah, adm ch	2:86
Terril	Molly	5 Aug	1810	Josi., adm ch	1:56
Terril	Molly	-	1822	wife of Josiah, member	1:83
Terril	Nancy	4 Mar	1808	d, wife of Horace, 22y	1:158
Terril	Oliver	17 Feb	1785	adm ch, dism to "Ohio" [could be error; "to Prospect" in	1:53
-	-	-	-	previous entry]	-
Terril	Oliver	20 Feb	1785	adm ch [sic, voted on 17 Feb]	1:9
Terril	Polly	23 Aug	1812	bp, ch of Molly wife of Josiah	1:175

Terril	Sally	5 May	1833	wife of Horace, adm ch	2:93
Terril	Sarah	8 Jul	1781	dau of Susannah, adm ch	1:6
Terril	Sarah	8 Jul	1781	dau. Susannah, adm ch, dism ["to Oxford" added]	1:53
Terril	Sarah	15 Oct	1830	wife of Horatio, d, 29	1:146
Terril	Shelby Wayne	23 Jan	1814	bp, son of Hannah wife of Elias	1:176
Terril	Statira	15 Mar	1818	adm ch	1:59
Terril	Statira	-	1822	wife of Alben, member	1:83
Terril	Statira	3 Feb	1837	voted to be requested to ask for letter of dism.	2:23
Terril	Susanna	21 Feb	1790	bp, ch of Irijah	1:165
Terril	Susannah	8 Jul	1781	Wid., adm ch, d 3 Apr 1794	1:53
Terril	Susannah	8 Jul	1781	widow, adm ch	1:6
Terril	Tirzah	30 Sep	1787	adm ch	1:11
Terril	Tirzah	30 Sep	1787	adm ch ["Martin Stevens" added]	1:54
Terril	Unice	4 Sep	1818	ch of Alben, bp	1:61
Terrill	Anna E.	27 Apr	1898	38 marr Robt W. Dibble 42	3:226
Terrill	Etta A.	-	1885	adm ch; dis 1890 to So Norwalk	3:49
Terrill	Etta A.	5 Jul	1885	bp, adult	3:157
Terrill	Etta A.	5 Jul	1885	adm ch	3:67
Terrill	Etta A.	8 Sep	1889	19 marr Harry A. Dalby 22	3:220
Terrill	Israel	May	1784	adm ch	1:7
Terrill	Letsom D.	2 May	1875	dism to 2d Cong, Waterbury	3:124
Terry	Cynthia E.	3 Nov	1869	of Ansonia marr Thos N. Seeley of Derby	3:209
Thatcher	Rev. Mr.	19 Oct	1844	voted to become pastor of this ch	2:49
Thayer	Antoinette Hunt	13 Apr	1817	bp, ch of Calvin	1:176
Thayer	Calvin	-	1816	adm ch; dis 1818 to Coventry NY	3:48
Thayer	Calvin	5 Dec	1816	cand for memb	1:73
Thayer	Calvin	22 Dec	1816	adm ch; rem 2 Jan 1818 to Coventry NY	2:87
Thayer	Calvin	22 Dec	1816	adm ch, dism 2 Jan 1818	1:57
Thayer	Calvin	22 Dec	1816	adm ch	1:73
Thayer	Charles Beecher	13 Apr	1817	bp, ch of Calvin	1:176
Thayer	Mary Ann	13 Apr	1817	bp, ch of Calvin	1:176
Thayer	Susan Lewis	13 Apr	1817	bp, ch of Calvin	1:176
Thomas	Bertha Ann	22 Apr	1850	d, dau of Eliza & Angeline [sic], 4 yrs, dysentery	3:250
Thomas	Charles Leroy	Aug	1836	bp, ch of Rebecca H. ["Wid"?], b 23 Feb 1830	2:105
Thomas	Elizebeth	12 Nov	1829	of Salem, marr Asahel Smith	1:153
Thomas	H.	-	-	husband of Margt Stevens	3:41
Thomas	Henry Lawrence	Aug	1836	bp, ch of Rebecca H. ["Wid."?], b 30 Aug 1824	2:105
Thomas	Hezekiah	-	-	husband of Margarette Stevens	2:87
Thomas	Isaac M.	-	1852	adm ch; dis 1855 to Cheshire	3:48
Thomas	Isaac M.	4 Jan	1852	adm ch	3:60
Thomas	Isaac M.	9 Sep	1855	dism to Cong, Cheshire	3:121
Thomas	Joseph	Aug	1813	d	1:160
Thomas	Julia	16 Mar	1834	died, 1y 1m	2:114
Thomas	Julius Everil	Aug	1836	bp, ch of Rebecca H. ["Wid"?], b 9 Feb 1833	2:105
Thomas	Lyman	28 Dec	1805	d, son of Eisha [sic], 21y	1:157
Thomas	Margaret	13 Mar	1828	rec to ch in Bethany	1:106
Thomas	Margaretta	-	1822	wife of Hezekiah, member; dism [entry crossed out]	1:83
Thomas	Margaretta	9 Jan	1825	w of Hezekiah to Episcopalians 13 Mar 1828 [entry crossed out]	2:94
Thomas	Mitchel	19 Oct	1828	ch d, putred fever, 7	1:145
Thomas	Mitchel	27 Oct	1828	another ch d, putred fever, 1	1:145
Thomas	Mitchel	17 Apr	1835	died, 40	2:114
Thomas	Naomi	-	1845	adm ch from Bethany; dec 1858	3:48
Thomas	Naomi	10 Aug	1845	adm ch from Bethany	2:99
Thomas	Naomi	10 Aug	1845	Mrs., adm from ch in Bethany	2:51

NAUGATUCK, CONNECTICUT, CONGREGATIONAL CHURCH RECORDS

Thomas	Naomi	18 Jun 1858	d, 82, nervous rheumatism, Hillside	3:252
Thomas	Rebecca H.	- 1836	adm ch; dis 1848 Cheshire	3:48
Thomas	Rebecca H.	3 Jan 1836	widow, adm ch; dism Sep 1848 to Cheshire	2:95
Thomas	Rebecca H.	3 Jan 1836	bp, adult	2:105
Thombleson	Hariet	8 Jul 1834	Mrs., letter to Episcopal Ch in Newtown	2:17
Thompson	-	-	see Tompson	-
Thompson	Agnes	27 Dec 1894	21 marr Fred K. Bradley 23	3:223
Thompson	Betsey	- 1802	adm ch, wife of Saml; dis 1812 to Burlington O.	3:48
Thompson	Betsey	31 Oct 1802	wife of Samuel, adm ch; rem 6 Sep 1812 to Burlington O.	2:86
Thompson	Betsey	31 Oct 1802	Sa., adm ch, dism 6 Sep 1812	1:56
Thompson	Betsey	6 Sep 1812	wife of Samuel, letter of rec. to Ohio	1:63
Thompson	Caroline	22 Jul 1804	bp, dau of Samuel	1:172
Thompson	Clarinda	19 Oct 1856	d, 44, consumption	3:251
Thompson	E.P.	1 Jul 1868	d, 50, dropsy, Hillside	3:256
Thompson	Edward P.	- 1866	adm ch; dec 1868	3:49
Thompson	Edward P.	2 Sep 1866	adm ch	3:63
Thompson	Edward P.	- 1868	appt'd Deacon; 1868 Dec	3:1
Thompson	Enos Hull	8 Jun 1806	bp, son of Samuel and Betsy	1:173
Thompson	Enos Hull	19 Jan 1807	d, son of Samuel Thompson, 9m	1:158
Thompson	Hull--	22 Aug 1809	d, ch of Samuel, 1y 7m	1:159
Thompson	Jane E. [sic]	8 Aug 1870	d (Mrs. E.P.) 47	3:256
Thompson	Jane H.	- 1866	adm ch, wife of Edw P.; dec 1870	3:49
Thompson	Jane Harriet	2 Sep 1866	bp, adult	3:153
Thompson	Jane Harriett	2 Sep 1866	adm ch	3:63
Thompson	Lauran	aft Aug 1812	bp, ch of Samuel & Betsey	1:175
Thompson	Marion W.	22 Feb 1883	marr Wm A. Lanson, both of Naug	3:215
Thompson	Rosa B.	-	see Moulton, Rosa B.	-
Thompson	Saml	- 1802	adm ch; dis 1812 to Burlington O.	3:48
Thompson	Samuel	31 Oct 1802	adm ch; rem 6 Sep 1812 to Burlington O.	2:86
Thompson	Samuel	31 Oct 1802	adm ch, dism 6 Sep 1812	1:56
Thompson	Samuel	6 Sep 1812	letter of rec. to Ohio	1:63
Thompson	Samuel L.	13 Oct 1857	of New Milford marr Elethea B. Couch of Redding Ct	3:203
Thompson	Sarah Jane	8 Sep 1850	marr Adam Scappa, both of Naug	3:200
Thomson	Betsy	31 Oct 1802	wife of Samuel, adm ch	1:34
Thomson	Mary Hull	31 Oct 1802	bp, dau of Saml	1:171
Thomson	Saml	1 Nov 1801	marr Betsy Hull, both of this place	1:151
Thomson	Samuel	31 Oct 1802	adm ch	1:34
Thrall	Charles	20 Sep 1826	marr Mary Matthews, of Cheshire	1:152
Tiltey[?]	Wm A.	21 Aug 1882	[Titley?] marr Abbie A. Randall, both of Naug	3:214
Tingley	Edna Bertha	29 Dec 1865	d, 3y, Typhoid [day could be 29 Nov]	3:255
Tingley	Otis	12 Sep 1865	d, 60	3:255
Tirrell	-	-	see Terrell, Tyrell	-
Tirrell	Alma	- 1833	adm ch; dis 1850 Waterbury	3:48
Tirrell	Alma	24 Feb 1850	dism to Cong, Waterbury	3:120
Tirrell	Ansel	- 1829	adm ch from Baptist; dec 1855 [actually adm 1828]	3:48
Tirrell	Damaris	- 1789	adm ch, wife of Oliver; dec	3:48
Tirrell	Esther	- 1801	adm ch, wife of Jared; dec 1839	3:48
Tirrell	Hannah	- 1800	adm ch, wife of Elias; dis 1814 to German NY	3:48
Tirrell	Henry L.	- 1828	adm ch; dis 1837 to Ohio	3:48
Tirrell	Irijah	- 1787	adm ch; Exc 1816	3:48
Tirrell	Israel	- 1784	adm ch; dec 1811	3:48
Tirrell	Lois	- 1789	adm ch, wife of Israel; dis 1816 to Southington	3:48
Tirrell	Loly	- 1801	adm ch, wife of Joseph G.; dis 1814 to Columbia O.	3:48
Tirrell	Mary	- 1852	adm ch, wife of Monroe; dec 1875	3:48

Surname	Given	Date	Event	Ref
Tirrell	Molly	1810	adm ch, wife of Josiah; dec 1863	3:48
Tirrell	Oliver	1785	adm ch; dis to Prospect	3:48
Tirrell	Sally	1833	adm ch, wife of Horace; dec 1869	3:48
Tirrell	Sarah	1781	adm ch; dis to Oxford	3:48
Tirrell	Statira	1818	adm ch, wife of Albin; dec 1845	3:48
Tirrell	Susanna	1781	adm ch; dec 1794	3:48
Tirrell	Tirza	1787	adm ch, wife of Martin Stevens; dis 1835 to Camden NY	3:48
Titley	-	-	see Tiltey	-
Todd	-	-	husband of Nancy Eliza Hitchcock	3:19
Todd	Chas N.	1882	adm ch	3:49
Todd	Chas N.	5 Nov 1882	bp, adult	3:156
Todd	Chas N.	5 Nov 1882	adm ch	3:67
Todd	Mary	1873	adm ch from Cheshire	3:49
Todd	Mary	4 May 1873	adm fr Cheshire	3:93
Todd	Mary	5 Jan 1873	adm fr Cong, Cheshire	3:92
Todd	Nancy Eliza	26 Jan 1868	(Hitchcock) dism to Cong, Arcola, Ill.	3:123
Todd	Rhoda	1787	adm ch, wife of J. Beebe Jr., dis 1806 to German NY	3:48
Todd	Rhoda	30 Sep 1787	wife of Joseph Bebee Jr., adm ch; rem to Gorman NY	2:83
Todd	Rhoda	30 Sep 1787	adm ch	1:11
Todd	Rhoda	30 Sep 1787	adm ch, dism [to "Ohio" added]	1:54
Tolles	Eliza M.	8 Sep 1880	marr Ira P. Bennett, both of Naug	3:213
Tolles	Emma F.	24 Jan 1875	(Stevens) d, 22, child bed fever, Hillside	3:256
Tolles	Fremont W.	8 Apr 1873	marr Emma F. Stevens, both of Naug	3:210
Tolles	Fremont W.	16 Nov 1875	marr Clara Dover, both of Naug	3:211
Tolles	Lulee J.	10 Jul 1889	23 marr William L. Ward 28	3:220
Tolles	Ralph	4 Oct 1876	marr Emma Osborne, both of Naug	3:211
Tolles	Ralph J.	8 May 1879	Mrs, d, 21, Fever	3:258
Tomlinson	John B.	1853	adm ch from Birmingham; dis 1858 to Birmingham	3:48
Tomlinson	John B.	6 Nov 1853	adm from Cong, Birmingham	3:90
Tomlinson	John B.	25 Apr 1858	dism to Cong, Birmingham Ct.	3:121
Tompson	Hull	21 Aug 1808	bp, son of Samuel & Betsy [see Thompson]	1:174
Townsend	L.	-	husband of Submit C. Byington	3:4
Townsend	Larman	-	husband of Submit C. Byington	2:86
Trautviller	Carl	3 Sep 1897	dism to 1st Pres, Patterson NJ [with Anna Mary F. Nielson]	3:129
Trautweller	Carl W.	1895	adm ch; dis 1897 to Patterson NJ	3:49
Trautweller	Carl W.	6 Jan 1895	adm fr Presb, Sharpsville Pa	3:97
Trowbridge	Angeline B.	21 Sep 1881	marr Denny A. Whitehead, both of Naug	3:213
Trumble	Benjamin	22 Feb 1781	one of the ministers constituting the church, from North Haven	2:79
Trumble	Benjamin	22 Feb 1781	supervised organization of ch	1:6
Trumbull	Benjamin DD	29 Sep 1801	Rev. Elder attending consociation in Salem, from N. Haven	1:25
Trumbull	Benjamin, DD	2 Dec 1800	Revd Elder attending Consociation at Salem, from North Haven	1:19
Tuller	Cornelia M.	24 May 1855	of Naug marr John S. Way of Woodbury	3:202
Tuller	Susan P.	17 Mar 1865	of Naug marr James H. Newman of New Haven	3:206
Turner	Chas E.	29 May 1882	marr Emma L. Mather, both of Naug	3:214
Turton	Emily A.	12 Mar 1886	(Hopkins), Mrs., dism to 1st Cong, New Britain	3:126
Turton	Emily A.	1899	adm ch from New Britain, wife of Wm H.	3:49
Turton	Emily A. (Hopkins)	2 Jul 1899	adm fr 1st Cong, New Britain Ct	3:98
Turton	Wm H.	27 May 1885	26 of New Britain marr Emily A. Hopkins 23 of Naug	3:216
Turton	Wm H.	1899	adm ch from New Britain	3:49
Turton	Wm H.	2 Jul 1899	adm fr 1st Cong, New Britain Ct	3:98
Tuttill	Josiah	1840	adm ch from Mattewan; dis 1841 to Mattewan [sic]	3:48
Tuttill	Josiah	1 Mar 1840	adm ch from Mattewan NY; dism 18 Jun 1841 to HumphreysVille	2:97
Tuttill	Josiah	18 Jun 1841	dism to ch at HumphreyVille	2:37
Tuttle	Adelaide Eliza	5 May 1854	inf bp; Julius & Eliza	3:151

NAUGATUCK, CONNECTICUT, CONGREGATIONAL CHURCH RECORDS

Tuttle	Amos A.	-	1854	adm ch; dis 1859 to North Haven	3:48
Tuttle	Amos A.	5 Mar	1854	adm ch	3:60
Tuttle	Amos A.	30 Jan	1859	dism to Cong, North Haven	3:121
Tuttle	Amos Allen	5 Mar	1854	bp, profession	3:150
Tuttle	Donald Seymour	5 Jul	1891	an inf, bp; Howard B. & Jeanette P.	3:160
Tuttle	Dwight F.	-	1854	adm ch; dec 1857	3:48
Tuttle	Dwight F.	5 Mar	1854	adm ch	3:60
Tuttle	Dwight F.	7 Apr	1857	d, 25, typhoid fever, at East Haven, Hillside	3:251
Tuttle	Dwight Francis	5 Mar	1854	bp, profession	3:150
Tuttle	Edward	12 Nov	1857	of Woodbury marr Harriet Peck of Naug	3:203
Tuttle	Eliza W.	30 Dec	1854	d, wife of Julius, 35, Fever	3:251
Tuttle	Eliza Wooden	29 Jun	1855	inf bp; Julius	3:151
Tuttle	Esther	23 May	1835	died, 4y	2:115
Tuttle	H.B.	-	-	wife Nettie Phelps Seymour	3:45
Tuttle	Hannah	-	1851	adm ch; dis 1862 to New Haven [see Goodyear, Hannah]	3:48
Tuttle	Hannah C.	6 Jul	1851	adm ch	3:60
Tuttle	Harriet	-	1860	adm ch from Seymour, wife of Wallace M.; dis 1861 to Wis.	3:48
Tuttle	Harriet	3 Nov	1861	dism to Cong, Kenosha, Wisconsin	3:122
Tuttle	Harriet E.	2 Sep	1860	w of Wallace M, adm fr Cong Seymour Ct	3:91
Tuttle	Howard B.	24 Oct	1888	marr Jeannette P. Seymour	3:219
Tuttle	Howard Beecher	3 Jul	1864	inf bp; Brunson & Mary	3:153
Tuttle	Julius	-	-	husband of Eliza Woodin	3:54
Tuttle	Julius	3 Oct	1852	marr Elisa Wooding, both of Naugatuck	3:201
Tuttle	Julius	-	1853	adm ch from Cheshire; dis 1867	3:48
Tuttle	Julius	8 May	1853	adm fr Cong, Cheshire	3:90
Tuttle	Julius	-	1863	appt'd Deacon; removed 1867 Dec	3:1
Tuttle	Julius	2 Jun	1867	dism to Cheshire	3:123
Tuttle	Julius	23 Mar	1868	d (in Cheshire) 45, diabetes	3:256
Tuttle	Mary A.	-	1861	adm ch, wife of Brunson B.	3:49
Tuttle	Mary A.	3 Nov	1861	bp, adult	3:152
Tuttle	Mary A.	3 Nov	1861	adm ch	3:62
Tuttle	Mary B.	-	1847	adm ch from Cheshire; dis 1855 to Cheshire	3:48
Tuttle	Mary B.	16 May	1847	adm ch from Cheshire	2:100
Tuttle	Mary B.	17 Jun	1855	dism to Cong, Cheshire	3:121
Tuttle	Muril Seymour	12 Jun	1892	an inf, bp	3:160
Tuttle	Olive	-	1801	adm ch, wife of Josiah Chatfield; dis 1806 Windham	3:48
Tuttle	Olive	4 Jan	1801	wife of Josiah Chatfield, adm ch; rem 4 May 1806 to Windham NY	2:86
Tuttle	Olive	4 Jan	1801	adm ch, dism	1:56
Tuttle	Olive	4 Jan	1801	adm ch	1:20
Tuttle	Ruby Seymour	13 Jun	1897	inf bp; Howard & Jeanette	3:162
Tuttle	Sarah M.	-	1854	adm ch; dis 1858 to New Preston	3:48
Tuttle	Sarah M.	5 Mar	1854	adm ch	3:60
Tuttle	Sarah M.	13 Jun	1858	dism to 1st Cong, New Preston Ct.	3:121
Tuttle	Sarah Maria	5 Mar	1854	bp, profession	3:150
Tuttle	Temperance	3 Oct	1863	d, w of Eben, 55, dropsy, Hillside	3:254
Tuttle	Vincent	25 Oct	1824	of Columbia, marr Mary Hitchcock, of Hartland	1:152
Tuttle	Wallace M.	-	1860	adm ch from Seymour; dis 1861 to Wis.	3:48
Tuttle	Wallace M.	2 Sep	1860	adm fr Cong Seymour Ct.	3:91
Tuttle	Wallace M.	3 Nov	1861	dism to Cong, Kenosha, Wisconsin	3:122
Twitchel	Jennette E.	16 Nov	1859	d, 40, Hillside, removed to Grove	3:252
Twitchel	Lavinia A.	1 Sep	1861	adm fr Cong, So. Coventry	3:91
Twitchel	Robert	24 Oct	1861	his inf d, 15 wks, Hillside	3:253
Twitchel	Sarah	27 Nov	1846	adm ch from Sharon	2:100
Twitchel	Sarah	11 Jun	1865	dism to 2d Cong, Bridgeport	3:123

NAUGATUCK, CONNECTICUT, CONGREGATIONAL CHURCH RECORDS

Surname	Given	Date	Year	Notes	Ref
Twitchell	Frank M.	7 Apr	1897	41 marr May Parker Spencer 26	3:225
Twitchell	Geo. B.	-	-	husband of Juliette A. Payne	3:36
Twitchell	Jennie G.	-	1885	adm ch; dis 1894 to Naug Episcopal	3:49
Twitchell	Jennie G.	5 Jul	1885	adm ch	3:68
Twitchell	Jennie G.	5 Jul	1885	bp, adult	3:158
Twitchell	Jennie G.	26 Oct	1894	dism to Episcopal, Naug	3:128
Twitchell	Lavinia	2 Apr	1897	Mrs. Hosmer, d, heart disease	3:261
Twitchell	Lavinia A.	-	1861	adm ch from So. Coventry, wife of Homer; dec 1897	3:49
Twitchell	Sarah	-	1846	adm ch from Sharon; dis 1865	3:48
Tyler	Antoinette E.	-	1877	adm ch; dis 1877 Meth Ch, Waterbury	3:49
Tyler	Antoinette E.	4 Mar	1877	adm ch	3:65
Tyler	Mary E.	29 Nov	1891	marr Walter L. Hannahe, both of Naug	3:213
Tyler	Nettie	2 Sep	1877	Miss, dism to Waterbury Ct Meth Ch	3:125
Tyrell	-	-	-	see Terrell, Tirrell	-
Tyrell	Ansel	3 Nov	1829	adm ch from Baptist [actually 1828]	2:93
Tyrell	Henry L.	6 Jul	1828	adm ch; rem 21 May 1837 to Ohio	2:92
Tyrell	Irijah	18 Nov	1787	adm ch; excomm	2:84
Tyrell	Oliver	20 Feb	1785	adm ch; rem to Prospect	2:82
Tyrell	Statira	15 Mar	1818	wife of Albin, adm ch; died Feb 1845	2:89
Tyrell	Tirza	30 Sep	1787	wife of Martin Stephens, adm ch; rem 7 Jun 1835 to Camden NY	2:83
Tyrill	Israel	May	1784	adm ch; died 8 Jan 1811	2:82
Upson	Emily	18 Jun	1837	Mrs., dism to Cong. Ch in Waterbury	2:26
Upson	Emily	-	1841	adm ch from Waterbury, wife of Merlin; dis 1854 to Waterbury	3:51
Upson	Emily	14 Nov	1841	wife of Merlin, adm ch from Waterbury	2:98
Upson	Emily	19 Feb	1854	w. of Merlin dism to 1st Cong, Waterbury	3:120
Upson	Isabel	23 Oct	1828	of Salem, marr Hector Porter	1:153
Upson	Israel	21 Apr	1851	of Waterbury marr Mrs. Maria P. Clark of Waterbury	3:200
Upson	M.	-	-	husband of Emily Beecher	3:5
Upson	Mary Cornelia	31 Oct	1852	inf bp; Merlin & Emily	3:150
Upson	Merlin	-	1841	adm ch from Waterbury; dis 1854 to Waterbury	3:51
Upson	Merlin	12 Nov	1841	and wife adm from ch in Waterbury	2:39
Upson	Merlin	14 Nov	1841	adm ch from Waterbury	2:98
Upson	Merlin	19 Feb	1854	dism to 1st Cong, Waterbury	3:120
Upson	Mertin [sic]	-	-	husband of Emily Beecher	2:93
Upson	Sarah	4 Oct	1855	of Seymour marr George W. Beach of Naug	3:202
Valentine	John C.	12 Nov	1899	29 marr Emma Distler 20	3:227
Valentine	William	-	1877	adm ch from 2nd Pres Albany NY; care withdrawn 1885	3:53
Valentine	Wm	7 Jan	1877	adm fr 2nd Pres, Albany NY	3:93
Veil	Gertrude	3 Feb	1884	marr Henry [Harry? Hurry?] Wicke, both of Naug	3:216
Veil	Rosa	24 Jan	1883	marr Joseph Spackman, both of Naug	3:215
Vredenberg	May	-	1890	adm ch; erased 1900	3:53
Vredenberg	May	5 Jan	1890	adm ch	3:69
Wadge [sic]	Stephen	8 Dec	1828	d, affliction of the liver, 41	1:145
Wagner	Robert	21 Feb	1882	marr Anna Marie Mussner, both of Naug	3:214
Wagner	Robert	-	1893	adm ch, wife also	3:56
Wagner	Robert	2 Jul	1893	and wife adm ch	3:70
Wait	Wm	6 Jan	1889	Mrs., adm ch	3:69
Waite	Ida	-	1876	adm ch	3:55
Waite	Ida	7 May	1876	adm ch	3:65
Waite	Ida J.	6 Oct	1886	26 of Naug marr Frederick W. Cooper 31 of Waterbury	3:217
Waite	Minnie Inez	-	1890	adm ch; dec 1892	3:56
Waite	Minnie Inez	9 Mar	1890	Miss, adm ch	3:70
Waite	Minnie J.	8 Sep?	1892	d, [day taken fr previous entry]	3:260
Waite	William	24 Nov	1878	marr Angie McGinnis, both of Naug	3:212

NAUGATUCK, CONNECTICUT, CONGREGATIONAL CHURCH RECORDS

Surname	Given	Date	Year	Notes	Ref
Waite	Wm	-	1889	Mrs. adm ch	3:55
Waldon	Mary	1 Nov	1890	23 marr W.S. Johnson 24	3:221
Walker	C.	-	-	husband of Sarah G. Spencer	3:44
Walker	Charles F.	14 Sep	1864	of Oxford marr Sarah G. Spencer of Naug	3:206
Walker	Sarah G.	30 Apr	1866	d, 24, Hillside	3:255
Wallace	Margaret	-	-	see Booth	-
Wallace	Thomas H.	7 Aug	1865	of West Haven (Orange) marr M. Eugenia Smith of W. Haven at W. Haven	3:207
Walters	Lena	-	1891	adm ch	3:56
Walters	Lena	1 Mar	1891	Miss, adm ch	3:70
Walthers	Rosa Paulina	8 Oct	1893	an inf, bp	3:161
Ward	Alice	20 Apr	1876	of Naug marr Chas Briggs of Waterbury	3:211
Ward	Elisa J.	29 Dec	1868	of Naug marr Eli C. Barnam	3:208
Ward	Elisa Jane	2 Sep	1866	adm ch	3:63
Ward	Eliza Jane	-	1866	adm ch, wife of E.C. Barnam	3:54
Ward	Eliza Jane	2 Sep	1866	bp, adult	3:153
Ward	Elizabeth A.	-	1866	adm ch from New Haven, wife of Wm	3:54
Ward	Elizabeth A.	1 Jul	1866	adm fr Chapel St., New Haven	3:92
Ward	Elmer James	27 May	1869	ch bp; James & Jane	3:154
Ward	Emily	-	1866	adm ch, wife of Lorrin; dec 1887	3:54
Ward	Emily	4 Nov	1866	adm ch	3:64
Ward	Emmie E.	-	1869	adm ch, wife of Walter Hatch; die 1888 Pullman Ill	3:54
Ward	Emmie E.	20 May	1873	marr Walter P. Hatch, both of Naug	3:210
Ward	Emmie Elisabeth	2 May	1869	bp, adult	3:154
Ward	Emmie Elizabeth	2 May	1869	adm ch	3:64
Ward	George S.	16 Aug	1866	marr Catharine Hill, both of Naugatuck	3:207
Ward	Hanah	May	1819	infant ch of Richard, bp	1:60
Ward	James	May	1842	bp, ch of Lewis	2:106
Ward	James B.	2 Dec	1862	d, 26, drunkenness, Hillside	3:254
Ward	Jane	-	1869	adm ch, wife of James	3:54
Ward	Jane	2 May	1869	bp, adult	3:154
Ward	Jane	2 May	1869	adm ch	3:64
Ward	Lauren	15 Mar	1818	ch of Richard, bp	1:60
Ward	Lauren	19 Jan	1887	Mrs, d, 74, old age	3:259
Ward	Lewis	15 Mar	1818	ch of Richard, bp	1:60
Ward	Lewis	13 Dec	1895	Mrs, d, 84	3:260
Ward	Maria	-	1836	adm ch; wife of Ralph Smith; dis 1843 Washington	3:54
Ward	Maria	3 Jan	1836	adm ch; [m] Ralph Smith; dism 10 Sep 1843 to Washington	2:95
Ward	Mary A.	-	1841	adm ch, wife of Lewis; dec 1895	3:54
Ward	Mary A.	12 Sep	1841	wife of Lewis, adm ch	2:98
Ward	Richard	-	1843	adm ch; dec 1851	3:54
Ward	Richard	4 Sep	1843	delegate to Humphries Ville	2:47
Ward	Richard	14 May	1843	adm ch	2:99
Ward	Richard	24 Jun	1849	on comm to visit Mr. Teele	2:60
Ward	Richard	1 Mar	1851	d, 63, Erysipelas, Hillside	3:250
Ward	Roxana	16 Nov	1817	wife of Richard, adm ch	2:87
Ward	Roxana	-	1822	wife of Richard, member	1:83
Ward	Roxanna	-	1817	adm ch, wife of Rich; dec 1865	3:54
Ward	Roxanna	5 Feb	1865	d, 78, Hillside	3:255
Ward	Roxany	16 Nov	1817	adm ch	1:57
Ward	William	20 May	1825	ch of Richard, bp	1:86
Ward	William L.	10 Jul	1889	28 marr Lulee J. Tolles 23	3:220
Ward	Willie Lewis	27 May	1869	ch bp; James & Jane	3:154
Warner	Adna	-	-	husband of Jennie E. Lewis	3:26

NAUGATUCK, CONNECTICUT, CONGREGATIONAL CHURCH RECORDS

Surname	Given	Date	Event	Ref
Warner	Adna	- 1878	adm ch; dis 1901	3:55
Warner	Adna	3 Mar 1878	adm ch	3:66
Warner	Adna D.	29 May 1897	37 marr Clarrissa S. Church 35	3:225
Warner	Andrew	8 Jan 1868	of Naug marr Mrs. Abbie F. Kenyan of Westerly RI	3:208
Warner	Annie R.	- 1893	adm ch from Whitehall NY, wife of Lucian D.	3:56
Warner	Annie R.	1 Jan 1893	adm fr Presb, Whitehall NY	3:97
Warner	Baldwin	28 Jun 1801	bp, ch of Stephen	1:170
Warner	Bennet	5 Apr 1835	died, 27	2:114
Warner	Burton C.	- 1891	adm ch from North Haven; dec 1896	3:56
Warner	Burton C.	4 Jan 1891	adm fr Cong, North Haven	3:97
Warner	Burton C.	27 Feb 1896	d, cancer of stomach	3:261
Warner	C.S.	22 Feb 1881	at centennial exercises	3:300
Warner	Carlton Sherman	Sep 1872	ch bp; Lucian D. & Julia M.	3:155
Warner	Clarissa	14 Nov? 1841?	adm ch [date unclear, written prob in pencil next to year 1842]	2:98
Warner	Clarissa	- 1842	adm ch; dec 1849	3:54
Warner	Edward	Jun 1828	ch d, dysentery, 3	1:144
Warner	Fred A.	Oct 1878	inf bp; L.D. & Julia M.	3:156
Warner	Fred A.	- 1893	adm ch	3:56
Warner	Fred A.	2 Jul 1893	adm ch	3:70
Warner	G. Dana	Oct 1878	inf bp; L.D. & Julia M.	3:156
Warner	G. Dana	- 1893	adm ch	3:56
Warner	G. Dana	2 Jul 1893	adm ch	3:70
Warner	Garry	23 May 1860	d, 57, fit, instantly, Hillside	3:252
Warner	Garry Smith	11 Sep 1803	bp, son of Stephen	1:172
Warner	Geo Adna	10 Jun 1894	inf bp; Lewis C. & Lucia B.	3:161
Warner	Grace	31 Mar 1898	23 marr Henry Newman 21	3:226
Warner	Halbert Dodge	- 1900	adm ch from Minneapolis Min	3:56
Warner	Halbert Dodge	4 Mar 1900	adm fr Westminster Pres, Minneapolis	3:98
Warner	Harriet	4 Sep 1814	bp, adopted ch of Lucretia wife of Reuben	1:176
Warner	Jennie E.	30 Aug 1893	Mrs. A.D.W., d, 37	3:260
Warner	Julia M.	15 Mar 1890	d, 46, consumption	3:260
Warner	Karl	6 Jul 1890	an inf, bp	3:159
Warner	L.D.	-	husband of Julia M. Lewis	3:26
Warner	Lewis C.	- 1885	adm ch; dis 1901 Beacon Falls	3:55
Warner	Lewis C.	5 Jul 1885	adm ch	3:68
Warner	Lewis Carter	16 Jun 1867	ch bp, L.D. & Julia M.	3:154
Warner	Lewis Carter	15 Sep 1892	25 marr Lucia Belle Warner 29	3:222
Warner	Lucia B.	- 1885	adm ch; dis 1901 Beacon Falls	3:55
Warner	Lucia B.	5 Jul 1885	adm ch	3:68
Warner	Lucia Belle	15 Sep 1892	29 marr Lewis Carter Warner 25	3:222
Warner	Lucia Eliza	1 Mar 1885	inf bp; L.D. & Julia M.	3:157
Warner	Lucian D.	- 1863	adm ch	3:54
Warner	Lucian D.	14 Sep 1864	marr Julia M. Lewis, both of Naugatuck	3:206
Warner	Lucian D.	1868	appt'd deacon	3:1
Warner	Lucian Dayton	5 Jul 1863	adm ch	3:62
Warner	Lucius A.	- 1891	adm ch from Brookville Kan; dis 1901 to Beacon Falls	3:56
Warner	Lucius A.	1 Mar 1891	adm fr Cong, Brookville Kan	3:97
Warner	Lucretia	- 1800	adm ch, wife of Reuben; dec 1857	3:54
Warner	Lucretia	24 Aug 1800	wife of Ruben, adm ch	2:85
Warner	Lucretia	24 Aug 1800	Ru., adm ch	1:56
Warner	Lucretia	- 1822	wife of Reuben, member	1:83
Warner	Lucretia	29 Jun 1857	d, 78, Apoplexy, Hillside	3:251
Warner	Lucy L.	- 1830	adm ch, wife of Obadiah; dec 1863	3:54
Warner	Lucy L.	21 Feb 1830	adm ch	1:59c

NAUGATUCK, CONNECTICUT, CONGREGATIONAL CHURCH RECORDS

Warner	Lucy L.	4 May 1863	d, 66, Hillside	3:254
Warner	Lucy S.	21 Feb 1830	wife of Obediah, adm ch	2:93
Warner	Mary	- 1835	adm ch; dec	3:54
Warner	Mary	1 Mar 1835	adm ch; died 1837	2:95
Warner	Mary	3 Feb 1837	voted to be requested to ask for letter of dism.	2:23
Warner	Minerva	- 1822	female, member adm since 1822	1:83
Warner	Minerva	- 1828	adm ch; dec 1867	3:54
Warner	Minerva	4 May 1828	adm ch	2:92
Warner	Minerva	4 May 1828	adm ch	1:59a
Warner	Minerva	4 May 1828	adm ch	1:106
Warner	Minerva	20 Mar 1828	propounded for adm	1:106
Warner	Minerva	28 Jun 1867	d, 66, Hillside	3:255
Warner	Minerva Johnson	28 Jun 1801	bp, ch of Stephen	1:170
Warner	Mrs.	13 Mar 1838	on comm	2:31
Warner	Nancy	23 Jul 1815	bp, ch of Lucretia wife of Reuben	1:176
Warner	Nellie A.	28 Jul 1888	21 marr Thomas J. Wylie 24	3:219
Warner	Obadiah	1 Apr 1838	Mrs, SS Comm	2:32
Warner	Obadiah	16 Jun 1864	of Naug marr Mary Jane Johnson of Seymour	3:206
Warner	Obadiah	23 Nov 1868	d, 76, Hillside	3:256
Warner	Obediah	Apr 1933	on committee for SS	2:9
Warner	Olive	3 Mar 1878	w of Oscar, adm fr Silver Lake Pres.	3:94
Warner	Olive R.	- 1878	adm ch from Presb Silver Lake Pa, wife of Oscar	3:55
Warner	Oscar	6 May 1877	adm fr Silver Lake NY Pres	3:94
Warner	Oscar L.	- 1877	adm ch from Presb Silver Lake Pa	3:55
Warner	Phebe	- 1785	adm ch, wife of Stephen; dec 1824	3:54
Warner	Phebe	26 Jun 1785	wife of Stephen, adm ch; died 22 Jun 1824	2:82
Warner	Phebe	26 Jun 1785	wife of Stephen adm ch	1:9
Warner	Phebe	26 Jun 1785	St., adm ch, d ["1824 June 22" added]	1:54
Warner	Phebe	22 Jun 1824	Wid, d, 96	1:161
Warner	Polly	- 1800	adm ch, wife of Richd; dis 1914 German NY	3:54
Warner	Polly	Apr 1800	Ri, adm ch, dism	1:55
Warner	Polly	Apr 1800	wife of Richard adm ch	1:15
Warner	Polly	1 Apr 1800	wife of Richard, adm ch; rem to German NY	2:85
Warner	Poly	2 Mar 1800	wife of Richard adm ch [date, sic]	1:16
Warner	Reuben	6 Oct 1805	bp, son of Steven	1:173
Warner	Reuben	- 1836	adm ch; dec 1862	3:54
Warner	Reuben	2 May 1836	adm ch	2:96
Warner	Reuben	23 Nov 1862	d, 89, Hillside	3:254
Warner	Richard Vincent	12 Jun 1892	an inf, bp	3:160
Warner	Ruben	24 Aug 1800	wife adm ch	1:15
Warner	Sally	28 Jun 1801	bp, ch of Stephen	1:170
Warner	Sally	- 1822	wife of Stephen, member	1:83
Warner	Sarah	- 1801	adm ch; wife of Stephen Jr.; dec 1847	3:54
Warner	Sarah	22 Feb 1801	wife of Stephen Jr., adm ch; died 18 Mar 1847	2:86
Warner	Sarah	22 Feb 1801	St., adm ch	1:56
Warner	Sarah	22 Feb 1801	wife of Stephen Jun. adm ch	1:21
Warner	Stephen	- 1810	adm ch; dec 1842 [sic]	3:54
Warner	Stephen	5 Aug? 1810	adm ch; died 21 Nov 1812 [adm day crossed out]	2:94
Warner	Stephen	21 Nov 1812	d, age 81	1:63
Warner	Stephen	13 Nov 1825	d, fever, 55	1:163
Warner	Stephen Charles	May 1818	son of Stephen, bp	1:61
Warner	Stephen Senr	- 1812	d	1:160
Warner	Winnifred L.	- 1885	adm ch; dis 1895 Torrington	3:55
Warner	Winnifred L.	5 Jul 1885	adm ch	3:68

NAUGATUCK, CONNECTICUT, CONGREGATIONAL CHURCH RECORDS

Surname	Given	Date	Event	Ref
Warner	Winnifred L.	18 Sep 1895	25 marr Geo B. Alvord 24	3:223
Warner	Winnifred L.	29 Nov 1895	(Alvord), dism to Cong, Torrington Ct	3:128
Warner	Winnifred Louise	May 1870	ch bp; L.D. & Julia M.	3:155
Warren	Elizabeth	- 1888	adm ch from Waterbury, w of Franklin	3:55
Warren	Elizabeth	4 Nov 1888	adm fr 2nd Cong, Waterbury	3:96
Warren	Frank	- 1890	appt'd Deacon 1890; resigned 1897	3:1
Warren	Franklin	- 1888	adm ch from Waterbury	3:55
Warren	Franklin	4 Nov 1888	adm fr 2nd Cong, Waterbury	3:96
Warren	George	10 Feb 1881	marr Lillie F. Lowes, both of Naug	3:213
Waters	Earle M.	- 1899	adm ch from Lyons Falls NY	3:56
Waters	Earle M.	2 Jul 1899	adm fr Forest Pres, Lyons Falls NY	3:98
Watkins	Hannah D.	21 Jul 1880	marr Frank E. Chamberlain, both of Seymour	3:212
Watrous	Addison R.	2 Jun 1898	22 marr Ada F. Wilcox 22	3:226
Watson	Jeannette Doolittl	- 1899	Mrs., adm ch from West Haven	3:56
Watson	Jeannette Doolittl	5 Nov 1899	Mrs., adm fr 1st Cong, West Haven	3:98
Watson	Wm H.	12 Jun 1899	26 marr Jeanette A. Doolittle 24 at West Haven	3:227
Way	John S.	24 May 1855	of Woodbury marr Cornelia M. Tuller of Naugatuck	3:202
Weaving	-	-	see Miller, Lillian Marguerite	
Weaving	Lizzie W.	3 Nov 1886	24 marr Chas H. Stahl 20, both of Naug	3:217
Webb	Benham	7 Jun 1789	bp, ch of Daniel	1:165
Webb	D.	-	husband of Sarah Benham	3:4
Webb	Daniel	-	husband of Sarah Benham	2:82
Webb	Daniel	-	m to Sarah Benham, [this added to 1811 membership list]	1:53
Webb	Daniel	5 Oct 1794	bp, ch of Daniel	1:167
Webb	David	5 Oct 1794	bp, ch of Daniel	1:167
Webb	Mansfield	7 Oct 1787	bp, ch of Daniel	1:164
Webb	Sally	19 Jul 1834	died, 81	2:114
Webb	Sarah	8 Jan 1792	bp, ch of Daniel	1:166
Webb	Thankful	27 Jan 1788	bp, dau of Dani[el]	1:165
Webber	Geo	4 Nov 1897	28 marr Rose Spachman 22	3:225
Weber	Martin	21 Apr 1874	bur, 71	3:257
Webster	Covert B.	25 Mar 1898	or 27 Mar, dism to Presb, Mishawaka Ind.	3:129
Webster	Covert Buckingham	- 1890	adm ch; dis Mch 1898 to Mishawka, Ind.	3:56
Webster	Covert Buckingham	9 Mar 1890	bp, adult	3:159
Webster	Covert Buckingham	9 Mar 1890	adm ch	3:70
Webster	Eliza	18 Nov 1883	bp, adult	3:157
Webster	Emmett	- 1895	adm ch; dis Mch 1898 to Mishawaka, Ind.	3:56
Webster	Emmett	3 Nov 1895	adm fr --	3:97
Webster	Emmett S.	25 Mar 1898	or 27 Mar, dism to Presb, Mishawaka Ind	3:129
Webster	Florence	- 1897	adm ch	3:56
Webster	Florence	2 May 1897	bp, adult	3:162
Webster	Florence	2 May 1897	adm ch	3:71
Webster	J.	-	husband of Orra P. Saunders	3:44
Webster	Joel F.	25 Dec 1867	marr Orra P. Saunders, both of Naugatuck	3:207
Webster	Mary Edith	20 Sep 1899	23 marr Asa Lewis Chamberlain 28	3:227
Wedge	Miner C.	5 Nov 1855	of Warren Ct, marr Melissa D. Merrells of Naug	3:202
Weeks	Holland	2 Dec 1800	Revd Elder attending Consociation at Salem, from Waterbury	1:19
Weeks	Holland	29 Sep 1801	Rev. Elder attending consociation in Salem, from Waterbury	1:25
Weeks	Holland	19 May 1802	bp Holland Weeks Chadwick, son of Rev. Jabez	1:171
Weeks	Holland	19 Aug 1804	Rev., bp ch [one of many, entered here to show given name]	1:172
Wener	John	1 Jul 1888	marr Tillie Wener	3:219
Wener	Tillie	1 Jul 1888	marr John Wener	3:219
Wertz	Annie L.	- 1893	adm ch, wife of -- Frisbie	3:56
Wertz	Annie L.	7 May 1893	adm fr Emanuel Chapel, Brooklyn	3:97

NAUGATUCK, CONNECTICUT, CONGREGATIONAL CHURCH RECORDS

Surname	Given	Date	Event	Ref
Weston	Mary Ann	18 Feb 1858	of Naug marr Charles Freeman of Bridgeport, both colored	3:203
Wheeler	--ddias	- 1807	d, 65y [entry above is 18 Sep]	1:158
Wheeler	Chas V.	7 Aug 1887	of Seymour 23 marr Hattie A. Parmalee	3:218
Wheeler	George	22 Nov 1887	22 marr Gabriella Brush 21	3:218
Wheeler	Grace B.	25 Dec 1856	marr David Smith, both of Naug	3:203
Wheeler	J.N. [sic]	3 Mar 1878	adm ch	3:66
Wheeler	John N. [sic]	- 1878	adm ch; withdrawn 1885 [John H. on 3:409]	3:55
Wheeler	Merritt	8 Mar 1862	marr Emerett Dougall, both of Naugatuck	3:205
Wheeler	Polly G.	- 1843	adm ch, wife of D. Smith; dec 1899	3:54
Wheeler	Polly Grace	2 Jul 1843	bp, adult	2:107
Wheler	Polly Grace	2 Jul 1843	adm ch	2:99
Whipple	Jessie L.	- 1885	adm ch; dis 1891 Bridgeport	3:55
Whipple	Jessie L.	5 Jul 1885	bp, adult	3:157
Whipple	Jessie L.	5 Jul 1885	adm ch	3:67
Whipple	Jessie L.	20 Feb 1891	dism to So Cong, Bridgeport	3:127
White	Emma	- 1828	adm ch, wife of Joel; dis 1832 to Hump.ville	3:54
White	Emma	6 Jul 1828	wife of Joel, adm ch; rem 10 Jan 1832 to Humphryville	2:92
White	Emma	6 Jul 1828	member	1:94
White	Emmi [sic]	10 Jun 1832	wife of Joel, given letter of rec to ch at HumphreyVill	1:119
White	Emmy	6 Jul 1828	Joel, adm ch	1:59a
White	Emmy	6 Jul 1828	wife of Joel, adm ch	1:106
White	Joel	- 1828	adm ch; dis 1832 Hump.ville	3:54
White	Joel	6 Jul 1828	adm ch; rem 10 Jan 1832 to Humphreyville	2:92
White	Joel	6 Jul 1828	adm ch	1:59a
White	Joel	6 Jul 1828	member	1:94
White	Joel	6 Jul 1828	adm ch	1:106
White	Joel	10 Jun 1832	letter of rec to ch at HumphreyVill	1:119
White	Wm J.	4 Jul 1875	marr Mary A. Cole, both of Naug	3:211
Whitehead	Denny A.	21 Sep 1881	marr Angeline B. Trowbridge, both of Naug	3:213
Whiteley	Samuel Jr.	13 Dec 1888	29 marr Anice F. Needham 21	3:220
Whitney	Betsey	31 Dec 1847	adm ch from Litchfield	2:100
Whitney	Betsey (Wooster)	- 1847	adm ch from Litchfield; dis 1854 to Plainville [dism not in rec]	3:54
Whitney	Edgar O.	3 Jan 1877	of Meriden marr Ella A. Hotchkiss of Naug	3:211
Whitney	Mary E.	21 Oct 1868	marr Edward T. Miller, both of Naug	3:208
Whittemore	Arthur Harris	16 Jun 1867	ch bp; J.H. & Julia	3:154
Whittemore	Gertrude Buckingha	Nov? 1875	ch bp; J.H. & Julia A.	3:155
Whittemore	Harris	21 Sep 1892	27 marr Justine Morgan Brockway 25	3:222
Whittemore	Harris	23 Dec 1894	bp; Harris & Justine	3:161
Whittemore	Helen Brockway	21 Dec 1899	inf bp; Harris & Justine Brockway	3:164
Whittemore	J.H.	- -	husband of Julia Spencer	3:44
Whittemore	J.H.	- 1869	adm ch	3:54
Whittemore	J.H.	2 May 1869	adm ch	3:64
Whittemore	John H.	10 Jun 1863	marr Julia A. Spencer, both of Naug	3:205
Whittemore	John Howard	Sep 1872	ch bp; John H. & Julia A.	3:155
Whittemore	Julia	29 Jul 1876	d, inf dau of Julia A. & J.H., 11 wks, cholera inf, Hillside	3:257
Wicke	Christina	23 Oct 1883	marr August P. Pallman, both of Naug	3:216
Wicke	Henry[?]	3 Feb 1884	[Harry? Hurry?] marr Gertrude Veil, both of Naug	3:216
Widge	Daisey	2 May 1886	bp, adult	3:158
Widge	Daisey	2 May 1886	adm ch	3:69
Widge	Daisey A.	22 Nov 1888	22 marr Henry P. Bird 28	3:219
Widge	Daisy	- 1886	adm ch, wife of Henry Bird	3:55
Widge	Delia	- 1886	adm ch, wife of Chas	3:55
Widge	Delia	2 May 1886	bp, adult, "Mrs"	3:158
Widge	Delia	2 May 1886	Mrs., adm ch	3:69

NAUGATUCK, CONNECTICUT, CONGREGATIONAL CHURCH RECORDS

Surname	Given	Date	Notes	Ref
Widge	Gertrude	– 1886	adm ch	3:55
Widge	Gertrude	2 May 1886	bp, adult	3:158
Widge	Gertrude	2 May 1886	adm ch	3:69
Widge	Gertrude Jane	14 Jun 1900	26 marr Hardy Massam Smith 35	3:228
Widge	Helen J.	1 Jan 1882	marr Edwd J. Scribner, both of Naug	3:213
Widge	Lena P.	26 Apr 1893	21 marr Frank R. Nichols 21	3:223
Wight	Wm K.	5 Jul 1899	66 marr Mary H. Rockefellonw 58	3:227
Wilbur	Geo W.	– 1886	adm ch from M.E. Birmingham; dis 1887 M.E. Shelton Ct	3:55
Wilbur	Geo W.	2 May 1886	adm fr M.E. Ch, Birmingham Ct	3:95
Wilbur	Geo W.	2 Sep 1887	dism to M.E. Ch, Shelton Ct	3:126
Wilcox	Ada F.	2 Jun 1898	22 marr Addison R. Watrous 22	3:226
Wilcox	Mary S.	5 Jun 1885	marr Walter L. Benham 23 of Naug	3:216
Wilcox	Russell W.	– 1876	and wife adm ch; dis 1877 Southington Cong.	3:55
Wilcox	Russell W.	7 May 1876	and wife adm ch	3:65
Wilcox	Russell W.	10 Jun 1877	dism to Cong, Southington Ct; also wife	3:125
Williams	–	2 Sep 1828	d, complicated diseases, 40	1:144
Williams	Charles	3 Jan 1802	marr Polly M'Donald, both of Columbia	1:151
Williams	E.S.	– –	husband of Mary W. Potter	3:36
Williams	E.S.	– 1877	adm ch from Cong. Plainville; "Diciplined" 1881	3:55
Williams	E.S.	– 1877	Mrs., adm ch from Cong, Plainville, dis 1897 Plainville	3:55
Williams	E.S.	6 May 1877	Mr., adm fr Plainville Ct, Cong,; wife also	3:94
Williams	E.S.	2 Aug 1881	Removed under certain conditions, "see folio 402 this book"	3:125
Williams	E.S.	– 1882	restored; dis 1897 Plainville	3:55
Williams	E.S.	5 May 1882	restored by vote	3:67
Williams	E.S.	15 Oct 1897	and wife dism to 1st Cong, Plainville Ct.	3:129
Williams	Elijah S.	– 1866	adm ch; dis 1867 to Easthampton Ms.	3:54
Williams	Elijah S.	22 Sep 1867	dism to Easthampton	3:123
Williams	Elijah S.	2 Jul 1881	church discipline re charges made by him against his brother, Horace	3:402
–	–	– –	–	–
Williams	Elijah Sherman	7 Jan 1866	bp, adult	3:153
Williams	Elijah Sherman	7 Jan 1866	adm ch	3:63
Williams	Harriet D.	1 Dec 1851	of Naug marr David K. Nichols of Waterbury	3:200
Williams	Horace	1 Jul 1866	dism to Appleton, Wis. (Conl.)	3:123
Williams	Horace	Dec 1876	appt'd Deacon; resigned 3 Dec 1880	3:1
Williams	Horace N.	– 1856	adm ch; dis 1866 to Appleton Wis.	3:54
Williams	Horace N.	2 Nov 1856	adm ch	3:61
Williams	Horace N.	– 1874	adm ch from So. Meriden Ct; dis 1881 M.E. Naug; also wife	3:55
Williams	Horace N.	5 Jul 1874	adm fr Cong, So. Meriden, also wife	3:93
Williams	Horace N.	4 Mar 1881	charges against him by his bro E.S. Williams	3:401
Williams	Horace N.	30 Sep 1881	dism to M.E. Ch, Naug; also wife	3:125
Williams	Horace Nelson	2 Nov 1856	bp, adult	3:151
Williams	Howard Gates	22 Sep 1878	inf bp; E.S.	3:156
Williams	James	5 Jan 1875	bur, 82, Hillside	3:257
Williams	Lewis	14 Jun 1801	marr Polly Porter, both of this place	1:151
Williams	Mary W.	22 Sep 1867	(Potter) [wife of] Elijah S., dism to Easthampton	3:123
Williams	Sabria	21 May 1825	d, lung fever, 30	1:162
Williston	Noah	2 Dec 1800	Revd Elder attending Consociation at Salem, from West Haven	1:19
Willis	–	4 Aug 1873	bur, 7 mos	3:257
Wilmot	Alice Pope	– 1898	adm ch, wife of B.N.	3:56
Wilmot	Alice Pope	1 May 1898	adm fr Windsor Ave, Hartford Ct	3:98
Wilmot	Asenath	– 1847	adm ch from Waterbury; dec 1887 [does not say "Mrs."]	3:54
Wilmot	Asenath	16 May 1847	Mrs., adm ch from Waterbury [ditto marks indicate "Mrs"]	2:100
Wilmot	Asenath	1 Feb 1887	Mrs, d, 98, old age	3:259
Wilmot	Aseneth	22 Feb 1881	at centennial exercises, 92 on 29 Apr 1981	3:300

Wilmot	Benneville Dayton	2 Jul	1899	inf bp; Benneville N. & Alice Pope	3:164
Wilmot	Benneville N.	-	1898	adm ch	3:56
Wilmot	Benneville N.	1 May	1898	bp, adult	3:163
Wilmot	Benneville N.	2 May	1898	adm ch	3:72
Wilmot	Cordelia E.	-	1885	adm ch	3:55
Wilmot	Cordelia E.	5 Jul	1885	bp, adult	3:158
Wilmot	Cordelia E.	5 Jul	1885	adm ch	3:68
Wilmot	Edmund B.	-	1885	adm ch	3:55
Wilmot	Edmund B.	13 Sep	1885	adm ch	3:68
Wilmot	Estella	24 May	1871	marr Hubert Chamberlain, both of Naug	3:209
Wilmot	Francis Noyes	12 Jun	1892	an inf, bp	3:160
Wilmot	John M.	-	1859	adm ch; care withdrawn 1885	3:54
Wilmot	John M.	2 Jul	1859	bp, youth	3:152
Wilmot	John Morton	3 Jul	1859	adm ch, age 14	3:62
Wilmot	Lauren	6 Jun	1888	Mrs, d, rheumatism	3:259
Wilmot	Lauren A.	3 Jul	1889	d, 38, Water or blood on the brain	3:259
Wilmot	Lorein	-	1878	Mrs., adm ch; dec 1888 ["Lawren" crossed out]	3:55
Wilmot	Lorein	-	1878	adm ch; dec 1889 ["Lawren" crossed out]	3:55
Wilmot	Lorein	3 Mar	1878	and wife adm ch ["Lawren" crossed out]	3:66
Wilmot	Louis Howard	15 Mar	1893	23 marr Lilian Jane Chamberlain 20	3:222
Wilmot	Mary A.	-	1866	adm ch, wife of Lucius	3:54
Wilmot	Mary A.	-	1885	adm ch, wife of Noyes S.	3:55
Wilmot	Mary A.	5 Jul	1885	Mrs, adm ch	3:68
Wilmot	Mary Amelia	2 Sep	1866	bp, adult	3:153
Wilmot	Mary Amelia	2 Sep	1866	adm ch	3:64
Wilmot	Ruby E.	-	1885	adm ch	3:55
Wilmot	Ruby E.	5 Jul	1885	bp, adult	3:158
Wilmot	Ruby E.	5 Jul	1885	adm ch	3:68
Wilmot	Ruby Estelle	7 May	1897	26 marr John M. Currie 24, both of Waterbury	3:225
Wilson	Emma	4 Feb	1898	32 marr Chas F. Morgan 27	3:225
Wilson	Sidney A.	22 Jun	1873	of Naug marr Evadene M. Porter of New Haven	3:210
Wilson	Warren	2 May	1827	of Harwinton, marr Dencey F. Rowe of Columbia	1:153
Wilton	Ellen	5 Sep	1883	marr Thomas Melbourn, both of Middlebury	3:215
Wimple	Wilson J.	14 Feb	1878	marr Eva Jones, both of Naug	3:212
Winslow	Anna	28 Jun	1899	30 marr Henry Sharer 40	3:227
Wirgand	Catharine	23 Mar	1851	of Port Chester NY marr Antone Kurreck of Naug	3:200
Wirth	-	-	-	see Wuth	-
Wistim [sic]	Mary	7 May	1891	marr James Carey	3:221
Woermer	Joanna Bertha	11 Aug	1895	inf bp; Vector & Abbelina [see Wormer]	3:161
Woermer	Johannes August	11 Aug	1895	inf bp; Vector & Abbelina	3:161
Wood	Agnes	-	1900	Mrs., adm ch	3:56
Wood	Agnes	2 Sep	1900	Mrs., adm ch	3:72
Wood	Amanda	26 Jan	1864	marr Lawrence S. Spencer, both of Naug	3:205
Wood	Chas N.	14 Sep	1893	25 marr Mary A. Foster 24	3:223
Wood	Fredk Arthur	8 Sep	1897	24 marr Margretta Hughes 23	3:225
Wood	Lottie E.	-	1885	adm ch from Waterbury, wife of A.J.	3:55
Wood	Lottie E.	3 May	1885	Mrs., adm fr 2nd Cong, Waterbury Ct	3:95
Wood	Luke	29 Apr	1817	Rev. Elder at Council re Rev. Dodd's removal	1:74
Wood	Luke, Rev.	5 May	1811	of Waterbury, invited to attend installation	1:51
Wood	Mary A.	-	-	see Foster	-
Wood	Wm Jr	15 Nov	1894	48 marr Emma M. Hooker 38	3:223
Woodard	Betty	1 Feb	1801	widow, adm ch [see Woodward]	1:20
Woodbridge	Joseph	3 Mar	1856	of Stonington marr Mary E. Curtis of Middlebury in Middlebury	3:203
Woodbury	Judith H.	8 Oct	1863	d, 46, tumor	3:254

NAUGATUCK, CONNECTICUT, CONGREGATIONAL CHURCH RECORDS

Woodcock	Thomas	-	1878	adm ch; dec 1892	3:55
Woodcock	Thos	30 Mar	1892	d	3:260
Woodcock	Thos.	3 Mar	1878	adm ch	3:66
Wooden	Henry	26 Feb	1854	inf dau d, 3 days [see Wooding]	3:250
Woodford	Rosa A.	-	1873	(sic) adm ch from W. Winsted, wife of Geo E.; erased 1900	3:55
Woodford	Rosa A.	6 Sep	1874	w of Geo E., adm fr 2nd Cong, Winsted Ct	3:93
Woodford	Rosa A.	2 Aug	1881	dism to Cong, West Winsted Ct	3:125
Woodhead	Cora F.	10 Apr	1883	d at Manaos S.A., billious fever	3:259
Woodhead	Florence Cora	-	1876	adm ch; dec 1883	3:55
Woodhead	Florence Cora	5 Mar	1876	adm ch	3:65
Woodin	Eliza	-	1841	adm ch, wife of Julius Tuttle; dec 1854	3:54
Woodin	Eliza	11 Jul	1841	adm ch	2:98
Wooding	-	-	-	see Wooden	-
Wooding	-	-	-	husband of Jennett Limburner	3:25
Wooding	-	-	-	husband of Harriet Hopkins	3:19
Wooding	-	-	-	husband of Jennett Limburner	2:98
Wooding	Anna	-	1900	Mrs., adm ch	3:56
Wooding	Anna	1 Jul	1900	Mrs, adm ch	3:72
Wooding	Elisa	3 Oct	1852	marr Julius Tuttle, both of Naug	3:201
Wooding	Florence Mabel	1 Jul	1900	adm ch	3:72
Wooding	Florina Mabel	-	1900	adm ch	3:56
Wooding	Harriet A.	7 Sep	1858	d, 32, congestion of lungs, Hillside	3:252
Wooding	Harriet A.	-	1869	adm ch, wife of Andrew Renz; irr Epis 1876	3:55
Wooding	Harriet Augusta	5 Sep	1869	adm ch	3:64
Wooding	Jennett	20 Feb	1859	dism to Cong, Cheshire	3:121
Wooding	Rebecca	6 Jul	1865	d, 27, consumption, Hillside	3:255
Wooding	Wales H.	2 Sep	1860	d, 13, bilious fever, Hillside	3:253
Woodruf	Selden	21 Sep	1845	delegate to Milford	2:52
Woodruff	-	-	-	husband of Ruth Andrus	2:89
Woodruff	Beah	8 Jan	1797	bp, ch of Jonah	1:168
Woodruff	Br	6 Nov	1829	on comm	1:109
Woodruff	Br	6 Nov	1829	voted to attend future conf	1:109
Woodruff	Catharine	-	1847	adm ch from Avon, wife of Wm Hess; dis 1860 1st Cong Waterbury	3:54
Woodruff	Catherine	31 Dec	1847	adm ch from Avon	2:100
Woodruff	E.	-	-	husband of Ruth Andrus	3:2
Woodruff	J.	Jul	1819	his wife adm ch	1:59
Woodruff	Jonah	-	1795	adm ch; dec 1830	3:54
Woodruff	Jonah	19 Apr	1795	adm ch; died 11 Oct 1830	2:85
Woodruff	Jonah	19 Apr	1795	adm ch	1:13
Woodruff	Jonah	11 Oct	1805	restored to fellowship	1:39
Woodruff	Jonah	-	1816	adm ch; dis 1828 to Windsor NY	3:54
Woodruff	Jonah	17 Nov	1816	adm ch; rem to Windsor NY	2:87
Woodruff	Jonah	-	1822	male, on list of members	1:81
Woodruff	Jonah	4 May	1827	on committee	1:102
Woodruff	Jonah	6 May	1827	appointed delegate to Consociation in Columbia	1:102
Woodruff	Jonah	30 Dec	1827	to attend conf at Wilton	1:105
Woodruff	Jonah	-	1828	and wife dism to Windsor NY	1:143
Woodruff	Jonah	12 Mar	1828	on comm	1:106
Woodruff	Jonah Jr.	-	1822	male, on list of members; dism	1:81
Woodruff	Jonah Jr.	1 Dec	1822	on committee	1:96
Woodruff	Jonah Jr.	5 Mar	1824	on committee	1:97
Woodruff	Jonah Jr.	10 Apr	1825	on committee	1:101
Woodruff	Jonah Jr.	13 Aug	1827	appointed messenger to conference at Southbury	1:103
Woodruff	Jonah Jr.	14 Oct	1827	appointed to attend conference at Reading	1:103

NAUGATUCK, CONNECTICUT, CONGREGATIONAL CHURCH RECORDS

Woodruff	Jonah Jun	31 Apr	1819	chosen Clerk	1:78
Woodruff	Julia	-	1819	adm ch, wife of Jonah Jr.; dis 1828 to Windsor NY	3:54
Woodruff	Julia	3 Sep	1819	2nd wife of Jonah Jr, adm ch; rem to Windsor NY	2:91
Woodruff	Julia	-	1822	wife of Jonah, Jr., member; dism	1:83
Woodruff	Mabel	-	1795	adm ch, wife of Jonah; dec 1831	3:54
Woodruff	Mabel	19 Apr	1795	wife of Jonah, adm ch; died 15 May 1831	2:85
Woodruff	Mabel	19 Apr	1795	wife of Jonah adm ch	1:13
Woodruff	Mabel	31 May	1795	bp, ch of Jonah	1:167
Woodruff	Mabel	11 Oct	1805	wife of Jonah, restored to fellowship	1:39
Woodruff	Mabel	-	1822	wife of Jonah, member	1:83
Woodruff	Mary	-	1858	adm ch; dis 1861 to Terryville [see Bunnell, Mary]	3:54
Woodruff	Mary	5 Sep	1858	adm ch	3:62
Woodruff	Mr.	13 Mar	1838	on comm	2:31
Woodruff	Ruth	3 May	1840	Mrs., left informally, joined Episcopal ch Waterbury; excomm	2:34
Woodruff	S.	4 May	1828	Mrs, on comm	1:106
Woodruff	S.	22 Mar	1833	appt'd Asst. Superintendant of SS	2:13
Woodruff	S.	5 May	1837	Mrs., SS Comm	2:25
Woodruff	S.	5 May	1837	Mrs., on comm "to attend to cases of unchristian walk...female members"	2:25
Woodruff	Seld	4 Apr	1830	to attend consociation at Humphr...	1:110
Woodruff	Selden	-	1811	adm ch; dec 1853	3:54
Woodruff	Selden	6 Dec	1811	cand for memb	1:62
Woodruff	Selden	22 Dec	1811	adm ch	2:87
Woodruff	Selden	17 Dec	1830	on comm	1:112
Woodruff	Selden	Sep	1831	on Visiting Committee	1:115
Woodruff	Selden	30 Dec	1832	on comm	1:119
Woodruff	Selden	30 Dec	1833	on comm	2:14
Woodruff	Selden	5 May	1837	chosen deacon	2:25
Woodruff	Selden	5 May	1837	SS Comm	2:25
Woodruff	Selden	20 Dec	1842	to be visited and laboured with	2:42
Woodruff	Selden	23 Feb	1843	on comm	2:45
Woodruff	Selden	24 Aug	1843	on comm	2:46
Woodruff	Selden	4 Oct	1847	delegate for annual meeting of Consociation	2:56
Woodruff	Selden	5 Mar	1847	appt'd to visit members	2:56
Woodruff	Selden	1 Jul	1848	on Standing Committee of the Church	2:58
Woodruff	Selden	12 May	1853	d, 70, Hillside	3:250
Woodruff	Seldon	-	1822	male, on list of members	1:81
Woodruff	Seldon	7 Oct	1827	on committee	1:103
Woodruff	Seldon	16 Sep	1827	appointed to attend conference in Middlebury	1:103
Woodruff	Seldon	4 May	1828	on comm	1:106
Woodruff	Seldon	30 Apr	1830	on Sabb School board, Librarian & Secretary	1:111
Woodruff	Statira	-	1811	adm ch, wife of Selden; dec 1861	3:54
Woodruff	Statira	6 Dec	1811	wife of Selden, cand for memb	1:62
Woodruff	Statira	22 Dec	1811	wife of Selden, adm ch	2:87
Woodruff	Statira	-	1822	wife of Seldon, member	1:83
Woodruff	Statira	30 Apr	1830	on Sabb School board	1:111
Woodruff	Statira	10 Dec	1861	d, 76, heart disease, Hillside	3:253
Woodruffe	John	5 Sep	1813	bp, ch of Lucy wife of Philo	1:176
Woodruffe	Jonah	19 Apr	1795	adm ch	1:55
Woodruffe	Jonah	17 Nov	1816	adm ch; dism 1828	1:57
Woodruffe	Jonah, Jun	1 Nov	1816	cand for memb	1:73
Woodruffe	Jonah, Jun	17 Nov	1816	adm ch	1:73
Woodruffe	Mabel	19 Apr	1795	J[onah], adm ch	1:55
Woodruffe	Selden	22 Dec	1811	adm ch	1:57

NAUGATUCK, CONNECTICUT, CONGREGATIONAL CHURCH RECORDS

Surname	Given	Date	Notes	Ref
Woodruffe	Selden	22 Dec 1811	adm ch	1:62
Woodruffe	Statira	22 Dec 1811	adm ch	1:57
Woodruffe	Statira	22 Dec 1811	wife of Seldin, adm ch	1:62
Woodward	-	-	see Woodard	-
Woodward	Betty	1801	adm ch; dec	3:54
Woodward	Betty	1 Feb 1801	Wd, adm ch; died	2:86
Woodward	Betty	4 Feb 1801	Wid., adm ch, dead [copy error in book, should be 1 Feb]	1:56
Woolworth	Frances D.	30 Jul 1861	of Naug marr Joseph H. Somers of Waterbury	3:205
Wooster	-	-	see Whitney, Betsey, also see Worster, Worcester	3:54
Wooster	Alonzo	13 Mar 1854	Mrs, d, 47, consumption	3:250
Wooster	Alson [sic]	13 Feb 1855	of Naug marr Olive Cosier of Woodbury	3:202
Wooster	Mattie	1893	adm ch	3:56
Wooster	Mattie	2 Jul 1893	adm ch	3:70
Wooster	Mattie	12 Dec 1898	20 marr Clarence E. McKinney 21	3:227
Wooster	S.D.P.	20 Feb 1860	d, inf of Benj, 16 mos, inflamm stomach	3:252
Wooster	Sarah L.	5 Apr 1857	w of Zenas dism to Cong, Easthampton [with Julia Ann Hotchkiss]	3:121
Wooster	Walter Dryden	17 Jan 1863	d, son of Benj, 9, inflam fever, Hillside	3:254
Worcester	Levi Alanson	28 May 1826	ch of David, bp in the Baptist Meetinghouse	1:86
Worcester	Walter	21 Jul 1829	d, 83	1:145
Worcester	Z.	-	husband of Sarah L. Hotchkiss [see also Worster]	3:19
Worden	Sylvester	1878	adm ch; "Reported dead;" in Bpt Nov 11/88; dec 1888	3:55
Worden	Sylvester	1878	Mrs. adm ch; Irr dis 1896 [see Sylvanus Wordner]	3:55
Worden	Sylvester	11 Nov 1888	reported died in Bridgeport	3:261
Worden	Sylvester	17 Apr 1896	Mrs, joined Episc ch in Bridgeport	3:128
Wordner[sic]	Sylvanus [sic]	3 Mar 1878	and wife adm ch	3:66
Wormer	Albertina Anna	11 Jun 1899	inf bp; Victor J. & Abbalina [see Woermer]	3:164
Wormer	Frederick Victor	19 Mar 1901	ch bp; John E. Victor & Abbalina; twin	3:165
Wormer	Grace	1 Aug 1897	bp, adult; [prob at chapel in Millville]	3:163
Wormer	Robert Henry	19 Mar 1901	ch bp; John E. Victor & Abbalina; twin	3:165
Wormer	Wilhelm John	24 Aug 1897	inf bp; Victor & Adeline G.	3:163
Worster	Polly	12 Apr 1805	d, wife of Levi, dau of Joel Terrel, 20 y	1:157
Worster	Z.	-	husband of Sarah Hotchkiss	2:97
Wright	Caroline A.	12 Apr 1866	of Derby marr Arthur M. Grant of Plymouth	3:207
Wright	Carrie	1898	Mrs, adm ch from So. Amenia NY	3:56
Wright	Carrie	4 Sep 1898	Mrs., adm fr Pres, South Amenia NH	3:98
Wright	H.E.	1886	Mrs., widow, adm ch from Greenwich Ct., dis 1891 Tacoma W.	3:55
Wright	H.E.	7 Aug 1891	Mrs., dism to 1st Cong, Tacoma W.T.	3:127
Wright	Harriet E.	3 Jan 1886	Mrs., adm fr 2nd Cong, Greenwich Ct	3:95
Wright	Harry B.	2 Jul 1900	24 marr Florence Mackey Stelle 26	3:228
Wright	J. Louise	8 Sep 1885	21 marr Wm H. Bristol 25, both of Naug	3:217
Wurtenburg	Fred Alderson	8 Sep 1897	ch bp; Fred & Laura	3:163
Wurtenburg	Laurina Mary	8 Sep 1897	ch bp; Fred & Laura	3:163
Wurtenburg	Wm George	8 Sep 1897	ch bp; Fred & Laura	3:163
Wuth[?]	Frank	1 Jun 1890	[Wirth?] 32 marr Anna Hirsch 21	3:221
Wylie	Andrew B.	11 Sep 1891	an inf, bp	3:160
Wylie	Barbara Williamson	Sep 1885	bp, adult	3:158
Wylie	Cathrine	26 Oct 1882	marr Hanford D. Freeman, both of Naug	3:214
Wylie	Isabel Godser	25 Jul 1880	inf bp; Andrew	3:156
Wylie	Kate J.	10 Aug 1889	d, 17, consumption	3:259
Wylie	Katie J.	1887	adm ch; dec 1889	3:55
Wylie	Katie J.	3 Jul 1887	adm ch	3:69
Wylie	Sibley	1887	Mrs., adm ch from Scotland	3:55
Wylie	Sibley	3 Jul 1887	Mrs, adm fr Ch of Scotland Mochnun [?]	3:96
Wylie	Thomas J.	28 Jul 1888	24 marr Nellie A. Warner 21	3:219

NAUGATUCK, CONNECTICUT, CONGREGATIONAL CHURCH RECORDS

Wylie	Wm Henry	11 Sep 1891	an inf, bp	3:160
Yackel	Frances Susie	29 Oct 1900	inf bp; Gustave & Eva	3:165
Yackel	Guslav John [sic]	12 Nov 1898	inf bp; Gustav & Eva M.	3:163
Yale	Charles T.	8 Mar 1865	of Cornwall marr Harriet M. Curtis of Middlebury at Middlebury	3:206
Yale	Jane L.	- 1858	adm ch, wife of W. Jones; dec 1892	3:59
Yale	Jane Lucretia	7 Mar 1858	bp, adult	3:152
Yale	Jane Lucretia	7 Mar 1858	adm ch	3:61
Yerks	Aaron	3 Oct 1888	33 marr Mary Staples 36	3:219
Yoerg[sic]	Fannie Lena	7 Nov 1897	inf bp; Wm E. & Martha	3:163
Yost	David	25 Aug 1883	marr Bertha Louwin, both of Naug	3:215
Young	-	- -	husband of Mattie Steeber	3:46
Young	Clarissa	18 Nov 1849	dism to ch in Prospect	2:62
Young	Cora Hunter	- 1898	adm ch	3:59
Young	Cora Hunter	1 May 1898	bp, adult	3:163
Young	Cora Hunter	2 May 1898	Mrs., adm ch	3:72
Young	Geo Penman	2 May 1898	adm ch	3:72
Young	Geo Penman	4 Apr 1898	22 marr Cora Della Hunter 20	3:226
Young	Geo Penmans	- 1898	adm ch	3:59
Young	Julia Clarissa	5 Oct 1858	d, dau of Truman, 33, typhus	3:252
Young	Katherine	3 Jun 1896	23 marr Henry M. Steinholtz 27	3:224
Young	Martha Steele	- 1900	adm ch	3:56
Young	Martha Steele	- 1900	adm ch, wife of Albert Horton	3:59
Young	Martha Steele	1 Jul 1900	adm ch	3:72
Young	Robert	- 1885	Mrs., adm ch from Jersey City NJ	3:59
Young	Robert	3 May 1885	Mrs, adm fr 3d Presb, Jersey City NJ	3:95
Young	William E.	11 Jan 1894	23 marr Martha Steiber 20	3:223
Zeigler	Annie	- 1891	adm ch	3:59
Zeigler	Annie	1 Mar 1891	Miss, adm ch	3:70
Zeigler	Christine	- 1891	adm ch, "Mrs. Kahl"; dis 1896 2nd C. Waterbury	3:59
Zeigler	Christine	1 Mar 1891	Miss, adm ch	3:70
Zeigler	Christine	19 Jun 1895	23 marr Fred W. Kahl 26	3:224
Zellar	Jennie M.	19 Jan 1882	marr Samuel E. Marshall, both of Naug	3:213
Zels	Josephine	23 Sep 1858	of Naug marr Jacob Deabler of Bethany	3:203
Zumpf	-	- -	see Sumpf, Smf	-
Zumpf	Charles Russell	9 Jun 1895	an inf, bp	3:161
Zumpf	Gladys Lillie	9 Jun 1895	an inf, bp	3:161
Zumpf	Wm Adam	9 Jun 1895	an inf, bp	3:161
Zwick	-	- -	see Cwick	-
Zwick	Amelia	24 Jul 1889	marr August Horn	3:220
Zwick	Rosa	1 Jan 1890	21 marr Henry Runpfen [Rempfen?] 20	3:221

www.ingramcontent.com/pod-product-compliance
Lightning Source LLC
Chambersburg PA
CBHW080404170426
43193CB00016B/2801